DIRTY WARS

Dirty Wars

Landscape, Power, and Waste
in Western American Literature

John Beck

UNIVERSITY OF NEBRASKA PRESS · LINCOLN AND LONDON

Library of Congress
Cataloging-in-Publication Data

Beck, John, 1963–
Dirty wars: landscape, power, and waste in western American
literature / John Beck.
p. cm. — (Postwestern horizons)
Includes bibliographical references and index.
ISBN 978-0-8032-2631-9 (cloth: alk. paper)
1. American literature—West (U.S.)—History and criticism.
2. American literature—20th century—History and criticism.
3. West (U.S.)—In literature. 4. Politics and literature—United
States—History—20th century. 5. Politics and culture—United
States—History—20th century. 6. War and literature. I. Title.
PS271.B43 2009
810.9'35878—dc22
2009024329

Set in Quadraat by Kim Essman.
Designed by R. W. Boeche.

For E

CONTENTS

ACKNOWLEDGMENTS

I would not have started on this book without the time and space made available to me during a research fellowship at Darwin College, Cambridge. I would not have finished it without the continued financial and collegial support of the School of English at Newcastle University. A British Academy award made it possible for me to travel extensively in the U.S. Southwest, and an Arts and Humanities Research Board Research Leave Award gave me the time to complete the project.

A good deal of the material for this book was tried out, in one form or another, at conferences in the United States and United Kingdom, and I would like to thank the people I had the good fortune to meet at those events, many of whom have become friends. Among those who organized events, shared panels, or generally showed an interest, particular thanks go to Linnie Blake, Neil Campbell, Audrey Goodman, David Holloway, Martin Padget, Steve Tatum, and Rick Wallach. I also want to thank Caroline Levander, Krista Comer, and José Aranda for their hospitality during a visit to Rice University in 2004, and John Armitage, Ryan Bishop, Dan Brooke, Darren Carlaw, Matthew Cornford, Paul Crosthwaite, John Dickie, Stacy Gillis, Steve Graham, Ruth Helyer, Colin Hutchinson, Allan Kristensen, Tom Theobald, Melanie Waters, Anne Whitehead, and Sue Wragg for conversation, correspondence, and advice.

Ladette Randolph and the Postwestern Horizons series editors helped me get the project into shape. Audrey Goodman, William Handley, and Sue Breckenridge offered invaluable criticisms and suggestions at crucial stages, while Kristen Elias Rowley and others at the University of Nebraska Press have made the publication process a pleasure. Needless to say, any shortcomings and errors remain mine.

Finally, thanks to Paula for living with my passions, and to Edmund, who arrived in the middle to become first among them.

INTRODUCTION
Dirty Wars

All profound changes in consciousness, by their very nature,
bring with them characteristic amnesias.
Out of such oblivions, in specific historical circumstances, spring narratives.
Benedict Anderson, *Imagined Communities*

In Richard Powers's novel *Prisoner's Dilemma* (1988), an account of the insular Hobson family's struggle with the deteriorating health of their eccentric father Eddie is broken up by italicized interchapters that make up Eddie's secret project, Hobstown. Over the years, Eddie has narrated into a tape recorder his personal history of World War II. Central to the Hobstown story is Walt Disney's patriotic wartime work, which, skewed by Eddie's damaged imagination, includes Roosevelt's commissioning of what Disney believes will be the greatest propaganda film ever made. It is to be called *You Are the War*. Considering the logistics of making the film, Disney, noticing for the first time the absence of Ralph Sato and Tom Ishi from a board meeting, is struck by the fact that Japanese Americans have been interned. Like some cornfed Schindler, an outraged Disney effects the liberation of ten thousand incarcerated Japanese Americans—by reminding Secretary of War Harold Stimson that he, Disney, is himself an American of Japanese ancestry and will demand his own arrest if his demands are not met—and puts them to work in a vast hidden studio where they are to make *You Are the War*.

Eddie Hobson is chosen as the representative all-American boy for the movie, and Disney proceeds to explain to the young man what the postwar order will be like. "We have reached the point," Disney says, "where we imprison ourselves by the hundred thousand, commonly agreed to be in the best collective interest. . . . The world is now so treacherous and immense that the private citizen in the postwar world will lock himself up rather than face the prospect of prison."[1] In the future, Disney goes on, war will continue in "livable doses, far away," while life will be a "closet hell: each person passive, static, too terrorized to leave the apartment."[2] In order to prevent this terrible fate, Disney proposes to "tell a fable" in the manner of Dickens's *A Christmas Carol* and Capra's *It's a Wonderful Life* that will show how the individual—Eddie Hobson—can make a difference.

Faced with the prospect of his own private life history carrying the redemptive message for the future, Eddie asks Disney what good his story will do. "The world is not millions," answers Disney, "it is one and one and one. It does not become an impasse until those *ones* start to renounce it. And they will have no cause to, if they stay tied to the good faith of others." [3] Eddie's life will change all the other lives it touches if he keeps the faith. In the fifth reel of *You Are the War*, Eddie, in the manner of Scrooge and George Murphy, is given a tour of the future by Mickey Mouse that reveals a montage of continuous war and destruction and the withering of human agency in the face of impossible threat. Asked how this happened, by way of an answer Mickey offers Eddie his version of the prisoner's dilemma, the non-zero-sum puzzle from game theory used by the RAND Corporation in the context of deterrence strategy that attempts to think through the conflict between individual and group rationality: "[i]t's really very simple: two men are put in separate rooms. They can play it safe or they can put their fate in the hands of another. Lack of trust begets lack of trust. The fear of being undercut trickles into the garden, as irreversible as falling. The choice of those first two people filters into four, the four eight, and the eight several billion." [4]

A frightened and appalled Eddie wonders how this suspicion started. Mickey shows him evidence proving that there was no military emergency to justify Executive Order 9066. In Hobstown the spiral of war and fear has its root cause in the betrayal of the constitutional protection of civilians in the wake of Pearl Harbor. For Eddie Hobson, the collapse of democracy begins there. Eddie's despair lies in his awareness that the individualism he grew up believing to be the bedrock of American virtue in fact serves to demolish ethical identification with others and sanctions the selfish pursuit of private salvation at the expense of other people's liberty. This is not merely a philosophical realization, however, but is grounded in Eddie's actual wartime experience. Eddie spent the last part of the war at Alamogordo and witnessed the Trinity blast. As an eyewitness to the moment when individual agency is voided by the nuclear sublime, Eddie's faith in democracy's capacity to provide social forms based on freedom from harm becomes, along with his physical health, the first casualty of the postwar world order: the only difference Eddie can now make lies in the narrative of defeat he constructs in Hobstown.

Eddie Hobson's account of his place in history, refracted through an imagination traumatized by violence and betrayal, is an attempt to give form to the chaos of experience, to shape barely comprehensible forces into a network of meaning that connects private struggles to broader and more intangible, though no less felt, events. The result is a fiction that, however bizarre, performs the service of a kind of truth in the sense that it is a record not just of what Eddie knows, but a manifestation—through its compromise formation of laterally spliced popular cultural references, personal memory, and historical events—of what he does not know. In the absence of a documentary record that would explain to him how things came to be the way they are, a record that either does not exist or has been suppressed, Eddie's narrative makes one up. As such, Hobstown is a mechanism that functions to make visible the intuited but not verifiable relations of power that have produced Eddie as the acme of postwar, permanently threatened, atomized individualism.

According to the media theorist Friedrich Kittler, the dematerialization of the transcribed record of the recent past caused by advances in information technologies makes it increasingly difficult to take stock of history by recourse to the archive. Not only are "the pertinent files" often classified "for exactly as many years as there remains a difference between files and facts," but "real streams of data" effectively bypass writing and writers altogether, and are nothing but "unreadable series of numbers circulating between networked computers." What used to be recorded in books, on records and film, is now "disappearing into black holes and boxes that, as artificial intelligences, are bidding us farewell on their way to nameless high commands." What we are left with, like Eddie Hobson, is "reminiscences, that is to say, with stories." The job of writing, then, for Kittler, is to record "[h]ow that which is written in no book came to pass," since when "[p]ushed to their margins even obsolete media become sensitive enough to register the signs and clues of a situation," and from these clues "patterns and moirés emerge: myths, fictions of science, oracles."[5]

It is no accident that Powers has Eddie Hobson combine the two major domestic events of World War II—the internment of Japanese Americans and the Trinity test—as the core actions that shape American postwar experience, since each in its own particular way inaugurates the emergence of the national security state. Recording devices such as cameras were banned from the internment camps, and the atomic program was top secret, both projects concealed from public view in the American West. For Eddie, truth is not only a casualty of war, suppressed by something called military necessity, but Eddie—including Hobstown—is also a casualty of truth as he comes to see it. The story Eddie tells himself braids, as Kittler says, the "signs and clues of a situation" into "patterns and moirés" that depict the ways the imperatives of security can function to render history accessible only through the speculative recombination of reminiscences. Under the self-erasing technologies of national security, fictions (an obsolete medium, like Eddie Hobson himself, pushed to the margins) become the only viable form of history in that they supply narratological structure, however complex or damaged, to knowledge of the world everywhere subjected to the obfuscatory concealments and erasures of power.

My purpose in this book is to explore the ramifications of this notion as it is played out across a range of literary texts concerned variously with the post–Pearl Harbor American West. If Powers is right that internment and the atomic bomb establish the contours of American postwar political and social organization, then it is in the West that the national security state takes its shape. As I hope will become clear, this is the view shared by writers as different as Cormac McCarthy, Don DeLillo, and Leslie Marmon Silko, who, along with the other writers examined here, encounter a West that has become, metaphorically and literally, the arsenal, proving ground, and disposal site for American military-industrial power. The myths, fictions of science, and oracles produced by contemporary writing about the West, I want to argue, provide signs and clues about the way the West, and the arid Southwest in particular, has become the self-erasing fulcrum of postwar American geopolitics. The Western literary landscape, from California through Nevada, Utah, and Arizona, across New Mexico to the panhandle and down to the plains of West Texas, is a landscape formed by the impact of wars visible and invisible.

Nothing shapes historical consciousness like a surprise attack. The Japanese attack on Pearl Harbor on December 7, 1941, and the terrorist attacks on the World Trade Center and the Pentagon on September 11, 2001, provide the historical frame for this book, which is concerned with literary interrogations of what, I will argue, has been the state of continuous war in the American West since the United States entered World War II.[6] By beginning with the American response to Pearl Harbor, I wish to locate the emergence of a new conception of the western United States as crucial to American global security that both overturns the perception of the West as geographically and politically remote from American centers of power and, at the same time, reinvigorates that remoteness as a geopolitical virtue. As such, the so-called "wasteland" discourse that can be said to have characterized negative Euro-American responses to much of the desert West up until World War II is given a new positive valence as the thinly inhabited areas of the region become the location for American military-industrial enterprise.[7]

Just as Pearl Harbor transformed America's understanding of its role in world affairs, with the United States emerging from World War II as a global superpower, the 9/11 attacks have likewise reshaped U.S. international relations and given a new urgency to American military priorities and operations. Recent anxieties over domestic security; the limits of executive power; the indeterminacy of the enemy; the human and financial cost of prolonged conflict; the relationship among politics, the military, and business interests; and the legitimacy of war itself are not new but are, in fact, contemporary intensifications of a set of issues that, as I hope will become apparent, have been played out in the American West in numerous ways in the years since December 1941. The internment of people of Japanese origin in the West in the immediate aftermath of Pearl Harbor; the location of America's atomic bomb project in Los Alamos, New Mexico; the progressive military withdrawal from public use of millions of acres of Western land; the hundreds of nuclear detonations at the Nevada Test Site and elsewhere, and the subsequent poisoning by fallout of people and land; the plans for permanent storage of contaminated waste in the Western desert; the "war on drugs" and intensive policing of the international border with Mexico: all of these indicate some of the ways in which the West has been at war.

The long Cold War with the Soviet Union occupies a central position in the reconstitution of the Western states as the core site of American military-industrial prowess, and the ideology, rhetoric, and material impact of covert operations and nuclear stand-off concerns a significant proportion of the works examined here.[8] The Cold War cannot, however, be conveniently bracketed off as a peculiar and definable period that comes to a close with the fall of the Berlin Wall in 1989. The impact of the Cold War cannot be undone anymore than the bomb can be uninvented, and the cumulative effects of what Joseph Masco calls the project of "radioactive nation-building" undertaken during the Cold War remain in the deep organizational structures of American life, not least in the commitment to secrecy "as a means of socially regulating American society."[9] The scale of the state infrastructure established with the nuclear program, argues Masco, is so immense that it "renders the security state largely invisible to its citizens who walk everyday in its infrastructure, rely on its technoscientific products, and unknowingly carry traces of its toxic effects in their bodies."[10] Just as internment and Los Alamos provide models for the Cold War security state, then, the preoccupations of the Cold War continue to structure much of post–Cold War life.

None of the writers discussed in this book were born before the 1930s, and a majority are part of the postwar baby boom of the 1940s and 1950s. This is a generation sometimes literally conceived in wartime and whose formative experiences are those of atomic threat, the civil rights movement, Southeast Asian conflict and resistance to it. These are, as W. J. T. Mitchell argues, the "children of postmodernism," whose conception of the world, much like Eddie Hobson's, "evolved within narratives of paranoia and melodrama," where any attempt to understand the forces at work in that world involve the "critical unveiling of 'hidden persuaders,' subliminal messages, and ideological codes."[11] For this generation, national security comes to be understood as something often, if not always, maintained and challenged by forces that are largely concealed and secret. The recognition that the freedom and transparency of democracy are underwritten by unseen and often unknowable powers might be said to be a defining characteristic of the postwar world, and certainly the grip of the hidden holds the attention of many of the books explored here. These are works concerned with the possibility of critically unveiling power in the post–Pearl Harbor West. I say "possibility" because it is by no means certain that such an unveiling is achievable, at least not with any completeness. Indeed, one might say these are less works that unveil than they are investigations of what such an unveiling might be like if it could occur. Taken together, however, what these works do provide is what, following Michel Foucault, can be termed a "counterhistory" of the post–Pearl Harbor West that interrogates the establishment of a permanent military-industrial presence in the area and explores the repercussions of this presence as it reconfigures social, political, and economic relations at local, regional, national, and international levels.

In chapter 1 I outline the terms under which the condition of permanent war can be understood and explain the way in which I see the West as central to the maintenance of America's open secrets. I connect this regional reimagining with recent analyses of neoliberal restructuring of the global economy and the concurrent reformulation of warfare under post–Cold War conditions. Of particular relevance in this discussion is the use to which Foucault's notion of biopower has recently been put by Giorgio Agamben, Michael Hardt, and Antonio Negri, among others. The production of "wasteland," I argue, includes the production of waste populations as the necessary structural threat that maintains the state of emergency under which contemporary capitalism operates.

Chapter 2 takes Cormac McCarthy's *Blood Meridian* (1985) as a conceptual starting point for this study. McCarthy's novel, while set outside my historical frame inasmuch as its subject is the mercenary expeditions of the 1840s that shaped the geographical parameters of the American Southwest, is an important articulation, I argue, of the process of rhetorical dehistoricization that substitutes the legacy of conquest with the deep time of Western geology. *Blood Meridian*, I suggest, self-reflexively reanimates the notion of permanent war that Foucault and Hardt and Negri claim precedes the emergence of the nation-state. Modern political legitimacy, according to this argument, is born as the state—in this case the consolidation of the continental geographical limits of the United States—pushes war to its borders in order to establish legitimacy within, thereby enacting a segregation of internal "friend" and external "enemy." What *Blood Meridian* achieves is an articulation of the moment when prehistory folds into history, when permanent war is placed under erasure at the service of history as the story of the nation at peace with itself. The history of the creation of the nation-state as an event underwritten by untrammeled violence is refigured as before time and therefore not part of the national story but external to it. Given that the novel was written and published in the years following the end of the Vietnam War and the rise of neoliberal conservatism in the United States, I argue that *Blood Meridian* offers an important analysis of the rhetorical underpinning that holds the legitimation of permanent warfare in place.

The internment of Japanese Americans after Pearl Harbor properly inaugurates the emergence of the permanent state of emergency that shapes the contemporary West. Justified as a necessary precaution in the interests of national security, enacted under the emergency powers claimed by the executive during times of war, waiving the constitutional protection of citizens, and utilizing the "wasteland" of the American West as repository for excluded populations, the internment is, I argue in chapter 3, the precursor event that shapes subsequent attitudes to people and place after World War II. Not only does landscape here function as the site for waste, it is often, in internment narratives, figured as actively participating in the concealment by burial of the interned through the fierce accumulation of dust on everything in the camps. In a disturbing twist, the destruction of Japanese social organization caused by internment is also seen as a mode of Americanization whereby traditional family and community hierarchies are scrambled by the imposition of a new order that privileges the native-born over the elder generation. While there are a number of notable nonfiction works that deal directly with impact of internment, I have chosen to focus on two recent novels by sansei women, Rahna Reiko Rizzuto's *Why She Left Us* (1999) and Julie Otsuka's *When the Emperor Was Divine* (2002). These are texts produced after the presidential apology and financial compensation for the internment policy and are as much concerned with the legacy of internment as they are with direct representation of the experience itself. As such, they are texts that move away from and complicate the testimonial form of works like Jeanne Wakatsuki Houston's *Farewell to Manzanar* (1973) and the documentary mode of internee fiction typified by Hiroshi Nakamura's *Treadmill*, written during internment but not published until 1995.

In chapter 4 I turn to the other paradigmatic site of World War II secrecy: Los Alamos. As the birthplace of the atomic age, the Trinity test in July 1945 positions the American West at the center of the global geopolitical map. Los Alamos is a site where contradictory considerations of landscape, power, and history converge: of past and future, experimentation and instrumentality, center and margin, country and city, private and public, secrecy and openness, local and international. I concentrate on three texts that foreground the emergence of what we might call a nuclear subjectivity; that is, an identity coterminous with the new dispensation inaugurated by the bomb. In Thomas McMahon's *Principles of American Nuclear Chemistry* (1970), and especially in Bradford Morrow's *Trinity Fields* (1995), the children of Los Alamos scientists are positioned as inheritors of a world poised in a state of perpetual threat of annihilation. Both novels consider the ethical and psychosocial ramifications of secret violent power and the dubious privilege bestowed on the scientists at the core of the project. Morrow goes furthest in exploring the aftereffects of the bomb's invention, following his protagonists through the 1960s and, in a sequel, *Ariel's Crossing* (2002), up to the present.

Ariel's Crossing concludes with the symbolic reclamation of a homestead evacuated to make way for the White Sands Missile Base, and the theme of homelessness is explored in the next chapter, which considers issues of dispossession and alienation in McCarthy's *Border Trilogy* (1992–98). Read alongside Edward Abbey's *Fire on the Mountain* (1962) and Alexander Parsons's *In the Shadows of the Sun* (2005), which work in some ways as bookends to McCarthy's novels, and including discussion of three defining texts of Native American and Chicano literature—N. Scott Momaday's *House Made of Dawn* (1966), Rudolfo Anaya's *Bless Me, Ultima* (1972), and Leslie Marmon Silko's *Ceremony* (1977)—I argue that McCarthy's trilogy is an extension and response to a tradition of exile narratives in recent Western literature. Together, these works compose a taxonomy of wasted lives, older Anglo warrior/cowboy values joining racialized populations as the unproductive residuum of Sunbelt economic and spatial restructuring.

The kind of nuclear subjectivity identified in the Los Alamos novels and rendered as the power-stripped and exiled remainder in McCarthy and others is approached from another angle in chapter 6, which examines two novels set in West Texas that register the amorphous dread produced by nuclear consciousness. Don DeLillo's *End Zone* (1972) and William Hauptman's *Storm Season* (1992) are novels that foreground connections between apocalyptic Cold War rhetoric and an evangelical obsession with end-times. While DeLillo pairs small-town football and the game theory of RAND Corporation deterrence jargon to produce an interrogation of linguistic opacity, Hauptman identifies a powerful convergence of political and religious rhetoric at work in the maintenance of business-as-usual in the military-industrial West of the 1980s. In both novels the banal regularity of small-town life is permeated with global geopolitical significance, and, particularly in Hauptman, the felt insularity of remote communities is belied by their crucial position in the nuclear weapons industry.

If rhetoric works as a prophylactic against the threat of nuclear devastation in DeLillo and Hauptman, the real impact of the West's nuclear business is felt in other invisible ways. The next two chapters focus on responses to the domestic catastrophes produced by the colonization of the West by military-industrial power. Chapter 7 looks at three novels—Martin Cruz Smith's Night Wing (1977), A. A. Carr's Eye Killers (1995), and Jake Page's Cavern (2000)—that address issues of despoliation of environment and community through the use of the gothic. These books work through the implications of invisible agents that restructure matter and attempts to dispose of contaminated waste by conjuring monsters awakened or produced by invasive extraction and burial. In these novels, I argue, waste, whether human or mineral, will not be buried as the toxic remainder of Western history but returns as the unsightly fact of a new, radioactive order of postnatural resistance.

Chapter 8 continues a consideration of "nature" in a militarized landscape, with extended analysis of three nonfiction texts by women variously engaged in environmental politics: Terry Tempest Williams's Refuge: An Unnatural History of Family and Place (1991), Rebecca Solnit's Savage Dreams: A Journey into the Landscape Wars of the American West (1994), and Ellen Meloy's The Last Cheater's Waltz: Beauty and Violence in the Desert Southwest (1999). Like gothic novels, these texts are all concerned with a nature retooled by science and industry. They mark, I argue, the emergence of a kind of nature writing that must include fallout within its remit. Drawing on Lawrence Buell's notion of "toxic discourse," I argue that Williams, Solnit, and Meloy are all compelled to attend to the unseen and unverifiable even as the conventions of the genre within which they are loosely working demands attention to the phenomenological fact of being in place.

Don DeLillo's Underworld (1997), a self-confessed "counterhistory" of the Cold War, is the focus of chapter 9. Explicitly identifying the West as the repository for the abjected remains of America's containment culture, Underworld offers an overt and complex consideration of the network of forces that have contributed to the West as waste-disposal site. The relocated Bronx "waste manager" Nick Shay works in postindustrial Phoenix, part of the emerging global disposal industries that rewrite Cold War antagonism as business opportunity. Recalling William Rathje's work on the Garbage Project at the University of Arizona in the 1970s, DeLillo's novel elaborates the notion of an archaeology of waste that stands in opposition to attempts to recuperate Cold War violence as the reified curatorial artifacts of American triumphalism. Shay's business trip to Kazakhstan, Nevada's nuclear double during the Cold War, demonstrates the always already global position of the American West in postwar geopolitics. While never named as such, DeLillo's twinning of U.S. and post-Soviet test sites is a reminder of the 1989 "Nevada-Semipalatinsk" antinuclear alliance discussed by Solnit that led to the cessation of testing in the Kazakh region through public pressure. Solnit compares the Kazakh protest's success with the relative powerlessness of U.S. campaigners, and DeLillo's post–Cold War assessment of the legacy of the arms race is no less bleak, as new forms of industry move in to extract further value from the contaminated residue of destruction.

While the waste business is one aftereffect of the end of the Cold War, the "enemy deficit" faced by the war economy after 1989 is another. Leslie Marmon Silko's Almanac of the Dead (1991), discussed in chapter 10, provides a grim assessment of the construction of another permanent emergency along the border with Mexico. The declaration of a "war on drugs" focused on the drug-producing countries of Central and South America, combined with nativist fears of a migrant "invasion" has served since the 1980s to legitimize the militarization of the border as a new war zone. At the same time, the fall of the Berlin Wall provided a powerful trope for a new era of inter- and postnational alliances. As Guillermo Gómez-Peña wrote in 1991, "in the middle of this fin-de-siècle earthquake" it may be possible to find "a new place to speak from, and a new vocabulary to describe this bizarre terra ignota we inherited."[12] *Almanac of the Dead*'s ambitious interrogation of neoliberal racism and the prospect of a global anticapital alliance led by indigenous revolutionaries is explored here as a reanimation of wasted populations that redraws the map of the West as a network of marginalized constituencies set to reappropriate the apparatus of invisibility that has rendered them disposable. In doing so, the conjured Anglo-capitalist terror of impending invasion is forced into being. Silko's work is read alongside Charles Bowden's account of a deep-cover drug agent in *A Shadow in the City* (2005) and Cormac McCarthy's *No Country for Old Men* (2005), two books from the point of view of the Anglo male that mark the anxieties produced by the permanent "war on drugs" as a state of emergency that challenges gendered, racialized, and economic structures of power once guaranteed by the boundaries of the nation-state.

Finally, I conclude by reflecting on the heightened relevance of recent Western history and politics in the light of domestic and foreign policy responses to September 11. Many of the concerns of the post–Pearl Harbor period explored here—the exclusion of perceived security threats and the indefinite internment of people constructed as of indeterminate status; the political deployment of fear and dread and the invocation of "evil"; the inferred presence of infiltration from outside and the strengthening of borders; the militarization of daily life through the implementation of a permanent state of emergency and the sense that everything and everyone is a potential target; the containment of dissent; and, not least, the expansion of corporate interests and executive power underwritten by the production of unspeakable human and environmental devastation—have reestablished themselves as issues of utmost significance. If, as both Sunbelt boosters and some critics have long maintained, the West is America, or at least a premonition of what America will become, then the recent history of the West as the hub of U.S. military-corporate power has never been more relevant.[13] In closing, I briefly discuss two post-9/11 novels that, I think, cast a revealing, if dystopian, light on recent history and its roots in the post–Pearl Harbor West. Cormac McCarthy's *The Road* (2006), though arguably more a Southern than a Western novel, is a spare bulletin from the other side of catastrophe, depicting the final march to the sea of a father and son who are among the very few survivors of an unnamed apocalypse. Perry Miyake's *21st Century Manzanar* (2002) imagines a near-future where Executive Order 9066 is reinstated in the aftermath of World War III and a failed economic war with Japan.

Fixated on corruption, duplicity, state violence, and aggressive policies of deracination, the books explored in this study catalog an ongoing series of dirty wars conducted in or emanating from the western United States. A "dirty war" is underhanded, not fought by the rules, and often considered unscrupulous; it is the sort of conflict where actions are unpredictable not just in a tactical sense but in a transgressive sense of being beyond recognized rules of engagement. To be "dirty" in this sense is to be unjust, and a "dirty war" stands in negative relation to the idea of a "just war," epitomized in the post–Pearl Harbor period by the moral legitimacy of World War II.[14] In the West, actions conducted in the name of justice have often been dirty.

If the necessary subterfuge and strategic underhandedness of war counts openness and fairness among its first victims, the proportionality of military actions introduces another dimension to issues of legitimate engagement. A war conducted through dirty tricks soon becomes dirty in another sense: transgressive actions may have the result of producing, whether by design or accident, a level of suffering and destruction considered disproportionate to the aim. In other words, the action produces more chaos than is required to achieve the intended outcome and is therefore dirtier than, say, a "surgical strike," which, as the term implies, is a "clean" or hygienic assault on a definable and limited target. As with the underhanded connotation of a "dirty war," however, the definition of what is disproportionate is relative to position, and all claims to sanitary or efficient warfare must remain open to interpretation. All wars are "dirty wars" in the sense that they produce material devastation and waste, and the jargon of clean and dirty is a familiar part of representations of military actions as combatants separate out the redeemable from the abject, friend from enemy, conduct "clean-up operations" to eliminate enemy presence from an area, and seek to produce some kind of containable order from the catastrophe of a combat zone. At an etymological level, dirt's relation to excrement reinforces the associations with waste as something produced and disposed of, a kind of creative destruction. The aim of war is always the restoration of order after the production of chaos: the purpose of producing dirt is to clean it up.

In the context of the works studied here, there is a further, more literal relevance to the use of "dirt" related to the often desert places in which the wars are said to occur: these are "dirty" wars in the sense that they are wars of and in dirt, an arid version of the notion of a "turf war." As a synonym for earth, then, there is a strong landscape dimension to the notion of a "dirty war" as it pertains to the American West, though territorial and jurisdictional interests clearly drive many wars elsewhere. As will become apparent, the specificity of the Western deserts as the site for the wars discussed here gives the notion of dirt a particularized resonance.

In short, then, the term "dirty war" calls forth a consideration of legitimacy, waste, and land. The contest of meaning over what is clean or just, what is dirty or excessive, in various ways, animates the texts examined here, and all turn around issues of justice, abjection, and place. Put differently, these are texts that investigate power as it works through three interrelated theaters of operation. First is the issue of sovereignty, the nature of authority and its legitimacy. The second issue is a function of the first and concerns the limits of sovereignty, where the line between inside and outside, friend and enemy, clean and abject, is drawn. Finally, inseparable from authority and its limits is the question of the place or site of sovereignty: where the contest for power and its limit is inscribed.

A dirty war implies a position; it is an evaluative, partisan critical term in the counterhistory of the post–Pearl Harbor West. The literature grouped here, shaped by the multivalent reverberations of World War II, the Cold War, and the civil rights movement, and by an awareness of the open secrets of the American West, is an adversarial literature in the sense that it calls attention to and explores the consequences of that which, according to the logic of military security, should remain hidden. The process of "critical unveiling" is a form of refusal since that which has been concealed has been hidden for a reason, even if the reason is also hidden. A critical representation of the workings of power is implicitly involved, then, in an articulation of the otherwise unspoken or unseen.

What I hope will become clear in this book is that what is often characterized as, in Benedict Anderson's words, a "change of consciousness" post-9/11 is more accurately understood as an intensification of longer-standing attitudes and practices that, while not invented by the experience of World War II, have deep roots in the transformation of the United

States as a result of that war. The emergence of the United States as a world power is coterminous with the rise of the American West as an economic, political, and military powerhouse, and the narratives that have, to recall Anderson once again, sprung from the "specific historical circumstances" of the post–Pearl Harbor West speak directly to the "characteristic amnesias" of those times. Faced with the erasure of the founding violence of postwar power—incarceration and secret superweapons—Eddie Hobson tells a story. The struggles of those "collateral casualties" of state power—"othered" populations of Japanese Americans, Native Americans, Latino/as, "downwinders," "undocumented entrants," economically redundant workforces—enter the official record only negatively, as absences. What the "myths, fictions of science, [and] oracles" gathered here offer, then, is a literature of waste, a collection of "signs and clues" that converge to produce a counterhistorical record of what has been remaindered by military-industrial enterprise.

The importance of points or lines of convergence is repeatedly stressed in the texts explored here. Silko, Hauptman, Carr, and Solnit, for example, explicitly discuss the convergence of ostensibly unconnected events and ideas as central to understanding the process of mystification that has rendered invisible not just the workings of power but the excluded subjects of that power. The coming together of signs and clues to provide a pattern of sense is the job of narrative, and the technologies of storytelling themselves often become a narrative preoccupation. Whether it is the oral traditions of Native Americans (Silko, Momaday, Carr) or the Mexican corrido (McCarthy); the empirical rigor of natural history (Williams, Meloy) or the fusion of public and private realms in the spiritual autobiography (Williams); the domestic permutations of the family saga (Morrow, Rizzuto); or the "paranoid" mode of what is sometimes called the "systems" novel (DeLillo); in all cases the construction and circulation of narratives is continuously emphasized as vital to the survival of collectivities capable of the kind of critical engagement with adversity mourned as already lost by Eddie Hobson in *Prisoner's Dilemma*. Faced with the erasures produced by security-driven policies of containment and secrecy in the West, the writing of what "is written in no book" becomes a necessary mode of, literally, exposition, a placing into view or setting forth of relations hitherto unseen.

As my outline of this book suggests, the work of Cormac McCarthy provides one notable element of continuity to this study. This is because I think McCarthy's career broadly follows a path that engages with the movement of Western history. McCarthy's geographic shift of emphasis after *Suttree* (1979) from the South to the Southwest follows the historical migration of southerners into the West in the nineteenth century. *Blood Meridian* tracks that shift as a largely Southern contingent of mercenaries and filibusterers works to establish U.S. sovereignty over the newly conquered Sonoran deserts. The mid-twentieth century setting of *The Border Trilogy* traces the disintegration of the ranching culture established by the inheritors of nineteenth-century expansionists. In these novels, the internal colonization of federal military-industrial power—glimpsed in the elliptical epilogue to *Blood Meridian*—makes redundant the self-reliant masculinity constructed out of the legacy of conquest and, in John Grady Cole's and Billy Parham's apparent empathy with other "vanishing Americans" (Indians and Mexicans), positions the cowboy as the latest population to be consumed and wasted by the United States. *No Country for Old Men*, in returning to the 1980s, offers an assessment of the emergent neoconservative order through the asymmetrical conflict between small-town law-enforcement officers wedded to "traditional" values and the transnational free trade of the ultraviolent drug business. Finally, *The Road* seems to provide a bleak coda to McCarthy's twenty-year meditation on the fate of the West, as the wasteland discourse used in *Blood Meridian* as expansionist rhetoric returns in literal form as the postapocalyptic landscape of a decimated United States. McCarthy's most recent novel seems to finally yield to the catastrophe his previous works had always threatened.

While I do not want to overly privilege McCarthy's place in this book, I do think that, along with Don DeLillo and Leslie Silko, McCarthy's work most consistently and powerfully articulates the concerns of power, conflict, and waste that animate this study. McCarthy's first Western novel, then, opens my discussion of the works brought together here. Before turning to *Blood Meridian*, however, I want to explore the broader cultural politics of the postwar West. In other words, I want to give some account of the way in which the emergence of the military-industrial West marks a profound shift in U.S. power relations, both nationally and globally, and how the particularity of the West's political and economic dominance is shaped by and benefits from the conditions of open secrecy provided by the desert West as it is constructed through the wasteland discourse. What this means is that the West provides the ground for an emplaced cultural politics of permanent war that functions not just rhetorically as legitimation for a permanent war economy but materially through the production of enemies and the maintenance of a perpetual state of emergency. It is the West, I argue, that provides the model for this kind of militarized neoliberal entrepreneurialism that has come to represent U.S. global relations, and it is out of this West that a counterhistory of U.S. hegemony can be located.

1. THE PURLOINED LANDSCAPE

Nature loves to hide.
Heraclitus

Michel Foucault's 1976 Collège de France lectures outlined the emergence, in the sixteenth and early seventeenth centuries, of a form of historical discourse that sought to counter the traditional function of history as a celebration and memorialization of sovereignty and sovereigns. Instead of reminding readers of the antiquity of kingdoms and the greatness of heroes and kings, claims Foucault, this new discourse was driven by a demand for rights; instead of claiming a unity among the sovereign, the nation, and the people, a new "principle of heterogeneity" emerged that sought to reveal the hidden story of conquest that the blinding light of power had cast into darkness.[1] This counterhistory is not a history of continuity and order but, as Foucault explains, a discourse that "tears society apart and speaks of legitimate rights solely in order to declare war on laws."[2] Given the concealed nature of its object, this must be a history of "deciphering, the detection of the secret, of the outwitting of the ruse, and of the reappropriation of a knowledge that has been distorted or buried."[3] While it would be a mistake, Foucault warns, to think of this discourse as belonging solely to the oppressed, its "strategic polyvalency" means that it is a "mobile discourse" of opposition that, situated in "perpetual interaction" with the history of sovereignty, produces a powerful expansion of historical knowledge.[4] What this contest over the meaning of history reveals, for Foucault, is that there is "no such thing as a neutral subject."[5]

The partisan, adversarial nature of counterhistory, according to Foucault's model, emerges out of an apparently achieved ideological consensus. The placid continuity between past and present in the form of a naturalized order is taken to belie the concealment of repressed, contending claims. In many ways, Foucault is articulating precisely the experience of the postwar generation's unraveling of the Cold War consensus since the 1960s. The rewriting of history that has taken place due to the force of that generation's attempt to make visible the concealed legacies of conquest, to borrow a phrase from one of the defining texts of the New Western history's particular assault on the memorialization of sovereignty, has been profound and far reaching.[6] But just as contemporary "wars" on drugs or terror are conceived as open-ended, perpetual struggles, so too must the "war on laws" that Foucault mentions be understood as a permanent condition. If capitalism requires the maintenance of a permanent state of emergency in order to protect and advance its interests, the business of critical unveiling must continue in earnest. This, at least, is what I believe the texts examined here engage in and what motivates this study.

One of the dangers of the countermemory excavated through Foucault's genealogical "effective history" is that, in refusing a unified narrative in favor of "the singularity of events," important connections and continuities between and across events are broken.[7] A refusal of coherence can lead, as George Lipsitz has argued, to an "atomizing [of] common experience into accidents."[8] In his modification of Foucault's project of finding countermemory "in the most unpromising places,"[9] Lipsitz maintains a concern "with the local, the immediate, and the personal" but sees this starting point building "outward toward a total story."[10] In grounding this study in an examination of writings about the post–Pearl Harbor West that are often ostensibly unconnected and speak from and to very different constituencies, I want to preserve the local ramifications of the texts while, through juxtaposition and the identification of shared concerns differently expressed, I construct a discursive network that, within the "total story" of the military-industrial overlay, makes up an articulation of the "unpromising places" of the West produced by U.S. economic and military global dominance. The local here is, therefore, not reducible to but produced by global power relations, and regional, ethnic, gender, and class constructions, however particularized and contingent, must be seen as constituted, though not exhausted, by wider historical forces.

If internment camps, military bases, bomb sites, ruins ancient and modern, and waste dumps feature heavily in the articulation of the contemporary West featured here and compose what might be considered an unduly negative assessment of the region's complex and multiform identities, it is because, I think, these places stand as the excluded double of the celebrated landscapes of the national and international Western imaginary. The paradox of an awareness of the hidden that is shown but not seen is what I will call the open secret of the American West.

What makes recent writing about the militarized West particularly striking is the way this literature is faced with a power that is at once hidden and exposed. It is no secret that America's military occupies vast stretches of Western space, nor are the nuclear and other tests (and their effects) entirely invisible. The histories of Japanese American internment, of Los Alamos, the bomb and the arms race, the drug war and border policing are all in circulation as continued subjects of intense critical interrogation. As Foucault argues, the "unitary discourses which first disqualified and then ignored" counterhistorical forms of knowledge can also be annexed and taken back "within the fold of their own discourse."[11] If Foucault is right, what is hidden that requires unveiling if the secret is open?

William Chaloupka has speculated on the meaning of the "open secret" in American political usage, arguing that to use this term "is to remind one's audience that this is something they already know, a significance they have already grasped."[12] While the history of internment, nuclear testing, and so on are "already known," the circulation of confirmed knowledge reiterates the practice of concealment as something already part of the discourse of security that gives meaning to those "already grasped" events. The absorption of counterhistories into the unitary discourse of the nation includes the exceptional as part of itself, negatively confirming "official" history through its embrace of the exception. The reminder of the secret that is already known both reconfirms secrecy as integral to national security and activates an awareness of the spectral threat that produces secrecy as a necessary defense.

The open secret of the American West, then, is that its open landscapes, so often the overdetermined signifiers of American liberty, screen off its military uses and their environmental and human consequences, supplemented and reinforced by a long-standing discourse of Western "wasteland" that further shields from view the contradictions produced by the inclusion of the excluded. The West is the screen upon which openness is projected and also the veiling screen that preserves secrecy.[13] The inherited overdetermination of "desert space" in U.S. culture as site of physical and spiritual challenge, as irrecoverably hostile "wasteland," and as physical evidence of an achieved apocalypse, makes the desert West an essential element of—indeed, perhaps the essential ground for—the military-industrial mystification of its own covert spectacle.[14] What I am discussing, then, is a purloined landscape, a space that, like Poe's letter, is hidden in plain sight. The landscape, like the letter, remains hidden, of course, because it is so flagrantly before one's eyes. That which has been taken is not taken away but rendered invisible by allowing itself to be thoroughly exposed to the field of vision.[15]

Before the mid-nineteenth century, the deserts between Texas and California were valuable mainly because they connected the east and west coasts. The southwestern desert, as Patricia Limerick notes, "found its initial significance as a place to cross."[16] The desert, then, is from the beginning conceived by Americans as a redundant space that receives its significance in negative terms. Limerick observes that while the overland trail was seen by many as an adventure and a challenge, "the desert went too far. In desert travel, hardship went past adventure and into ordeal." This hardship led many travelers to feel betrayed by the land's intractable reality: "[t]he desert passage was an interlude of shaken confidence; the visual distortion of mirages was only one of the ways in which nature, in the desert, seemed to cheat." For a nation concerned with agricultural expansion as the primary civilizing force, hitting arid lands meant that "the project of mastering the continent seemed to have reached a nonnegotiable limit."[17] While Spanish explorers in New Mexico, as Yu-Fi Tuan points out, made little mention of climatic aridity in their reports, often remarking on the presence of water, Anglo-Americans, by contrast, seem from the outset to have been preoccupied with the perceived emptiness of the desert.[18]

Nevertheless, even as the idea of the desert as ordeal seemed to contradict Anglo-American notions of the United States as nature's nation, the arid lands did serve to confirm other aspects of Protestant America's discourse of spiritual mission. The American desert, like its biblical counterparts, could be a test, a site for overcoming the temptations and excesses of civilized life. While the desert became, after the mid-nineteenth century, a site of economic value due to the discovery of minerals,

by the turn of the century growing dissatisfaction with American capitalist culture among the well-off, educated middle classes also made
the deserts inviting as a purgative space of Romantic sublimity and aesthetic purity.[19] Even as evangelical Progressive irrigationists became increasingly confident that they could redeem the terrain through cultiva-
tion, aesthetes like Rutgers art historian John C. Van Dyke were writing
about the visual splendor of a land that should remain untouched by base
economic interests.[20]

The conflict between exploitation and conservation is, then, present
from the beginning of U.S. interest in its desert lands, yet both positions
derive at least part of their authority from the imposition of ideas of vacancy onto the terrain. Both read the space as empty and see this emptiness as its source of value. This notional vacancy, saturated in Hebrew
and Christian desert iconography, functions also as a form of selective
blindness that eliminates consideration of indigenous populations and
traditions and values that may have prior claim to the land. Speculators
and aesthetes alike need the tropes of emptiness and uselessness in order to validate their construction of the landscape as available space. As
a place meaningless in itself and useful only in its very expendability,
the desert becomes a facilitating site evacuated of any significance other
than the instrumental.[21]

This designation of desert as wasteland makes the arid West an abject
place that, by World War II, can serve as the necessary differentiating sacrifice that maintains the national order. In withdrawing land, the nation
identifies a site that is, as Julia Kristeva writes, "something rejected from
which one does not part."[22] That which has been withdrawn continues to
be the necessary structural other that gives shape to what is being protected through the act of exclusion. Abjection, Kristeva explains, "does
not radically cut off the subject from what threatens it—on the contrary,
abjection acknowledges it to be in perpetual danger."[23] The sense of danger maintained by a permanent state of emergency is served by the indispensable existence of places out of sight but definitely there that signify the containment of externalized threats to security. The withdrawn
land, then, is both guarantor of security and an oblique and uncanny signifier of that which is feared.

Pearl Harbor and the Military Occupation of the West

It is with Pearl Harbor that the "wasteland" conception of the desert West is firmly rearticulated as a function of national security. The Japanese attack revealed America's vulnerability to external threat and soon became symbolic of American innocence in a dangerous world. Isolationists could no longer appeal to geographical distance as a guarantor of national security, as Roosevelt explained to the nation two days after the attack: "[w]e cannot measure our safety in terms of miles on any map anymore."[24] The compression of distance and devastation caused by modern bombers became the source of increasing anxiety as the United States anticipated further and more terrible surprise attacks. The imaginative power of possible danger inaugurated a range of civil defense measures, including blackouts, air raid drills, ID cards and fingerprinting, and the beginnings of the hypersensitivity to issues of domestic security that would come to characterize the postwar years.

The absence of real evidence of further external attacks did not prevent the incarceration of 120,000 Japanese Americans in concentration camps, a policy justified as a security measure but that really served as a symbolic punishment for the only visible trace of the enemy. Indeed, in a remarkable feat of paranoid reasoning, the very absence of sabotage became itself evidence of the scheming inscrutability and devious ingenuity of Japanese Americans.[25]

The procedure of eliminating undesirable social elements through removal and containment had been a tactical element in the securing of U.S. hegemony since the concentration of Native Americans on reservations in the nineteenth century. The removal of Japanese Americans through a modified version of this internal colonization functions similarly to identify and eliminate social excess as dangerous waste that must be cordoned off and held in place.[26] As such, threats to security are made visible and then removed and rendered invisible.

The majority of internment camps were located in remote regions of the American West, away from urban centers in inaccessible and, as internment narratives repeatedly emphasize, inhospitable areas.[27] The secreting of hazardous human elements in the desert West was soon followed by the establishment of the nuclear weapons project in New Mexico and the expansion of military bases and test sites throughout the West. World War II made the desert West the secret receptacle of national security. Pearl Harbor, then, triggered fear of the military-technological sublime, activated a xenophobic distrust of imagined enemies within, kickstarted the permanent military mobilization of the United States, and led to the geographical and tropological location of much of that mobilization in the deserts of the Southwest.

The radical transformation of the West during World War II is well documented. As Carl Abbott argues, until the war the West was "a colony of the Northeast," good for raw materials but with little investment capital or industrial output.[28] The massive federal and military involvement in the West during the war changed all that, as the public works projects of the New Deal were extended, and reclamation projects, agricultural subsidies, interstate construction, and maintenance of public lands effectively restructured, as Gerald D. Nash claims, "a natural resource–based colonial economy into a technologically oriented and service economy."[29] The rate and extent of growth in the West during the war was, Nash argues, on a scale not seen since the Gold Rush.[30]

It was Western wartime production that drove massive westward migration, with cities like Las Vegas, Tucson, Phoenix, Albuquerque, and El Paso doubling their populations.[31] Postwar housing policies, new highways and airports, and the invention of air conditioning sustained and accelerated urban and suburban growth.[32] Increasingly, the marginal, land-based communities described by writers like McCarthy, Anaya, and Silko found themselves adjacent to, if not consumed by, New Western corporate hubs like DeLillo's Phoenix. The maintenance of a large military presence in the West after the war, along with federal social support in the form of the GI Bill and continued investment in large public works projects such as dam and reservoir construction, cemented the physical and economic transformation of a region that saw the population grow from thirty-two to forty-five million in the fifteen years after 1945.[33] It was as if, as Richard White has written, "someone had tilted the country: people, money, and soldiers all spilled west."[34]

Military spending in particular underpinned the West's economic and political ascendancy. Local capitalists knew that it would be federal military spending rather than the operation of the free market that would determine the location of new plants, army bases, and scientific research facilities.[35] The West became what Nash calls "the nation's military bastion" with training grounds, airfields, supply depots, and weapons test sites sprouting throughout the region, installations sunk underground and into mountains, entire communities relocated and new ones of scientists and soldiers created.[36] The military's nuclear program also reshaped the region's extraction industries, with the federally sponsored Atomic Energy Commission creating an artificial uranium-mining boom during the 1950s when the mineral was found in Colorado, Utah, and New Mexico, and on the Navajo reservation in Arizona.

If federal money drove military-related scientific and industrial expansion in the early postwar period, the rise of the Sunbelt and its high-tech, postindustrial base also emerges out of the apparently contradictory mixture of military Keynesianism and the antilabor, antiwelfare entrepreneurialism of Southern and Western conservatism.[37] Heavy government investment in military and security sectors has been accompanied by sustained disinvestment in social services that produces, alongside the jackpot economy of the federally manufactured military-industrial boom, an "other" West characterized by structural poverty, underdevelopment, and despoliation. As such, the "colonial" economy of the West is not so much replaced by the industrial, high-tech and service sectors as it is obscured by them. The preservation of "other" Wests inside the military-industrial New West as, for example, tourist attractions or disposal sites, complicates the narrative of the West's spectacular postwar economic transformation and demands consideration of the region as emblematic of the intensified asymmetrical social relations produced by state-supported military-industrial capitalism. These relations, as the literature of the postwar West variously makes evident, must be properly understood as constituting a condition of permanent war.

Locating the Militarized West

The part of the American West that is the focus of this book is commonly known as the Southwest, one of the last areas to be incorporated into the continental United States by Euro-American settlers and a region that, due to its unique landscapes, has long been ambivalently figured in the national imaginary as both repellent and sublime. While the Southwest is by no means the only part of the West transformed by post–Pearl Harbor militarization, the particularity of the Southwest's desert spaces—its relative isolation, sparse population, and mineral wealth—has meant that it has been especially useful for the siting of some of the most deadly aspects of modern military-industrial enterprise.

No geographical region is more indeterminately locatable than the Southwest, and the definition of where and what the Southwest is continues to provoke disagreement. It is worth repeating here Reed Way Dasenbrook's obvious but essential question: "Southwest of What?"[38] The geographer D. W. Meinig wrote in 1971 that the Southwest "is a distinctive place to the American mind but a somewhat blurred place on American maps, which is to say that everyone knows that there is a Southwest but that there is little agreement as to just where it is."[39] While the difficulty of locating the Southwest is generally perceived as a problem, since the vague set of assumptions and imaginings associated with the region can leave it open to misrepresentation, cultural colonization, and exploitative caricature, fixing the Southwest spatially may not be the most appropriate response to the dangers of locational indeterminacy.[40] Michael J. Riley, for example, rejects any attempt to locate a Southwest that is external to its discursive formation, arguing instead that it is in the necessarily fluid and malleable zone of cultural space that the Southwest is ultimately to be found, and the "culture of touristic displacement" and "commodification of the Other" are unavoidably embedded in the discourses and practices that have produced the region as a spatial construct.[41]

The Southwest is distinctively heterogeneous in terms of what is conventionally referred to as its "tricultural" combination of indigenous, Hispanic, and Anglo histories and cultures. While the combination of remarkable landscapes, ancient ruins, and "colorful" indigenous traditions has provided the Southwest with valuable tourist-industry capital, the "untouched" quality of the region is made possible in large part by the structural poverty brought about by underdevelopment.[42] If the desert is the place that makes possible the testing and disposal of hazardous products, it is also the place where social waste is most likely to be deposited. As such, the romantic anticapitalism that animated the desert aesthetic of writers like John C. Van Dyke, Mary Austin and D. H. Lawrence can be efficiently converted into the reified romance of the "old

Southwest." In a curious double bluff the historically marginal status of the Southwest can be symbolically maintained as the Chamber of Commerce face of Western identity even as it is denied by the fact of Sunbelt military-industrial prosperity and confirmed by the experienced marginality of those wasted populations and landscapes screened off by tourist industry simulations of them.

The importance of display and concealment in the production of the Southwestern imaginary is, then, not merely a consequence of relatively recent military-industrial occupation but is also a functional aspect of the region's long-standing reputation as a space of great natural beauty. The "untouched" Southwest so attractive to nature-lovers and Indian-watchers is preserved as such because, as Sylvia Rodriguez has argued, it is "a rugged, isolated geographical zone where marginal ethnic enclaves persist in subordinated relation to members of the national society."[43] The whole of the U.S-Mexican Southwest is, for Rodriguez, a "refuge region" within which enclaved minority populations socioculturally "retain a colonial, sometimes pseudoaboriginal character." Because of their remoteness and ecology, such regions "remain sparsely populated and isolated and become progressively underdeveloped and backward in relation to mainstream urban society."[44] This constructed backwardness, while applying primarily to indigenous populations, also, as McCarthy's novels illustrate, comes to include an increasingly outmoded cowboy culture, and might in addition serve to characterize the disposability of "downwinder" communities and other casualties of Western military-industrial blight. This economically and ethnically heterogeneous population is a class of wasted lives that is at the same time visible and invisible, productive and nonproductive; it is the human resource that produces the optical effect of an untouched nature outside history. Such forms of internal colonization must be understood as dialectically related to the ascendancy of postwar Sunbelt capitalism and its capacity to construct and consume "other" people as well as "other" places.[45] Indeed, as DeLillo and others suggest, it is even possible for the region's nuclear legacy to be absorbed into the commodified Southwest of the touristic gaze.

While the wasteland discourse claims to have found a wilderness of waste, then, what in fact has happened is that the discourse itself makes the land into waste as it produces order through differentiation: waste is, as Zygmunt Bauman argues, echoing Foucault and Kristeva, the "refuse left after the world has been cleanly cut into a slice called 'us' and another labeled 'them.'"[46] The condition of threat generated by this ordering is, for Bauman, "a toxic side-product in the production of semiotic transparency. Irrationality, chaos, strangerhood, ambivalence are all names for that nameless 'beyond' for which the dominant powers that identified themselves as reason, as forces of order, as natives, as meaning have no use."[47] If part of this ambivalence is what gives the tourist view of the Southwest its edge, it is also what drives the critique of consumption of people and places as spectacle in the West's "mobile discourse" of opposition. What narratives concerned with internees, Native Americans, downwinders, cowboys, and illegal migrants share is the sense of being simultaneously inside and outside the dominant order; they are identities both defined by and excluded from the exercise of sovereign power as it shapes the postwar Southwest as the space within which national security is maintained.

Arjun Appadurai argues that the local, from the point of view of modern nationalism, functions "principally to incubate and reproduce compliant national citizens."[48] As such, the overdetermined symbolic "Southwest" could be said to operate for the United States both as "a site of nationally appropriated nostalgias, celebrations, and commemorations" and as "a necessary condition for the production of nationals."[49] The importance of the local or regional in the production of national identity is echoed by Dasenbrook when he refers to the "Southwest" as an area southwest of U.S. federal power: "a perfect representation of the dependent status of the whole area."[50] While the growing economic and political strength of the Southwest since World War II may have challenged that dependence, the persistent notion of an "Old" dependent Southwest does help to screen off the fact that the "New" Southwest houses the means by which U.S. global authority is rigorously maintained. It is through these terms that colonized or abjected populations and places can function as "local color" in the national imaginary and remain inside American national identity even as they stand in exceptional relation to it. Bearing in mind the imbrication of the "Southwest" in the discourse of the nation, it follows that there can be no local contingency that is not always already bound up with national or international affairs. Any attempt to bracket local environmental, political, or literary concerns as of merely regional interest reproduces the subordination of the periphery that gives definition to the center.

The paradox of the West as both peripheral and central to American national identity helps explain why terrain often considered to represent the quintessence of American openness and potentiality is also the most federally managed part of the United States. Indian reservations, New Deal public works, military-industrial installations and bases, National Park management, and border-policing are all aspects of the federal government's production of Western space, and over 80 percent of Nevada, over 60 percent of Utah, and between a third and half of Colorado, New Mexico, Arizona, and California continue to be federally owned.[51] This is a federally constructed landscape, and the conception of emptiness that facilitated its creation is a federally constructed emptiness.

Not all of the areas discussed in this book belong properly to the most particular definition of the Southwest that takes as its center the Four Corners and radiates out to include New Mexico, Arizona, southeastern Utah, and southwestern Colorado. Instead, following Riley, the Southwest is conceived here as a discursive space or nodal point that intersects with other regional, national, and international zones. Nevertheless, there is one particular use of the "Southwest" as a definable place that connects with the textual geography explored in this book, and that is the so-called Southwest Defense Complex, a grouping of labs, bases, ranges, and airspaces stretching from West Texas through New Mexico and Arizona to Southern California and up into Nevada and Utah.

The area, defined by the lobby group Southwest Defense Alliance, includes Edwards Air Force Base, China Lake Naval Air Warfare Center, Vandenberg Air Force Base, the Air-Ground Combat Center in Twentynine Palms, and the Fort Irwin National Training Center, all in California; the Yuma Proving Grounds and Marine Corps Air Station in Arizona; Naval Air Station in Fallon and the Weapons Tactical Center and Electronic Warfare Ranges at Nellis Air Force Base in Nevada; the Utah Test and Training Range; and the White Sands Missile Range in New Mexico. The sites and installations of the Southwest Defense Complex are, as described by the alliance, "in close proximity to each other, operate with each other quite often, and are linked to each other by a unique array of telecommunications, electronic and optical connections." Taken together, the complex "provides unencroached geography, national laboratories, expanses of dedicated airspace, and millions of acres of buffer lands thus assuring our nation the best place on Earth to conduct military research, testing, and training."[52] The cost-effectiveness of maintaining all the major installations in the same region is clear, but it is the kind of landscape provided by the Southwest that truly justifies the location of the sites there, as this description of the complex demonstrates:

> Physical space is vital to the type of testing and training [required by a high-tech military force]. A single open-air test range requires nearly two million acres of open land. The Southwest is the only region of the country that offers land of this size, as well as air and sea space needed for other kinds of testing. The Southwest offers over 335 million acres of federally owned land. Over 490 thousand square miles of air space is available in the Southwest, and 484 thousand square miles of sea are open for training activities. This land can be used without the interference from civilians or substantial electromagnetic interference—both of which are a problem in the rest of the country.[53]

This boosterism reveals the perpetuation of long-held perceptions of the Southwest as vast, unused and empty. The wasteland discourse is in full operation here and pitched directly as a strategic advantage to American national (and, by implication global) security. With plenty of "buffer" lands and no "interference from civilians," the Southwest as defense complex is the ultimate open secret. As the alliance's 2005 full-color brochure makes plain—depicting a map of the major installations flanked by images of fighter planes, bombers, and a number of explosions—this is the space in which U.S. military power is realized in its most spectacular forms. Screened out by images of utterly decontextualized pyrotechnics is any consideration of environmental impact or acknowledgment that many of the installations are positioned adjacent to large metropolitan centers, Indian lands, or National Parks and other historic and recreational sites. While such a rampant example of military-industrial corporate self-promotion cannot realistically be expected to address those absences, the imagining of a Southwest Defense Complex as both regionally distinctive and globally significant does serve to pin down a construction of the Southwest that speaks to the cultural politics of this study. The brochure's map of major military installations is an overlay that conceals the markers of military-industrial conquest and the socio-economic conditions produced and sustained by it. If the tourist Southwest, to recall Appadurai, functions to service "nationally appropriated nostalgias, celebrations, and commemorations," then the Southwest Defense Complex establishes the "necessary condition for the production of nationals."

The Southwest of this book is indeed, then, a "distinctive place" but blurred on the maps. Imbricated in the defense complex map is the counterhistory of the postwar West that is produced by the writers included here. The site occupied by the complex includes, for example, the Tucson and Laguna Pueblo of Leslie Marmon Silko's *Ceremony* and *Almanac of the Dead*, the Phoenix of Don DeLillo's *Underworld*; the New Mexican landscapes of Thomas McMahon's and Bradford Morrow's Los Alamos novels; the Nevada Test Site and northern Utah discussed by Terry Tempest Williams, Rebecca Solnit, and Ellen Meloy; the West Texas and northern Mexico of Cormac McCarthy's borderlands; and the Texas panhandle around Amarillo imagined by William Hauptman. In addition, the map must include Manzanar and Tule Lake in California and other Japanese American internment camps as markers of the inauguration of the permanent state of emergency that calls into existence the Southwest as a defense complex. Furthermore, as a March 2007 update on the alliance Web site reminds us, the international border with Mexico must be entered as a crucial location for developments in U.S. militarization.[54]

What the Southwest Defense Complex brochure illustrates, especially in its combination of a map of the Southwest on one side with a global map of the Americas on the other, is the reach of American military and economic power. In the sense that part of the argument of this book is that what happens in the West makes a difference everywhere else I think we must accept the alliance's positioning of the Southwest Defense Complex as the hard core of American geopolitical dominance. As I have already claimed, however, this demarcated region is shot through with a counterdiscourse that challenges the legitimacy of the complex's overlay and the implications of its global authority. While Appadurai's reading of the regional suggests a straightforward manufacturing of consent, he goes on to note that the local is in actuality a very hard site to police and "subversion, evasion, and resistance" are widespread and pluriform.[55] What I hope will become clear through the course of this book is that the power of the local stands in complex and often subversive relation to the national and global constructions that would render a region like the Southwest uniformly compliant in the surrender of its particularity to any metanarrative of assent.

The "Southwest" referred to throughout my discussion is necessarily contaminated both by what might be considered properly external to it both in terms of geography—those areas some commentators would exclude from a regional definition focused on the Four Corners—and demographics (not all of the writers here hail from or live in the West). Such contamination refuses the notion of a "pure" Southwest and allows for some geo-conceptual slippage. It recognizes that the Southwest is produced in dialectical relation to other places. It also signals a concern not just for actual places but for the power of connotations produced by the idea of places that are not necessarily of the place itself but nonetheless inseparable from it. The Southwest that emerges here is at the same time sublime and abject, overdetermined and thoroughly vacant, prehistoric and futuristic, utopian and apocalyptic, saved and wasted.

How the West Was Withdrawn

The Southwest as defense complex is the result of over fifty years of federal imagineering that has called into being a space of extraordinary power predicated on the exceptional authority conferred on the executive during times of war. As James Madison wrote in 1795, enhanced executive power has long been a consequence of war, where "executive will" directs "physical force" and "the executive hand" dispenses "the public treasures."[56] Under the military Keynsianism of the West's post–Pearl Harbor war economy executive power has become part of what Chalmers Johnson calls a "feedback loop," whereby a strengthened military-industrial complex concentrates power in the executive, who is then predisposed to further military investment.[57] War calls forth executive power that can remain legitimate only insofar as the war footing is maintained.

As commander-in-chief, the president can use the military for police actions without the formal declaration of war, but only Congress has the authority to declare war.[58] As head of state, however, the president has authority to declare a state of emergency and in so doing summons executive power otherwise held accountable to the other branches of government. Outside a formal declaration of emergency, the president also has recourse to the executive order, which amounts to direct presidential action that does not require congressional support. Taken together, the executive order and emergency powers constitute broad executive authority that has been used directly to reshape the territorial, economic, and social environment of the American West according to the conditions of permanent war.[59]

Since presidential power is fully realized in wartime, the metaphor of war, as Georgio Agamben argues, has become increasingly integral to the way presidents justify political action.[60] In the American West, executive power has been used to redefine the boundary between inside and outside in terms of populations (Roosevelt's Executive Order 9066) and in terms of space itself, with the withdrawal of land for military bases. Executive powers have also been invoked to deal with immigration as a perceived national emergency, contributing to the intensified policing of the border with Mexico as a form of military conflict.[61] The broad remit given to such powers by the need for security demonstrates how a state of exception can produce populations and places that can be literally withdrawn from the field of vision and reinscribed as outside the desired limits of "normal" social circumstances.

The practice of federal land withdrawal is fundamental to an understanding of how the state of emergency is given spatial form by executive order and how the desert West is thereby constructed as the site of permanent war. From 1940, when President Roosevelt created what is now called the Nellis Range in Nevada, through the 1950s, the Department of Defense expanded its control of land from three million to over thirty million acres.[62] Between January 1955 and June 1956 alone the military applied for over fourteen million acres of public land. While congressional disquiet at the scale of land withdrawal led to the passage of the Engle Act in 1958, which required congressional approval of any withdrawal over five thousand acres, in practice security demands have often trumped congressional restraint.[63]

Once captured by executive order, the release of withdrawn land back into the public domain is rare. The Military Lands Withdrawal Act of 1986 extended for fifteen years a number of withdrawal extensions that had previously failed to get through Congress, giving the military over seven million acres of land in Alaska, Arizona, California, Nevada, and New Mexico. A further act of 1999 renewed the withdrawal for another twenty-five years after 2001. While the 1986 act made the Department of the Interior responsible for the management of these lands, ensuring provision for grazing, wildlife management, recreation, fire control, and the preparation of environmental impact statements, the military was given authority to close the ranges for operational, safety, or security reasons.[64]

Withdrawn Western land remains, like Poe's letter, in place but hidden, still part of the United States but in a relation of exception to it. Again the desert has been bestowed with negative value, the wasteland that gives form to the "inside" of security.[65] The desert is no longer a hostile enemy but, as Bauman puts it, the abjected stranger "who 'joins in,' the outside that enters the inside, the difference that turns into identity."[66] Once the exception—war—becomes the rule, the exceptional powers called upon by the sovereign in a state of war are normalized. It is this paradoxical condition of modern sovereignty as, in Agamben's words, "at the same time, outside and inside the juridical order," that produces the purloined landscape of the Southwest Defense Complex.[67]

Embraced through withdrawal, militarized land, like Bauman's stranger or Agamben's "bare life," a form produced by the state of exception that is subject to the law but not protected by it, is a kind of waste generated during the production of friends and enemies.[68] While the indeterminate status of the wasted stranger is not quite an enemy, he or she or it does constitute a threat to security inasmuch as the stranger (the excluded land and its inhabitants) represents, from the point of view of security-driven order, what Hardt and Negri call a "fleeting and ungraspable" danger that is "ever present, something like a hostile aura."[69] The wasted lives and spaces produced by the process of withdrawal, then, persist as the necessary threat that justifies the continuation of the emergency that has caused their exclusion in the first place.

The Biopower of Permanent War

Paul Virilio claims that World War II did not conclude with Allied victory in 1945 but has, in fact, never ended.[70] Eisenhower knew as much when he warned of the power of the military-industrial complex and its grip on what Seymour Melman in 1974 called the "permanent war economy."[71] In the same year, Daniel Bell noted that between 1950 and 1970, 80 percent of federal research and development money was spent on "external challenge" at the expense of social and environmental needs at home.[72] Melman and Bell, reflecting on the repercussions of the long Cold War and the cost, financial and social, of the Vietnam War, might have been forgiven for thinking, as relations with the Soviets began to thaw and U.S. troops withdrew from southeast Asia, that nearly thirty years of military-industrial domination of the American economy could be coming to an end. Yet, with the failure of Jimmy Carter's "reality check" and the election of Ronald Reagan in 1980, another wave of military spending and Cold War rhetoric commenced. While there have been four major postwar booms in defense spending—during the wars in Korea and Vietnam, during Reagan's presidency, and finally in the wake of the 9/11 attacks—it is worth noting that from 1955 to 2002 defense spending never declined to its pre–Cold War level.[73] It would seem, as Thomas Pynchon observed the year before Melman and Bell, that the "real War is always there," and this "true war is the celebration of markets."[74]

Foucault calls this permanent war a "coded war" with battle lines running "through the whole of society."[75] While modern political theory promised the separation of war from politics, encrypted in "peacetime" politics is the "real War" that continues to structure relations of power the nation-state claims to have banished beyond its borders.[76] Mobilizing the external threat of war achieves the establishment of military institutions ostensibly removed from the civil order but in fact entirely constitutive of it. From military institutions, as Madison was aware in the eighteenth century, "proceed debts and taxes; and armies, and debts, and taxes are the known instruments for bringing the many under the domination of the few."[77] Preparedness for war produces the entire civil order, even as war is figured as the exception to that order.[78] Understanding war not as a disruption of order but as the condition upon which order is constructed "makes society intelligible," Foucault argues, since a "history that takes as its starting point the fact of war can relate all these things—war, religion, politics, manners, and characters—and can therefore act as a principle that allows us to understand history."[79]

Madison believed that by strengthening executive power, war eroded democracy and led to a "degeneracy of manner and of morals." "No nation can preserve its freedom," he concludes, "in the midst of continual warfare."[80] Everyday life, under such conditions, is produced through the maintenance of a sense of imminent danger that Hardt and Negri, drawing on Foucault and Agamben, describe as a "regime of biopower."[81] For Foucault, biopower reaches beyond the merely negative power of disciplinary separation and exclusion to achieve the convergence of life and politics through a thoroughgoing regulation of all aspects of life.[82] Biopolitical governmentality gives shape and order to entire populations not primarily through laws but tactically through the complementary triangulation of "sovereignty-discipline-government."[83] While the function of biopower is to sustain rather than to take life, the paradox here is that if war is a regime of biopower, then the threat of violence and death must somehow be written into the regulation of life, normalizing the exceptional conditions of war as part of everyday affairs.

In order to protect and sustain life, biopower needs to maintain within itself as real the threats it promises to protect against. The presence of militarized land is one way that invisible threats can become materialized, the fact of a secure installation's existence seemingly confirming the danger it purports to protect against. Routinized acts of civilian preparedness are another, as William Chaloupka explains in his description of school duck-and-cover drills during the Cold War. These drills, he writes, while "purporting to further chances of survival, were actually exercises in the utility of terror." Perfecting the moves required during the drill was motivated out of a "pervasive respect for military capabilities inextricably combined with an awesome fear and an empathy with Hiroshima's fate." While the drills produced "citizens ready to dive under the desk 'in a flash,' [students also] internalized [a] calibrated, produced fascination with modernity, adopting the conditions of control as their own 'motives' (to attend college and study science, for some; for others, to enter the military and go to Vietnam)." These "nuclear-inspired micro controls," successfully "labeled as repressed and unspeakable," become the "invisible" conditions of everyday life: "[w]e ducked, and it covered."[84]

Here, knowledge of recent history (Hiroshima) connects with collective values (obeying the teacher, respecting the military), instinct (survival) and performative gestures (distinctive postures and positions), to reproduce the conditions of the Cold War as integral to ordinary domestic life. The broad structures of global geopolitics—Hiroshima's legacy, Soviet threat, militarized economy—are reiterated at the level of individual choices and actions, each of which further shapes life under the permanent state of exception. Tactics for fostering life entail the taking of life, as the memory of Hiroshima and its discursive configuration as the necessary event that saved American lives and stopped the war reveals.[85] Under permanent war, being capable of killing to go on living is the principle that defines the strategy of states since wars, as Foucault argues, "are no longer waged on behalf of a sovereign who must be defended" but are fought "on behalf of the existence of everyone."[86]

The decisive move that justifies death in the pursuit of life is, for Foucault, "to create caesuras within the biological continuum addressed by biopower" through racism, by which he means the process of othering.[87] Racism makes the relationship of war—"If you want to live, the other must die"—compatible with the application of biopower, since racism renders the relationship between self and other biological rather than political: the death of the other will make life healthier. Thus conceived, enemies are no longer political adversaries but "threats, either external or internal, to the population and for the population," and as such, in a "normalizing society, race or racism is the precondition that makes killing acceptable," not just in terms of literal murder but in terms of exposure to death, increasing the risk of death, and through expulsion or rejection.[88] It is precisely through this process of othering that postwar Western territorial and social space effectively normalizes sites of exclusion—internment camps, secret weapons facilities, military bases, and toxic mines—as part of the "natural" environment. Creating insecurity through the implementation of security measures invokes the threat of death or expulsion that justifies asymmetrical relations between sections of the population and discontinuities of land use and freedom of movement. Understood as a regime of biopower, the permanent war economy is more than the sum of its business transactions, it is the condition for life itself.

After Vietnam: Full Spectrum Dominance

The collective memory of World War II is that it provided clearly externalized, justified enemies and definable, real threats to national security. The basis of the rhetoric of war deployed since Pearl Harbor resides in that collective memory of a "just" war, which, as Michael Rogin argues, "laid the structural foundations in politics for the modern American empire."[89] Only for a few years during and after America's defeat in Vietnam, notes Rogin, "were the fundamental assumptions about America's role in the world established during World War II ever challenged by significant sectors within American politics." Since World War II "celebrated the undercover struggle of good against evil," it prepared the way for an awareness and acceptance of covert military activities—the known but not seen, what Rogin calls the "covert spectacle"—as the hidden necessary violence that underwrites American security.[90]

It is not surprising, then, that since it was World War II that retooled the Western United States as the defense complex of the national security state, that recent writing about the West so often returns to World War II as the source of many contemporary conflicts. While the war is obviously fundamental to Japanese American internment narratives, the impact of World War II is also central to works by Silko, Momaday, Anaya, Abbey, McCarthy, McMahon, and Morrow. Like Joseph Heller's Catch 22 (1961) and Kurt Vonnegut's Slaughterhouse 5 (1969), Vietnam-era novels like Ceremony, House Made of Dawn, Bless Me, Ultima, and Principles of American Nuclear Chemistry, invite connections to be made between World War II and contemporary foreign policy and its domestic ramifications. In later works like Morrow's Trinity Fields and Ariel's Crossing, the continuities between World War II and Vietnam are made explicit, and McCarthy's Border Trilogy, though less overt, likewise calls for a relational understanding of the post–World War II rationalization of Western space as the precondition for a militarized international border in the 1990s.

In turn, the haunting of post-1970 novels by the Vietnam War makes sense when Vietnam is understood as the disaster that fatally corroded the consensus culture of the period from the end of World War II and through the 1950s. Vietnam, as a "dirty" war, retrospectively casts a more dismal light over the triumph of World War II and activates a scrutiny of military-industrial values and practices occluded by the stand-off of the Cold War. If World War II marks the break with the peacetime past, Vietnam renders problematic the justifications for that break as well as exposing as a fiction the nuclear-age notion of an end to conventional warfare. Gary Harkness, the protagonist of DeLillo's *End Zone*, is obsessed with nuclear devastation, but it is being sent to Vietnam that poses the real threat to his safety. In *Night Wing*, Cruz Smith's Youngman Duran is a Vietnam veteran court-martialed for sabotaging the war effort after he, like Silko's Tayo, comes to identify with the enemy.

The parallels between Vietnam and the conquest of the West are also evoked, though never explicitly, throughout McCarthy's *Blood Meridian*. The realignment of military strategy toward guerilla warfare prompted by the American experience in Vietnam also places *Blood Meridian*, I think, squarely as a novel of the 1980s, since Ronald Reagan's counterinsurgent adventures in Latin America during that decade seem to be another way of allegorically positioning McCarthy's scalp hunters. Along with the reactivation of apocalyptic Cold War rhetoric that preoccupies Hauptman in *Storm Season*, Reagan's anticommunist policies south of the border, combined with an intensified "war on drugs" and determination to curb illegal immigration, served to position Latin America as a winnable Vietnam.

The failure of the state during the Vietnam era to control foreign policy and dominate the economy forced a defensive nationalism that turned increasingly, as Rogin argues, to "covert action and the spectacle" in order to achieve what in contemporary parlance would be called Full Spectrum Dominance: "in the political economy of the military-industrial complex; in a nuclear-dominated military strategy, where weapons function as symbols of intention in war games rather than as evidence of warfighting capabilities; and in the permeation of public and private space by fiction-making visual media."[91] The notion of the post-Vietnam covert spectacle, then, is a sign of vulnerability, a "symbolic gesture" that "reflects the persistence of dreams about American dominance in the face of the erosion of the material and ideological sources or American preeminence in the world."[92] If the executive order characterized the early mode of intervention that put in place the spatial structure of the Southwest Defense Complex, the Vietnam era intensified the importance of the display of secrecy as a weapon.

While conventional wisdom locates the fall of the Berlin Wall and the dismantling of the Soviet Union as the key moments when global geopolitics realigns toward American neoliberal hegemony, Hardt and Negri identify the shift instead with the Anti-Ballistic Missile Treaty of 1972.[93] Here, they argue, the "specular contest of nuclear threat had reached its apotheosis," and the strategic importance of the threat of the missile began to wane, replaced by "proliferating mini-threats."[94] Instead of a preoccupation with the destruction of the enemy, the "production of the enemy," so evident in No Country for Old Men and Almanac of the Dead, became paramount, the United States sidestepping nuclear stand-off in favor of police actions in Vietnam and Latin America.[95]

The shift in the forms and aims of war in the early 1970s also coincides with a period of transformation in the global economy.[96] The economic crisis of the early 1970s was accompanied by the beginning of the dismantling of welfare provisions and the shift of economic production from the factory toward the more flexible, mobile, and "immaterial" sites of post-Fordist production.[97] A new focus, away from the Soviet Union and toward the Middle East, also sought to establish the United States as a negotiator rather than an aggressor. While the struggle against the Soviet Union did not end, covert action—as a military form of mobile, flexible, low-intensity post-Fordism—increasingly replaced the arms race as the means through which the United States sought to maintain the strategic upper hand. Nevertheless, while the SALT I agreement (1972) limited the number of ICBMs, it did not limit the number of warheads a missile could carry, so although missile numbers froze, warhead numbers continued to grow, suggesting a continuity at the core of the permanent war economy even as the rhetoric shifts to accommodate a weakened faith in the legitimacy of the arms race.[98]

From the end of Vietnam, then, through to the first half of the Carter administration, the United States retreated from Cold War rhetoric and the doctrine of containment. A number of factors, however, including conservative elements within the Carter government, the targeting of Western Europe by Soviet medium-range nuclear weapons, and the Soviet invasion of Afghanistan in 1979, shifted U.S. foreign policy rightward. While Carter initiated the military build-up inherited by and credited to Ronald Reagan, it was Reagan who successfully reimagined the permanent war economy as a viable post-Vietnam project.[99]

With Reagan, claims Rogin, the men "whose consciousness was formed by World War II revived the American empire after Vietnam."[100] During the Reagan era, the suspicion of technology that accompanied disenchantment with U.S. foreign policy in Vietnam was brushed aside as new technologies, especially computers, revived the economy.[101] What has been called Cold War II "seized once again on containment's formula for global politics as the bipolar, apocalyptic struggle of a radically bounded closed world, radically divided against itself."[102] In the name of national security, huge increases in defense spending followed, much of it on technology-related modernization.[103]

Reagan's revival of the Cold War has its origins in World War II as a "just war" in which America's national security state triumphed.[104] The decline of American prominence during the 1970s led Reagan to attempt to actively forget Vietnam and to symbolically restore the certainties of Cold War national security as justified by World War II "innocence." This was achieved by the stockpiling of symbolic weapons that cannot be used and equally symbolic "low-intensity" military activities in the Third World. Even top-secret operations can be made to work, Rogin argues, as "therapeutic politics," since that which is repeatedly shown is "normalized to invisibility," becomes "absent and disappeared" even as it remains politically useful as a spectral security threat.[105]

The Reagan-Bush desire to kick the so-called "Vietnam Syndrome" by rolling back American life to the 1950s while funding futuristic high-tech weapons systems served, in the end, if anything, to produce more dissent than it stifled. The lessons of the civil rights movement and the anti–Vietnam War protests, buttressed by the experience of second-wave feminism, shaped a more politicized environmental movement sharply focused on the nuclear West. Neither did concessions to downwinders and World War II internees at the end of the 1980s, and the cessation of underground nuclear testing in 1992, draw a line under the excesses of post–Pearl Harbor militarization. Instead, the afterburn of the arms race continued to shape post–Cold War anxieties as the dilemma of toxic waste disposal supplanted the weapons themselves as the live threat to security.

The literal and political fallout produced out of World War II remains, then, a permanent threat, in the literal form of toxic landscapes and waste that cannot be destroyed, but also in the persistence of economic and political modes of organization operating according to a war model. Domestic and foreign policy responses to the post-9/11 world order have, indeed, tended to confirm and intensify the sense that continuous war underpins the organization of the U.S.-led world order. If World War II never really ended, then the state of emergency that war invoked has remained and continues to regulate every aspect of economic, political, social, and cultural life. While the Southwest Defense Complex is the screen upon which the permanent war economy projects its spectacle of full spectrum dominance, the Western counterhistory of waste produced by that spectacle persists as a kind of excessive remainder, inviting scrutiny of the technologies of domination that would prefer to be self-erasing.

Reading the Letter

"No space ever vanishes utterly, leaving no trace," writes Henri Lefebvre.[106] The persistence of the waste produced manufacturing the conditions of permanent war is precisely the material out of which any form of counterhistory can be conceived. "It is not that life has been totally integrated into techniques that govern and administer it," Hardt and Negri contend; rather "it constantly escapes them."[107] Part of what is elusive within biopower is what they call "immaterial labor," or "the production of social relations and social order" through culture in the form of "information, communication, cooperation."[108] This involves an extension of Foucault's conception of power as a network to include the oppositional power of "those who seek [power], want it, or want to overturn or destroy it."[109]

Inasmuch as the military-industrial complex has appropriated the aesthetic legacy of the desert West along with the land itself, it has become the function of much cultural work produced in and about the region to discover the presence of the purloined landscape. This work must of necessity involve itself with a space that, like Poe's letter, has been turned, like a glove, "inside out, re-directed and re-sealed." Furthermore, following

Dupin's double-bluff in the tale, where the letter is replaced by a "fac-simile" that turns the tables on the sinister D——, in many cases, the works discussed in the following chapters might be said to, literally, do likewise.[110] In other words, literature must seek ways of representing back the duplicity of the purloined terrain and its contested histories as critical substitutes for the original act of appropriation. In this way, the works I discuss ought to be conceived as acts of countersurveillance, as double agents, or as modes of cognitive and representational disturbance that might warp, fold, or rend the military-industrial desert screen. The prospect of the desert as site of resistance to the U.S. warfare state even as it is the prime location for the reproduction of that state is, confus-ingly but necessarily, a function of the cultural legacy of the desert West as cognitively destabilizing and physically perilous.

Stephen Paul Miller argues that "reality" in post–World War II Amer-ica was "difficult to separate from the federal government and the Cold War." Until the Vietnam escalation, Miller claims, for most people most of the time the federal government played a largely benign role.[111] Dur-ing the Vietnam War, however, a gap opened up between "those who still identified themselves, if somewhat nervously, with 'official' reality and those who did not."[112] As World War I generated the (anti)forms of Dada and Surrealism, the broken frame of modernism, and often a nos-talgia for the preindustrial, so World War II might be expected to pro-duce an adversarial culture committed to the "critical cognition of re-ality," as Peter Bürger has put it.[113] Certainly, as Philip Nel argues, the "ambivalent legacy" of Dada and Surrealism might be "uniquely suited to revealing the ideological underpinnings of the Cold War period" be-cause the "emotional attitude of the Cold War [itself] is surreal."[114] What Nel is suggesting here is that the Cold War produced contending ver-sions of reality that, as Miller also argues, increasingly come into con-flict with one another. Like the surrealist combination of disparate real-ities positioned within the same space, after World War II America kept and enlarged its peacetime military forces for the first time and, by cre-ating the CIA, established, in Nel's words, "invisible channels of power that competed with public ones"; increasingly, an invisible government challenged a visible one.[115] As DeLillo has so precisely put it, "there was a split between reality and what we couldn't quite accept as reality but could come to be so at any time."[116]

For Pynchon, American reality is intrinsically split, producing an ideologically contained reality of the visible world (the world made possible by the descendants of the Puritan "saints") that exists alongside an uncanny invisible world of the preterite, the abjected outcasts and strangers of the dominant order. These economically and socially unwanted "other" populations, in their structural relation with the elect, function to define the elect by negation. In *Gravity's Rainbow*, World War II is merely part of the ongoing "real War" that continues to kill "the right people" even when armies are not fighting.[117] Pynchon's work seeks to make visible the "other" America, the consumed and wasted America discarded and buried under ascendant military-industrial capitalism. A characteristic of many of the texts discussed below is their similar commitment to exposure, a determination to make visible the war against what Martin Heidegger calls the "standing-reserve" of consumable human resource. Alongside U.S. "manifest destiny" is an ongoing struggle against the campaign of containment and attempted removal of other "latent destinies."[118]

The desert West, as the screen for the open secret, trades under what Lefebvre calls the "illusion of transparency" where space is "innocent" and "free from traps and secret places."[119] Combined with the "realistic illusion" of "natural simplicity," the open spaces of the West are constructed by the exigencies of the national security state to produce a naturalized rationality.[120] At the same time, this illusion is continuously revealed as an illusion in order to display the power of secrecy as a guarantor of security. The dilemma for any counterhistorical response to this dance of the seven veils is not so much to locate the hidden, though this must also remain imperative since the sheer heterogeneity of what is hidden defies a simple one-time exposure, but to engage with the discourse of hiddenness itself as the shifting ground of permanent war. It is here that literature can function as a vital mode of interrogation in that it is precisely through form that literature works against the grain of conventional logic. What is at issue in my analysis of the texts gathered here, then, is not merely to inventory the ways in which narratives about the post–Pearl Harbor West document the processes of exclusion that characterizes much of recent Western history. More interesting, perhaps, are the ways in which these texts seek to reshape those processes as narratives that turn the discourse of hiddenness inside out, find new moments of concealment and exposure, and suggest ways in which the wasted places and populations of the West refuse to be recycled as a function of the screen.

It is often out of ruptures in the screen that alternative readings of history emerge, as in the failure of the Vietnam war to contain dissent. The end of the Cold War is another instance when the rationale for the maintenance of a permanent war economy is temporarily threatened by events. In two pieces of legislation enacted at the end of the 1980s, the federal government belatedly accepted responsibility for American policies during World War II and the Cold War. At the same time, the demise of the Soviet Union accelerated a process of military downsizing already underway before the collapse of the Berlin Wall.

After years of campaigning, the passage of the Civil Liberties Act of 1988 provided a presidential apology and symbolic payment of twenty thousand dollars to those "evacuated" and interned under Executive Order 9066. The first payments were made in 1990, the year the Radiation Exposure Compensation Act also provided fixed payments to individuals who contracted serious diseases as a consequence of exposure to radiation produced by above-ground nuclear tests or through employment in uranium mines.[121]

In addition to these acts of compensation, in 1989 Congress approved the first round of military base closures. The Defense Base Closure and Realignment Act of 1990 authorized three further rounds of realignments and closures for 1991, 1993, and 1995. Together, the four rounds of Base Realignment and Closure (BRAC) resulted in decisions to close 97 of 495 major defense installations in the United States and the realignment of many others.[122] A fifth round took place in 2005, recommending a major consolidation of forces in large bases. While this was a significant reshuffling, it eliminated only 5 percent of the military's installation structure.[123] The widespread negative economic repercussions that inevitably hit local communities with each round of BRAC serves to illustrate how reliant the U.S. domestic economy is on military investment, and changes to military installations continue to be fraught with local problems even as they rarely represent a real reduction of overall military presence. As commentator Tom Engelhardt noted in 2005, with over six

46

thousand bases on American soil, the United States remains "in some ways a vast military camp."[124]

Concessions to some of the wasted populations of the permanent war economy and acknowledgment of the environmental impact of sustained military activity are invariably hard won and not without consequence. But just as military "realignment" is more a reconfiguration of resources than a step down toward demilitarization, so too must compensation and recognition of responsibility be seen as strategic acts that can function to maintain consent and absorb challenges to legitimacy.[125] Official acceptance of responsibility for harm is often belated and guarded, and structural causes are generally not addressed. As Foucault reminds us, the unitary discourse of the nation-state is always ready to annex counterhistories. In many of the works explored here, the ramifications of permanent war and its security restrictions become ontological inasmuch as the conditions of existence are underwritten by structural inequality, powerlessness, and estrangement. Recuperation back into the official national narrative is no solution, but instead identity must be forged in what Lorna Dee Cervantes calls the "abandoned lots"—"en los campos extraños de esta ciudad"—"where I'll find it, that part of me / mown under / like a corpse / or a loose seed."[126] The reverberations of past injustice are not calmed by moments of official contrition but persist in shaping the conditions of possibility within which place, identity, and agency, however abjected, are constructed and contested.

2. THE PREHISTORY
OF THE PERMANENT WAR ECONOMY

In history, the great moment
is when the savage is just ceasing to be the savage.
Ralph Waldo Emerson, "Power"

Blood Meridian, published in 1985, is Cormac McCarthy's first novel set in the Southwest. While the subsequent volumes that make up *The Border Trilogy* are concerned with the period from the 1930s to the present, *Blood Meridian* is temporally located in the 1840s, in the years following the Mexican War and the Treaty of Guadalupe-Hidalgo that ceded much of what had been northern Mexico to the United States. Along with the Gadsden Purchase (signed 1853, ratified 1854), American victory against Mexico served to consolidate the continental national body articulated by the expansionist ideology of Manifest Destiny and the Monroe Doctrine. With the demarcation of an international borderline across the two thousand miles from the Pacific to the Gulf of Mexico, the United States for the first time achieved a national definition of unbroken continental totality.

McCarthy's novel, then, is quite clearly located during a decisive moment in the process of national identity formation, the moment when the desert lands of Sonora are incorporated into what has become the American Southwest. If *The Border Trilogy* will focus on the dispossession of Anglo ranching culture by the oil industry and the military-industrial complex, *Blood Meridian* is grounded in a concern with the consequences of possession. The novel is certainly unequivocal in its assessment of the nature of this acquisition: it is unrepentantly violent and chaotic, ruthlessly opportunistic, and driven by the necessarily unchecked libidinal forces of a rampant primal individualism tacitly legitimated by the absent presence of Anglo capitalist democracy.[1]

The importance of *Blood Meridian* for this study lies precisely in its construction of a kind of prehistory of the American Southwest. The novel is highly sensitive to the peculiarities of time and space as they are understood in the desert West and how spatiotemporal measurement is imbricated in modes of representation bound up with national ideology. Set as it is when the meaning of a specific territory is transformed by a change of ownership, Blood Meridian is concerned in part with how space is formed into landscape, how anterior readings of that space become overwritten in the process of acquisition, and how this overwriting enables and per-petuates forms of representation that lay waste to the referent and all pos-sible counterreadings. In other words, the novel is concerned with the es-tablishment and maintenance of a sovereign discourse. Such a discourse is inseparable in the novel from a particular conception of war.

As I suggested in the previous chapter, among the promises of the mod-ern nation-state is the externalization of war beyond its boundaries. But if Foucault and others are right that this promise merely represses the fact of war's continuation by other means, the establishment of the state's boundary—and the cessation of war this boundary serves to mark—is, in fact, the point at which the repression of war's continuation takes place. In recent times, as Hardt and Negri assert, "we seem to have been catapulted back in time into the nightmare of perpetual and indetermi-nate war."[2] Our "postmodern state of war," they claim, "resembles the premodern wars."[3] Published during Reagan's campaign of low-inten-sity conflict in Latin America and revival of apocalyptic Cold War rhet-oric, Blood Meridian is a response, I intend to argue here, to the moment when the desire to overcome the "Vietnam Syndrome" that afflicted Civil Rights era military-industrial legitimacy is achieved through a neocon-servative, neoliberal catapult back in time whereby the externalization of war promised by the nation-state is disavowed in favor of war's perma-nent state of emergency. As such, Blood Meridian's tendency to move be-tween the historically specific and the indeterminately prehistoric works to expose the contemporaneity of the prehistoric as a mode of temporal distancing that is, in fact, strategically useful in maintaining the open secret of permanent war.

In a way, Blood Meridian is a kind of creation story: it marks the moment when chaos becomes form, if we consider, from the viewpoint of the ex-pansionist, the Southwest to be meaningless before it is given shape by occupation. In this view, the agents of Manifest Destiny call place into being, at the same time violently removing contradictory signs of prior habitation; space is made void in order for its re-presentation as place to occur.[4] The notion that the novel may be concerned with the production of order and meaning from a site imagined as feral and vacant goes some way to explaining the curious temporal fluidity of the text, which, while being rooted in verifiable historical time, as I have said, also plunges into geological deep time in a way that moves the book far beyond the precincts of any conventional historical novel.

Blood Meridian is rightly celebrated for its descriptions of landscape, which produce a space that is both precise in its geophysical and climatological particularity and irreducibly strange and otherworldly. Barrenness has never required such detail. The lengths to which McCarthy goes in the construction of the desert borderlands serve, I think, to foreground the immense importance of modes of landscape representation as integral to the understanding of the site's function in the national imaginary. For the representation of landscape in Blood Meridian, in its particular and otherworldly doubleness, suggests ways in which history is both revealed and concealed simultaneously through the articulation of space. In the first place, as geographically remote from centers of U.S. power, the border territories are literally far from view, enabling the brutal process of conquest to continue out of sight and providing the distance that marauders like Holden and Glanton need in order to claim authority for their deeds that cannot be verified by the institutions of law they notionally serve. Whether or not U.S. authorities sanction the actions of filibusterers and scalp hunters is simply irrelevant since the end result—the clearing of the land for Anglo occupation—erases the means by which the end is achieved. More than the simple fact of remoteness from authority, however, it is the representation of the landscape as already wasteland that fully enables the completion of the process of conquest. As such, representations of the border landscape conspire to screen off alternative readings of desert space as anything other than dehistoricized, prehistoric, primal, and "naturally" empty: "[t]hey rode through regions of particolored stone upthrust in ragged kerfs and shelves of traprock reared in faults and anticlines curved back upon themselves and broken off like stumps of great stone treeboles and stones the lightning had clove open, seeps exploding in steam in some old storm. They rode past trapdykes of brown rock running down the narrow chines of the ridges and onto the plain like the ruins of old walls, such auguries everywhere of the hand of man before man was or any living thing."[5]

The precision of terms in a passage like this—"traprock," "anticlines," "chines"—draws from the language of geology and geomorphology and combines with a vocabulary of age—"some old storm," "the ruins of old walls"—to produce a terrain that is both eminently describable yet somehow beyond human comprehension. The readable signs "of the hand of man before man was" cements the paradox of marks made before mark-making, a kind of impossible history of inscrutable ruins. What agency there is here is primordial and requires unusual words like "kerf" (a cut or stroke) to register its remoteness. The chines and ridges are only "like" old walls, and the trace of occupancy is a chimera produced by a simile that invokes only to deny prior habitation. One might pass through such a place, but no one, it seems, has ever lived there.

While Blood Meridian is carefully researched and draws on a range of historical sources, stylistically it withdraws from any form of conventional historical realism.[6] Instead, the text appears to be hurled outside measurable human history and into a form of epic or cosmic spatiotemporal realm. This is the view of the novel put forward by Dana Phillips, who argues that "the American West in McCarthy's fiction is not the New World but a very old world, the reality of which is bedrock." As such, we might place him, Phillips goes on, "as a writer not of the 'modern' or 'postmodern' eras but of the Holocene, with a strong historical interest in the late Pleistocene and even earlier epochs."[7] Thomas Pughe makes a similar point when he claims that McCarthy presents us with "a history of the earth into which human history is sucked."[8] It is this prehistoric sensibility that links McCarthy to the epic, for the lack of interiority that characterizes epic narrative is similar, according to Phillips, to the descriptive practices of the earth sciences. By this he means the strategies of description that seek to depict the stuff of the world that exists prior and indifferent to, and also independent from, human agency. It is Blood Meridian's "adherence in its descriptions of events to the protocols and paradigms of natural history that gives it epic resonance. The present world as McCarthy describes it is an ancient world not of myth but of rock and stone and those life forms that can endure the daily cataclysms of heat and cold and hunger, that can weather the everyday round of random, chaotic violence."[9]

Phillips is right, I think, to argue that McCarthy's understanding of Western history is natural history, one of forces and processes only barely adequately comprehended by human understanding. Certainly, McCarthy responds to the West with a sensitivity to geological duration and terrestrial violence that would not be out of step with someone like the geological catastrophist Clarence King. And as *The Border Trilogy* makes clear, this fascination with the extrahistorical and nonhuman extends to the feral world of animals, notably wolves and horses. In *Blood Meridian* the human protagonists, not to mention the countless unnamed Mexicans and Indians, are similarly rendered so as to evacuate all but the barest libidinal drives, leveling human intentionality to little more than the instinctual impulses of beasts.

The problem with this reading is that it does not take into account the historical specificity of the novel's events and the deliberate appropriation of historical figures like Glanton and Holden. As Richard Godden and Colin Richmond argue, citing Captain White's flagrant argument for an imperial policy of extermination and terror in Sonora, "[o]n such evidence it would be a mistake to read *Blood Meridian* simply as a baroque exercise, anymore than it is adequate to read *Moby Dick* (1851) as a romance."[10] The fictional space of *Blood Meridian* is indeed an ancient world of forces and processes, but it is also, at the same time, an inescapably particular historical space. Alongside the primal forces work historical forces, and McCarthy presses hard together the deep temporal dimension with the historically verifiable to produce a kind of fold in time whereby the prehistoric and the late 1840s appear to exist in the same place. Holden, Glanton, and others are both historically identifiable figures and also prehistoric, "of an order imperative and remote" (BM 152). Sometimes the dating of events is excessively precise, such as the scalp hunters' arrival in Ures on "the second of December of eighteen forty-nine" (BM 199), while often the men are described as stone age with nothing about them "to suggest even the discovery of the wheel" (BM 232). More than once they are figured as evolutionarily regressive, sitting "among the rocks without fire or bread or camaraderie any more than a band of apes" (BM 148), and are indistinguishable from "the rawest savage of that land" (BM 120). Spatially, of course, this effect can be produced through the setting of the geologically exposed Southwest, a place where the ground is a persistent reminder of its long duration. But *Blood Meridian* does more than just imply that this is an ancient place upon which history occurs. The bleeding of prehistory into history produces human life forms that are themselves "[l]ike beings provoked out of the absolute rock . . . mute Gorgons shambling the brutal wastes of Gondwanaland in a time before nomenclature was and each was all" (BM 172). These are not, to be precise, actually creatures provoked out of rock but "like" such beings. The extended simile, while appearing to pull the text back into prehistory, reminds us that there is a critical difference between wandering across Gondwanaland and the Mexican desert of the 1840s. The power of the prose is such that metaphors and similes in McCarthy are easily read as straight description. While, as Phillips maintains, McCarthy's drive toward a disembodied depiction of the natural world bespeaks a determination to move through subjectivism toward the absolute rock of things as they are, the strategy produces more metaphorical slippage than documentary observation.

One result of this is to imbue the historical content—filibustering and scalp hunting in the wake of an imperial war of conquest—with an almost inconceivable temporal depth. On one hand, the 1840s is made to feel far away, while on the other, the eons of geological time are telescoped into the recent past. Another consequence of this telescoping of time is to alienate American history from any discernible connection with the present; the past here is not so much another country as another world. At the same time, it is also clear that it is the representation of Southwestern space itself, its geology, landforms, and climate, that facilitates this apparent annihilation of history, demanding that we take full account of the nonhuman environment in order to properly understand the site of human activity. The land, thus, is inseparable from the creatures and the deeds they perform upon it. Physical space is not the setting for but *is* history inasmuch as the life-forms, human and nonhuman, that occupy this space are of the same nature, made of the same stuff. McCarthy's strategy in folding history into the prehistoric reveals a powerful sense of environmental contingency, and in combining the epic resonance of the geological record with the specificity of the historical record, the prose demonstrates the fusion of geography and history, space and time, necessary to properly articulate the appropriation of space into the national imaginary.

In this way, I think, McCarthy's text pulls in two directions at once. Pushing the 1840s into prehistory moves the acquisition of the Southwest so far back in time that there is no perceptible thread of connection between the process of conquest and the present. Confusing and complicating temporal causality in this way produces a sense in which the barbarism of the novel's protagonists can be read as "natural" rather than cultural, taking place in a time outside connection with the affairs of human civilization. As Phillips notes, *Blood Meridian* "treats darkness, violence, sudden death, and all other calamities as natural occurrences."[11] This reading suggests a conservative undertow to McCarthy's text as it erases the link between imperial wars of the past and the subsequent history of the United States: what happened in the past is long gone. Such a reading situates *Blood Meridian* among the classic literary and cinematic Western texts, where an unremarked upon gap separates the violence of domination that "broke" the land and its people and the moment of production and reception of the text that represents that past from a point of achieved domestication. The temporal arc of this narrative locates the beginning of history with the suppression of resistance; all that came before—"wilderness," "savages," wild animals—must therefore be "primitive" or prehistoric. This reading is enabled and reinforced through *Blood Meridian*'s utilization of many stock Western tropes: the alienated kid falling in with bad men, the corrupt soldiers, the ex-priest, the desert battles, the power-hungry charismatic leader, the unregulated economy of violence, and so on. The epic resonance of the text that Phillips locates in natural history is, furthermore, a masterly prose rendering of the classic Hollywood Western's choice of location.

It is appropriate to be suspicious of McCarthy's production of an arcane West as an effect that distances the text from complicity with the political and racist justification of imperial violence. But I do not think this is the only direction the text leads us. There are other implications behind McCarthy's use of geography to collapse history. For in some respects, the text deliberately makes visible the way the representation of space—such as descriptions of landforms and biota, the sensory effects of light and temperature, and the phenomenological and cognitive experience of distance—produces temporal confusion and dislocation. In particular, the trope of the desert as external to human culture, a notional neutrality outside the affairs of history, is presented in *Blood Meridian* as precisely the place where U.S. history comes into being. Even the conservative reading of the West as wasteland to be redeemed follows this line of argument, but McCarthy, I believe, pushes this conception of "empty" space until it cracks. For the desert serves a double function in western culture; it is both the space of apocalypse and the site of an arduous revelation. The place that most completely blanks history might, then, also be the site where history is most glaringly revealed. While *Blood Meridian* on the one hand leads us toward an atemporal, inaccessible prehistory, on the other we are persistently reminded of the historical locatability of the events depicted. The novel exposes how a vocabulary of vacancy and always already wastedness is put to service in the erasure of temporal connections between violent conquest and its retelling as creation myth. The novel, however, is not explicit about this and indeed confounds all attempts to resolve or synthesize its temporal disjunctions.

The doubleness of McCarthy's text has been a subject of analysis for critics since Vereen Bell's early study noted that *Blood Meridian*'s many similes produce a divided "double image."[12] The identification of bifurcating trajectories in the novel does not mean, however, that there is any kind of straightforward dialectical relationship between them. Indeed, as I am suggesting with relation to the temporal fissure that opens up between prehistorical and historical time in *Blood Meridian*, contradictions generated by the text tend to be preserved and held in tension for the duration rather than resolved. One effect of this stasis is to reinforce the sense of unchanging, intractable inertia in the text to the extent that the reader soon abandons expectations of plot and character development. It is more than tempting at this point to position the novel as a deliberately negative critique of the attributes it patently does not provide. Susan Kollin, for example, points out that "[u]nlike the classic Western, *Blood Meridian* does not offer a region whose promise and possibility were somehow lost at a certain point in history, but a West fully corrupted from the moment Anglos arrived."[13] It is true that there is nothing "lost" in the West of *Blood Meridian*—unlike the novels of the *Border Trilogy*, the earlier work is not even interested in thinking through the ramifications of an imagined organic relationship with history—but construing the novel as an "anti-Western" as Kollin does tends to preserve and merely invert the moral aspect of the genre the book purportedly operates within. As such, *Blood Meridian* can be made to function fairly straightforwardly as a negative critique of the "myth" of the West.[14]

This, I think, would be a mistake, and a number of critics of the novel have identified the difficulty of generating an oppositional position from the text. Kollin herself acknowledges that, just as classic Westerns have been said to be "divided texts," so too "anti-Westerns . . . are often unable to escape the very thing they seek to dismantle but instead are drawn into an intimacy and affiliation that destabilizes the critical effort."[15] Others have noted the "inert" (Peter Josyph) or "stalled" (Steven Shaviro) dialectic in *Blood Meridian*.[16] As Shaviro explains, there is no transcendence in *Blood Meridian*, and McCarthy refuses both the "rational mastery" of the Enlightenment and romantic "apocalyptic transfiguration."[17] What is revealed instead is the "ironic dependence" of the dream of transcendence "upon the very (supposed) mysteries that it claims to violate."[18] The result, as David Holloway proposes, appears to be a form of "willful self-cancellation, a writing from which any claim to determinate meaning or hermeneutic engagement with the world has been willfully expunged."[19] If the text's contradictions have rendered any possibility of resolution or direction impossible then it would be more accurate, Holloway argues, to refer not to the novel's contradictions but to its antinomies.[20] Frederic Jameson explains that a contradiction "is susceptible of a solution or a resolution" while an antinomy "states two propositions that are radically, indeed absolutely, incompatible," where "contraries are unable to enter into antagonistic contact and therefore develop themselves."[21]

This appears to be where we are with regard to *Blood Meridian*'s temporal doubleness: it is prehistorically indeterminate and historically specific both at once. The former distances events by pushing them to the horizon of deep time (primordial, geological, and biological), while the latter pulls the action up close and imbricates mid-nineteenth-century nation-building—once history is admitted—within an ongoing process that includes American imperial enterprise since 1848, including Vietnam and the Central American adventures of the Reagan years.[22] What is suggestive about both of these temporalities is not just that one seems to cancel out the other but, more strikingly, that they both tend to represent a repetition of the same. *Blood Meridian*'s epigraph from the *Yuma Daily Sun* that reports the discovery of a scalped three-hundred-thousand-year-old skull signals at the outset that the novel will have little to say about historical change. Rather, the *longue durée* here seems merely to strengthen the implausibility of an historical alternative to wars of conquest. Gondwanaland becomes an echo of "the ashes of Gnadenhutten," from where the generations who "learnt war from warring" pour forth to the "bloodlands of the west" (BM 138) and on to the charred wastelands of North Vietnam and the jungles of Central America. Here *Blood Meridian*'s spatiotemporal confusions add up, since, as Godden and Richmond observe, "East meets West if viewed from the perspective of imperial ambition."[23] Again, folding history into prehistory appears to serve political realism's acceptance of human conflict as somehow "natural" and beyond the reach of liberal mediation. But this is to convert an antinomy back into a contradiction, and *Blood Meridian* will not quite allow that to happen.

Holloway argues that *Blood Meridian*'s antinomies should properly be seen as "historical symptoms" produced by a "world context where contradiction of a very worldly kind does indeed appear primordial and monolithic: a world where history itself, as a narrative movement through and beyond existing social contradiction, has become almost unthinkable."[24] When Godden and Richmond locate in Phillips's and Pughe's readings of the novel a disavowal of history in favor of geology, they are right to insist that McCarthy's "geological dimension does not decline from the human."[25] Instead, they argue that McCarthy's geology "most typically involves that which will become sand, grit or dust, each speck or grain of which has been, or will be, stained with blood." These are "the bedrock of McCarthy's terrain" and "are human in so far as they are monuments to killings, past, present and future."[26]

McCarthy's descriptions of landscape work inside a tradition of writing about the southwestern deserts that is nothing if not historical in its reliance on a particular combination of positivist scientific ambition and nationalist mystification. For John C. Van Dyke, whose *The Desert* (1901) has become a classic of Western nature writing, to enter the desert is to step back in time and feel the thrill of possession "by right of original exploration and conquest." In the desert, life "begins all over again, starting at the primitive stage. There is a reversion to the savage."[27] The savagery is immanent in Van Dyke's landscape, the sun, wind, and sand themselves fiercely aggressive and annihilating: "[t]he sunshafts are falling in a burning shower upon rock and dune, the winds blowing with the breath of far-off fires are withering the bushes and the grasses, the sands drifting higher and higher are burying the trees and reaching up as though they would overwhelm the mountains, the cloud-bursts are rushing down the mountain's side and through the torn arroyos as though they would wash the earth into the sea."[28]

Life in the desert is also "peculiarly savage," with a "show of teeth in bush and beast and reptile" and everywhere "the presence of the barb and thorn, the jaw and paw, the beak and talon, the sting and the poison thereof." Here everything is "at war with its neighbor, and the conflict is unceasing."[29] McCarthy borrows this kind of rhetoric of perpetual struggle and natural aggression to good effect—the novel is full of snub-nosed descriptions of things like "deadlylooking bayonet plants," "shrubs blasted under the sun," and "deathcamas hanging in a small and perilous garden" (BM 57)—but, as Godden and Richmond suggest, this is not to say that the ahistoricizing tendencies of the natural scientist are to be taken at face value.

The events narrated in *Blood Meridian* take place around the time when the notion of the "prehistoric" was emerging as a category in the developing modern discipline of archaeology.[30] Closely aligned with Lyellian and Darwinian natural science as well as, later, the Spencerian notion of evolutionary progress that marks Van Dyke's feral vision of the desert, American archaeology configured all of pre-Columbian America as prehistoric.[31] One consequence of this thinking, of course, is that it compresses deep time and configures contemporary indigenous populations as living fossils. In the desert West not only does the landscape appear to be primordial but the human inhabitants are made to confirm this impression.

As a means of systematizing the strewn and buried debris of the past, archaeology provided a means of assembling order from pre-textual chaos. Alice Beck Kehoe sees American archaeology as a mode of "post hoc justification of the doctrine of Manifest Destiny," a bourgeois science that legitimated capitalist domination.[32] It did this by providing empirical evidence that supported the notion of human progress "crowned by the Western nations' awesome machines."[33] Pre-Columbian civilizations could be factored into this argument through the countervailing notion of degeneration, which helped explain why nineteenth-century Indians seemed to have regressed from the achievements of the Aztecs and Anasazis.[34] Judge Holden is patently abreast of developments in archaeology, as his mania for cataloging artifacts suggests. And while he may be an agent of manifest destiny he does not necessarily subscribe to the ideology of progress. In the Anasazi ruins he sees a "judgment on the latter races" and, in a clear articulation of degenerescence, notes that "progressions from a higher to a lower order are marked by ruins and mystery and a residue of nameless rage" (BM 146). What McCarthy allows the judge to say here is that a geology of dust is indeed, as Godden and Richmond contend, made of the remains of the dead whose "spirit is entombed in the stone" (BM 146). McCarthy's description of the desert borderlands is as much archaeological as it is geological and is therefore historical inasmuch as it refers to the deeds of human beings. This is a qualified historical record, however, for it remains extratextual and thus, according to the archaeological rubric, is prehistoric and requires natural scientific articulation. This may be where history folds into geology and where time folds into space: if the traces of historical conflict—and here we must include the violent conquest of the Sonoran borderlands and the post–Pearl Harbor militarization of Western space, as well as its global extensions—are literally ground into the dirt, proof of their existence lies not in the pages of any historical account but in the rocks themselves. Taking this to be the case, it could be argued that McCarthy's description of geophysical and climatological conditions is indeed a mode of history inasmuch as the desert surface is the site upon which history is graven.

In Blood Meridian there does appear to be something of a conspiracy between the killers and the land when it comes to the destruction of evidence, and here the active erasure of the trace of violent deeds colludes with the construction of desert space as already empty. The scalp hunters actually aid in the production and preservation of empty desert by actively clearing the land of inhabitants, who are either killed or flee. Even Glanton is surprised at the efficiency with which "nineteen men had evacuated an area of ten thousand square miles of every living human" (BM 148). Equally, the desert makes its contribution to the voiding of evidence of mass killing. After the Tigua massacre, we are told that within days the blood of the dead "would crack and break and drift away so that in the circuit of few suns all trace of the destruction of these people would be erased. The desert wind would salt their ruins and there would be nothing, no ghost nor scribe, to tell to a pilgrim in his passing how it was that people had lived in this place and in this place died" (BM 174).

The desert is littered with the brittle remnants of departed communities; as Godden and Richmond observe, McCarthy's Southwest "is a cemetery."[35] What is striking about the different kinds of remains is that they soon become historically indeterminate. Godden and Richmond describe the Sonoran landscape as at once "conspicuously genocidal" and "spectacularly . . . monumental," suggesting that "[i]t takes time for acts of genocide to be turned into monuments."[36] On the evidence, though, it does not appear to take much time, though the monuments may be modest in the extreme. The fact is, descriptions of vacated or destroyed settlements are more or less the same whether the site is a recently abandoned Apache village (BM 148–49), an ancient Anasazi site (BM 139), or a still used cemetery (BM 175).

Geology must be seen, in the light of *Blood Meridian*'s scalp hunters' murderous granulation of any evidence of prior occupation, as empirical evidence of those events even as they are converted from history into landscape. They make history disappear through the annihilation of all evidence, relying on its inevitable ossification into geology.[37] This landscape—embodied history rendered invisible *as* history—subsequently acts as the open secret of American conquest. The antinomies of geology and history, prehistory and history, space and time are, as Holloway puts it, historical symptoms in a world where movement "through and beyond existing social contradiction has become almost unthinkable." McCarthy's antinomies may result in a stalled dialectic, but the text's lack of movement must stand as a function of what we might call the negative unconcealment of history. In other words, the screening off of the facts of conquest by landscape is as much as can properly be shown without returning to a metaphysics of transcendent revelation the text simply is not willing or able to perform.

Pandemonium of the Sun

Blood Meridian's creation story of U.S. continental consolidation is also at the same time a tale that marks the end of that consolidation, and here the function of the novel's description of geological, meteorological, and astronomical conditions is not to remove the narrative from history but precisely to scrutinize it. As I have suggested, the question of what time it is in *Blood Meridian* is confusing, and the novel appears to slip its temporal moorings and drift back across the millennia. However, there is surely no better way of telling the time than to follow the sun, and it is the novel's heliocentrism, with the sun as source of illumination and thus of visibility, that properly reveals *Blood Meridian*'s spatiotemporal concerns.[38] The sun offers a model for timekeeping that relies on cosmic movement rather than chronological measurement and tends to reinforce the sense that events in the novel do not advance but repeat and return. At the same time, though, the sun's movement can be reckoned from a human vantage point, enabling the conversion of cosmic movement into segmented chronological units of duration: dawn, meridian, evening. The sun is the source of enlightenment and offers a means of regulating the temporal dimension of the objects it makes visible, but in the inevitability of its glare the solar presence is also a sign of the repetition of the same.

For Georges Bataille, the supreme power attributed to the sun lies in the fact that, in the figure of noon, it represents "the most *elevated* conception." At the same time, the sun is also "the most abstract object, since it is impossible to look at it fixedly at that time of day." The power of the sun, then, lies in its "poetic meaning of mathematical serenity and spiritual elevation." Yet these values can only be bestowed upon the sun so long as it is not seen directly; serenity and elevation are appreciated only by indirection, through reflection. To look directly at the sun is an act of "certain madness" that yields not illumination but "refuse and combustion." The sun not looked at is beautiful, the one gazed at is "horribly ugly." Bataille's implication is that the authority of the sun as an elevated symbol of power is only made possible by a willful blindness that prefers the abstract indirectness of concepts to direct experience; indeed, to remain sane one must look away. The fact that the sun has been mythologically expressed "by a man slashing his own throat, as well as by an anthropomorphic being *deprived of a head*" (emphasis in original) suggests an awareness of the catastrophic consequences of peering directly at the source of power. "All this leads one to say," Bataille concludes, "that the summit of elevation is in practice confused with a sudden fall of unheard-of violence," a fact he illustrates with reference to the myth of Icarus, which splits the sun into two: the inviting glow that beckons Icarus's ascent, and the one that melts the wax when he gets too close.[39]

The doubleness of McCarthy's novel begins with the title, which apparently offers a choice: *Blood Meridian, or, The Evening Redness in the West*. This choice bespeaks, I think, the text's forking political pathways. The dominant image is clearly that of the bloody sun, yet are we to read this bloodiness as the sign of the meridian, of the highest point in the sun's altitude, or of sunset, where the day ends? Temporally, it is not clear whether the text is positioned at midday or sunset, highpoint or lowpoint. In *Blood Meridian* there is more than an echo of "high noon," the point of reckoning, of purgative violence, while the *Evening Redness in the West* signals a waning, an ending. The "or" of the title seems to invite interchangeability and mark a point of uncertainty. The title could be a question or simply an offering of equivalences. That "or" as choice and uncertainty presents an ambiguity that haunts the novel.[40] The Treaty of Guadalupe-Hidalgo could be read as the ultimate line of partition that finally fences off the United States as an achieved historical totality, the meridian of Manifest Destiny after which the heroic phase of nation-building is over and now there must be only decline. Alternatively, this moment could signify the nadir of imperial barbarism, the historical moment where, thankfully, the sun is now setting. Perhaps the consolidation of empire is the beginning of the end.[41]

This doubleness is glossed at least once in the narrative, where we are told that while the "way of the world is to bloom and to flower and to die," for men "there is no waning and the noon of his expression signals the onset of night. His spirit is exhausted at the peak of his achievement. His meridian is at once his darkening and the evening of his day" (BM 146–47). The sense here is that the pinnacle of human expression signals an imminent decline, just as noon suggests the highest and hottest the sun is going to get. Every noon is thus latent with darkness; in one is written the other. Temporal unfolding is countered here with simultaneity, the movement of human history being no more than an illusion of natural progression from bloom to flower to death. The "affairs of men" appear to be divorced from cosmic time, doomed to spiritual exhaustion, the blaze of achievement promising no radiant afternoon glow but simply the "onset of night."

A bloody sun is precisely what Bataille knows we will see if we look upon it: an authority that shines benignly in our thoughts but which cannot be looked at directly without the danger that we will see too much, that the horrors of that power will pour into our eyes and reveal the rottenness at the core of its celestial sovereignty. For Bataille, the sun is the logos, the principle of earthly power and mastery. It is the sign of the father, the glaring phallus of domination. McCarthy's travelers similarly labor under a sun that can cast runs of color "like blood seeping up" and which rises "at the edge of creation . . . like the head of a great red phallus until it cleared the unseen rim and sat squat and pulsing and malevolent behind them" (BM 44–45). As well as bloody, in the morning the sun can be "urinecolored" (BM 47); it is "remorseless" (BM 243), a "distant pandemonium" (BM 185); it "lay in a holocaust" (BM 105).

There is something fraudulent about the glow from sources of light, or at least about the truth claims made in the name of illumination, in the literal sense that what we see when we look at objects is not their materiality but the effects of light cast upon them.[42] In *Blood Meridian*, that which enlightens does not truly reveal but merely casts a light upon things. This should not be taken as an unveiling but as simply another form of distortion, a "will to deceive that is in things luminous" that may "post men to fraudulent destinies" (BM 120). Distortion of the past by false light, it seems, can send us off in the wrong direction.

The other way in which the sun's action upon the desert deceives is through the production of mirages. For the majority of the novel, McCarthy's wanderers barely seem to register the look of the landscape they traverse. But there is a point after the Comanche massacre of White's filibusterers where the kid and Sproule, after a typically punishing spell in the desert, appear to come across a lake and a distant city. As the sun falls, the lake and city "dissolve," and when they wake the next morning they find "only a barren dusty plain" (BM 62).

The sun as power, then, is duplicitous. The deceptiveness of luminous things, and the fact that the source of illumination can only be perceived indirectly, suggest that the source of power can only be intuited, never actually seen. What knowledge we have is obtained always already mediated through indirection, reflection, or "in retrospect," after the fact. If McCarthy favors the "absolute rock" of experience, the corrosive power of violent history, then the novel must court madness by looking into the sun.

The overwriting of American Manifest Destiny on the Southwest inscribes the narrative of acquisition on a land where for millennia the sun has expended its energy without recompense. The moment of McCarthy's narrative marks the point where a space of libidinal expenditure is converted into a place of production, where violence yields scalps and gold as forms of wealth to be accumulated rather than released back into the solar energy flows.[43] On the pivot of this turn into history stands Judge Holden, who represents both the acme of Enlightenment rational domination of the life-world and the ultimate warrior king. The judge straddles both worlds, and like his literary precursors from Natty Bumppo to Ahab, he must facilitate the safe arrival of the rational management of nature through his very acts of metaphysical violence. Claiming that "[w]hatever in creation exists without my knowledge exists without my consent," the judge speaks fulsomely for the totalizing power of encyclopedic knowledge (BM 198). He will document and destroy in order to convert material into fact. Yet later he will speak of war not as the instrument of domination but as a noble dance that has become dishonored (BM 331). The judge is both warrior and imperial functionary, spokesman of, in turn, expenditure and accumulation: "[e]very child knows that play is nobler than work"; "[w]ar is the ultimate game" (BM 249). He would restore the bloody nobility of sacrifice yet will also absorb the world into himself as property. While keeping notes on geology, fauna, and fossils, the judge can also observe that "[b]ooks lie" and that the truth is "in stones and trees, the bones of things" (BM 116).

In making this distinction the judge appears to prefer the empirical world before him, trusting the apparently unmediated truth of appearances. Yet those appearances are revealed only due to the light cast by the power of the sun. To look at stones and trees is not really to see them but to see the temperatures of the objects as their brute matter is animated by the heat of solar light. The notional directness of vision required by the Enlightenment scientist is not direct at all but mediated by that object—the sun—that can only be known through indirection.

The sun is nowhere more powerful than in the desert, where the ferocity of the unsheltered gaze pitilessly illuminates the world of things. Stripped of defining shadow under the meridian sun the terrain becomes a "neuter austerity," and distinctions between objects appear to have been removed, "bequeathed a strange equality" (BM 247). The "very clarity" of things "belied their familiarity, for the eye predicates the whole on some feature or part and here was nothing more luminous than another and nothing more enshadowed and in the optical democracy of such landscapes all preference is made whimsical and a man and a rock become endowed with unguessed kinships" (BM 247). Critics have identified this celebrated passage as a form of metacommentary on the "horizontal" way in which the novel itself refuses to make distinctions between classes of objects (rocks and men, men and animals) or between kinds of activity (riding, eating, killing).[44] As such, landscape is not a background or stage upon which human agency is played out. Instead, natural forces and human actions are equally represented as both violent and motiveless.

This assessment of *Blood Meridian*'s style is consonant with the argument put forward here in that it confirms the way in which McCarthy's precision of description actually blurs rather than defines the place and time of the narrative. What I would stress about McCarthy's "optical democracy" is that the passage is about the perception of objects rather than about the material fact of the objects' existence. This is a passage about phenomenology rather than epistemology. We are warned that clarity does not mean that we know more about things; indeed, familiarity is given the lie by clarity, and what equality the lack of shadow bequeaths is "strange." What the direct light of the sun actually produces is an uncanny effect whereby familiar objects are made to appear otherwise. Indeed, what the desert sun illuminates is not the world of things but the contingency of vision, since the kind of light cast upon things changes the sense of what those things are and what they mean. There is an argument here, I think, about exposure and concealment, with "optical democracy" functioning as a sort of ideological special effect. The unforgiving illumination of an all-pervasive light might be described as power (the sun, the state) showing itself, revealing its capacity for unifying its subjects (revealing the "unguessed kinships" between discrete entities). In this way, total illumination functions as a trope for total transparency and a promise of unambiguous correspondence between what is shown and what is seen (what you see is what you get). We might conclude, then, that the sun as provider of an "optical democracy" works to produce a plane of vision where everything appears to be revealed in its actuality and where each thing seems to be the kin of everything else. The sun's bald illumination creates an apparent totality where everything is connected, unambiguous, and shown as it really is: a state of nature uncomplicated by the shadows of cultural or political doubt. But as I have already said, this apparent clarity is strange, the complexity of things rendered overly simple by excessive illumination. The passage registers a skepticism toward the noonday sun that ought to be identified as a nascent form of critique.

If one of the things *Blood Meridian* manages to do is fold American history into natural history in order to interrogate the implications of naturalizing a process of imperial conquest, the maintenance of an optical (perceived) democracy based on illumination invites an analogy between cosmic power (the sun) and historical power (the state). One of the planks of liberal democracy is that its institutions operate according to the will of the people. Transparency of government is a precondition for the legitimacy of power since the exercise of that power is accountable to its source, the electorate. What the emergence of the national security state in the wake of Pearl Harbor inaugurated, as I argued in the previous chapter, was the seemingly paradoxical notion of secrecy and dissemblance as a necessary device for the protection of democracy, effacing transparency as a virtue. The Vietnam War and Nixon's adventures in Cambodia, not to mention Watergate, temporarily unraveled the justification for legitimate secrecy in pursuit of national security. The disillusionment with the institutions of government during the 1960s and 1970s indicates that in part the tacit Cold War acceptance of the hiddenness of power had been at best a mistake. What *Blood Meridian* suggests is that transparency produces what can only be a *perceived* and "strange" equality. To mistake this strangeness for clarity is to invest too heavily in the value of notionally empirical evidence and the facts before one's eyes. It is to privilege the source of illumination over the thing illuminated and to mistake the glow of direct penetrating (as illumination is often described) light as enlightenment. As Bataille makes clear, we cannot look directly at the source of power but can only perceive its effects. And what we learn when we look at its effects is that we can never look directly at the source. In other words, what is really powerful about power is the way it conceals itself through the act of revelation. To look directly at the clarity of the articles illuminated makes them strange rather than familiar, and suggests that what we are seeing is not the truth about things "as they are" but only as they have been made to appear to be. "Optical democracy" is a good term because it qualifies democracy as an effect. The sun of McCarthy's title is the sun as power, conceived at its zenith (casting no shadow) and at its lowest (too much shadow). Just as this doubleness in the title means we cannot know what time of day it is (or where in time we are), only what color it is, neither can we be comfortable with whether what the novel shows us in its horizontality is the truth about power and history or only an effect of that power and that history. Nor should we be comfortable. This may be the limit of what McCarthy's book can do as "revisionist" history since the very idea of a revisionist reading infers that something can now be revealed which was once hidden. If my understanding of McCarthy's notion of optical democracy—and Blood Meridian—is right, any historical "truth" the novel may be imparting in its description of the bloody pursuit of America's Manifest Destiny (Sonoran and Saigon versions) can only be read by looking awry.

As I have suggested in my reading of McCarthy's representation of landscape, the novel demonstrates how agency can be effaced by the recoding of historical space as prehistoric. A similar action is performed, I think, through the judge's rhetoric of ritual and sacrifice as mystifications of war's political economy. The judge's view of war as a noble game with no end outside itself situates him within an economy of expenditure with links to the notion of sacrifice. For Bataille, sacrifice is put forward as a critique of production that gives back a noninstrumental meaning to objects that have been reduced to inanimate things by the productive world. The freedom offered here "is given in destruction," claims Bataille, "whose essence is to consume profitlessly whatever might remain in the profession of useful works. Sacrifice destroys that which it con-secrates."[45]

In this view, the warrior stands outside the world of productive labor and in contradiction to it. Discussing war and sacrifice in ancient Mexico, Bataille quotes the missionary and compiler of the Florentine Codex Bernadino de Sahagún:

> [The midwife would say to the newborn boy:] I cut your navel in the middle of your body. Know and understand that the house in which you are born is not your dwelling. . . . It is your cradle, the place where you lay your head. . . . Your true land is elsewhere; you are promised for other places. You belong to the countryside where battles are fought; you were sent to go there; your function and your skill is warfare; your duty is to give the sun the blood of your enemies to drink and to supply the earth with the bodies of your enemies to eat. As for your native land, your legacy and your happiness, you will find them in the house of the sun in the sky.[46]

This passage bears comparison with the opening description of the kid in *Blood Meridian*, who is also born into a house that is not his dwelling: "[h]e can neither read nor write and in him broods already a taste for mind-less violence" (BM 3). At fourteen, the kid runs away to where battles are fought, to the house of the sun in the sky. The judge's grievance against the kid at the end of the novel is that he has turned away from his birth-right as warrior: "[i]f war is not holy man is nothing but antic clay" (BM 307). Later, the judge continues his accusation that the kid has dishon-ored the warrior caste by not following his destiny. The true warrior is he "who has offered up himself entire to the blood of war, who has been to the floor of the pit and seen horror in the round and learned at last that it speaks to his innermost heart" (BM 331).

As Bataille's use of Sahagún suggests, linking the birthright of a war-rior with a land of war fuses identity to place as part of an organic ritual of violence between the sun as power and earth as site. In Sahagún's ac-count, warfare is sanctioned as the noninstrumental fulfillment of libid-inal destiny. Jay Ellis's point that the meridian of McCarthy's novel is the line between untrammeled bloodletting and a more constrained and in-stitutionalized violence is right, I think, and the judge's castigation of the kid is part of the former's awareness of the bureaucratic foreclosure of war's ecstatic dimension as the nation becomes fenced in, with the kid's reticence, if that is what it is, as a sign of the kind of internalization of social norms that makes the pursuit of sacred violence untenable.[47] Once violence becomes instrumental it is no longer natural but merely functional and the legitimizing force of war-as-sacrifice hard to maintain. The judge must kill the kid in order to erase this evidence of compromised holiness, but it is a final purgative gesture that cannot restore the primordial state of war the judge has been instrumental in dismantling. Any remnant of the warrior's sacred function left in the aftermath of the externalization of war by the demarcation of the limits of the nation-state serves only as a legitimation effect for continued bloodshed.

A Geopolitics of Primordial Return

The parable-like epilogue to *Blood Meridian* appears to imply, as some critics have suggested, the imposition of mathematical regulation onto the nonhuman order of the Southwestern landscape. It is by no means clear what the epilogue is about, and the critical discussion has not been conclusive.[48] What is clear is that the insertion of an epilogue provides a narrative space outside of what Holloway calls judge Holden's "totalizing energy."[49]

In the epilogue, a man "progresses" over the plain by means of the postholes he is digging, one after the other. Space is being produced in accordance with the progression of incremental measure. The wanderers behind him mechanistically either search or do not search for bones, as if they are part of some kind of clock. Again, this appears to be the spatialized movement of temporal measurement. The wanderers cross the track of holes one by one, the track itself seeming to be "the verification of a principle, a validation of sequence and causality" (BM 337). Each hole verifies all the others, owes its existence to the principle of sequence rather than to its physical existence. Nothing is categorically demonstrated here, no real key to events is given: everything "appears," "seems," is "as if " there is meaning. However, it is hard to avoid the conclusion, as Phillips accepts, that this is a description of a more modern world than that of the 1840s, the time during which *Blood Meridian* is set, and that the world of the epilogue is one "in which the western plains have been rationalized—settled, fenced, and punctured."[50]

In a sense, the epilogue could be said to function as a bridge between the feral world of the 1840s and the heavily managed space of the twentieth century McCarthy goes on to explore in *The Border Trilogy*. The epilogue is a bewilderingly obscure but necessary device that demands we read the novel back through this final puzzle. It insists we understand the world of the novel as anterior to the act of measurement, before postholes and the very idea of sequence and causality. The posthole digger, then, serves to represent the construction of history: the delineation and regulation of time and space by the imposition of abstract systems of measurement. The epilogue, as Ellis argues, "demands both a mythic, and a historical, interpretation," since it calls forth a consideration of the broad symbolic and historically particular forces within which the novel's actions are situated.[51]

If Holden carries the double burden of Enlightenment rationalism and fallen warrior priest, this cocktail of logic and mysticism provides a vivid emblem of the military-industrial sensibility as it became manifest in the United States during the mid-twentieth century. The thorough domination of the Western lands could only be achieved through such a doubleness: brutal force and painstaking classification together ensnare the world of things and put them to use by using them up. While *The Border Trilogy* marks off the dispossession of the remnants of an older order, there is no aspect of that process that is not already at work in the years following the Mexican War.

The "chief Western preoccupation of the national government during the era of Manifest Destiny," claims William Goetzmann, "was a grand national reconnaissance of the entire trans-Mississippi country." The expeditions conducted by the Corps of Topographical Engineers, supervised by the Topographical Bureau, itself under advisement from scientific societies, were ordered to examine the plants, animals, Indians, and geological formations of the country they crossed. The plan was to "comprise a total geographic inventory of the West which would have meaning and utility for Westbound Americans, whatever their needs."[52] Materials were collected and brought "back East" to be classified and organized in order to chart a "Linnaean cosmic order."[53]

This inventory functions in part to contain the previously unknown and unpredictable, to mark out the perimeter of what is possible. The physical removal of specimens for classification further implies a process of containment and abstraction. Such a practice is at odds with McCarthy's sense of a kind of deep political ecology, and the assessment made of science by someone like T. E. Hulme would not be out of place in *Blood Meridian*. "The aim of science and all of thought," writes Hulme, "is to reduce the complex and inevitably disconnected world of grit and cinders to a few ideal counters which we can move about and so form an ungritlike picture of reality—one flattering to our sense of power over the world." Unity is made in the world, according to Hulme, "by drawing squares over it" in the manner of a "sorting machine."[54] The idea that the order charted upon this map contains everything is, however, a fiction of rational unity. Not only can the representation not grasp and fully contain that which it describes, but things are deliberately left out.

What is left out of the ordering of space in the aftermath of territorial wars is the granulated remains of the exterminated, turned into landscape by the violence left unchecked by an expansionist politics that articulates itself as a force of nature. The ostensible "thereness" of land as outside human history and the notionally primordial depravity of unregulated human beings in their "natural" state are made to work, in fact, as the legitimizing agents of the process of domination that renders them finally as waste. "Nature" and its human counterparts are thereby consumed and excluded even as their excessive otherness is reinvested as the necessary sacrificial component of the orderly state. This process is by no means completed with the consolidation and mapping of territorial limits that concludes *Blood Meridian*. Rather, as I argue in the following chapters, the delimiting of Western space as "wasteland" is a necessary precondition upon which can be built a national order based on the perpetual sacrifice of its abjected waste.

3. DUST BREEDING

Narratives of Inter(n)ment

Half the sky was dark with a tide of sand pouring toward us.
Jeanne Wakatsuki Houston

Blood Meridian's epilogue signals the conversion of space into a legible resource through its delineation as a grid of consumable packets. This reterritorialization of "wasteland" overwrites the open space of prehistory as part of the map of the nation, an integration of the outside into the form of the state. The eradication of prior inhabitants by wars of conquest reconfirms the designation of such a space as empty while the material remains, like the petroglyphs McCarthy's cowboys in *The Border Trilogy* constantly walk over, are figured as ancient, illegible, and decontextualized rather than recent and historically locatable. The usefulness of the desert as a place that produces accelerated ruins, making recent devastation seem "like some more ancient ossuary" (BM 175), suggests that inside the newly gridded United States exists a site capable of processing the extraneous or unwanted by-products of national formation. The wasteland of prehistory can be made to serve as the waste site of history.

In the wake of the attack on Pearl Harbor, the internment of people of Japanese ancestry in camps located predominantly in the "waste" land of the Western interior is one way in which the desert as resource can be put to use as the excluded inside of American self-definition. In this chapter I want to explore how the particularity of the Western desert landscape functions, as it is depicted in narratives of internment, as an agent of erasure that collaborates in the enforcement of security measures designed to conceal in plain sight the presence of the excluded. In two very different novels by sansei (third generation) writers, Rahna Reiko Rizzuto's *Why She Left Us* (1999) and Julie Otsuka's *When the Emperor Was Divine* (2002), internment functions as both the agent of exposure that forces the contradictions of Japanese American cultural formation into the open—including the institutionalized generational divide produced by a history of American anti-Japanese policies on one hand and the inherited Japanese patriarchal order on the other—while at the same time deepening and complicating those contradictions. In each novel, internment effectively decapitates the existing Japanese American social order (recall Bataille's image of the sun as an anthropomorphic being deprived of a head) by inverting the traditional generational hierarchy. A reconfigured Japanese American identity emerges post-internment—after exposure to the sovereign Western sun of disciplinary power—predicated on the accelerated "Americanizing" experience of internment as a mode of "pioneer" existence that granulates prior attachments and disperses the abjected, atomized subject back into the national body. The desert wind that salts the ruins in *Blood Meridian* continues to operate in the mid-twentieth century as an instrument for the manufacture and dispersal of dirt that provides cover for the interment of the interned refuse of the national imaginary.

Executive Order 9066 was signed by President Roosevelt on February 19, 1942, authorizing the prescription of exclusion areas by virtue of military necessity. While no specific group was named, the designation of the western halves of Washington, Oregon, and California, including all of California south of Los Angeles, and the southern half of Arizona as military exclusion areas on March 2 meant that it was clearly the Japanese who were to be removed. Another proclamation on March 16 named Idaho, Montana, Nevada, and Utah as military areas. The War Relocation Authority (WRA) was established two days later and selected ten isolated sites, mostly in desert areas, for relocation centers that it described as "a pioneer community, with basic housing and protective services provided by the Federal Government, for occupancy by evacuees for the duration of the war."[1]

To describe a concentration camp as a pioneer community reveals something of the inventiveness of the WRA's conception of their task, signaling the way "evacuation" is reconceived within an existing discourse of adventurous Westering. The invocation of the "pioneer community" directly establishes internment as a Western formation inseparable from the experience of being in a particular landscape that is challenging and, by inference, character building. Inadvertently, the choice of the figure of the pioneer as the model for the internee activates, following the Turner thesis, the notion of the West as the site of Americanization.[2] The regulation of life in the camps and the unraveling of Japanese identity caused by internment has, in fact, been seen by some as the decisive constitutive moment in the production of Japanese American identity, a fact made explicit in internment narratives like Jeanne Wakatsuki Houston's *Farewell to Manzanar* (1973). With the internee-as-pioneer, the WRA enlists the Western landscape, and the collective memory of it, as the place where the excluded can be contained and possibly converted by the redeeming openness of American space.

The reinvention of evacuees into pioneers required the divestment of all that could not be carried, effectively wiping out for many their stake in the U.S. economy. The rapidity with which removal was effected, sometimes within a few days of notification, meant that many people were forced to sell off their businesses and possessions at a fraction of their worth or leave them with trustees. Taken together, racialized exclusion, geographic displacement, and economic impoverishment function to effect in the interned an erasure of prior attachments and commitments before submission to the dubious blandishments of the dusty, windswept landscape of Americanization.

Dirty Camps

The pervasiveness of dust is a recurrent trope in internment narratives. Whipped up by the winds cutting across the desert, dust relentlessly pummels away at the internees, and barracks must be continually swept to clear the recurring film of dust that accumulates over everything. Together, the wind and the dust collaborate to assault both the bodies of the interned and the integrity of Japanese social, especially familial, organization. As John Y. Tateishi claims, the common experience at all ten of the internment camps was the wind, which at Manzanar created "great dust storms" that descended "like a tidal wave wreaking havoc over the land."[3] On arrival at Topaz in Utah, Miné Okubo notes that "it was impossible to see anything through the dust."[4] In Edward Miyakawa's novel *Tule Lake* (1979), the "dry heat burns the dirt loose from the earth" in order to gather in "gusts and whirlwinds" that attack the "eyes and throats, burning and strangling."[5] The "slightest breezes raise clouds of dust" and "[p]eople scurry about to signs of whirlwind sandstorms that whip the camp."[6] The "capricious crosswinds that have blown us together in this bleak flatland" also conspire to wear the camp away; while

Tule Lake is "a new city, yet already it looks aged, with buildings, poles, and bodies all coated with sedimentary layers of dust and sand."[7] Exposure to dust is not confined to outdoor space, which also infiltrates the inside of the barracks. Jeanne Wakatsuki Houston, in *Farewell to Manzanar*, describes icy gusts of wind "sending fresh dust puffs up through the floorboards"; sand creeps through knotholes in the floor and walls, and a "different kind of sand" comes through cracks. Sweeping "could barely keep up with it."[8]

Peter Suzuki expands on the notion of an encroaching and debilitating environment as a defining characteristic of the internment experience when he uses the term "desertification" to describe the process of withering that takes place in Hiroshi Nakamura's *Treadmill*.[9] The family depicted in that novel are punished by a landscape that causes them to physically "wilt" in the heat while their belief in America "wither[s]." The stasis and resulting enforced passivity strips the interned of meaningful agency; they are seemingly placed out in the sun simply to shrivel away.

While the problem of dust is unremarkable enough in arid places, Patricia Limerick has noted that the internment camps were mostly in areas where strong winds are common, and that the bulldozers used in building the camps had destroyed the ground cover, "exacerbat[ing] the interaction of wind and dirt."[10] The very construction of the space of incarceration activates a hostile environment, the landscape "on the offensive, actively intruding on the observer."[11] Ansel Adams, however, who photographed the Manzanar relocation camp in 1943, offers a more sanguine reading of the desert environment and its challenges: "I believe that the arid splendor of the desert, ringed with towering mountains, has strengthened the spirit of the people of Manzanar. I do not say all are conscious of this influence, but I am sure most have responded, in one way or another, to the resonances of their environment. . . . The huge vistas and the stern realities of sun and wind and space symbolize the immensity and opportunity of America—perhaps a vital reassurance following the experiences of enforced exodus."[12] Internees did indeed respond to the "resonances of their environment," though as the observations noted above suggest, more in one way than the other. Often it was less the "arid splendor" they registered than the extremities of heat and cold and the pulverizations of wind and dirt.[13]

For Mary Douglas, dirt is "matter out of place." It is "never a unique, isolated event" but "the by-product of a systematic ordering and classification of matter, in so far as ordering involves rejecting inappropriate elements."[14] Similar to Agamben's notion of the exception, dirt for Douglas is a "residual category," an anomaly which serves to define order through its own negation: "[w]hen something is firmly classed as anomalous, the outline of the set in which it is not a member is clarified."[15] Julia Kristeva argues that what causes abjection is that which "disturbs identity, system, order," something that "does not respect borders, positions, rules. The in-between, the ambiguous, the composite."[16] The removal of people of Japanese ancestry to the dustblown regions of the Western interior, in these terms, trades on the wasteland discourse that figures the desert as a residual category within which further anomalies might be deposited. With the classification of the Japanese population as "out of place" within the circumscribed definition of American order brought about by the state of emergency caused by Pearl Harbor, the functional anomaly of the desert can be recruited as the inside outside space for the containment of rejected "inappropriate elements" notionally injurious to national security.

As a challenge to the maintenance of social order within the camps, the desert dust threatens to accelerate the erosion of domestic space that might otherwise provide a site of continuity between everyday life as it was lived prior to internment and the deracinated experience of the barracks. The constant sweeping noted by Wakatsuki Houston thus becomes a strategy of refusal that seeks to minimize the impact of the external environment and preserve the domestic order of the family. The relationship between sweeping and household dust, however, is dialectically complex, and the action of constant sweeping in the context of Western wartime internment is revealing not only of the struggle between desert dirt and Japanese identity—landscape as adversary—but of the erosion of social organization experienced inside the domestic sphere between generations and between men and women.[17]

Household dust is a particular kind of dirt in that it seems to come from nowhere. In fact, as Jake Kennedy has suggested, dust is produced "by the very processes of domestic action that strive to keep it hidden and controlled." Dust both represents "the 'domestic' (it is the everyday signifier of the bourgeois home) and threatens to erase, or at least contaminate, that very space as it connotes imperceptible, paradoxical 'invasion' from *within*." While other kinds of dirt can usually be seen, "dirt in its dust-form 'descends' and is nearly as ubiquitous as oxygen. Thus 'the domestic,' in its most general sense of a home environment, *is* dust."[18]

In 1920 Man Ray photographed the reverse of Marcel Duchamp's *Large Glass* (1915–23) as it lay in Duchamp's New York studio. They called the image—a flat, crustaceous plane resembling an aerial shot of a desert landscape—*Dust Breeding*.[19] The title combines the seemingly contradictory notions of static neglect and dynamic organic production. *Dust Breeding* suggests a process of accumulation even in inactivity, of a barely perceptible aggregation of sedimented matter that, rather than being moribund and inert, is in fact an encroaching, proliferating stratum of dirt. The image makes visible the actions of the environment upon objects, suggesting that neglected or forgotten things are far from untouched when human attention is directed elsewhere. Indeed, *Dust Breeding* reveals a universe of force in which dust becomes the material residuum of duration, the literal embodiment of time having passed. Time coats the glass, which, while static, becomes the repository for entropic actions working around and upon it.

It may seem out of place to introduce Duchamp's *Dust Breeding* in the context of a discussion of Japanese American internment. However, the notion of dust as a kind of dirt that constitutes the domain that simultaneously seeks to remove it—the domestic—is a useful way of thinking about how the desert landscapes into which Japanese Americans were deposited function as that part of the homeland that is already excluded ("wasteland"), contains the excluded (Japanese Americans), and conceals that exclusion (by removal from centers of habitation and by interment, the landscape of dust "breeding" to cover everything upon it) at the same time. If *Dust Breeding* is domestic dust that turns into a landscape—turns an inside into an outside—the barracks of the internment camp are displaced domestic sites given over to a landscape of dust. The desert is the dust of the homeland, both of and apart from the domestic (inside the nation, outside the cultivated): it is *unheimlich*, both homely (inside) and uncanny (outside). The desert and the camps located there are the disorder that defines order and the places where disorder is concentrated.

Like Agamben's sovereign exception, they are "the fundamental localization" that "traces a threshold (the state of exception)" between "outside and inside, the normal situation and chaos," making the "validity of the juridical order possible."[20]

The physical incarceration of the Japanese American population during World War II might be seen, then, as the moment when the state of exception (the emergency of Pearl Harbor) becomes the norm, when the exceptional status of a racialized other is, literally, concentrated, brought to the center of American national identity. The exception, as Agamben explains, "is an element in law that transcends positive law in the form of its suspension."[21] In other words, the exception is the apparently contradictory condition of law being suspended in order to protect the law. The exception is, Agamben goes on, "truly, according to its etymological root, *taken outside* (*ex-capere*). And not simply excluded."[22]

The camp as the space of exception has a "paradoxical status" for Agamben since what is "excluded in the camp is . . . included through its own exclusion." What is exceptional outside the camp becomes the norm inside: the camp is "the structure in which the state of exception—the possibility of deciding on which founds sovereign power—is realized *normally*."[23] The birth of the camp is thus decisive of "the political space of modernity itself" since it comes at the point when the "functional nexus" between the nation-state and the land it occupies enters a crisis that leads to the state's assumption of "the care of the nation's biological life as one of its proper tasks."[24] When otherness is seen to be structurally in excess of the imagined order of the state, then, and a threat to the maintenance of that order, the camp becomes "the new, hidden regulator of the inscription of life in the order." More to the point, it is "the sign of the system's inability to function without being transformed into a lethal machine."[25] The point of biopower, to recall Foucault, is to regulate life rather than take it since death is beyond power's reach. The camp is a crisis measure that excludes without killing and introduces a new category of outside insiders, indeterminate prisoners without trial.

The process of interning people of Japanese ancestry first used racial classification to segregate the population to be excluded. Classification by national origin (and, de facto, by generation) enabled the division of "enemy aliens" from citizens. The insistence on tests of "loyalty" hardened divisions by producing classes of "loyal" and "disloyal" internees, even though many respondents answered the loyalty questionnaires on pragmatic rather than ideological grounds—in order to keep the family together or so they would not have to move again. This process of separation creates different orders of exclusion: all people of Japanese ancestry are excluded, but within that group, issei (immigrants from Japan) are more excluded than nisei (sons and daughters of Japanese immigrants), "disloyal" nisei are more excluded than "loyal" nisei. The transformation of Tule Lake from a relocation to a segregation camp where the "disloyals" could be held introduces another physical demarcation within the camp system.

Caroline Chung Simpson has argued that while little was written about internment in the popular press during the war, when it was considered postwar "it threatened to undermine the reputation of U.S. democracy because the internment exposed the arbitrariness of the very enterprise of national history and the myth of exceptionalism that history sustains."[26] Although many of the interned remained silent about their experience after the war due to a mixture of shame, continuing anti-Japanese sentiment, and a general disquiet about the dubious legality and deep injustice of the policy, Simpson contends that the media, "far from simply burying the news of Japanese American internment as the war ended, sometimes actively engaged the concept of Japanese Americanness both as a discomfiting challenge to national ideologies and histories and as a means of recasting national boundaries."[27] Nevertheless, the visibility of internment in public discourse, especially in the decade following the end of the war, belies, as Simpson argues, "a surprising lack of discussion of the function of the national remembering of that event."[28] In short, internment is "everywhere in the immediate postwar as a vacated history" that is remembered by forgetting, what Simpson calls an absent presence "of discursive inclusion that works to evade or displace."[29]

After the war, then, the wartime threat of the Japanese is replaced by the fact of internment itself as a threat to democracy. As Simpson explains, internment "so clearly threatened the ideal of the American nation that it created an undeniable uncanny effect by seeming to dissolve the difference between America as a symbol of democratic freedom and the tyranny of a police state represented by the Axis powers."[30] The contradiction of the incarcerated citizen makes visible the dilemma of the national security state: that the emergency that is called in order to protect democracy has the effect of dismantling the democratic process it is intended to preserve. What Simpson reminds us is that the knowledge of the secret that is already known—in this case that the internment of American citizens as well as "aliens" has taken place—reinforces an awareness of secrecy as implicit in the promise of security while keeping alive the threat that legitimates secrecy as a defense. It is in this sense that Simpson can argue that the postwar and Cold War American nation are, in fact, "reproduced and renewed through the narrativity of the internment discourses." [31]

This renewal is already evident in Ansel Adams's ambivalent photographic memorial to Manzanar published in 1944. In the accompanying text, Adams imagines how Manzanar will look when the internees "have resumed their places in the stream of American life." In a peculiarly elegiac register, Adams pictures the desert reclaiming the site: "flimsy buildings will vanish," plants will "wither," orchards will "grow older," "foundations and terracing will gradually blend into the stable texture of the desert," and "the cemetery monument will assume the dignity of desert ruins." Once again, "the wind will move over the land and the snow fall upon it." [32] Though this is not a battlefield, Adams's attention to the natural erosion of evidence of sovereign power anticipates McCarthy's reading of the Tewa massacre: "[t]he desert wind would salt their ruins and there would be nothing, no ghost nor scribe, to tell to a pilgrim in his passing how it was that people had lived in this place and in this place died" (BM 174). If Adams is such a scribe, his hope that Manzanar is only a "rocky wartime *detour* on the road to American citizenship," despite his obvious disquiet, effaces the fact that two-thirds of the interned are already citizens in the same way that the desert functions to erase the camp. What Adams, "in his passing," insists upon is that "we know that the human challenge of Manzanar will rise insistently over all America—and America cannot deny its tremendous implications." [33] As Simpson's argument suggests, what Adams manages to do here is celebrate the resilient Americanness of the internees even as he concedes the threat to democracy internment has already posed. Disturbingly, the interned are both potential enemy and confirmed ally, sharing "our" aspirations even as they are excluded in order to reinforce the values that underpin such aspirations. Functioning proleptically, memory of the internment serves as evidence of what has and will happen under a state of emergency. While the desert will convert the site back into landscape, the political threat internment poses is not so easily buried. As Adams himself observed, "the future is only a hope, no longer an assurance."[34]

Given the profound ambivalence produced by internment in the years following the war, not to mention the radical impact of incarceration upon the interned themselves, it is not surprising that narratives dealing with the wartime experience of Japanese Americans are placed somewhat awkwardly in the American literary canon. While a number of nonfictional testimonies and memoirs by ex-internees—Miné Okubo's *Citizen 13660* (1946), Monica Sone's *Nisei Daughter* (1953), and, probably the best known and most widely read, Wakatsuki Houston's *Farewell to Manzanar* (1973), for example—have been rightly celebrated, fictional accounts of incarceration have been few and largely, though not exclusively, produced by subsequent generations. Hisaye Yamamoto's stories, collected in *Seventeen Syllables and Other Stories* (1988), are an exception, as the earliest of which were originally published in the 1940s and through the 1950s in mainstream American literary journals. John Okada's *No-No Boy* (1957) remains the best-known novel dealing with the aftermath of imprisonment, though there was no paperback edition of the book published until 1976.[35] Nakamura's little known novel *Treadmill* has been claimed as the first novel about the camps and was actually written during the period of internment but remained unpublished until 1995. Miyakawa's equally marginal *Tule Lake* is the first novel set in the camps themselves, published in 1979 by a small Canadian press.

Since the redress movement gathered momentum in the 1980s, the number of fictional narratives of internment has grown, though the most visible of these have also been somewhat unrepresentative in terms of the experience of most Japanese Americans. The most celebrated internment novel, Joy Kogawa's *Obasan* (1983), has become the canonical text, but it is striking that Kogawa deals with the Canadian experience. As Sau-ling Wong writes, there is no comparable U.S. novel to *Obasan*, and "no one quite knows why."[36] David Guterson's award-winning best seller *Snow Falling on Cedars* (1994) takes internment as its context and is set on an island

82

on Puget Sound that stands in for Bainbridge Island, but this is really a novel about interracial romance that has found little favor among Japanese Americans.[37] Other non–Japanese Americans have also published internment novels, including Wyoming writer Gretel Ehrlich's *Heart Mountain* (1988) and Marnie Mueller's Tule Lake–based *The Climate of the Country* (1999), while Wakatsuki Houston recently returned to the subject of the camps thirty years after the publication of her memoir in the novel *The Legend of Fire Horse Woman* (2003).

The two novels that will be my focus here, Rahna Reiko Rizzuto's *Why She Left Us* (1999) and Julie Otsuka's *When the Emperor Was Divine* (2002), self-consciously come after the memoirs and testimonies written by those who actually experienced internment firsthand. The authors' explicit acknowledgment of historical accounts and other sources positions their texts as both posterior to the events themselves and also foregrounds the already-textual nature of the material they have drawn upon. While citing sources confers some sort of verifiability to the fictions, it also signals the secondariness of these works. At the same time, then, they claim authority through reference to research conducted, while removing the likelihood of the narratives being mistaken as anything other than fiction. This strategy of authenticated inauthenticity, while a common gesture in contemporary historical fiction that serves to show that previous research has formed a carefully emplotted impression of the past, signals something in Rizzuto's and Otsuka's fictions about the instability of truth claims that is revealing of the exceptional nature of internment itself.

In the context of existing internment narratives, Rizzuto's and Otsuka's are distinctive in that they eschew the reportorial realism of earlier works like *Treadmill* (subtitled *A Documentary Novel*) and *Tule Lake*, even as they draw on the conventions of memoirs like *Farewell to Manzanar* to structure their narratives. Instead, more dislocated narrative strategies serve to foreground not just the scrambling of identity experienced by internees but the rifts produced between family members, between generations, and between Japanese Americans and the rest of American society by the process of internment and its repressed reverberations as they continue to regulate Japanese American social relations. As such, *Why She Left Us* and *When the Emperor Was Divine* function recursively to repeat the story of internment in its familiar stages—"evacuation," containment, relocation, return—and through its stock of common themes—the loss of home and possessions, the emasculation of the patriarch, the divided loyalties of children, the punishing environment, poor diet, cramped communal living conditions—but differently.

The way in which they are different is in the attention placed on the problem of truth-telling. The titles of these works promise straight answers—*why* she left us, *when* the emperor was divine—that the texts themselves refuse or are unable to give. In fact, the titles are interrogatives disguised as demonstratives: why did she leave us? when was the emperor divine? The promise of clarity has written into it questions about causation and history that position these novels as posterior investigations into how things came to be the way they are. If the function of previous realist novels of internment such as *Treadmill* and *Tule Lake*, and their nonfiction analogues like *Citizen 13660* and *Farewell to Manzanar*, is to testify to the fact of internment as it was experienced—the prohibition of cameras in the camps means that, outside of the work made by visiting professionals like Ansel Adams, there is no photographic record of internment from the inside—the later novels absorb and redirect that testimony toward a probing of consequences.[38]

Why She Left Us and *When the Emperor Was Divine* are revealing works not least because they repeat the familiar trajectory of the internment memoir but in ways that put under pressure the representational claims of the chronological, developmental account of "what happened" that realism ostensibly promises to deliver. The problem with the chronological account is that it can serve to order and thereby domesticate the experience of internment, inadvertently reproducing the pioneer narrative of American becoming that internment in so many ways contradicts. Krista Comer has made this point in relation to *Farewell to Manzanar*, where the internment regime liberates the narrator from a dominating father, making the camp the site "for this girl's articulation into female subjectivity" that "is deliberately American."[39] While *Farewell to Manzanar*, as Comer goes on to explain, is a more complex text than this, what Rizzuto and Otsuka are interested in is scrambling the narrative of ascent (and, more cautiously, assent) implicit in the chronological account of struggle and survival.

Rizzuto figures this difference of approach by troping on the theme of dirt and cleaning so embedded in internment narratives. Discussing the complex intergenerational response to a forthcoming redress payment, Kim (born 1950), the stepsister of Mariko (born 1942 and interned), explains to Mariko's daughter that "the difference between us and your mother" is the younger generation's refusal to euphemize incarceration as internment—"a horse stall is a horse stall," Kim insists.[40] Mariko's daughter is an artist, and Kim explains to her that "[a]rtists rub the dirt into things to see the definition. Mari cleans them up, hoping they'll disappear" (WSL 20). This harsh assessment links Mariko to her own mother, the ill-treated Emi the novel's title refers to as the one who "left us." Emi was placed into domestic service during the Depression at twelve years of age because she "was so meticulous at finding dirt" (WSL 61), and this removal from the family in effect produces much of the strife that drives the novel. The capacity to discover and remove dirt is thus situated as the catalyst for family breakdown, and Kim's assessment of Mariko suggests that an obsessive denial of disorder at some level implicates the previous generations in their own removal.

If a chronological, realist account of internment courts the danger of formally cleaning up the dirt its content exposes, the more broken narratives produced by Rizzuto and Otsuka are more inclined to rub it in. In many ways, *Why She Left Us* and *When the Emperor Was Divine* are works of what Marianne Hirsch calls "postmemory," by which she means "the response of the second generation to the trauma of the first." Postmemory is, of necessity, characterized by its secondariness, its "basis in displacement, its vicariousness and belatedness." It is memory mediated "through representation, projection, and creation—often based on silence rather than speech, on the invisible rather than the visible."[41] Postmemory is, importantly, relational, "an intersubjective transgenerational space" that connects past events to the present through an ethical relation of identification with the experience of others.[42]

If postmemory is characterized by the belated aftereffects of traumatic memory transmitted across generations, then it may be, as Hirsch suggests, that it is "only in subsequent generations that trauma can be witnessed and worked through, by those who were not there to live it but who received its effects, belatedly, through the narratives, actions and symptoms of the previous generation."[43] As I observed earlier, the experience of internment remained critically uninterrogated after World War II despite its position as the defining event of Japanese American identity formation. The belated effects of internment's coercive severance of connections with Japan and Japanese cultural life and the inversion of traditional family structures—the privileging of the English language over Japanese, children over their parents, and individualized loyalty oaths over collective allegiance—are registered in *Why She Left Us* and *When the Emperor Was Divine* not by testimony but by modes of estrangement. Each novel eschews a central narrative position, preferring to signal the collapse of family hierarchy through a dispersal of focalization across family members. The nonlinear nature of the narratives further unhinges the stories from any developmental logic, exacerbating the sense of dislocation and ruptured continuity caused by the emasculation of the patriarch and the dismantled social relations produced by the impact of internment. In *Why She Left Us*, in particular, the narrative is positioned at the point of official recognition of government culpability, using the claim for compensation as the lever that opens a repressed history of destroyed relationships and shameful violence. What is also striking about these novels is the way they withdraw from an unambiguous negative assessment of internment, which is presented as heterogeneous in its effects. While the impact on the fathers is unequivocally catastrophic, for mothers and children the effects are more ambivalently registered, opening up spaces for a complex dialectical reading of internment as enabling even as it remains devastating.

The Abject Pioneer

David Leiwei Li argues that there is an "inextricable but often repressed relation between the acts of Asian exclusion and American national formation."[44] It is worth considering Li's argument here since his reading of racialized exclusion helps shed light on the politics of expulsion that not only drives internment as an embodiment of security-driven identity production but also normalizes that exclusion as the concealed guarantor of biopolitical sovereignty. Just as *Blood Meridian* scrutinizes the legitimacy effects of the sort of landscape representation that naturalizes (and thereby dehistoricizes) violence as a prehistory of national becoming, I think that the wartime removal of Japanese Americans stands as a moment of wish-fulfillment in the history of American waste management in the West.

The "repressed relation" Li locates between pre-internment Asian exclusion and the internment itself should also extend to include the continued repression of the relation between internment and post-internment cultural politics. The desire to bracket internment as a wartime aberration belies the necessary continuation of the state of emergency into "peacetime" that sanctions other modes of exclusion, exemption, and withdrawal that have come to characterize the use of Western space. In these terms, fictions of internment not only register wartime "evacuation" as a foundational moment in the construction of Japanese American identity, they also reveal how the state of exception becomes written into postwar social organization. While I am not suggesting that the specificity of Japanese American experience should somehow be reductively generalized in any way, I do think that there are indications in internment fictions to suggest that the reconstitution of Japanese American identity that is forced into being by internment has reverberations beyond an ethnically specific politics of difference.

Li divides the history of the management and control of Asians in the United States into two periods. The first, from 1856 to 1943/1965, he terms the period of "Oriental alienation," whereby Asian American citizenship is regulated through a series of legal prohibitions and exclusions, rendering the "Oriental" foreign to the United States. As the excluded other of the imagined Euro-American national body, the Asian, according to Li, has a "spectral centrality" in the definition of the "formative European American *ethnos*" that cements "the historical consanguinity between racial essence and national legitimacy."[45] Following Gramsci, Li's second period (1943/1965 to the present) is marked by the rejection of disciplinary exclusion in favor of manufactured consent. From the end of World War II and the Immigration Reform Act of 1965, the enforced alienation of "Orientals" has been replaced with the construction of the "Asian American," legitimized by the neo-orientalist discourse of the "model minority." Li notes that this reinvention of the Asian other coincides with the globalization of capital and the decline of the nation-state as the model for economic organization. Drawing on Kristeva, Li's second period is termed "Asian abjection," since, he argues, despite the legal inclusion into the United States of the Asian as citizen or legal alien, culturally the recognition of the Asian American as "possibly representative of the United States' national imaginary" has failed to materialize. Instead, the Asian American has been turned into an "abject," no longer the objectified external threat but still culturally excluded from the imagined community.

In *Why She Left Us*, the consequences of Oriental alienation have enabled the reproduction of a rigid Japanese patriarchal order in the Okada family to remain unmediated by the promise of a more liberal American social order. Children who feel American "on the inside" are depicted as trapped in a "Japanese" domestic sphere or cast out due to their adaptation to Caucasian ways. Internment forces the family back together, and the threat of the father, and the order he represents, is removed, but the Asian American identity that is produced post-internment carries the legacy of Oriental alienation as an absence—maintained by the mother's codependent relationship with the alienated order she has survived—that is exacerbated by the experience of interned abjection. Application for official redress for internment by the third generation is not a sign of belated inclusion into the U.S. national imaginary in the novel but instead a marker of achieved abjection inasmuch as redress does not fill in the blanks in the family history but merely reconfirms them.

On application Mariko is told there is no record of her entering the camp, meaning she must approach her taciturn mother for the number assigned to the family by the War Relocation Authority. While Mariko discovers that her cousin Eric is in fact her brother, neither the identity of her father nor the cause of her mother Emi's youthful waywardness is ever revealed. Nobody in this novel ever willingly explains anything. Though the point of view of the novel shuffles between Mariko's grandmother Kaori, her uncle Jack, brother Eric, and Mariko herself, and covers events between 1941 and 1990, and despite the family tree the novel provides, a straight answer to the question of Emi's real and symbolic estrangement from the family is never offered. The catastrophes of the past and the inability of the family members to address their distance from one another are perpetually explained by displacing that failure onto others' refusal to mention it. Kaori reflects that there were so many

secrets in the family because "we never told the truth" or wanted "to understand what had happened to our lives" (WSL 63).

Although this admission implies a personal or cultural resistance to
candor, it also points toward a broader sense of resignation in the face of
inscrutable events. Kaori believes that "things went wrong for Emi early
and they had to get worse. It was part of God's plan," as was Pearl Harbor (WSL 63). Kaori's attitude of *shikata ga nai*, or "it can't be helped," may
be read as a refusal to accept responsibility for her own actions or determined perseverance in the face of unavoidable suffering, but toward the
end of the novel Emi is unconvinced: "I never believed her," she says (WSL
241).[46] Family strife is so bound up with the broader politics of Japanese
American experience in the novel that it is as difficult for the reader to
tell the difference between personal motivation and sociopolitical forces
as it is for the characters themselves.

It is possible, for example, to locate the source of the Okada family's
misery in the brutal behavior of the patriarch, Mitsuo, who rapes his
wife in front of his children, though whether the father's behavior is a
direct consequence of his own abjection in America or a manifestation
of a much more deep-seated misogyny is unclear. Kaori's contempt for
Emi, who is sent out to clean houses at twelve years old and is later spot-
ted by her mother on the street as a "vulgar and crude" pregnant, Americanized monster—her neck "impossibly long and light" and the "vast-
ness of her skin" is bewilderingly "new" and "free" (WSL 62–63)—can be
accounted for by the profound gap between issei parent and nisei daughter but is also borne out of the mother's own incapacity for empathy. By
the time of Pearl Harbor, the animosity between generations, genders,
and ultimately, nationalities, in the family is so longstanding and deep-
seated that as Jack translates the news bulletin reporting on Pearl Harbor
for his parents, his alienation from them can now legitimately be given
form: they are "Japs, sitting in a foreign land" (WSL 31).

Being American on the "inside," the invented world Jack has imagined
for himself over the years has been a form of covert action against the
enforced Japanese identity he has had to display at home. The problem
with being American on the inside, though, is that it does not provide
the right kind of evidence of belonging that Americans require to prevent his, as well as his parents', internment. Jack's privatized American

identity—"his own world"—is not the same as belonging to the outside world, and while his individuation from his parents is sanctioned by war, his urge to flee cannot be followed through.

Why She Left Us is a frustrating novel in that it refuses to give the information needed to make sense of the domestic abuse suffered by the female members of the family. Neither does it explicitly make the links between Emi's original removal from the family, the patrimony of her children, the enfeeblement of the father, and the particularities of Japanese American internment experience that would help reveal the historical continuities that have produced a damaged family underwritten by institutionalized racial exclusion. Life before internment in the novel is patently no better than it is after Pearl Harbor, and the book's refusal to position internment as a fall importantly serves to demonstrate the already conflicted position of Japanese Americans in the United States before the war. What is most troubling about *Why She Left Us*, then, is what the novel leaves out. What is left out, in the end, is the resolution of conflicts the narrative puts into place. The novel offers no redress for the abjection of its characters and refuses the kind of closure that would dispel the mysteries it leaves in place. In Otsuka's *When the Emperor Was Divine*, a similar interest in absences produces a more measured sense of disquiet, this time not through the repression of family secrets but directly through the ostensibly innocent experiences of family members as they are themselves secreted in the Utah desert.

Don't Fence Me In

When the Emperor Was Divine is distinctive among fictional representations of internment in its refusal to pile up the facts and construct a character- and plot-driven narrative. Its five short chapters shift focus among the unnamed members of a single family. The father has already been arrested at the novel's opening, and the book follows the family as they pack (from the mother's perspective), leave Berkeley for Topaz in the Utah desert (daughter), languish in the camp for the war's duration (son), and return in 1945 (a collective "we"). The brief final chapter offers the broken father's bitter assessment of the experience.

As the *New York Times* noted in its review of the novel, the concluding chapter breaks with the rest of the book's studied refusal to register any kind of appraisal of the legitimacy of the internment process, and the shift in tone is indeed jarring.[47] The father's rage stands in contrast to the first chapter, which is rendered in such as way as to be almost an embodiment of the mother's attitude of *shikata ga nai*. Titled "Evacuation Order No. 19," the chapter opens with the statement that the "sign had appeared overnight."[48] There is no explanation of who put up the sign or why, or even what the sign says. The woman reads the sign "from top to bottom" and then takes out a pen and reads it "from top to bottom again." She makes a few notes then goes home and starts packing (WED 3). There is no gap between reading the instructions and carrying them out, leaving the reader no space to make any kind of assessment of the situation or of the woman's response to what she has read. It is not possible to gauge from the information provided whether the woman is doing as the sign instructs her or if she is packing to escape the consequences of what the sign says. She could be responding to a command or taking steps to evade or resist. The title, of course, provides the information missing from the description itself and gives the reader enough context to place the woman's actions, but the almost continuous present of the prose refuses to yield more in the way of affect. Instead, the accumulation of prosaic details—shopping for soap and face cream, considering whether to buy a shovel or hammer, failing to purchase a duffel bag—constructs a familiar pattern of activity that withholds the significance of those details as acts of preparation prior to compulsory relocation. The soap, face cream, and duffel bag will be essential items for any "evacuee," and the shovel, it transpires, is required to kill the family dog, who cannot be taken along. "Play dead," the woman commands the dog after feeding him and before clubbing him to death with the shovel: "[b]etter, she thought, than a hammer" (WED 11).

The underplaying of the first chapter produces a disturbing, uncanny effect as the rhythms of domestic life are shot through with a barely detectable but undeniable strangeness. The incident of the dog and the shovel is clearly the most striking indication that things are not quite as they should be, and the jolt produced by the killing of the dog ripples backward and forward through a chapter that is in fact wrinkled throughout with signs. The woman insists on paying straight away in the hardware store even though the shopkeeper says she can pay later. Her words

to him sound "strange to her. Wrong, almost" (WED 6). She thinks people have been staring at her because there is something wrong with her
face. A siren wails in the distance.

The sense of withheld significance in *When the Emperor Was Divine* reproduces the bewildering causal disjunction effected by the suddenness
of the evacuation order. In Yamamoto's "Death Rides the Rails to Poston," serialized in the Poston, Arizona, relocation camp newspaper the
Poston Chronicle in 1942, the detective work required to make sense of internment's absent cause is made plain through the self-conscious use of
the mystery genre.[49] When a much disliked man dies suddenly aboard the
train to Poston, a young man uses skills learned reading detective fiction
to expose the death as murder. In the manner of an Agatha Christie who-
dunit, everyone in the carriage becomes a suspect as the self-appointed
detective sifts through the possible motives for the crime. What Yamamoto captures is something of the suspicion, anxiety, and paranoia en-
gendered by forced removal; despite the outward appearance of life being
lived as usual, everyone on the train is in fact a potential criminal.

The detective work of deciphering the concealed significance of ordinary things drives the narrative of *When the Emperor Was Divine*. The second chapter, "Train," like Yamamoto's story, deals with the journey to
the camp at Topaz in the Utah desert. The discrepancy between normalcy
and the exceptional nature of relocation continues to shape the narrative,
this time through the difference mediated by the train windows. As the
transport passes through Nevada, the girl watches houses and lawns and
cottonwood trees with hammocks swinging in the breeze. From this orderly bucolic scene the desert appears unannounced from behind a house:
beyond a dry lake "there was nothing but the scorched white earth of the
desert stretching all the way to the edge of the horizon" (WED 23). On the
map the girl is using to follow the route, as if somehow this will verify the
existence of the world beyond the window, she sees the lake is called "Intermittent Lake." She cannot see the lake, which has been dry for two years
"but she did not know that," nor does she know the meaning of the word
"intermittent" (WED 24). Authorial intervention here steers the reader,
unlike the first chapter's refusal to help, to consider the relationship between the documented designation of places and the truth of the senses.
The map names something that is apparently not there, even though the

name it has been given admits it is not always there. The name remains even when the lake is not. If there is an echo of "internment" in "intermittent" this may be no accident, for the internees are also there but not there. They have been named and registered as potential enemy aliens, and this naming has made them visible. Once named they have been removed from sight, behind the houses and into the desert where the dust covers over them. Like the lake, the Japanese Americans are there or not there depending on conditions.

This liminal state is reinforced by the guard's insistence that the shades on the train's windows go down. Whether this is to protect the passengers from the hostile gaze from without or to prevent the passengers seeing where they are going is not explained. Either way, with the shades down the passengers are fully erased from view, and their own sense of space and time is evacuated, severing the causal chain that links the points of departure and destination. They are now travelers without a map:

> Now she could not see anyone at all and no one outside the train could see her. There were the people inside the train and the people outside the train and in between them were the shades. A man walking alongside the tracks would just see a train with black windows passing by in the middle of the day. He would think, There goes the train, and then he would not think about the train again. What was for supper, maybe, or who was winning the war. She knew it was better this way. The last time they had passed through a city with the shades up someone had thrown a rock through one of the windows. (WED 28–29)

Screening off the internees is seen to restore domestic order for those on the outside and provide safety for those inside. Encapsulating the logic of the internment project, this passage identifies the way the state of emergency is normalized and rearticulated as reasonable: because people of Japanese ancestry are perceived as a threat, they should be removed for their own protection. Revealingly, though, to see it as "better this way" the Japanese must be assumed to share the reasonable justification for the constitution of themselves as a threat. In order to believe that it is "better this way" those inside the train must have once been outside the train, wondering what was for supper. Compulsory relocation, then, relies on,

93

or at least benefits from, a shared culture of duties and responsibilities in order to obtain consent for the segregation of people of Japanese ancestry for their own good. The same discourse of security and protection works to give meaning to relocation to those inside American society and those excluded from it. The sheer ordinariness of response to the evacuation order in *When the Emperor Was Divine* and the commonsense understanding of why it is better for the shades to be down powerfully conveys how the exceptional can work inside, and indeed supplant, the normal organization of everyday life.

Another example of how the text works with the estrangement of the familiar is through the father's postcards home from prison, first in Fort Missoula, Montana, and then in Fort Sam Houston, Texas. The girl reads his postcards during the train journey: "[o]ne of them showed a tiny man fishing on the bank of a river. Beneath him were the words *Greetings from Montana. The Treasure State.* Another one showed the highest stack in the world. The highest stack in the world was in Anaconda, Montana. She flipped through the pictures of the Indian pueblos and the ancient cliff dwellings until she came to the postcard of the largest and finest auditorium in New Mexico: the Seth Hall Gymnasium at Santa Fe High School. Seth Hall looked like an enormous adobe house only with cross bars over the windows" (WED 42). In the banality of the postcard images and their rhetoric of tourist preoccupations—fishing, landmarks, antiquities, municipal buildings—these could be mail from dad's business trip, checking in at home on his travels in Montana and New Mexico. The father's writing is equally devoid of anything that might suggest the nature of his absence, mentioning the weather, the girl's upcoming birthday and the promise of a gift from the Paris department store in San Francisco (by mail order). Only the "cross bars" on the gymnasium building and the blacked out censor mark at the bottom of one card signal the fact that these are letters from jail.

Yet the postcards also carry an unwritten message of Western destruction, from the extraction industries of Montana to the marginalized or extinct tribes of the Southwest. The father's forced removal from one jail to another (Fort Sam Houston providing a further allusion to the West's violent history, this time the annexation of Texas from Mexico) also echoes the serial displacement experienced by the West's indigenous peoples.

Like the view from the train window, the postcards are, on one hand, evidence of a culture the family has been removed from. As tokens of sights seen, the postcards suggest an enjoyment and celebration of the fruits of liberty—abundance, prosperity, industry, history, and civic institutions—entirely at odds with the experience of the interned. Chances are that the father has in fact seen none of those things, the postcards thus becoming a coded signal of what has been removed from sight, each card an index of a lost world. On the other hand, the images provide an inventory of extraction, displacement, and domination that connects the internment experience to the longer history of the region.[50]

Arriving at Topaz, the reader is offered what vista is available to the interned: "[t]he girl looked out of the window and saw hundreds of tarpaper barracks sitting beneath the hot sun. She saw telephone poles and barbed-wire fences. She saw soldiers. And everything she saw she saw through a cloud of fine white dust that had once been the bed of an ancient salt lake" (48). As with everything in *When the Emperor Was Divine,* the emphasis here is on reporting the bare visual information. In quick succession the inventory of the camp is sketched out, including the mediating scrim of dust and the "blinding white glare of the desert" (WED 48) that conspire to impair the sight of any who would look upon the militarized encampment.

The time spent in Topaz is depicted from the point of view of the girl's younger brother, whose repertoire of images from an American childhood in California leaves him ill-prepared for camp life. This is unlike any desert he has read about; there are no palm tress, oases, or camels, "only the wind and the dust and the hot burning sand." The heat is hostile, rising "up from the ground in waves" making the air shimmer (WED 53). Time has stopped and they do nothing but wait—the girl stopped winding her watch when they got off the train, and it has been six o'clock for weeks (WED 65)—even though his mother says that the sun "made you grow old" (WED 63). The dust is aggressive and deceptive, "soft and white and chalky, like talcum powder," but it "made your skin burn. It made your nose bleed. It made your eyes sting. It took your voice away" (WED 64). The dust "seeped under doors and around the edges of windows and through the cracks in the walls." The mother seems to be continuously sweeping, a rearguard action against erasure. The boy writes his name in the dust before bed, but while he sleeps "more dust blew through the walls" (WED 64), erasing any trace of his marks.

The curious continuous present of childhood is made to function, in this chapter, as an analogue for the arrest of time achieved by removal to the desert. The nocturnal erasure of the boy's name by the incremental and apparently invisible sedimentation of dust recalls Adams's fantasy of Manzanar being reclaimed by the land after the war, though for the boy the dust that gets into your dreams merges desert sand with fairy-dust to become the erasing slumber brought by the sandman. Focalizing this chapter from the point of view of the boy enables Otsuka to imbue internment with a strange innocence that manages to capture something of the otherworldliness produced by the sleight of hand that has conjured away an entire community to a place where human time stops and natural time takes over. The child's capacity to charge everything with mysterious significance, a mixture of the empirical and the magical, opens a space through which the profoundly estranging experience of internment can be properly registered by the text.

Another instance of ostensibly innocent childhood observation recalls *Blood Meridian*'s meditation on the sun, perception, and power. Watching the sunset, the girl instructs the boy to "[l]ook. Look away. Look. Look away" (WED 65). This, she tells him, is the correct way to look at the sun, for to look at it "straight for too long" will make you go blind. The emphasis on intermittent looking here recalls the lake that is there but not there, the blinds that are pulled down on the train, and the glare of the sun that occludes direct perception of the camp. Looking "straight" is not possible, prevented by the source of illumination itself. The fact of things can only be seen intermittently if one is to avoid what McCarthy calls the "will to deceive that is in things luminous" (BM 120).

When the Emperor Was Divine is a novel about looking and seeing, but it refuses "straight" testimony in favor of intermittent, oblique observation. Only indirectly can the uncanny fact of internment be properly registered since direct looking causes blindness. Direct looking reveals life going on in difficult circumstances, an acceptance of necessity, military or otherwise, that reasonably requires the safe removal of threat, both to "Americans" from the Japanese other and to the Japanese themselves from angry Americans. What the injunction to "[l]ook. Look away" calls for is a rupturing of continuous, empirical reckoning, the instances of looking broken by the reflective action of looking away. In this manner perceptions are caught momentarily and held rather than allowed to unfold in logical sequence, as if things, like time, move uninterrupted from one state to another. The act of looking away before again looking suggests that peripheral vision and unexpected configurations are given priority over a sustained fixed-point gaze. Looking and looking away might reveal something to be there and then, like the name covered by sand, gone. This, I think, for Otsuka, is how the removal of Japanese Americans must be apprehended.

The outburst of the father's "confession" that concludes *When the Emperor Was Divine* is incongruous largely because it so defiantly punctures the bland stoicism of the mother's chapter and the innocent wonder encountered by the children. Bitter and ironic, the father admits to the plethora of charges and stereotypes that constructed issei men as fifth columnists in order to gain his freedom. While it is true, I think, that this final chapter damages the care with which the preceding narrative maintains a knowing distance from the events it depicts, it is an equally knowing sabotage of what precedes it. In eschewing "literary" tact for overwrought indignation, the father's "confession" violates the clean, minimal space of the text with its dirty truths. It also articulates the depth of the shame experienced by issei men with a directness never registered by books like *Farewell to Manzanar* or *Why She Left Us*, which represent tyrannical and raging fathers mostly through their violent effects on the family. In giving the father the last word, *When the Emperor Was Divine* suggests that, as the first target of the post–Pearl Harbor policy of arrest and interrogation, the dismantling of male issei authority, already severely curtailed by their exclusion from citizenship and landowning, is not only key to understanding the reconfiguration of Japanese American identity during and after internment, but that this emasculation has been absorbed as part of the compensation deal. The actions of the brutal Mitsuo Okada in *Why She Left Us* are never properly explained, but the survival of his family depends on the dissolution of his power, just as Wakatsuki Houston's American identity is likewise predicated on the camp's removal of paternal authority.

If it was largely the women's job in the camps to combat the encroachments of the concealing dirt, the clean, well-lighted place provided by works like *When the Emperor Was Divine* exposes deep divisions within Japanese American identity that cannot straightforwardly be blamed solely on the internment experience but instead stem from modes of social organization with deep roots in Japanese culture exacerbated by the institutionalized exclusion of Japanese immigrants in the United States. The post-redress narratives explored here, in embodying the strategies of concealment and exposure dramatized by, but not exclusive to, internment, do not resolve the damaged social forms produced by Japanese American history but instead render divisions between men and women, between issei and nisei, as complexly structural. If one of the effects of internment was to engineer an Americanized post-internment subject, it is, in these narratives at least, a body without a head. The improvised family structures that gather in and after the decapitation of the head of the household brought about by the process of internment do offer, it is true, more liberal alternatives to the patriarchal domination experienced before the war. What the final "confession" chapter of *When the Emperor Was Divine* reminds us, however, is that the restitution of a more flexible and "Americanized" Japanese American identity post-internment—a social order, for example, that can embrace Emi as an unmarried mother who abandons her children and can also countenance narratives about internment as an absorbed historical given—is built on a founding patricidal violence (the father here symbolizing not only authoritarian masculinity but the demonized threat of the alien Japanese national other) that remains only partially laid to rest. The real and symbolic erasure of the father in internment narratives throws up the troubling proposition posited by Horace's famous line "dulce et decorum est pro patria mori" (it is sweet and becoming to die for one's country), with the indeterminate national status of issei men making the sacrifice ring fatally hollow.

If Mitsuo's brutality reveals him to be irrecuperable within American civil society, the danger is that this violence is made to stand in for "Japan" and the arcane ideology of imperial divinity that legitimized atrocities against all enemies of the homeland. The title of Otsuka's novel both delivers the text and the reader from the threat of patriarchal authority—the emperor is no longer divine—while reminding us that he once was indeed considered so. The content of the novel, of course, renders the title ironic in the sense that there is no trace of anything like divine imperial power anywhere to be seen in it and no evidence that the characters ever held such beliefs; the bathos of the title is ultimately underscored by the tawdry treatment of the emperor's notional subjects. While Rizzuto shows Mitsuo's vicious imperial reign over his family as the repressed truth internment serves to reveal, Otsuka, by giving space to the father's expression of shame and anger, goes some way to reveal the height from which the Japanese patriarch has been made to fall. While the rest of the family are invited to remake themselves as Americans through coerced pioneering, the father's abjection is completed by compelling him to die (always symbolically and often in fact) for a country he does not have. Neither Japanese nor American, the issei patriarch remains the exception that enables the construction of Japanese American identity in his absence. The collapse of "literary" control in Otsuka's novel with the flaring up of the father's angry presence at the end refuses the assimilationist revisionism that would mark internment as an achieved historical moment and issei emasculation as, at best, collateral damage that clears the way for the postwar invention of Americans liberated from the tyranny of antiquated despots.

If internment found some sort of legitimation in invoking the "pioneer" lifestyle of the West, a similar sense of Western utopian identity formation is evident in the creation of an advanced scientific community at Los Alamos. In the next chapter, the estranging impact of security-driven isolation in the desert West experienced by Japanese Americans is registered, albeit in a radically different form, by the children of scientists in novels by Thomas McMahon and Bradford Morrow that, like Rizzuto and Otsuka, attempt to reckon with the reverberations of the West's deployment as the site for the creation of America's postwar social order.

4. LEARNING FROM LOS ALAMOS

Everyone was now caught in what had become: The Land of Entrapment.
Ana Castillo, *So Far from God*

Maj. John H. Dudley, charged with locating the site for America's secret nuclear program, came to Los Alamos, as Peter Bacon Hales observes, "seeking a contradiction." The colony had to be remote yet convenient enough for the construction workers, scientists, and machinery to access: "[i]t had to be a place between wilderness and civilization—a place on the frontier."[1] The invocation of Western myth, here, while it is somewhat ironically utilized by Hales, recalls the way the discourse of the "pioneer" became an enabling fiction for administrators of internment. While the kind of pioneering undertaken by the atomic scientists at Los Alamos can in no way be compared to the forced incarceration of a racially excluded population, the tendency to associate Western space with the frontier spirit continues in postwar depictions of how the bomb was developed in the New Mexican desert.

If the race to win the war through superweapons created a threshold between worlds—the pre- and post-bomb eras that bifurcate the twentieth century—the nature of the installation at Los Alamos also established a precedent for the militarization of science and the military construction of secret zones of operation that would shape the permanent war economy in the West. As with internment, wartime emergency generated at Los Alamos new kinds of spatial and social organization that, like the bomb itself, would remain long after the war was over.

The withdrawal of land for the atomic program, at Los Alamos and also at Oak Ridge, Tennessee, and Hanford, Washington, is analogous to the withdrawal of populations through internment inasmuch as in both cases executive authority overrules prior claims to protection under the law. In both cases military authority takes over the management of civilian activity, fences it in, and posts guards. In both cases, withdrawal is justified in terms of security and with the intention of secreting the contained object in a place difficult to access. In both cases the freedom of the populations contained within the installations is restricted and disciplined;

movement between inside and outside is controlled, communication is censored or prohibited.[2] In both cases conventional habits and practices, relationships and allegiances are scrambled or severed. If internment inadvertently produced new forms of Americanized identity due to the undermining of traditional Japanese cultural hierarchies, the conditions of life at Los Alamos also produced new social formations that prefigure in a number of ways Cold War society's internalized modes of self-surveillance and security-consciousness, and its celebration of managerial, corporate, and scientific elites as manifestations of a thorough-going patriarchal and paternalistic order.[3] Finally, just as internment and its consequences can be seen as the sign of sovereign power's emergence under the state of exception, so too must Los Alamos be understood as a marker of law's suspension in the interests of security. The facilities at Los Alamos were not dismantled after Japan's surrender but, in fact, continued to grow as a vital component in the general economy of permanent war. The defense establishment has, beginning with Los Alamos, as Hugh Gusterson claims, "created an enormous secret world next to but separate from the everyday world inhabited by the rest of us."[4]

Ambivalence toward the legacy of Los Alamos is understandably profound, and the literature produced about this remarkable and peculiar site is immense. Along with the steady stream of histories, biographies, and memoirs detailing every aspect of life on the Hill, novelists have been writing about Los Alamos since the war ended. An inventory of those novels would include, but by no means be exhausted by, Pearl S. Buck's *Command the Morning* (1949), Michael Amrine's *Secret* (1950), Dexter Masters's *The Accident* (1955), Frank Waters's *The Woman at Otowi Crossing* (1966), Martin Cruz Smith's *Stallion Gate* (1986), Robert Cohen's *The Organ Builder* (1988), Roberta Silman's *Beginning the World Again* (1990), Joseph Kanon's *Los Alamos* (1997), and Millicent Dillon's *Harry Gold* (2000).[5] Many of these, including Waters's, attempt to combine elements of the thriller and romantic genres, and it is striking how few dwell on the magnitude of the bomb's actual devastating power. In fact, Waters's novel is characteristic of many Los Alamos novels in that it seems more concerned with psychic damage and ethical crisis than attempting to describe material destruction. The following quotation from *The Woman at Otowi Crossing* is fairly typical of Waters's attempt to fuse the psychological with the physical impact of the bomb: "[t]he similarity of this implosive-explosive process objectively in the A-bomb and subjectively as it happened to Helen Chalmers is at once casually apparent. Fear, worry, guilt, dread, shame, financial failure—all this psychological dynamite accumulated within her, recalled with pain and anguish, and brooded upon, seemed suddenly on a quiet day to be detonated from all directions; to be driven in upon her, implosively, with immense psychological force."[6]

The bomb itself is described here only through analogy, remaining more of an absent ontological threat than an actual object or event. Social and psychological injury, however, is widespread in Los Alamos novels, as if the invention and construction of the device is enough to have already caused profound damage. It is this rending of the social fabric through the manufacture of a community dedicated to the single-minded creation of unspeakable violence that is really the subject of much Los Alamos fiction, the strangeness of the place itself often positioned as a model for what will become the common atmosphere of post-Trinity life in the United States.

Aside from the legacy of profound ethical crisis, Los Alamos also established institutional secrecy as part of the new order. The disinformation generated to reassure witnesses of the Trinity blast that it was an accidental munitions explosion became, as David Nye argues, typical of postwar weapons research, which proceeded to develop increasingly more powerful bombs free from public scrutiny. Paradoxically, decisions made in the defense of democracy were made undemocratically, in secret by a small elite: "[a]fter the war, on grounds on national security, ordinary citizens were denied the chance to discuss or to vote on the desirability of weapons of mass destruction."[7]

Los Alamos, then, has come to represent the concealment of power in its most deadly military form, a power folded into the deep time of the Southwestern landscape. *The Woman at Otowi Crossing* sums up the provocative metaphorical significance of Los Alamos when Waters writes that the site is "the birthplace of the oldest civilization in America and the newest." Nowhere else in the world "were juxtaposed . . . all the values of the prehistoric past and the atomic future."[8] This was the "hub of time," Waters concludes, and his combination of archaeologists, scientists, and soldiers struggling for position is a common feature of fiction concerned with the postwar West.[9]

Here, I want to concentrate on three Los Alamos novels that deal with the emergence of a generation born into the secrecy and dread of the nuclear age. In Thomas McMahon's *Principles of American Nuclear Chemistry* (1970) the narrator's teenage years are spent around the scientists working on the Hill, bomb technology, and erotic awakenings joining to produce a damaged adulthood that displaces the trauma of the bomb's destructiveness, which is again never mentioned, with an obsessive longing for his father's wartime mistress. In Bradford Morrow's *Trinity Fields* (1995), the entwining of bomb and birth is even more complete, the novel's protagonists being two boys born in Los Alamos in the months before the Trinity test. The burden of their birthplace animates the novel and its sequel, *Ariel's Crossing* (2002), which follows the reverberations of the boys' complex relationship through to the 1990s.

Locating Los Alamos as the site for nuclearism's bildungsroman is apt given the project's appropriation of the Los Alamos Ranch School, founded in 1917 by Ashley Pond for wealthy city boys to build character before taking up their position among America's ruling elites. Sent West due to frail health before seeing action as one of Teddy Roosevelt's Rough Riders, Pond went on to design a school that combined, according to Peter Bacon Hales, a "philosophy of masculine pantheism" with the disciplinary regime of the Taylorist factory system of individual efficiency.[10] In the novels discussed below, the mix of intensely symbolic landscape, the machismo of hard science, the ruthlessness of modern warfare, and its insinuation into the social fabric characteristic of the project coalesce to produce a nuclear subjectivity conceived in and damaged by a climate of secrecy—like nuclear research, "classified at birth" or "born secret," in government parlance—that has become foundational of postwar identity.[11] In approaching Los Alamos from inside the compromised sphere of the literal nuclear family, McMahon's and Morrow's novels explore the peculiar braiding of professional and domestic lives experienced by scientists and their families, indicating the ways in which military and scientific affairs, and their consequences, can no longer be separated from private relationships. The novels mark, then, an intensified point at which the demands of the national security state are internalized and

function to regulate all aspects of private life. In their narration of familial fragmentation brought about by the biopolitical regime of the weapons laboratory, these works identify the ground zero of post–Pearl Harbor American governance.

Thus Passes the Glory of the World

Principles of American Nuclear Chemistry is told from the point of view of Tim
MacLaurin, the son of a Los Alamos physicist. By 1960, when Tim reflects
on his experiences growing up at Oak Ridge and then Los Alamos during
the war years, he is a twenty-eight-year-old scientist who has returned to
the parental home after losing his low-level technical job due to what his
employers construe as a nervous breakdown. Taking long toilet breaks
in order to find some privacy where he can read in the regulated environment of the lab, this simulated constipation eventually draws the attention of Tim's boss and he is fired.[12] Tim is literally paralyzed by the
experience of Los Alamos, both professionally due to his belief that the
spirit of free intellectual adventure he saw there is over and unrepeat-
able, and emotionally because of his obsession with his father's wartime lover, Maryann. His time is spent painting the family barn, making
twice-weekly visits to his psychiatrist, and working on scientific problems set by his father.

The narrative trades on the conventions of the coming-of-age genre and
the complex emotional, eroticized experiences of the adolescent boy as
they are recalled from the highly colored perspective of a troubled adulthood. As such, the novel is more interested in the process of representing
the recent past and the continuing reverberations of history than with a
documentary reconstruction of life of Los Alamos, though the author's
credentials—McMahon was a professor of both applied mechanics and
biology at Harvard—mean that the text is convincing in its depiction of
the scientific milieu. What Tim's position as an overawed teenager in the
entirely manufactured environment of Los Alamos enables is a consideration of what unlimited resources and freedom from extraneous responsibilities are capable of accomplishing.

What Tim, or the novel, never directly addresses, is the particular application of scientific knowledge that Los Alamos is constructed for—the
atomic bomb—or its terrible consequences. Enthralled as he is with the

domestic and intellectual adventures of the scientific community, Tim's perspective echoes the mixture of fascination and intimidation that constitutes the public's perception of advanced science and its practitioners. The men (there is only one "lady scientist") and their work is not only protected by the state and top secret, but very few outside the Los Alamos community could be expected to understand much about it even if they were told. Local bemusement and military disdain for the exotic scientists establishes de facto compartmentalization of the community that is also implemented among the scientists themselves, both in the professional pecking order and domestically. The ramifications of atomic weapons are further displaced by the scientists' tendency to discuss the bomb entirely as an intellectual proposition—engineers and technicians take over once the theoretical work has been achieved. While it is never stated that it is the fact of the bomb itself that is the cause of Tim's malaise as an adult, the inference is unavoidable. Tim stands for, I think, a general postwar acquiescence toward the necessity of the bomb that manifests itself negatively; that is, in a silent awareness of its presence as part of the ideological and ontological atmosphere of postwar American life that is barely registered in any direct way, but which inflects and shapes behavior and action.

Tim's partiality—toward Maryann and "pure" science as he sees it practiced at Los Alamos—means that unpleasant facts about the community and its task remain unexplored in any explicit way. Tim's obsessions, however, cannot conceal a casual indifference among the scientists toward their families and nonscientists, a widespread and stifling misogyny, and a complete evacuation of context in order to make space for the abstract creativity of the elite.

The kind of space constructed by the military for the atomic program constituted, Hales suggests, "a new form of American culture," different in "laws, beliefs, customs and myths" than anything known prewar or even elsewhere outside the sites themselves.[13] Produced out of the conflicting interests of the military and the scientists, and manufactured at speed, life at Los Alamos was heavily policed, managerially regulated, and also intensively singleminded and removed from the extraneous pressures of everyday concerns. Nevertheless, the social order shaped by military compartmentalization according to level of security clearance and importance to the project helped stratify Los Alamos along fairly conventional class, gender, and race lines, with officers and scientists at the top and Native and Mexican American laborers at the bottom.[14] "As a geographic space," argues Gusterson, "the laboratory is divided into zones of greater or lesser exclusion that relate to the system of classifying information and clearing people."[15] As the son of a scientist, Tim is in a privileged position and can move more or less freely across the social divisions of the site. The intensification of prevailing social attitudes toward women at the installation, not to mention the high level of social lassitude enjoyed by the scientists, means that Maryann is considerably more vulnerable to abuses of power. While women provided a necessary labor force and produced the social conditions within the camp that made life bearable, these very qualities constituted, from the military point of view, a danger to the success of the program. Women introduced threatening social complexities to the efficient prosecution of the project, and, as Hales observes, "like other unwanted but necessary 'populations' who came to the sites"—African Americans, Indians, Mexicans—brought with them an unpredictable otherness that posed a challenge to the regime's program of social control.[16]

In the novel, the elect status of the scientists is precisely registered through the expendability of their spouses. Tim's mother refuses to join her husband on the project—tellingly, her name is never given—so his father, Harold, gets a Los Alamos job for his mistress. The road trip to the Southwest effectively erases Tim's mother from the text, since no one at Los Alamos ever speaks of Harold's wife, though her absent presence remains as a periodic intrusion, notably when her prematurely born baby dies at seven months old, and Harold reluctantly has to return home for the funeral. Harold refers to life outside Los Alamos as "the old troubles, the old worries," which Maryann knows means "[h]ouses, wives."[17]

As a scientist's mistress, Maryann's position at Los Alamos is more volatile than that of a wife, and her increasing frustration at her marginal position serves to expose the extent to which social relations have been skewed toward the needs of the project. To Harold she complains, echoing the broader obscuring of accountability at the site, that "everything you do somehow implies that I have all the responsibility and you have none" (PNC 100). The control that Harold has over his relationships, however, has been conferred upon him by both his wife and Maryann themselves and reinforced by the collusion of everyone else at Los Alamos and the insulation from the world provided by the authorities. "Tell me as much as you think I have to know" (PNC 29), Maryann says of Harold's marriage before they leave for Los Alamos, indicating her acquiescence to the requirements of ignorance by consent. For Harold's wife, Maryann is an open secret from the beginning: she knows he is living with Maryann, but they will never meet and after the war she is never mentioned. During their postwar reconciliation there is an "unspoken agreement" between the MacLaurins to forget Maryann, though Tim is disturbed by the ease with which his father seems to have achieved this forgetfulness, and Tim himself, of course, can think of no one else.

The fact is that the military only grudgingly accepted the wives and families of scientists onto the Los Alamos site in the first place, and the strict security that prevented husbands from speaking about their work, not to mention the regulation of movement, censorship of mail, removal from friends and community, and the general climate of condescension toward nonparticipants drove the creation of what Hales calls a female "countercommunity" within the camp. Produced out of a sense of uselessness and valuelessness, a "shadow-culture . . . existed among the women during the day and extended to all the family members at night."[18] This transgressive shadow culture is particularly marked in McMahon's depiction of marital infidelity and out-of-hours bohemianism among the Los Alamos scientists, though this licentiousness also works as an enabling safety valve that in fact functions to reinforce discipline, as the truth about the affair between Harold and Maryann reveals.

As Maryann eventually discovers, she is entirely without agency, and the relationship with Harold was engineered by another scientist, Nelse Nachtigall, to ensure Harold's productivity. Even Harold is unaware of this, but Maryann's expendability—once her relationship with Harold dims, she enters an ill-advised marriage with Nachtigall before becoming the object of a military police gangbang—is symptomatic of the erasure of human value under the exceptional conditions of Los Alamos. The aloofness and misogyny of the men in the novel is almost without exception, and the exploitation of Maryann only the most visible. On reflection, Tim thinks it was "for the best" that his mother was not at Los

Alamos during the war because of the "feeling of infidelity" there at the time (PNC 154). His mother, with an unexpected sense of patriotic propriety, corrects him by saying she does not "believe everyone of my generation regards the atomic bomb as having been a debauch" (PNC 154). The sense of infidelity Tim felt at Los Alamos is about more than sexual adventure, though patently that was a part of it, as his own awakening sexuality among the female "countercommunity" suggests; rather, he is thinking of a broad "sense of abandon" that involved "throwing away the rules" (PNC 154). While this is Tim's long-percolated nostalgic memory of a creative environment he cannot recover, he seems unable to assess the extent of the trade-off between intellectual liberty for the scientists and the desolation (personal and historical) it produced.

The case of Sandeman, the project leader, is instructive in this regard, with the story that triggers his downfall framed in a chapter with a parable-like dimension. The absent-minded Sandeman is called back urgently to San Francisco by a troubled ex-girlfriend, but he loses his wallet en route and ends up wandering the streets of San Francisco trying and failing to cash a paycheck. Encountering a man beating a three-legged dog, Sandeman buys the dog in order to save it, only to discover that this is a con and that the dog, out of love for its master, allows itself to be beaten.[19] After a humiliating episode with a former colleague, Sandeman returns to Los Alamos promising to wire the cash the next day. The ex-girlfriend commits suicide the moment he leaves.

This is a tale, we are told, that Tim "learned years later" (PNC 168), and he does not comment on the significance this story might have. Not only does Sandeman's incompetence cause the death of the young woman, a fact that, typically, is of little consequence at Los Alamos, but it draws him into a federal investigation—the authorities believe the girl's new lover is a Communist spy—that contributes to his discreditation after the war. A laundry bag discarded in the desert by Tim's father containing, unbeknownst to him, letters between Sandeman and Russian scientists, seals Sandeman's fate. Many of the scientists blame Harold for ruining Sandeman, but it is Tim who carries the burden, since, in a conspiratorial conversation that turns into a personal attack, Sandeman had blamed Tim for the falling off of his father's work toward the end of the project: "I think he's sad about you," Sandeman charges (PNC 220).

Scapegoating Tim in this way typifies the kind of manipulative engi-neering of mood that the scientists undertake to ensure the unimpeded flow of creativity from their top performers. While Sandeman appears humane—he rushes to the aid of his ex-lover, saves the dog, and offers himself as Tim's confidante—his actions are characterized by an inabil-ity, whether feigned or real makes little difference, to read circumstances correctly. The abdication of responsibility Maryann accuses Harold of is systematic at Los Alamos. Sandeman always forgets his wallet because there are others ready to pay for him, but ultimately this indifference to everyday necessity results in a suicide and, in the end, his career. This in-fidelity, a lack of faith in anything other than the protected and privileged work of atomic physics, makes the bomb but at the same time becomes its precondition. The compartmentalization of labor, which allows San-deman to think only about the idea of the bomb without having to worry about its instrumental function, just as his indifference to money means that someone else has to pay, patently has catastrophic effects even as it absolves any individual from responsibility for the consequences of ac-tions removed from their cause.

After Los Alamos, the novel invites us to consider, the normalization of deception, concealment, and denial that the management of the proj-ect achieved has become perhaps the most enduring part of the bomb's legacy. Furthermore, the idealization of abstract, "pure" thinking is ex-posed as a fabrication that is preserved by militarized social hierarchies to enable what is essentially the work of making bombs. Maryann's com-plaint about Harold's off-loading of responsibility accurately articulates the condition that makes it possible for nuclear scientists to imagine they are involved in ideas and not weapons. Blaming those who make possible the work of the scientists shifts responsibility onto those in whose name the bomb is made—the American people and their security—while ab-solving the scientists themselves as somehow above the worldly impli-cations of their enterprise.

Tim, in his paralyzed adult state, fixated on the afterimage of faunlike Maryann as atomic muse, cannot see this even as he utters the truth of it in every line. He wonders, for example, why he was amorphously afraid of things during the war, even though he is living in a top secret military installation devoted to the invention of superweapons. He complains that the army eroded morale due to their secrecy and hypocrisy, when it is evident that the scientific community was adeptly secretive and hypo-critical. Most of all, Tim remains awed by Maryann as the embodiment of an erotized and uncontaminated scientific creativity despite witness-ing her treatment first by the scientists, including his father, and then by the military policemen.

The truth of the situation is that Tim's notion of Los Alamos as the cru-cible for free scientific adventure is brought to an end by Los Alamos it-self. The war transformed "pure" science from the free transmission of ideas across an international network of experts disinterested in prac-tical applications to, by the middle of 1941, what Hales describes as "a highly complex, vertically structured bureaucracy under the aegis of the military."[20] This transformation is a conversion of science from "an infor-mation system to a system of power," driven not so much by a desire for efficient movement from theory to practice but by a corporate and man-agerial takeover that pushed scientists to the periphery of what soon be-came an industrial-factory organizational model.[21]

The National Defense Research Committee and the Office of Scientific Research and Development that soon superseded it were set up early in the war to manage scientific activity in the production of weapons and implement military codes of secrecy and security. Free movement of sci-entists and the free and open exchange of ideas were now potentially treasonous, and new bureaucratic structures isolated individual scien-tists who might be lower down the command structure. The consolida-tion of scientific work in discrete and containable sites was increasingly seen as the most fruitful way to maximize and regulate production, "or-ganized under the rubric of a confident and unambiguous power struc-ture, presided over by the military, operated by the corporate sphere, and coordinated by the contract system."[22]

With this in mind, the "sense of abandon" Tim mourns for is already lost at the point that he believes it to have been achieved. The end of what the scientists imagined as a utopian community with the conclusion of the project is paralleled in the novel with the death from cancer of Richie Mundi's wife, perhaps the only woman in the book to be held in any es-teem by her husband and friends. In naming her Gloria Mundi, McMa-hon may be working too hard, but Tim's psychiatrist notices how Tim dates things by saying whether they happened before or after her death. The end of an idea among the scientists, Tim suggests, "would leave people in something very much like mourning for a period, as if it were a true death" (PNC 238), and the "death of a beautiful but impractical idea," like Gloria's death "diminished the total hope, diminished each individual hope" (PNC 238).

The treatment of Maryann; the scapegoating of Tim by Sandeman and then of his father by the other scientists for Sandeman's downfall; the callousness, legitimated by camp security, shown by Harold toward his wife; and, ultimately, the erasure of Maryann and the whole Los Alamos "debauch" by Harold and his wife in the years after the war, suggest a far more compromised endeavor than the utopian community remembered by Tim. What *Principles of American Nuclear Chemistry* reveals is how the military instrumentalization of science produces a corrupting mode of social organization founded on security-driven secrecy. The distortion of conventional social forms by the bleeding of organizational compartmentalization into every aspect of domestic as well as professional life is seen to sanction the disposability of anyone not central to the prosecution of the project and to enable the deployment of covert manipulation in order to further the needs of those at the top of the operational hierarchy.

Given the retardation of agency the Los Alamos regime achieved, it is no surprise that Tim suffers from constipation. In Bradford Morrow's two novels centered on Los Alamos, the damaging effects of the national security state are given wider scope, with Los Alamos located as the hub of what has become America's permanent war.

Splitting the Adam

Trinity Fields is a love story and a parable of postwar America, as childhood friends Kip Calder and Brice McCarthy, born on the same day in 1944 in Los Alamos, grow up into a divided 1960s that also presents a forking path for the young men: after both attend Columbia, Kip leaves for Vietnam while Brice becomes an antiwar activist. The novel deals, then, with the ethical legacy inherited by those inextricably bound to the Manhattan Project, and while Kip and Brice are, of course, unusually tied to the bomb, their responses—acquiescence to the war machine and resistance to it—are intended to be representative of the generation entirely constituted by Cold War technology.

Kip's and Brice's attempts to work through their inheritance not only destroy their friendship but are also intended, I think, to demonstrate a bifurcation in the Cold War mind. As a boy, Brice confuses the splitting of the atom with Adam, understanding that the atom "preferred to remain whole, would never want to be broken in two."[23] For the young Brice, the explosion resulting from the smashing of "Adam the atom" is a manifestation of his unhappiness: "when I asked my father what your name meant and he told me, That which cannot be cut, didn't I shout it was wicked to harm you?" (TF 26). Kip and Brice, who share the given name William, are the atom and Adam (first man of the new age) split by the gadget's Fall; postwar America is the wilderness into which they are cast.

Atomic power, argues Alan Nadel, could be understood "within the same tropic scheme as the Christian Almighty, whose gifts and demands had, even prior to the nation's formal declaration of independence, constructed an important narrative of Euro-American culture. The 'American Adam' in this latest covenant thus took possession of the American atomic bomb, invoking in the process holy blessings."[24] Arguing along the same lines, Hales calls the story of the Manhattan Project "the origin myth of the atomic age and the atomic culture." In this myth, he continues, "quintessential Americans—immigrants fleeing the dangers of a fetid European civilization—find on these shores the opportunity to convert their abstract knowledge into practical form. With the assistance of a benevolent government . . . they form a new, utopian community in the fastnesses of the West. And in this new utopia they invent a product that saves the world from barbarism by transforming Nature into Culture. In the process, they *become* Americans, and in that transformation, they serve to signify the soon-to-come Americanization of the globe, the new, postwar Family of Man."[25] Brice and Kip become Americans at Los Alamos, but the kind of postwar dispensation they inherit is characterized less by the unification made possible by a pax Americana and more by violent divisions, which are not simply played out through the rupturing of the bond between the boys but are recognized as structural in the novel, a kind of atomizing of individuals for security reasons.

As in McMahon's novel, secrecy in Trinity Fields functions as a prophylactic against any family or community intimacy that might compromise the project: "[n]ations aren't any more indivisible than the folks in them" (TF 114). A pact has been made "between the government and each of the men" that keeps even their wives "in the dark" (TF 15). Brice's mother, like all the other women on the Hill, is educated, sophisticated, comfortably off, and untroubled by the fears for her husband suffered by millions of other women during World War II. Yet there is a "mediating sadness" about her, a "misery she has always kept to herself " and nurtured by private drinking (TF 17). Tellingly, even the adult Brice is unable to ask his mother about the "enigma" of her sadness, "out of embarrassment or a fear of knowing the truth" (TF 18). While mother is sad, father is seldom seen, and the project is out of bounds as dinnertime conversation: "[s]tealth from dawn to dusk, stealth was all and everything to these men" (TF 18). On the Hill everyone "developed a deep detachment, a separateness" that remains throughout their lives (TF 24), and for Brice silence comes to be seen as a form of cowardice.[26]

The management of communication at Los Alamos through compartmentalization by role, censorship, enforced ignorance, and the proliferation of shifting codes was intended to discipline free speech, as much as was possible, out of existence. The extreme sensitivity of the project meant that even conventional military censorship was out of the question, since marked up letters or resealed envelopes themselves exposed the secret they were intended to disguise. At Los Alamos all letters were read and returned with suggested corrections if security was considered to have been breached. Self-censorship and the internalization of codes of speech and action were necessary, and subsequently, in many cases, the fear of saying the wrong thing led to people saying nothing at all.[27]

In the end, Hales argues, since espionage could have been achieved by other means, the censorship regime's real aim was to create "a persuasive fictitious world, into which Los Alamos residents were to immerse themselves, pretending it was their reality."[28] Gusterson's study of nuclear laboratories in the 1980s confirms this assessment, noting that while the prevention of information leaks to foreign governments is the ostensible reason for high security, "regulations also have a role to play in the construction of a particular social order" both inside the laboratory itself and between scientists and the outside world. The result is the production of a classic "secret society" where practices of secrecy create "loyalty and community" within, while producing "a radical sense of separation from those they exclude."[29] By remaking identity through initiation into a secret society, what ends up uniting the members of such a society is not the goal of the project but secrecy itself. The silence that Brice prefers to read as cowardice is rather a result of internalized censorship that represses the communication of anything that might endanger the continuation of the work.

By the late 1950s the mixture of containment and guilt by association has become too much for the young teenage boys. They have been "coralled at birth by barricades, censored and surveilled, isolated and cloistered, sworn to silence, and guarded by military police in hutments and on horseback" (TF 6). Finally understanding the nature of their exile, that they were associated with "things so buried in the dark, the sun didn't know how to make them manifest," the boys take off in a stolen car (TF 5–6). While the Trinity explosion may have been the "birth of a new religion" in which, while the end of the world is near, "no repentance would provide for repentance" (TF 153), Brice and Kip appeal to an older authority, breaking into El Santuario de Chimayó and literally eating dirt, seeking absolution by partaking of the "magic purifying soil" at the church (TF 10).

As Willa Cather and Mary Austin had observed of Southwestern churches in the early years of the twentieth century, themselves seeking a kind of authentic, earthbound spirituality in opposition to industrialized abstractions, Brice also sees such holy places are "worldly and pagan, made of earth, of dust and water" (TF 57). The modest organicism of Chimayó—the hole in the ground from which dirt is taken being a sacred Tewa site related to the Pueblo place of emergence—stands in firm opposition to the annihilating science of the Hill, merely an hour from the church.[30]

While Brice and Kip are punished for stealing the car, no formal charges are ever brought, the incident buried. "We'd risked everything," Brice reflects, "to purify them by performing a civic rite on behalf of their arrogant souls, and what had they done in return? Whitewashed our crimes," made disapproving noises and then "finally exonerated and so enfeebled us" (TF 97). Brice's adolescent resentment that his defiance has been ineffectual is an early lesson in the indifference of power toward dissent that informs his adult views of the arrogance of the nuclear industry: "[o]ur land may be poisoned with thousands of unmarked dump sites, we may hear the stories about Indian women who continued to dig from our canyons clay for their pottery and now have all lost their hair, and we may many of us be cancerous, but look here, it is *our* land, they were radioactive toxins fabricated by *our* hands, and they are *our* carcinomas, so stand out of our glowy light that we may continue to see as we desire" (TF 98).

The bifurcating paths of the split Adam are revealed at Columbia, where Brice studies and Kip becomes cynical. Brice reads Clausewitz, Kip spits that "[s]ociology is the study of the murdered and political science is the study of murderers" (TF 149). While Brice clings to liberalism's faith in progressive change, Kip embraces a universe of flux and perpetual war where even microbes are "locked in mortal combat inside your body" (TF 149). Brice's commitment to open dissent leads him to become a visible activist while Kip literally disappears into the covert bombing campaign in Laos as someone who "engineered strikes" (TF 296).

Kip moves from one secret to another, his life "bound together into a single iridescent winding sheet of stealth" (TF 237). He has become a "spook," an "invisible man, a specter" (TF 295); his life "was being lived inside an integument" (TF 238). Officially no longer part of the service, Kip effectively does not exist, swathed in the same kind of double-speak and denial that had enveloped him and his family back on the Hill: he is at the same time "running away from and toward his childhood" (TF 275). Flying over the Plaine des Jarres, "an earthen pan" scattered with ancient fragments of stone jars, Kip thinks of the Anasazi and the "potency" of the New Mexican landscape (TF 290). The Hmong remind him of the Pueblo Indians, both "made captive in their own worlds" (TF 338). Like Los Alamos, everyone went under assumed names in Laos; both are landscapes of euphemism, overlaid with codewords, duplicity, and an unspoken dread. "None of this was lost on Kip. Los Alamos, the most secret place in the world when he was born. Long Tieng, Laos, the most secret place on earth during the Vietnam war, his war, now that he was a man" (TF 292–93). Indeed, the word Laos "was hidden twice inside the words Los Alamos. Islands in the sky. Laos, Los Alamos" (TF 293).

Secrets, thinks Kip, "remind us of what we know too well" (TF 294), including the fact that places animate people (TF 316). The erasure of Kip in Laos is the manner of him becoming himself, a wolf "always on the move, a migrant on the prowl for prey." Los Alamos had never been home and he is now "as near the edge of the world as he could ever get," fighting a war he has no stake in (TF 295). As a forward air controller, Kip's job is far more dangerous than that of the bomber crews. He is "the avant courier, the scout," the mission being to "fly out over unknown terrain and make that terrain known, mark it with smoke, call in assaults from the fighters stacked in the skies above." He literally calls the shots, his "almost consummate" independence a form of imperial liberty that maps in order to destroy (TF 296). Kip's refusal of allegiance makes him a good functionary for the warfare state—Los Alamos has animated him: "[w]ar was home; or else, this place that war infected, this place was home" (TF 339).

Brice is also animated by the circumstances of his upbringing: his work as an attorney makes him one of those "breed of men to whom truth was open not just to minor revisions and nice distinctions, but to management" (TF 317). Children of scientists, Brice observes, "learn early on just how relative everything in the universe really is" (TF 317). Relative, but also connected, and Brice's studies in law lead him back from the anti-Vietnam protests to World War II, to the Treaty of London that made wars of aggression illegal, to the Nuremberg trials, and to the case of *Mitchell v. the United States*. Refusing the draft for Vietnam, Mitchell had argued that American foreign policy was being prosecuted in violation of a number of treaties, including the Treaty of London, which states that an individual is not exempt from responsibility for participating in a war of aggression. So, like the German officers whose defense at Nuremberg had been that they were just following orders, American soldiers could not be blameless. Since a person was always accountable, Mitchell decided to refuse to participate in what he saw to be criminal acts of war (TF 346–47). While Brice admires Mitchell's insolence and "brass-balls reasoning," nothing comes of the case; principled refusal, as Brice learned in the Chimayó incident from his childhood, is defeated by being largely ignored.

In different ways, then, Kip and Brice embody the culture of secrecy-driven security established at Los Alamos. Combined, Kip and Brice's contingent responses to their own historical moment represent the entwined relationship between war and sovereignty that gives form to the national security state for which Los Alamos served as a proving ground.

Berserk Terminus

Ariel's Crossing (2002), the second volume of Morrow's proposed New Mexico trilogy, continues the interrogation of the abiding legacy of Los Alamos. The narrative focuses on Ariel, the child produced by Kip and Jessica before he disappears in Vietnam but raised by Brice and Jessica in New York City. Now in her mid-twenties and working at a New York publishing house, Ariel is finally told the identity of her biological father after Brice is entrusted with Kip's father's Los Alamos journal by a broken-down Kip, now dying from lymphoma. While it is Ariel's quest to find Kip that drives the plot of the novel, it is Kip who is really the center of the narrative, for while he appears to be close to death as the book opens, he is rescued by the benign Montoya family who live in the Nambé Valley close to Los Alamos and is nursed back to health to the point where his cancer is in remission.

If *Trinity Fields* demonstrated the hurling apart of relationships and the traumatized exile of those produced by Los Alamos, *Ariel's Crossing* is concerned with an inexorable magnetic force of place that pulls those exiled and broken remnants of family and community back to the site that created them. While Kip is described often as a "runner" and Ariel comes to believe that she has inherited this tendency to flee responsibility, in the end all running converges back to Los Alamos as the unavoidable point of beginning and end. One of the novel's central tropes is that of circling, and Nambé, Kip tells us early on, means "circle of earth" in Tewa.[31]

Just as *Trinity Fields* played on the doppelganger effect of Kip and Brice as versions of each other and on the incestuous permutations of the trinity—Kip, Brice, and Jessica being the most obvious—*Ariel's Crossing* is similarly disposed to producing doubles and triples. This strategy is abetted by the theme of duplicity and secrecy, which, though often motivated by necessity or self-preservation, inevitably produces strife. Brice, of course, is the primary double, standing in for Kip as Ariel's father, but there are plenty of others. Mary Carpenter, for example, flees her violent father in Gallup and recreates herself as Franny Johnson (after Salinger and the hotel chain), a Santa Fe waitress with dreams of escaping to California; despite herself, she falls for Marcos Montoya and finds herself living on the Montoya ranch along with Kip. Marcos loves Franny, not Mary, and when she is compelled to come clean, she is rejected in favor of the newly arrived Ariel, whose own background and character uncannily fits the fabricated model Mary has invented for herself. Kip becomes Mary's surrogate father even as she fills Ariel's place for him. Mary's father, Russell Carpenter, is the only one of four brothers not to have fought in Vietnam—4F on account of an irregular heartbeat, like Billy Parham in *The Crossing*—and displaces his guilt by exacting Marine-style discipline on his children. Two of his brothers died, one never to be recovered, while the third, Clifford, is forgotten in a local convalescent home.

Convalescence from the traumas of war defines the novel, with the home becoming one of the key sites of convergence in the novel, along with the Montoya ranch, El Santuario de Chimayó, and Delfino Montoya's old ranch in the middle of the White Sands Missile Range. It is at the convalescent home that the domestic complications of the novel are finally resolved, but if the convergences that ease the plot's tensions appear to rely too heavily on fortuitous coincidence, it is nothing that is not remarked upon by the novel's characters themselves. Reflecting on her own curious fortunes, Mary wonders quite how much agency she has over her choices. While she sees her decisions as producing a causal chain, she has to conclude that "Kip was coincidence" (AC 149), and the novel is less interested in realism than in the barely concealed metafictional movement of pieces into alignment.

Certainly, the plot's overdetermined coincidences are matched by the burden carried by Ariel's name. As the progeny of a Los Alamos trinity, Ariel is portentously marked as an emanation from the Prospero-like sorcery of the Hill. Brice is described as commenting on the daily news in Elizabethan doggerel, and his hand in the naming of his adopted daughter is plain. "You're a view from above," he explains, only half-playfully, "an airy spirit" (AC 39), a benign version of Kip's Laos-era spook. While Ariel herself is as confused as anyone else in the novel, this aerial prospect is provided for the reader, who is privy to the web of connections holding the plot together.

The fact is that Kip and Brice have always been overly aware of their symbolic significance as atomic Adams. It is this burden that sets Kip running and leads Brice to become an activist and defense lawyer for protesters. Similarly, Ariel's literary bent enables a self-conscious troping, not just on her own name but on her quest, that gives Morrow an opening through which to make clear some of the references embedded in the novel. The source of a recurrent reference to ghost limbs, for example, is provided when Kip's old motel room reminds Ariel of the house in which Melville wrote "his great novel" (AC 199). If it seems that the characters are sometimes too busy explaining the text for the reader, it is partly because they are all too aware of themselves as constructions of the self-consciously manufactured laboratory of Los Alamos, which, in its own way, redrafted history to include mass death as synonymous with the enchantments of New Mexico. The deceptions and substitutions that Morrow's novels engineer—Brice substitutes for Kip, Mary becomes Franny and substitutes for Ariel, Kip tries to substitute himself for Delfino in the symbolic reclaiming of the Dripping Spring ranch from the army—serve to show how the unmooring of identity produced by the fact of the bomb has set in motion a spiraling of deception as characters struggle to put right something that is out of their control. The free associating that characters indulge in, piling up the connections—Oppenheimer liked The Tempest; the play was written while Santa Fe was being settled; Mary plays Miranda in a production of the play—is a function of what is configured as their exile from home, a primary sense of abandonment that leads to a surfeit of self-scrutinizing interpretation but little direction.

In a much cited essay, Jacques Derrida points out that because a nuclear war can never be described after the event, since there would be no one left to describe it, the "non-event" of nuclear war has existence "only through what is said of it." It is a fable, "a pure invention," yet at the same time we cannot "fail to recognize the massive 'reality' of nuclear weaponry." The fable of nuclear war "triggers this fabulous war effort" and structures "the whole human socius today."[32] The real is structured by the fable on the basis of an event that has never happened (and which must be prevented from happening even as we prepare for its happening). This hypothesis of a total nuclear war "conditions every discourse and all strategies," installing "humanity—and through all sorts of relays even defines the essence of modern humanity—in its rhetorical condition."[33]

The purely textual existence of nuclear war is no less threatening because it is not (yet) real, because the imagination of the event produces the devices that can make it happen. Oppenheimer's literary interests dress the work at Los Alamos in the stuff of civilization even as it makes real the apparatus for the obliteration of the history that gives it form. What Morrow's novels are faced with, then, is the collapse of the real—New Mexico as a site for dwelling—into the fable of Los Alamos that has overwritten all that precedes and follows it. Made in Los Alamos, Brice, Kip, and all associated with them, are produced out of nuclearism's "rhetorical condition": they are, like nuclear war, the textual doubles for which there can be no referent. They are exiled in an overdetermined text that must always circle back to the site that produced them; that is, the laboratory of Los Alamos as the proving ground for a plot resolution that can never be allowed to be written.

What *Ariel's Crossing* offers, then, is the meager compensation provided to the nuclear condition by the shadow cast by the now-inaccessible meanings of pre-nuclear culture. The "view from above" that may once have been available through literature's capacity to describe human agency in the world is now impossibly occluded. All language and interpretation leads back, as it must, to Los Alamos, for it is that site that "conditions every discourse and all strategies." It is little wonder that Morrow's characters have little choice but to follow the pull of the agent that conceived them. Kip's willingness to fight in Vietnam and ultimately to perform the ritual confrontation at White Sands, demonstrates the extent to which he understands his own fate. As a boy he hacked off the head of a contaminated buck so it could be hung on a wall as a reminder that "[t]he death of every creature is the promise of your own" (AC 240). Facing his own death, Kip is, like the buck, "little more than a footnote in the history of restricted-only installations" (240). His struggle to reach Dripping Spring is his "berserk terminus" (AC 233), a conscious embrace of the forces that have shaped his life: "[i]sn't it a way of looking at World War Two from its altruistic, damnable birth down in the Jornada by staring straight into the teeth of Vietnam, finally?" (AC 192).

Kip's desire to take on Delfino's burden is a measure of how much Kip has internalized the guilt of America's post-Hiroshima warrior condition. Delfino, more than Kip and Brice, embodies the exiled state of the West's surplus population: unlike their fathers, Delfino did not work on the project, "the Project worked on [him]" (AC 172). One of the 150 families evicted from their homes as White Sands Missile Range was established and then expanded since World War II, Delfino and Agnes Montoya persistently refused to enter the new script drawn up for Western history by the military-industrial complex. Refusing to touch the compensation payment forced upon them, they spend decades petitioning for their land to be returned, a campaign that becomes more futile and symbolic as the years progress.[34] When Agnes finally dies of cancer, Delfino vows to retake the ranch. For years he has been watching the strange lights emanating from the range through a night-vision monoscope, its singular eyepiece emblematic of what has become his own Ahab-like obsession with the unreachable object beyond the fence. Delfino has become well versed in the history of casual destruction wrought by the military and can recount details of tests conducted and casualties produced. He knows the stories of all the families who attempted in vain to resist eviction and, more than anyone, understands how the military has used the area to erase its own traces and cast doubt on those who might look directly on its activities.

Delfino's stories are "about how a moment in history defined by communications, by digitized and microprocessed interfacing," produces a "black hole" in the desert "where the fracture between what was known within and what was known without couldn't have been more complete." Looking over the fence does not reveal anything, and even if something can be seen it will remain "incomprehensible" and impossible to credibly describe to others (AC 296). What the base has produced is "stealth," both the bomber and the effect, that is conceived as an obfuscatory and sublime fusion of landscape and technology that recalls Heidegger's observation that the enframing of the lifeworld has come to be mistaken for the world in itself. Doubt is cast over appearances so extensively that even the sunset might be "their doing" and evidence of witnessed military exercises disappears so quickly as to be little more than another bad dream (AC 297).

Even if the sunset is not modified by technology, there is no longer any way of being sure. The line between observation and imagination has been fogged to the extent that anything is possible. The test flights are cognitively distant and function mainly as a form of peripheral spectacle, at once dazzling and absent. Life goes on regardless, but it is life shot through with nameless insinuations and evacuated of agency and purpose. "Thanks to you and the people you represent," Delfino tells government officials, "me and my wife live in a necropolis" (AC 317), but one without remains.

The estranged and exiled condition that Delfino describes as a necropolis characterizes the post–Los Alamos condition for Morrow's and McMahon's protagonists, who are set adrift not just by the fact of the bomb's devastating potential but also by the security-driven dissimulations. The secret conditions under which the bomb was developed contradict, as McMahon and Morrow make clear, the idea of technology, as Heidegger explains, as "a mode of revealing" and unconcealment.[35] What is distinctive about modern technology's process of revealing is that it "does not unfold into a bringing-forth in the name of *poiesis*" but is instead a challenging "which puts to nature the unreasonable demand that it supply energy that can be extracted and stored as such."[36] The militarization of science has led to a technology that has enframed the world; everything in nature has been determined by technology as a "standing reserve" of "calculable forces" ready to be put to use: "[e]verywhere everything is ordered to stand by, to be immediately at hand, indeed to stand there just so that it may be on call for a further ordering."[37] This includes the human as well as the nonhuman realm, with human beings as the mere "orderers" of the lifeworld as standing-reserve.

Tim MacLaurin's adult incapacity to do anything but paint the barn suggests a stasis that has its root in the disabling fact of an ineffable technology that elevates his father's generation, as Heidegger says, on the mistaken assumption that they are "lord[s] of the earth." The sense of abandonment felt by Tim and by Morrow's Brice and Kip is that they are forced to live in world enframed by the bomb created by their fathers but dissimulated as "natural," as if, to all intents and purposes, everything is as it was before. The final delusion, according to Heidegger, caused by technology's enframing of the lifeworld is that it is not enframed at all but the way things naturally are.[38] As Rob Wilson paraphrases, "technology quietly *technologizes* feats of human knowing, reducing the mind to robotic gestures as an analogous force of nature."[39] Enframing effectively "entraps" the world and knowledge of the world under the "disguise" of setting in order everything that is standing reserve.[40] It is impossible, then, to know anything outside of the enframing, and the very process of ordering the things we think we know is a function of technology's enframing. Not only is the earth forever on call as a potential technological resource, so too has human life become "human resources" to be deployed.

Kip's embrace of war in *Trinity Fields* suggests a fated understanding of this at some level, while Brice holds out in the hope that the structure of the law can yield some hope for redemption. Nevertheless, each, like Tim, is called into being by Los Alamos as the by-product of atomic science's regime of secrecy, which has entwined itself as part of the DNA of postwar identity. Since World War II, the products of Los Alamos—the bomb and the society that has emerged in its shadow—have remained on call, standing by.

5. GRIDLOCKED AND HOMELESS

When there is enough out-of-placeness in the world, nothing is out of place.
Don DeLillo, Mao II

The restructuring of Western space during World War II as part of a nascent security-driven defense complex displaces and disperses populations even as it contains and polices others. While the wasteland discourse encourages a conception of federally withdrawn spaces as always already vacant, ready to be filled with detainees or military-industrial labor, this vacancy is in fact achieved through clearing and dispossession. In novels as different as Edward Abbey's *Fire on the Mountain* (1962), Cormac McCarthy's *The Border Trilogy* (1992–98), N. Scott Momaday's *House Made of Dawn* (1968), Leslie Marmon Silko's *Ceremony* (1977), and, most recently, Alexander Parsons's *In the Shadows of the Sun* (2005), a combination of economic and military forces strip away prior claims to the land. Violence toward a sense of belonging is inflicted by the direct experience of warfare in the Pacific and the impact of the return of the traumatized veteran on an unprepared and often uncomprehending community. At the same time, the progressive appropriation of land by the federal government for military purposes during and after World War II literally removes the ground upon which any kind of reintegration might have been possible. In all these texts, the intensely local sense of place that has served to underpin traditional values and practices is dismantled by the intrusion of global geopolitics and advanced militarized capitalism.

To varying degrees and in different registers, the response of these novels to the destruction of what is usually conceived as a prior state of organic, if not uncomplicated, dwelling is to articulate the quest for a kind of symbolic realignment between the dispossessed subject and his (this is a largely male dilemma in the books) environment. This pursuit may take the form of employing traditional healing rituals and shamanistic intervention (Momaday and Silko), of attempts to retrieve and reinstall that which is perceived to have been lost (McCarthy), or even of a stubborn and necessarily doomed refusal to budge, as seen in Delfino's one-man war to reclaim his homestead in *Ariel's Crossing* that is also the central concern of Abbey's and Parsons's novels. What is true in all cases is that the ground has been or is about to be taken away, either literally through military appropriation or through a traumatic rupturing of the relationship between lived experience and place caused by the experience of warfare.

The process of appropriating the land and removing the inhabitants is plainly one of clearing, of emptying the site prior to its reemployment as proving ground or military base. The wasteland discourse is a powerfully enabling device for the redefinition of habitat as empty and useless. Indeed, in many cases the newly appropriated land literally disappears off the map, all physical markers expunged from the record. In a seemingly paradoxical move, the military-industrial interests now occupying space in order to further the development of advanced scientific and technological devices have taken themselves out of the domain of the rational inventory of what is there.

The Map and the State of Exception

Planning the rescue of a kidnapped friend who has been squirreled away in a disused government installation, two men in Thomas Pynchon's *Vineland* (1990) study maps of the area: "[t]hey peered at the maps, each with that enigmatic blank in the middle, like the outline of a state in a geography test, belonging to something called 'the U.S.,' but not the one they knew."[1] The unmarked space on the map has become a common trope in writing about the West in recent years, a double motif that speaks on the one hand of the shroud of secrecy covering military-industrial activity and on the other of the resistant spaces beyond the inventory of the U.S. standing reserve. In Terry Tempest Williams's *Refuge*, "[a] blank spot on the map translates into empty space, space devoid of people, a wasteland perfect for nerve gas, weteye bombs, and toxic waste."[2] Similarly, in DeLillo's *Underworld*, the white places on the map "include the air base, the army base, the missile range, the vast stretch to the northwest called the Jornada del Muerto and the interdunal flats as well." The flats themselves are perversely "map-white, on the page and in living fact," so that their absence on the map does in fact represent their physical condition. In an uncanny twist, the blank space on this map tells the truth even as it continues to lie, since the few low buildings and propane tanks that are visible "service the underground operation in the Pocket, where weapons were conceived and designed."[3] The blank space on the map is the achieved truth of the wasteland discourse whereby the nothing that is the land is reproduced as a nothing on the map. But of course there is something there, it has simply been removed from view. Indeed, what is there—advanced military technology—is defined by its wasteland environment in the sense that waste (that which is removed and discarded in the process of making something) is the concealed other of production. The removed inhabitants, displaced in order to install the invisible machinery of production, must also be thought of as waste in that they are surplus to requirements. They are, in Zygmunt Bauman's words, the "collateral casualties" of progress.[4]

For Bauman, the "factory of knowledge is incomplete without waste disposal sites." Knowledge is gained "thanks to the laying out of the blank spots of lack of interest, and the precision, exactitude, pragmatic utility of knowledge grows with the size of those spots." The blank spaces on the map and the dispossessed inhabitants who used to dwell in the places those maps now refuse to represent, like all "things excluded—thrown out of focus, cast in the shadow, forced into the vague or invisible background—no longer belong to 'what is.' They have been denied existence and a room of their own in the *Lebenswelt*."[5] If the separation of waste is "the trade secret of modern creation," there can be no order without the removal of the disorderly.[6] Waste is "an indispensable ingredient of the creative process," endowed with "an awesome, truly magical power"—it is unwanted and discarded but no order can be made without it. Waste, then, is "an embodiment of ambivalence," simultaneously "divine and satanic."[7]

The map with the blank spaces on it defines the wasteland as an absent presence—such spaces are excluded from the "what is" of representation but remain on the map in negation. This kind of wasteland is complicated, however, since its strategic value lies in its representation as waste, so the blanks on the map are not Bauman's "blank spots of lack of interest," because in that blankness is located (but hidden) the very "factory of knowledge" that has excluded the wasteland in the first place. What is really at issue here is the dividing line between the visibly mapped terrain and the erased information, the edge where representation stops and power exempts itself from the rules of rational and orderly plotting of space.

In withdrawing land under eminent domain the government's justification must be that the property be taken for, as the Fifth Amendment states, "public use." In the case of military withdrawal, that public use is the maintenance of security. Those members of the public who reside on the land in question may be financially compensated, but property rights are effectively voided. In a sense, those people removed from their property are excluded from the protection afforded the rest of the "public" and become collateral casualties of the state's exceptional powers. In *Fire on the Mountain*, the recalcitrant rancher John Vogelin is reminded by the army that "all property rights are derived from and depend upon the sovereignty of the State."[8] Asked which is more important, "your property or the national safety?" Vogelin replies that "[n]obody's safe when the Government can take away his home" (FM 142). Indeed, but the condition of nobody-being-safe is precisely the state of emergency that sanctions the exceptional withdrawal of private property in the first place. If one of the effects of the long Cold War was the institutionalization of the anxiety and fear produced by World War II and infinitely extended by the threat of nuclear conflict, state power must function in a perpetual condition of emergency. For Bauman, power is precisely about the production of what he calls "official fear," the requisite fear of vulnerability and uncertainty that allows safety and security to be felt as exceptions achieved by power's successful employment.[9] The exclusion of Vogelin and his land from "the public" produces a security effect whereby his private insecurity is offset by the security felt by the establishment of a military-industrial facility dedicated to the continued protection of national security.

The blank space on the map, then, is a visible marker of the state of exception that, as Agamben explains, "represents the inclusion and capture of a space that is neither outside nor inside."[10] The "topological structure" of the state of exception, claims Agamben, is defined by being-outside yet also belonging.[11] This seems to me to be precisely the condition of the map's blank spaces, which simultaneously refuse the function of the map's signifying purpose while also confirming this function: the blank space is where the hidden is emplotted, where the suspended norm gives shape to the normative representation of the world that surrounds it. The blank space is neither inside nor outside the nation-state of the United States; it ruptures the continuous spatial indexing that produces the narrative sense of the map as a record of all there is while also indisputably being in that space.

A fundamental mistake made by those landowners and inhabitants who insist on the fact of ownership and occupation as the unimpeachable guarantor of their rights is to believe that lived experience is sanctioned by law rather than the other way round. "We came to a fence," narrates Vogelin's grandson in *Fire on the Mountain*, "the west boundary of the old man's deeded property." Beyond this line are the summer ranges used for nearly a century by the old man and his father before him, and which are leased according to the provisions of the Taylor Grazing Act, which provides grazing districts on federal land. On the other side of the fence, the land "did not, however, reveal in any way its legal status: it was rocky and dry and sunny and almost though not quite worthless—it looked perfectly real and natural." This impression of a state of nature means that "[y]ou could never have guessed, looking at it, that it belonged to the United States of America and was colored a uniform green on maps" (FM 34). The grazing district is not yet a blank space on the map, but the uniform green already indicates that the space is defined by invisible rules that precede and take priority over the material facts of its existence. "The rule," explains Bauman, "precedes reality. Legislation precedes the ontology of the human world. The law is a design, a blueprint for a clearly circumscribed, legibly marked, mapped and signposted habitat."[12] The map, we might say, following Baudrillard, precedes the territory. Discussing the standoff between Vogelin and the Air Force, Lee Mackie points out to the old man that "they have the papers and the law. They have Acts of Congress, national emergency, eminent domain, right of condemnation, declaration of taking. What do you have?" Vogelin's reply is that "I have the land" (FM 22). But of course he does not have the land, since the law that entitles him to it invents the very notion of "having" and contains within itself the possibility of the exception. Representation of space in the form of the map might be said to be the first "declaration of taking," an announcement that the law calls the land into being, not as "real and natural" but as the domain of the state.

"It's always quite a shock to have your property pre-empted," Colonel DeSalius observes to Vogelin, the word "pre-empted" confirming the prior claim of the state to the land and also containing an acknowledgment of the legal history of preemption that assisted the colonization of the territory in the first place (FM 78). It was the Pre-Emption Act of 1841 that gave squatters the right to buy 160 acres at $1.25 per acre before the land was auctioned. The Homestead Act of 1862 made preemption an accepted part of U.S. land policy, providing 160 acres of public land free to any adult citizen or head of family who had lived on the land for five years. Here again is presented the doubleness of the state of exception, since preemption is both the basis of Vogelin's defense and also the cause of his dispossession. The novel admits as much when Mackie notes the arbitrariness of ownership: "[d]oes the land belong to anybody? A hundred years ago the Apaches had it, it was all theirs. Your father and other men like him stole it from the Apaches. The railroad company and the big cattle companies and the banks tried to steal it from your father and from you. Now the Government is going to steal it from you. This land has always been crawling with thieves" (FM 143). While Mackie is prepared to take the long view and insist on the endurably brute fact of the land as "the same dried-out burnt-up parcel of sand and cactus" irrespective of who "owns" it, Vogelin's response is to align himself with the Apaches—"That's the tradition around here" (FM 143)—and go down fighting in the manner of previous generations of vanishing Americans.

A similar scenario is rehearsed in Alexander Parsons's *In the Shadows of the Sun* (2005), a novel that is in many ways a composite of narrative strands from Abbey, McCarthy, Silko, and Momaday. Telling the story of the Strickland family as they endure both eviction from their homestead by the government and the loss of eighteen-year-old Jack in the Philippines, the novel is divided between White Sands and the war in the Pacific and deliberately draws parallels between the doomed struggle with the military the Strickland brothers Ross and Baylis experience, and Ross's son Jack's abuse and torture at the hands of the Japanese on the Bataan Death March. As Abbey's and McCarthy's protagonists realize from experience, and as Silko's and Momaday's know by inheritance, the line between friend and enemy is thin and easily broken. On receiving a letter warning them of possible removal days after Pearl Harbor and the declaration of war, the Stricklands feel like "they have been lumped to-gether with the enemy."[13] In a replay of Vogelin's complaint, Ross protests that "[e]victing citizens is a hell of a way to fight a war" (ISS 119).

If, as we will see, John Grady Cole and his father in Cormac McCarthy's *All the Pretty Horses* have cause to cast themselves as the remnants of a fad-ing civilization (Comanches), *In the Shadows of the Sun* makes the identifi-cation literal. Jack's life is saved because the Apache Conrad substitutes himself at the last moment when it is clear there are to be summary ex-ecutions along the road. Conrad has already explained to Jack, in terms that would not be out of place in McCarthy, that there is no meaning in words or things, tearing off Jack's dog-tags and hurling them into the bush. All there is left that is relevant, according to Conrad, is "what you do" (ISS 12). After Conrad's death, and for no obvious reason, Jack takes on Conrad's identity. The dehumanizing treatment the prisoners' expe-rience is so complete that the life Jack's name represents is over: "[e]very man had been prized free of the life that previously held them," and a new name signified a division between who you had been and what you now must be (ISS 145). This self-erasure results in the Stricklands back in New Mexico receiving a telegram recording Jack's death, and the family orders a headstone and conducts a funeral service on the ranch even as soldiers insist that they vacate the premises.[14] Jack is saved by, at least in terms of what is written on the tags, becoming Indian. Before rejecting the name on his army identification, Conrad explains that "Apache" means "fight-ing men" to the Yuma and "enemy" to the Zuni, while Apaches know themselves as "The People" (ISS 12). Being inside or outside depends on where you stand, and this fluidity of subject positioning keeps Jack alive, even though he has no idea what Conrad is talking about. What Conrad gives Jack is the mantle of vanished American: Jack is saved by being al-ready destroyed.

The implication here is—as it is in Morrow, Abbey, and, as I will sug-gest below in relation to McCarthy's *Border Trilogy*, as well as, in a differ-ent register, in Silko and Momaday—that World War II destroys prewar American identity and produces a new mode of wasted subjectivity in accordance with the post-Trinity world order. This new nuclear identity, predicated on the notion of the civilian soldier—everyone everywhere is always already a target—positions prewar Western populations, along with the land they live and work on, as the collateral casualties sacrificed in order to protect national security. Like Indians—and in Silko and Momaday, the analogy functions as a mere repetition—the old Western order must be put to use through being made to vanish.

Wasted Lives

While Vogelin is finally evicted, he soon returns to his cabin from his daughter's house in Alamagordo only for the journey to kill him. Mackie, in a final act of defiance, burns the cabin, and the old man's body within it, to the ground, returning Vogelin "cell by cell, atom by atom," to the elements (FM 180). This dispersal of the wasted warrior back into the landscape, along with Mackie's reading of Western history as a series of violent dispossessions, recalls Blood Meridian's notion of the land as graveyard. In the novels of The Border Trilogy, McCarthy pursues in extended form the theme, immanent in Blood Meridian and sketched out in Fire on the Mountain, of the state's expropriation of the land as it maps the extent of its domain at the expense of modes of life extraneous to the demands of national security. John Grady Cole and Billy and Boyd Parham, McCarthy's preternaturally aged youths, are far more complexly placed than Abbey's old-timer, though they carry Vogelin's ferocious loyalty to the simple virtues of the homestead in their blood as a kind of depleted agitation that compels them to roam the borderlands in fruitless pursuit of an order of things no longer historically sustainable. What is implicit in Abbey's novel—that the source of the law that entitles Vogelin to his spread in the first place is also the agent of his dispossession—is developed in The Border Trilogy as McCarthy probes the question of entitlement through his protagonists' sense of loyalty to "country." Through the numerous crossings they undertake back and forth between the United States and Mexico, McCarthy's youths test the limits of their exceptional condition—Agamben's oxymoronic state of ecstasy-belonging, being outside and inside—and in doing so articulate themselves as the necessarily wasted life called into being by the map of the national security state.

Vogelin's dilemma—how can homesteading, a way of life so thoroughly imbricated in the American national imaginary, be canceled by the very structure of power that gives it form?—is replayed in The Border Trilogy as an embodied contradiction of postwar American life. Unlike Boyd, who is dispersed into Mexican folklore as a transhistorical, postnational out-law even as his physical remains are returned to American soil, and de-spite sympathies of blood (the Parhams have a "fullblooded" Mexican grandmother) and culture (however caricatured they may sometimes be, the virtues of vaquero life and family honor are largely approached with-out irony), John Grady Cole and Billy Parham stay American. It is in this attachment to "country" as nation maintained by the protagonists, re-gardless of the borderless continuity of terrain and lifeways shared by the United States and Mexico, that the novels achieve the pathos of the state of exception. Successful, sustainable life in Mexico is not made available to Cole or Parham by the narratives, which frustrate in particular Cole's desire to settle there, by insisting upon the Americans' inability to accept the limitations of Mexican class and gender codes. Only by returning to the United States can Cole's and Parham's homelessness be properly con-firmed as the necessary condition upon which American territorial se-curity is predicated. The biopolitical regulation of life, however wasted, necessitates that people do not just leave. To make structural sense, the blank spaces and bare life have to be in country.

World War II, the encroachments of the extraction industries and U.S. military, and the widespread industrialization and militarization of the Southwest during the postwar period rarely feature directly in the tril-ogy, though the first and third volumes provide enough information to show that Cole's diminished prospect of living the cowboy life has mate-rial historical causes, and while *The Crossing* is arguably the most esoteric of the novels, the final false dawn of the Trinity test that leaves a bereft Parham weeping by the roadside is likewise real enough. Unlike Abbey's treatment of the confrontation between tradition and militarized mo-dernity in *Fire on the Mountain* or even the material and psychological re-flux of the war featured in Momaday and Silko, McCarthy's novels do not front the fact of material dispossession in any sustained and explicit way. However, recent and impending events permeate the atmosphere of the books, shape individual and family histories, establish economic and ex-istential limits, and well in the pores of the narratives. As such, as critics such as John Wegner and Jacqueline Scoones have noted, "[w]ars and ru-mors of war" (CP 61) saturate and animate the trilogy.[15]

John Grady's father is a survivor of a Japanese POW camp and the Bataan Death March, sick and damaged as a result of the experiences that also contributed to the breakdown of the marriage that will leave his son without an inheritance. The war forecloses on John Grady's future, which can exist only in his dreams of the ranch as it was before he was "disinherited by war and war's machinery" (CP 204). Others are also either lost or broken by the war, like Blevins's father, who did not return (APH 64), and the sense of bewildered abandonment is reiterated throughout the trilogy. Proleptically, Mr. Sanders tells Billy that "[t]here's no way to calculate what's to come" (C 345), and Billy goes to sleep that night knowing "that there was no certainty to any of it. Not just the coming of war. Anything at all" (C 345). "The world will never be the same" says the rider Billy meets prior to his final return to the United States. "I know it," he replies. "It aint now" (C 420). In *Cities of the Plain*, Troy is discharged at the end of the war only to aimlessly wander the country before winding up in a small town Texas jail for nine months after a fight. When he is released, his horses have been sold to pay the feed bill (CP 23). The final novel of the trilogy repeats as achieved alienation what the earlier books forewarned, Billy echoing John Grady's father's discomfort at the beginning of *All the Pretty Horses* when he observes that "this country aint the same. Nor anything in it. The war changed everything. I dont think people even know it yet" (CP 78). Asked how the war changed things, Billy can only say that "it just did" and insist on the irreversibility of that change: "[i]t aint the same no more. It never will be" (CP 78). The MacGovern ranch—"right in the middle" of the "sorriest land" the army could find (CP 11)—has not yet been claimed by the military, but its withdrawal is a foregone conclusion.

The most extensive effect of the militarization of everyday life registered in the trilogy is the destruction of security. People "dont feel safe no more" (APH 25), observes John Grady's father, comparing the remnants of the ranching culture to "the Comanches two hundred years ago. We dont know what's goin to show up here come daylight. We dont even know what color they'll be" (APH 25–26). Registering the emerging threat of Communist China (this is 1949), the Bataan veteran's racialized geopolitical anxiety is paired with Vogelin's identification with prior generations of "vanishing" Americans in a way that acknowledges the inevitability of the Anglo cowboy's demise while positioning him as victim of the same forces that legitimized his presence in the first place. The identification with the Comanches also acknowledges that the arguments used to justify Indian removal—their construction by racial science and history as an antique residue of a previously proud civilization, effectively naturalizing their supercession as inevitable—now apply to outmoded methods of production and modes of life.

Under the technocratic postwar dispensation, traditional modes of employment, habits, and practices are made redundant, along with the vocabularies used to describe them. The land itself is withdrawn from public usage and annihilating weapons exploded upon it, and nowhere is there any sense of an explanatory narrative or evidence of the agents of this transformation. The veterans of previous conflict and the remains of a deracinated civilian population persist in a state of resignation or bewilderment. Robert L. Holmes has suggested that "the paradox of contemporary civilization is that beyond a certain point the individual's security begins to vary inversely with the power embodied in the systems meant to ensure that security."[16] While this may be a paradox, it is not necessarily an unforeseen one. As Bauman reminds us, echoing Foucault and Hardt and Negri, "vulnerability and uncertainty are the principal raison d'être of all political power."[17]

In the postwar period, with the rollback of New Deal and wartime emphasis on collective endeavor and a reinstatement of the individual as the core unit of democratic freedom, while vulnerability and insecurity may be pervasive across society, the consequences are left with the individual as a private problem. In this way, as Ulrich Beck explains, "how one lives becomes the *biographical solution of systemic contradictions*."[18] All sorts of experts, Beck continues, "dump their contradictions and conflicts at the feet of the individual and leave him or her with the well intentioned invitation to judge all of this critically on the basis of his or her own notions." The collapse of traditional social structures and the increased impact of global forces on local experience means that "biography is increasingly removed from its direct sphere of contact and opened up across the boundaries of countries and experts for a *long-distance morality* which puts the individual in the position of potentially having to take a continual stand." Even as the significance and agency of the individual shrinks, "he or she is elevated to the apparent throne of a world-shaper." While biography is "opened to the world society," this world society "becomes a part of biography, although this continual excessive demand can only be tolerated through the opposite reaction of not listening, simplifying, and apathy."[19]

In The Border Trilogy the mysterious agents of market forces and national security drive Cole and Parham away from any possibility of secure and settled life. They are examples of Bauman's "collateral casualties" of capitalism's creative destruction that dismantles existing "forms of 'making a living'" that are "broken up into components meant to be reassembled ('recycled') into new forms." Some of these "components are damaged beyond repair, while of those that survive the dismantling phase only a reduced quantity is needed" to operate the new economic organization.[20] Cole and Parham are unlikely to reassemble themselves as functionaries of the military-industrial West. "What would you do," Cole asks Parham, "if you couldnt be a cowboy?" Neither of them can come up with anything, but Parham responds that they "may all have to think of somethin'" (CP 217). Cole is soon to come to a bloody end in the backstreets of Juarez, while Parham is confronted in "the oncoming years" with a drought that kills off the cattle business. There was "no work in that country anywhere," and he wandered "[t]ill he was old" (CP 265). At the end of Cities of the Plains, he has just finished a stint as a movie extra. This final role for Parham confirms both his marginality (a non-acting part) and the indispensability of that marginality (the non-acting part that makes up the numbers in order to ensure the veracity of the illusion of realism required by the mode of representation). Parham looks "real" but is without agency, and in this condition he is a necessary cipher in the reproduction of everyday life.

The glimpse of John Grady's father offered in passing in Cities of the Plain reveals a man of more substance than the sick and damaged veteran of All the Pretty Horses. As John Grady explains to Mac Johnson, his father was "one of the best" poker players, who, despite knowing the pitfalls of gambling, continued because he was good at it. The only other thing he was good at was being a cowboy, and given John Grady's rigor, his assessment of his father's skills ought to be taken as a fair measure: "I've heard of some that was supposed to be better and I'm sure there were some better. I just never did see any of em" (CP 214). While John

Grady does not play poker (though he does play chess), he shares his father's willingness to place himself in high risk situations on the basis of following his natural inclinations—doing something because he is good at it. John Grady is "some kind of specialist in spoiled horses" (CP 14), and this proclivity for stubbornly pursuing lost causes includes his doomed attempt at saving the epileptic Mexican prostitute that will lead to his death. We are told at the beginning of *All the Pretty Horses* that Cole loves the same quality in horses and people: "the blood and the heat of the blood that ran them"; his "reverence," "fondness," and "all the leanings of his life were for the ardenthearted and they would always be so and never be otherwise" (APH 6).

This unstinting commitment to the truth of the heart leaves John Grady singularly adrift from convention: he has "his own notions about things," and his methods are considered "unorthodox" at best (CP 20, 15). His pursuit of both Alejandra and Magdelena is driven by a self-destructive passion that overrides all sense and disregards all social restrictions. Cole can proceed in this unquestioning manner because he trusts the ardenthearted to be true and the true to be good; if he believes that a "good horse has justice in his heart" (CP 53) then his own desires can be pursued because they are emanations of a similarly just passion. Cole follows his blood into impossible situations because, like his father's poker playing, risk is a necessary but ultimately irrelevant condition of doing what comes naturally. He has inherited, as Gail Moore Morrison observes, "an unwavering commitment to a set of significant values" that places Cole as "an unlikely knight errant, displaced and dispossessed, heroically tested and stubbornly faithful to a chivalric code whose power is severely circumscribed by the inevitable evil in a hostile world."[21]

This assessment of Cole's character positions him as a remnant of a lost world of righteous action and just causes. McCarthy sets up this reading by describing, at the outset of the trilogy, the boy riding, after his grandfather's funeral, along the old Comanche road that "shaped before him . . . like a dream of the past" where "that lost nation came down out of the north . . . each armed for war which was their life and . . . all of them pledged in blood and redeemable in blood only" (APH 5). This lyrical passage invokes the ghosts of those people Cole's father will shortly identify with himself, "passing in a soft chorale across that mineral waste to darkness bearing lost to all history and all remembrance like a grail the sum of their secular and transitory and violent lives" (APH 5). As Cole turns south down the old war trail he inescapably becomes bound up with this elegiac narrative of honorable warriors—the sun even obliges by "coppering his face" to effect some kind of racial identification—who were, like the ardent-hearted John Grady, "pledged in blood." While modern warfare has irrevocably damaged the father, the son bears all the attributes of the chivalric warrior, someone who, as Foucault explains, "could be recognized from afar" by the "natural signs of his strength and his courage," whose movements and attitudes "belonged for the most part to a bodily rhetoric of honor."[22] If John Grady is "like a man come to the end of something" (APH 50), that something is the final gesture of a warrior caste (the authentic and righteous cowboy) about to be written out of the legend by the managerial rationalization of the permanent arms economy.

The warrior as "man of honor" remains a staple of popular constructions of nationalist masculine purpose in military and civilian forms alike—the incorruptible cop or lawyer, the righteous vigilante, and the extralegal but morally virtuous veteran all continue to animate accounts of individual masculine becoming in popular narrative—and the trope, especially in its Western form, became endlessly enabling during the 1940s and 1950s (the period in which The Border Trilogy is set) as a means of reinforcing the innate nobility of the American mission to protect democratic freedoms from Cold War enemies.[23] Technologically advanced warfare, however, does not require soldiers to be discovered as physically and morally ready-made. Instead, the soldier is a "machine" that "can be constructed" through the disciplining of the body.[24] Furthermore, after World War II and the fusion of military and civilian values and practices that it brought about, the distinction between solider and civilian, especially under the permanent threat of nuclear conflict that configures the entire globe as battlefield, becomes to a large extent irrelevant as a condition of what Harold Lasswell has called "civilian militarism" is established.[25] The recrudescence of the Western, and of the cowboy as warrior in particular during the Cold War, can, under these circumstances, be seen as symbolic compensation for the subjection of the social body to the disciplinary regimes of a permanent civilian army in which individual or inherited moral values and practices might themselves be construed as waywardly at odds with the strategic goals of the nation at war. The containment and exploitation of material and human resources by the military-industrial complex that drove and sustained the postwar boom confirms Foucault's sense that discipline "increases the forces of the body (in economic terms of utility) and diminishes these same forces (in political terms of obedience)."[26] Under these circumstances, the wasted lives of The Border Trilogy's protagonists are the human analog of the wasteland that is appropriated and sacrificed in order to preserve national security: they are outside and yet also belonging to the symbolic order, the externalized waste product that confirms the productivity of the inside.

The Border Trilogy may be set in the mid-twentieth century, but its publication across the 1990s signals yet another sense in which the narrative is concerned with belatedness. For just as Cole and Parham are out of step or behind the times, unable to find a place in the postwar global order, so too McCarthy's text seems to emanate from another time. The collapse of the Berlin Wall and the end of the Soviet Union put an end to the deterrence argument as justification for huge defense expenditure, and while McCarthy's cowboys represent the remnants of a social order made redundant by the postwar oil business and Western military-industrial power, the novels themselves depict an emergent Cold War–driven spatial management that is already in the process of realignment by the time the first volume is published. I think that just as Blood Meridian has been read as a response to Vietnam, The Border Trilogy continues to explore the ways American geopolitics are written into the Western landscape. If, as I believe, McCarthy's first Western says as much about the rhetorical deployment of a dehistoricized fundamentalism of conquest in the 1980s as it does about Vietnam, I also think his approach to the "last cowboy" genre in the 1990s is in part a reflection of how the 1950s Cold War Western topos served to reanimate Cold War fears in the 1980s by a self-styled cowboy president.

Theodore Roosevelt was inaugurated as the first "Cowboy President" with a reputation founded on actual deeds as a stockman, sheriff, and Rough Rider. Ronald Reagan's claim as cowboy president was, as Richard Slotkin suggests, "based entirely on references to imaginary deeds performed in a purely mythic space." The Reagan Revolution, Slotkin continues, "represented an authentic recrudescence and revision of the Frontier Myth," whereby supply-side economics and reenergized assaults on enemies of freedom—"anti-American" forces in the Soviet Union, Libya, Grenada, Nicaragua—replayed the righteous euphoria of Manifest Destiny for a postindustrial United States soured by "stagflation" and the culture wars.[27]

The nostalgic quest undertaken by John Grady Cole, Billy Parham, and their fellow travelers for uncorrupted forms of labor and human relationships leads them to criminality, pauperism, and/or death. Despite the tragic power of this pursuit the desire to make an honorable life within corporate America must also be considered in the light of the cowboy-warrior ideology of the reanimated Cold War. These are books written in the aftermath of the Reagan and George H. W. Bush presidencies, men who also played out a nostalgia for clear moral positions, for a rugged individualism within a "new world order" disturbingly like the old one.

John Grady and Billy enact, in their easy movement to and fro across the U.S.-Mexico border, the unrestricted, unregulated movement enjoyed by the existential American individualist able to construct "down there" as the proving ground for sanctified missions of rescue and restoration no longer possible in the United States.[28] Even the most dispossessed of U.S. citizens can move from the status of victimized to that of mythic cowboy once they loose themselves from the federalized containment of the postwar big government West. Read this way, the *Border Trilogy* gives back the libertarian dimension of open Mexican landscape as the blank space on the map even as that space is withdrawn on the U.S. side. While I think there is more to the trilogy's consideration of Anglo dispossession than that, and McCarthy's treatment of Mexico and Mexicans is more nuanced and sympathetic than I am at present giving him credit for, the books do court the prospect of an authentic Latin American wilderness still open for Anglo adventurism.

If There's Anything Left of This Life It's Down There

The blank spaces of the map are, for Terry Tempest Williams and Don DeLillo, the pernicious signs of concealment and subterfuge. For McCarthy's travelers in *All the Pretty Horses*, however, this absence signifies the promise of a kind of escape from the impinging gridlines of bureau-cratized U.S. space onto the other, undrawn side of the map. On an oil company road map John Grady Cole and Lacy Rawlins see "roads and rivers and towns on the American side of the map as far south as the Rio Grande." Beyond that, however, "all was white." The youths' reading of this map is a willful but enabling misreading, the blankness confirming their need to imagine the land beyond the border as a void of untranslat-able, extrarational experience:

> It dont show nothin down there, does it? said Rawlins.
> No.
> You reckon it aint never been mapped?
> There's maps. That just aint one of em. I got one in my saddle-bag.
> Rawlins came back with the map and sat on the ground and tracked their route with his finger. He looked up.
> What? said John Grady.
> There aint shit down there. (APH 34)

Rawlins's map of Mexico confirms the findings of the oil company map that leaves Mexico blank: as far as the boys can see, there is nothing there to map, at least not according to the criteria that governs the mapping of the American side. Cole and Rawlins fully intend a movement from cen-ter to periphery, away from the plotted landscape of the United States, marked up on the map and in fact by fences—symbolically broken up and burned as firewood by Billy and Boyd in The Crossing—and roads of privatized nature. The Mexican side may be a convenient fiction of emp-tiness, but it is out of American jurisdiction; while the youths may carry unrealizable U.S. fantasies of an unreconstructed and authentic Mexi-can "experience" with them, their desire to be rid of the American man-agement of space is not in doubt.

Throughout the trilogy, Mexico is consistently figured as barren, mys-terious, and strange. In The Crossing, on Billy's first movement across the border, to return the female wolf to its rightful place, the novel notes that the land they enter is as "undifferentiated in its terrain from the coun-try they quit and yet wholly alien and wholly strange" (C 75). The coun-try is "changeless" (C 88), "depopulate and barren" (C 134). Mexico as an embodied alienness suits the state of estrangement experienced by the cowboys. Tramping the land, Billy, his horse, and dog "looked like what they were, outcasts in an alien land. Homeless, hunted, weary" (C 296). In Mexico, Billy's home "had come to seem remote and dreamlike" (C 135), but the fact is that he has no home, as both Billy and Boyd concede when challenged. Having no home in the United States does not mean that they expect to find one in Mexico, which seems to function more as a space of confirmation, the place where homelessness is. When the hacendado asks Billy if he thinks Mexico is a country where he can come and do as he likes, he answers that "I never thought about this country one way or the other" (C 119).

While John Grady and Billy and Boyd share a respect and affection for ordinary Mexicans, they have little time for Mexican institutions, and it is the fact that American law does not extend south of the border that causes them to become outlaws in Mexico more than an innate inclination to break the law as such. When Boyd asks why the law cannot go into Mexico and apprehend their parents' murderers, Billy's answer is "[c]ause it's American law. It aint worth nothing in Mexico." Boyd wonders if Mexican law might do something for them, but Billy explains "[t]here aint no law in Mexico. It's just a pack of rogues" (C 176). Later, presenting the papers for one of their stolen horses to its new owner, the man simply dismisses the papers as of "no value" and takes the horse. "What the hell good are the papers without the horse," Billy asks when Boyd questions what they are to do without the documents: "you just got done seein what papers are worth in this country" (C 248). "It aint like home down here," Billy explains conclusively.

Given their insistence that they are homeless, it is suggestive that when faced with the absence of legal protection Billy invokes home as somewhere that Mexico is not. And given Billy's determination to repatriate Boyd's remains, it is clear that some notion of a home place continues to animate his actions. When Quijada questions the need to move Boyd's body, he suggests that "the dead have no nationality." Billy agrees, but adds that "their kin do" (C 387). In fact, Billy's nationality remains a marker of belonging despite his protestations of homelessness. "I'm an American," he tells the border guard at Columbus, New Mexico, even "if I don't look like it" (C 333), and his determination to enlist is an attempt to claim a home by right of citizenship, even if it is thwarted. The border guard tells Billy the country is at war, though Billy has already said he is going to sign up if he can "find an outfit that'll have me" before he hears the news (C 333). The intention to join the army is not an act of patriotic duty but a simple desire for reintegration. McCarthy's cowboys want to escape, but they want to come back.

The novels appear to endorse the free movement of Americans across international borderlines while accepting the static decrepitude of a "timeless" Mexico either uninterested or unable to cross into the modern world of the north. All crossings are undertaken by Anglos, and no border guards check Billy and John Grady's papers or question their travel plans; there are no spot checks or shakedowns, no customs officials. The unregenerate fantasy space of Old Mexico seems to lie before them with a passive historical vacancy, a land read only through the eyes of, even despite their apparent sympathy for the Mexican way of life, Anglo tourist-adventurers, counterinsurgent forces in Latin America seeking an authenticity foreclosed at home.[29] The mysterious women, the strange, picturesque peasants and cripples, the proud landowners, the corrupt officials, the occult tonalities of this dark fairy kingdom of good and evil offer John Grady, Billy and Boyd a space within which their domestic abjection can be injected with existential performative gravitas. Mexico offers, in its alterity, the right kind of evil to conquer, and the pimp, during the climactic duel in Cities of the Plain, sees straight through John Grady's Anglo fantasy. Functioning as a kind of self-deflating conclusion to the trilogy, Eduardo's speech appears to expose the novels' efforts to elevate McCarthy's down-at-heel cowboys to the status of chivalric heroes. In death, Eduardo suggests, "perhaps the suitor will see that it was his hunger for mysteries that has undone him." Drawn south by "[w]hores. Superstition. Finally death," behind the exotic projections the Mexican world "is very plain indeed." In a final sneering threat that calls up contemporary American fears of lawless Latin American hordes, Eduardo concludes that "we will devour you, my friend. You and all your pale empire" (CP 253).

It is tempting to hold on to the reading of Cole and Parham, Cole in particular, as carriers of American expansionist ideology and representatives of a wasted cowboy individualism retooled and recycled as agents of neoliberal redemption in the third world. Even the abject failure of their respective missions into Mexico does not undermine this conception, since an inability to control the chaos of the radically othered space south of the border has never been considered reason enough to doubt the righteousness of the effort. Certainly, Cole and Parham's disregard for the institutions of Mexican law and custom in favor of the "natural" justice of an ardent-hearted pursuit of the restitution of property and the object of one's desire suggests a willfully blind arrogance in the face of practically insuperable obstacles. If this were all The Border Trilogy offered then it would stand as an ambivalent and powerful indictment of American military and economic overreach.

What complicates this reading is the extent to which Cole and Parham are othered within the United States, despite their potential as symbolically recuperable markers of innate American values and their tendency to want to find a home in the United States. Like the blank spaces on the map produced by postwar security, they are the outside that remains inside, the waste that confirms productivity. They are homeless at home, strangely familiar. To an extent, Cole's inability to abide by the practical logic of the grid, even though he seeks confirmation of his legitimacy through its institutions—the lawyer at the beginning of All the Pretty Horses, the judge at the end; Mac Johnson in Cities of the Plain— reveals to the reader, if not to Cole himself, the contradictions of a national ideology mistaken as "natural."

While Cole continues to trust his instincts and follow his heart, for Billy Parham the heart is precisely what dispossesses him. If Cole is ardent-hearted, a measure of how he understands his actions as justified, Billy Parham is literally brokenhearted. Parham looks, we are told, "filled with a terrible sadness. As if he harbored news of some horrendous loss that no one else had heard of yet. Some vast tragedy not of fact or incident or event but of the way the world was" (C 177). On his third attempt to enlist at a third recruiting station, Billy pleads: "I dont have anyplace to go. I think I need to be in the army. If I'm goin to die anyways why not use me? I aint afraid" (C 341). By this point the army offers the only available home to Billy, but his heart's "irregularity" prohibits him from entering the disciplinary regime that would reconstruct him as a soldier and as a citizen. This failed attempt at submission to the dominant order—in order fulfill the "need" for a home and to be given a "use"—marks Parham as irrecoverably outside. Although he says he is not returning to

Mexico, by the spring of 1945, when "there was hardly a ranch house in all of that country that did not have a gold star in the window" (C 351), Parham heads back south to find Boyd. Discovering only bones, the retrieval of Boyd's body performs a symbolic repatriation for Billy that the army cannot offer: the dead may have no nationality, but their kin do, and Boyd's reburial on American soil—after the issue of a death certificate that reinstalls Boyd (and Billy) within the American legal framework—seals a hole in the border between order and chaos Boyd's disappearance had opened up.

Bauman argues that the nation-state, like all forms of sociation, is produced by separating inside from outside, by deciding on a division between us and them, friends and enemies.[30] Alongside the opposition of friend and enemy, however, Bauman places a third term, the stranger, an "undecidable" that disrupts the order produced by the opposition between us and them, "poison[ing] the comfort of order with suspicion of chaos."[31] Cole and Parham are both dispossessed and made homeless; they are made strange to the extent that in modern America, Billy looks like "something out of the past," an "outlandish figure" who represents what contemporary Americans "envied most and what they most reviled. If their hearts went out to him it was yet true that for very small cause they might also have killed him" (C 170). On his second return to the United States any vestige of empathy has gone and cars give him a wide berth; Billy is "a thing wholly alien in that landscape, something "from an older time" Americans have only heard or read about (C 334).

It is not surprising, given this throwback quality, that Cole and his father compare themselves to the Comanches, and the attraction of Mexico is not just that south of the border there might remain vestiges of a ranching culture that retains meaning for them. Mexico is also the excluded outside of the United States, the Mexicans and Indians that live there representing for Cole and Parham, I would argue, a mode of noninstrumental existence that the discarded youths come to identify with. José Limón has argued as much in his discussion of Cole's "impeccably fluent" Spanish as a sign of John Grady's Mexicanness, and Billy is proud of his "fullblooded Mexican" grandmother "who didnt speak no English" (C 419).[32] While Cole and Parham may well read Mexico as a fictional site of authenticity, at the same time Mexico provides a space in which their wasted lives are corroborated by the wasted landscapes and people they find there. They are not and cannot be Comanches and Mexicans, of course, however much they may come to identify with that which is outside the dominant discourse of the United States. If they are strangers at home, in Mexico Cole and Parham are read simply as "Americans." Paradoxically, it is only when they are outside the United States that they are recognized as properly belonging on the inside. They make sense as Americans only when they are not in America. The serial crossing of the border, then, operates as an oscillation between being outside inside (stranger) and inside outside (American). Cole and Parham are outside American society when they are in America and inside (to the extent that they are representative of American society) when in Mexico. It might be said that for Cole especially this is an attractive proposition inasmuch as his heroic romantic actions in Mexico perform an American natural virtue that at home would be read as a mere simulation (the "all-American cowboy") while in Mexico they can continue to function as if they retain their force, performing justified civilizing acts upon an unregenerate nature.

What is also clear from this is that Cole and Parham are in fact no more at home in Mexico than they are in the United States; in each country they remain excluded. In *The Crossing*, an old Indian warns Parham that although he is "huérfano" (orphan), "he must cease his wandering and make for himself some place in the world" (c 134). It is worth pointing out that Billy does not know at this stage in the novel that he is, in fact, an orphan; the old man either has access to some sort of supernatural knowledge or he reads Billy as existentially orphaned. He continues to counsel Billy that since the world can only be known through people, he should "live with men and not just pass among them" (c 135). The problem, of course, is that "passing among" people, as opposed to living with them, is a fairly good way of describing the nature of modern social organization.

The Point of Convergence

While World War II and its aftermath shape the narrative of *The Border Trilogy*, the direct effects of the war itself on returning combatants, while registered, is not extensively addressed by McCarthy, whose protagonists are either too young or too damaged to fight. Nevertheless, just as Abbey's Vogelin comes to identify with the Apache, John Grady Cole and Billy Parham likewise imagine themselves, and are imagined, to be updated versions of the nineteenth-century "vanishing" Indian. The *Border Trilogy*'s interrogation of the deracinated relationship to place felt by the newly extraneous Anglo population during and after World War II mirrors, I think, earlier influential narratives by Native American writers similarly concerned with the impact of military-industrial power on traditional social forms.

The irreparable rupture between past and present produced by the experience of war overseas and the militarization of Western space is the subject of two of the defining works of the so-called Native American literary renaissance of the late 1960s and 1970s: N. Scott Momaday's Pulitzer Prize–winning *House Made of Dawn* (1966) and Leslie Marmon Silko's *Ceremony* (1977). Rudolfo Anaya's influential Chicano novel *Bless Me, Ultima* (1972) also directly addresses the impact of the war on traditional rural life and, like Momaday's and Silko's works, approaches the trauma visited upon soldiers, local communities, and the land by means of a culturally syncretic novelistic reworking of folk rituals of witchcraft and healing. Published at the point when the Cold War justification for sacrifice (of land and prior claims to it; of constituencies with issues at odds with national security) in the name of American nuclear supremacy was dismantled by Vietnam, these novels return to World War II as a means of articulating the moment when that justification crystallized the state's formation of the West as integrally other. If the war makes McCarthy's Americans into Indians, these novels explore the way the war made Indians into Americans.

For Native American and other minority servicemen returning from combat in the Pacific to the newly militarized West, the physical displacement registered by Abbey and McCarthy is complicated in a number of ways. The cultural violence experienced through enlistment in the American military serves to underscore, in Momaday, Silko, and Anaya, the always already exceptional status of Indians and Mexican Americans, who are placed simultaneously as inside (Americans) and outside (the racialized other) nationally defined military identity. The promise of inclusion and escape from structural poverty offered at recruitment as the payoff for a demonstration of patriotic solidarity is in all cases never realized. Instead, existing racialized divisions are reinforced and further confused by, especially in the case of Silko's Tayo, troubling identification with the Japanese enemy. Indeed, on return home, Tayo, Momaday's Abel, and Anaya's farmers find themselves not only threatened by the proximity of expanding military bases and uranium production, but abandoned to their private suffering by inadequate veteran services and communities that have no means of comprehending the experiences that have produced broken men rather than assimilated heroes.

Abel and Tayo are, like Bauman's anomalies, strangers on their return from World War II. They are psychologically damaged, traumatized by their experiences of war and by being hurled outside the contained and traditional world of the pueblo. They are both troubled by involuntary memories of violence that prevent them from reentering life in the United States. Abel has a recurring nightmare of a German tank looming upon him; the least sensory provocation reminds Tayo of his half-brother Rocky's death at the hands of Japanese soldiers and his conviction that it was his uncle Josiah and not a Japanese prisoner that was shot in his presence. In both cases, official help in the form of doctors and medication for Tayo, social workers and relocation to Los Angeles for Abel, fails to reach them. The Indians remain in a purgatory where past and present are scrambled and their lives prior to the war beyond reach, even if they can be recalled. Abel can remember everything before his departure for the army "whole and in detail." But the recent past is an "intervention of days and years without meaning, of awful calm and collision, time always immediate and confused, that he could not put together in his mind."[33] Tayo, similarly, "could get no rest as long as the memories were tangled with the present." The more he tries to untangle things, the more they become entwined so that he "had to sweat to think of something that wasn't unraveled or tied in knots to the past."[34] Both are frequently drunk and violent, "inarticulate" (HMD 57) or "invisible" (Ce 15).

The tortured Lupito in Bless Me, Ultima is yet another instance of the war damaged veteran, who ends up pursued by his own townspeople after his inexplicable murder of the sheriff. "'Japanese sol'jer, Japanese sol'jer!' he cried, 'I am wounded. Come help me,'" but despite Narciso's plea that "[y]ou know that the war made him sick," he is shot dead.[35] The "war-sickness" is recognized in all who return, like Antonio's brothers, who become dissolute and agitated, wasting their service money in the pool hall. "They were like lost men who went and came and said nothing" (BMU 65). Of the three veterans, León suffers the most, howling and screaming in the night "like a wild animal" so that his mother has "to go to him and hold him like a baby until he could sleep again" (BMU 66).

While it is clearly the war that has caused this destruction of self and connection with the communities to which they have returned, the war is not read as a discrete historical event with singular consequences. Instead, the war is positioned as a particularly brutal instance of a far longer process of deracination. Like *Blood Meridian*, both *House Made of Dawn* and *Ceremony* are concerned to embed the events of their respective narratives into a deeper and vaster conception of time. As in McCarthy's novel, this is in part achieved through an attention to cosmological movement and an insistence on the long duration of the landscape. Both *House Made of Dawn* and *Ceremony* begin and end with sunrise, signifying not only the cycle of regeneration completed by each protagonist as he achieves ceremonial healing but also, more generally, the persistence of repetition and continuity despite the incursions of Anglo teleological history into the lives of Indian communities. While *Blood Meridian* conjures with a discourse that would naturalize violent conquest as a manifestation of the condition of being, the two Indian novels insist on a long historical context as necessary for understanding Indian belonging—a "house made of dawn"—and resistance to conquest. As such, World War II is in neither novel the root cause of the protagonists' dispossession but simply the latest manifestation of a five-hundred-year struggle for survival.

In *House Made of Dawn*, even imported animals—"the beasts of burden and of trade, the horse and the sheep, the dog and the cat"—are "late-coming things" and "have an alien and inferior aspect, a poverty of vision and of instinct, by which they are estranged from the wild land, and made tentative" (HMD 56). This is a place where ancient remains are not the detritus of a dead past but signs of temporary abandonment, "as if the prehistoric civilization had gone out among the hills for a little while and would return." Then everything "would be restored to an older age, and time would have returned upon itself and a bad dream of invasion and change would have been dissolved in an hour before the dawn" (HMD 56). The temporary nature of white conquest is registered by both *House Made of Dawn* and *Ceremony* (a notion Silko pursues in *Almanac of the Dead*), duration itself being put to the service of resistance: what is five hundred years compared to a "tenure" of "twenty-five thousand years" (HMD 56)? The refusal of the Indians to change their "essential way of life" and their capacity to absorb outside influences, such as Christianity, rather than allow them to obliterate the old customs, is offered as a model of tenacious defiance that attempts at material and ideological domination cannot overcome. The Indians "have assumed the names and gestures of their enemies, but have held on to their own, secret souls; and in this there is a resistance and an overcoming, a long outwaiting" (HMD 56). In *Ceremony*, when one of the doctors reads a report blaming alcohol and the war for the growth of violence among Indian veterans, Tayo senses that there is more to it than local circumstances, that "[i]t's been going on for a long time" (Ce 53).

What complicates things further is that the long struggle to maintain the singularity of tribal identity is compromised biologically by Abel and Tayo, who are both mixed blood. Abel's absent father was from an unknown tribe, "an outsider," making him and his mother "somehow foreign and strange" (HMD 15). It is also likely that his great-grandfather was the corrupt priest Nicolás. Tayo's mother, dead by the time of the novel's opening, ended up a Gallup prostitute, his father undoubtedly one of her white clients. Brought up by his mother's sister, Tayo for her is shameful evidence of the loss of blood integrity and collective unity. In each case, then, postwar return is blocked at the outset by the protagonists' inherent strangeness; they are, in Julia Kristeva's words, strangers to themselves.

When Rocky, the full blood he enlists to protect, is killed in the war, Tayo must return to the family with yet more evidence that he is in the wrong place. Tayo has a more profound connection with the old ways than Rocky, despite or perhaps even because of his divided inheritance. Like Abel, Tayo is a "longhair" (HMD 135) who is driven to adhere to the traditional rituals of attachment even as those rituals seem unattainable and scrambled. Abel is not aware enough of the nature of his confusion when he kills the albino he believes is the embodiment of the evil that pursues him. He still thinks he can safely identify the enemy, and the mistake lands him in jail and then parole in Los Angeles. Tayo, on the other hand, through the long mediation of Ku'oosh, Betonie, and Montano, manages to avoid becoming another victim, "a drunk Indian war veteran settling an old feud" (Ce 253), by refusing to kill Emo.

Tayo's rejection of murder is a sign that the tangled forces he has failed to understand throughout the novel have begun to make sense. Geopolitics begins at home in *Ceremony*, and the novel seeks to map the global network that links the interiority of its protagonist with environmental despoliation at home and war overseas. Runoff from uranium mines has ruined the land, and a generation of Pueblo men has been destroyed by the conflict overseas. Ku'oosh, the old medicine man, tries to heal Tayo with the old ceremony but has to admit that "there are some things we can't cure like we used to . . . not since the white people came" (Ce 38). Neither science nor tradition can reach Tayo, but ostensibly more unorthodox methods are more successful. Both Betonie and Montano offer Tayo instruction and love. As symbol of the Corn Mother, Montano gives Tayo a power "emanating from the mesas and arroyos" that replaces "the rhythm that had been interrupted long ago" (Ce 227), but the reintegrative power of Monano's lessons can only make sense after Tayo has worked through the complex argument put forward by the shaman Betonie.

Living in the hills overlooking the shanty town where Tayo and his mother used to live along the river next to the Gallup dump, Betonie still wears the traditional clothes, creates the curative sand paintings, and uses the old ceremonial paraphernalia. But Betonie also uses modern things as healing devices: Coke bottles, phone books, and calendars with pictures of Indians on them. When Tayo questions the use of such nontraditional items for his ceremonies, Betonie responds that the intrusion of white people meant "the elements in this world began to shift; and it became necessary to create new ceremonies." While Betonie's innovations are mistrusted, "things which don't shift and grow are dead things" (Ce 126), and fear of adaptation only serves the enemy. Being half Mexican positions Betonie, along with Abel, Tayo, and Billy Parham, as another stranger, suggesting that it is in fact the impure of blood that carry the means of survival. Just as an unwillingness to adapt rituals to circumstances is seen by Betonie as a form of suicide, so too his hybrid identity and willingness to live in full view of the depravity of contemporary

Indian poverty are suggestions of ways in which the medicine man might be politically configured as a figure of engaged opposition to both ossified tradition and capitalist development. Indeed, as Betonie understands things, the reification of tradition is in fact a function of domination: "[t]hat's what the witchery is counting on: that we will cling to the ceremonies the way they were, and then their power will triumph, and the people will be no more" (Ce 126).

While the Pueblos cannot ignore the impact that white contact has had upon their culture, neither can they completely abandon their old rituals and still survive. Betonie's solution is an assemblage of elements from both cultures, a deliberate contamination of ethnic purity. As the sorcerer, Betonie is the anomaly who overturns received definitions of value and waste. Anglos refuse to live on the garbage-strewn periphery where the Indians live, but for Betonie the dump is not the excluded margin, it is "that town down there that is out of place" (Ce 118). The bricolage of Betonie's ceremonial paraphernalia is no more or less than a junk pile of dead objects irradiated by his will to produce a counterhistory from the excluded detritus of the dominant order.

It is Betonie's notion of contaminated enlightenment that gives Tayo the insight to read across the fragments of his experience and grasp the constellation of forces that has produced him. At its epicenter is the bomb. After his long and painful debriefing, Tayo's healing ceremony is complete when he cries with relief "at finally seeing the pattern" that connects the alienating deterioration of the Pueblo and military operations overseas: the Trinity site is a mere three hundred miles southeast, and "deep in the Jemez Mountains, on land the Government took from Cochiti Pueblo" squat the laboratories that created the bomb. The "simplicity" of the connections Tayo makes between his own wartime trauma, the "powdery yellow uranium" in the rocks wrenched from the earth around him, the atomic program, and the devastation of Hiroshima and Nagasaki, "struck him deep inside his chest" (Ce 245–46). Tayo had been "so close to it" that the open secret of ascendant American military-industrial power and his place within it had been impossible to see. Standing at his own ground zero, Tayo "had arrived at the point of convergence where the fate of all living things, and even the earth, had been laid" (Ce 246). The apocalyptic power of nuclear weapons has not only been achieved by yet another assault on Indian sovereignty, cordoning off and irradiating great swathes of terrain; this power has, in a crushing inversion, brought everything together in one final communion. After Los Alamos, "human beings were one clan again, united by the fate the destroyers planned for all of them, for all living things; united by a circle of death that devoured people in cities twelve thousand miles away, victims who had never known these mesas, who had never seen the delicate colors of the rocks which boiled up their slaughter" (Ce 246).

Not only does Tayo's awakening confirm that the Southwestern desert has become a fulcrum upon which global geopolitics turns, he also identifies the fluidity with which power surges without hindrance: "no boundaries, only transitions through all distances and time" (Ce 246). This realization is a kind of liberation inasmuch as it frees Tayo from the trauma of atomized existence produced by an apparently absent cause. But it is also a curse since the immensity of the threat, as we have already seen in Morrow and McMahon, is so profound as to offer solace only in death. Betonie has trained Tayo to see the pattern, and this knowledge does indeed preserve him. But the contaminated enlightenment achieved here through a counternarrative that shows "the way all the stories fit together" (Ce 246) offers only momentary relief from the pulverizing fact of achieved catastrophe.

For Billy Parham, who inadvertently witnesses the Trinity blast at the end of The Crossing, the strangeness of the explosion as a false dawn suggests both the skewing of the natural order achieved by the bomb and the impossible light cast upon the world in its aftermath. Tarantulas are caught stricken and birds awaken in the "white light of the desert noon" that rapidly draws away even as Parham watches. Noon becomes "an alien dusk and now an alien dark," leaving an "inexplicable darkness" until "the right and godmade sun did rise, for all and without distinction" (C 425–26).[36]

The Crossing ends not with Tayo's cry of "relief" but with Billy weeping in the road, for his own ceremonial wanderings have not yielded the same capacity to connect up the fragments of his story with their wider significance. Whether this weeping is an expression of mourning for his dead brother, his lost family and home, or of a more profound desperation, it is hard to say. But, as is common in The Crossing, the reader is privy to things Billy cannot know or fails to know: in this case, that the flash of unnatural light inaugurates a new age of insuperable dread and anxiety. Billy's long quest for order—for things (horses, graves) to reside where they belong—is now, finally, entirely incommensurate with the death of certainty produced by the bomb. Today the "right" sun rose, but it may not rise tomorrow.

Parsons's *In the Shadows of the Sun* extrapolates on Silko's linking of Hiroshima and Trinity by doubling the act of witnessing. Jack sees the Hiroshima blast from a POW mining camp in Omuta, while Baylis experiences the Trinity explosion "like a primitive witnessing an eclipse" (ISS 181). While there is no response from Jack to what he has seen, Parsons borrows verbatim the dialogue recorded by the Los Alamos physicist Joseph O. Hirschfelder to describe the response to the Trinity blast by the locals: "[y]ou boys must have been up to something this morning. . . . Sun came up in the west and went on down again" (ISS 182).[37] Baylis himself offers the response we do not get from Billy Parham: "'You see something like that and it feels wrong. Like you ain't supposed to be seeing it.' He shook his head. 'No. More like it ain't supposed to happen, [something] that don't have no place in the way of things'" (ISS 195).

While Billy and Baylis witness the false dawn of the blast itself, Tayo sees a combination of its historical preconditions and aftershocks, a pattern he "ain't supposed to be seeing" that underscores the global reach of American power and the enfolding of the local concerns of the Pueblos into international geopolitics. Here the Japanese victims of Hiroshima and Nagasaki and the Pueblo Indians become modalities of wasted life, "the lines of cultures and worlds . . . drawn in flat dark lines on fine light sand, converging in the middle of witchery's final ceremonial sand painting" (Ce 246). The Trinity blast has produced a world map of catastrophe on the surface of the New Mexican desert, the blank space that marks the eradication of collateral casualties. Betonie has trained Tayo to read such a map but, despite the instruction Billy has received on his travels, he appears to remain unequipped for anything other than mourning. Silko intends a more adversarial response than McCarthy and imagines an achieved ceremony that can turn the destroyers' own witchery upon themselves, a proposition pursued at length in her next novel, *Almanac of the Dead*.

The portents of a nuclear winter registered at the end of *Ceremony* and *The Crossing*, of course, does not come to pass, at least not in the form of global annihilation the Trinity test appeared to foreshadow. Instead, what Tayo and Billy, along with Jack and Baylis, witness is the beginning of a long proleptic fall: the condition of anticipated disaster. As Ryan Bishop and John Phillips have suggested, with the invention of the bomb, "modern existence occurs entirely within the rhetoric of the false dawn, warding off at all costs some actual dawn, some dawn that would end all dawns."[38] This rhetoric is what concludes *The Crossing* but notably not the trilogy; what remains after Trinity is, as Tayo already knows, the permanent dread of a disaster that can only be imagined, never experienced.

6. LOOMINGS

Dread in West Texas

What is a pure war? It is a war of a single utterance: Fear! Fear! Fear!
Paul Virilio

Confronted with the permanent prospect of imminent nuclear destruction, the reassurances of 1950s civil defense literature that "your tomorrow may depend on today's preparedness" are little more than nostalgia for a time when vigilance could avert disaster. Dwarfed by the immensity of nuclear war, inert anticipation instead replaces future-oriented thinking. While Paul Boyer argues that acceptance of the bomb came quickly after initial protests, Allan Winkler contends that the threat of the bomb pervaded the postwar period, albeit with varying levels of intensity, through to the end of the Cold War.[1] Boyer's point is well taken, but a waning of concern is not necessarily the same as a dissipation of the sense of threat. Although the high anxiety of the early 1950s attempted to muster a practical response to nuclear threat by finding domestic applications for atomic power and by mobilizing the civilian soldiers of the Cold War to build or buy shelters and take part in evacuations and drills, the simple absence of the object of fear could only result in a settling of concern into a quieter but no less disturbing unease.

The state of being becalmed ought to suggest peace, but what the unstable security of the Cold War actually manufactures, as we have seen, is an uncanny covert spectacle of wasted land and people that stand for the realized catastrophe that looms in peripheral vision as the proleptic threat of what might still come to pass. Furthermore, despite the fact that there was no hiding place from the bomb, the notion of an ICBM specifically dedicated to the annihilation of Albuquerque or Amarillo gives special potency to the sense of imminent danger experienced by those living in the militarized West. In this chapter I want to focus on novels that, at very different moments of the Cold War, register the pervasiveness of nuclear dread even as it is displaced into the ritualized dangers of, respectively, football and storm chasing. Don DeLillo's *End Zone* (1972) and William Hauptman's *Storm Season* (1992) both feature protagonists with an obsessive fascination with the end of the world and the jargon of destruction invented by the U.S. military-scientific institutions of the Cold War. Both are interested in what we might call the theology of the bomb as an object of sublime contemplation and as an agent of actual and linguistic apocalypse. Both novels are set in Texas: *End Zone* in the deserts of west Texas, *Storm Season* in the panhandle towns around Amarillo. The location is important in each case, for both novels are interested in ostensibly remote and isolated places as the sites of an unexpected proximity to nuclear dread. Even the most particularized scraps of dusty Texan landscape—indeed, precisely in such places—is the locus of Cold War cultural formation to be found, whether in the militarized passion plays of Vietnam-era small town football in *End Zone* or in the blue-collar anomie of *Storm Season*'s Reagan-generation protagonists.

In each of these novels, then, the dreary monotony of everyday life is shot through with an awareness of possible catastrophe where, as Melville writes in *Moby-Dick*, the calm that "only apparently" precedes the storm is more awful than the storm itself, for "the calm is but the wrapper and envelope of the storm; and contained it in itself."[2] This terrible sense of stasis is what Paul Saint-Amour has called the "conditional space of catastrophe."[3] Discussing the uncanny and apparently inexplicable sense of dread experienced in Hiroshima before the atomic bomb was dropped, Saint-Amour explains that such "weird anticipation" became a "general characteristic" of Cold War experience in the sense that symptoms of trauma associated with disaster were registered in advance—indeed, in the complete absence—of the traumatic event itself.[4] As such, Cold War dread can be described as a "proleptic traumatic symptom, of a repressed that returns from the future."[5] This symptom is a calm without a storm whereby agency is retarded by a scrambling of temporal order that gives a dreadful glimpse of the future.

The institutions and practices of small town life have long offered an index of so-called middle American values that is predicated on continuity and stability. While urban centers have long functioned as a source of moral panic, small towns operate as a guarantor of the survival of bedrock American virtues—in particular, individual liberty enjoyed within a self-regulating democratic community—that are somehow inoculated from the incursions of subversive external forces. In *End Zone* and *Storm*

Season, however, the calm of relatively isolated small town existence does not produce security but instead generates the sense of proleptic dread described by Saint-Amour.

While DeLillo is vague about the precise location of *End Zone*'s Logos College, H. G. Bissinger's *Friday Night Lights* (1990), his bestselling narrative of the 1988 high school football season in Odessa, Texas, captures the fanatical devotion the sport enjoys in a region distinguished by little else besides a historical contempt for its climate and a legacy of economic instability produced by the extraction industries' boom and bust cycles. Odessa "was still a place," writes Bissinger, "that seemed on the edge of the frontier, a paradoxical mixture of the Old South and the Wild West, friendly to a fault but fiercely independent, God-Fearing and propped up by the Baptist beliefs in family and flag but hell-raising, spiced with the edge of violence but naïve and thoroughly unpretentious."[6] This combination of conservative values, frontier grit, and what Bissinger calls a "feel of lingering sadness" produced by geographical isolation is precisely what *Storm Season* identifies as the maximal conditions for Reagan's born-again Cold War.[7] Embodying the contradictions of neoliberal conservatism, the high rates of crime, alcoholism, suicide, and divorce in Odessa sit side by side with anti-government, anti–civil rights sentiment. This is perhaps closer to the truth of small town existence. As Bissinger notes, Odessa "evoked the kind of America Ronald Reagan always seemed to have in mind during his presidency, a place still rooted in the sweet nostalgia of the fifties," where high school girls are expected to be dumber than their boyfriends and teenage honor is measured in beer consumption rather than cocaine snorting.[8]

DeLillo does not venture too far off campus in *End Zone*, preferring to focus on the notionally monastic isolation of the football team's warrior-priest mentality, the wasted environment providing the necessary ascetic edge to the game's militarized devotional machismo. Hauptman's panhandle is more directly engaged with the particular cultural matrix noted by Bissinger. Amarillo's pivotal role in the production of America's nuclear arsenal makes the Texan location of these novels significant as examinations of yet another remote Western point of convergence in global geopolitics. Even in its remoteness, the region is defined by its status as a prime target for Soviet missiles throughout the Cold War.

While the facts of nuclear testing were kept secret, this secrecy was mediated in the national consciousness by a narrative of "containment" anticipated in the social organization of the Los Alamos installation and developed, as Alan Nadel argues, "to control the fear and responsibility endemic to possessing atomic power." Through such a narrative, whereby "insecurity was absorbed by internal security" and "apocalypse and utopia by a Christian theological mandate," rhetorical containment could "foreclose dissent, preempt dialogue, and preclude contradiction. The United States, empowered by the binding energy of the universe, was to become the universal container."[9] It became the task of the United States to both guard the power it had created and to monitor the possible employment of power others might obtain. Nuclear guardianship and the containment of its dangers thus involved both concealment of what the United States possessed and a watchful eye directed against what others could get their hands on. As such, as Nadel claims, "the atomic age mandated a gaze—a nuclear gaze—that defined the difference between dangerous and nondangerous activity, universal and specific jurisdiction, containment and proliferation. At the same time, this gaze was also the product of the universal jurisdiction that it was supposed to create, because that jurisdiction was the only possible condition under which the nuclear gaze could perform its most important task: to prohibit actions with ambiguous motives."[10] Suspicion of ambiguity as a security threat patently requires an elimination of anything considered undecidable, and the choreographed moves of DeLillo's footballers, and the way football is figured in *End Zone* as an analog for the rational dreams of deterrence theorists, offers one instance of how the attempt to minimize unpredictable outcomes can be read as symptomatic of the Cold War nuclear gaze. Nuclearism's structuring of the entirety of everyday life is, as Heidegger put it, the "grossest of all gross confirmations" of the enframing of the lifeworld by technology.[11]

While nuclear weapons and the threat they pose are real, the paradox that gives nuclearism an eschatological, not to mention literary, dimension is that nuclear war has never occurred and remains the threat from the future. Derrida's point that the logic of deterrence is one of "rhetorical-strategic escalation" is confirmed by the interpretive excesses of containment discourse, where all aspects of social and cultural as well as political life are scrutinized in order to identify possible latent threats.[12] The proliferation of narratives about security and nuclear disaster defers the moment when all narrative must stop: the moment when nuclear war annihilates everything. The paradox of total nuclear war is that attempts to historicize it must fail because it is the event that ends historicity.[13] What is left is the fable of nuclearism and its interpretations, the social and cultural texts that produce the simulacrum of nuclear annihilation that must endlessly defer and displace the "real" thing. If the point of containment culture's nuclear gaze is to identify and eliminate "actions with ambiguous motives" and thereby maintain a nervous stability of meaning, it is a project doomed to failure since the problem with fables is that they refuse any singularity of interpretation. At the same time, rhetorical escalation succeeds inasmuch as it substitutes fables for bombs and imagined threats for actual war.

The Eschatology of Football

Containment culture's dream of a language made safe from ambiguity is exposed in End Zone, a novel awash with jargon of various kinds, each hopelessly wedded to a metadiscourse of war it both confirms and displaces. DeLillo's Gary Harkness, not unlike McMahon's Tim MacLaurin and Morrow's Kip and Brice, is an alienated college footballer compressed to near-nothingness by the weight of his culture's nuclear dread. Drawn to the stripped-down ethos of systematic clarity offered by the coach at Logos College, Harkness conceives of his place on the team as a form of desert exile that provides respite from anomie through "simplicity, repetition, solitude, starkness, discipline upon discipline."[14] Football functions as a metonym for DeLillo, and for many of the characters in End Zone, for American managerial capitalism in its military-industrial mode, and the novel yokes sport, nuclear threat, and self-sacrifice together as a kind of metaphysics of victory that absorbs individuality into the comfort zone of complete acquiescence.[15]

The intricate strategy of the football game is, like the Cold War arms race, a system of complex moves and countermoves that relies on its own regulatory logic, its own self-legitimating vocabulary of technical jargon and euphemism. Football is seen as a "paramilitary complex" (EZ 22) known "for its assault-technology motif " (EZ 111). One of the players, Bing Jackmin, satirically describes the team as comprising "substandard industrial robots" (EZ 35). The players are like "things with metal claws," reified war machines, yet also somehow related to ancient ritualistic combat, involved in "psychomythical" or "hyperatavistic" warriorship, a cult "devoted to pagan forms of technology" (EZ 36, 63). "What we do on that field harks back" (EZ 36), says Jackmin, who sees football as an antiquated form of gladiatorial combat: "they fatten us up and then put us in the arena together. They train us to kill, more or less" (EZ 63).

If football harks back, Harkness embodies this condition of nostalgic attachment to authentic action in his name, an abstract noun that also situates him as a listener or sentinel, someone waiting for a message or sign. As part of the standing reserve of the Cold War, Harkness is, like everyone else, on guard. Along with the Air Force ROTC classes in modern warfare Harkness audits but will not, literally, take credit for, football trains a submission to systematic and logical yet unseen networks of abstract purity while at the same time appealing to rituals of blood and honor. The discipline inculcated at Logos is geared toward submission to Cold War rationality as the necessary means of preserving the status quo; in effect, the End Zone of nuclear stalemate and citizenship evacuated of agency.

At the same time, a longing for an end to the dread of nuclear apocalypse leads Harkness and others in the novel to become fascinated with representations of horror. After reading a book for a course "in modes of disaster technology," Harkness is worried to find that he enjoys the reading: "I liked reading about the deaths of tens of millions of people. I liked dwelling on the destruction of great cities. Five to twenty million dead. Fifty to a hundred million dead. Ninety percent population loss" (EZ 20). The nuclear sublime for Harkness is experienced in the dizzying statistics and catastrophe scenarios produced in the book that, clearly, cannot be about nuclear war (which has not taken place) but about the "possibilities of a nuclear war" that might happen. The impossibility of translating the unthinkable has produced a lexicon of euphemisms that become terms in a poetics of the ineffable. The names of weapons also hark back—"Titan, Spartan, Poseidon"—and terms like "thermal hurricane, overkill, circular error probability, post-attack environment, stark deterrence, does-rate contours, kill-ratio, spasm war" (EZ 21) produce an "almost sensual" thrill of pleasure and fascination that "nourished itself on the black bones of revulsion and dread" (EZ 43).

The asceticism encouraged by football and the desert itself appears to have produced an excessive desire for apocalyptic purgation. The west Texas desert is described as being "in the middle of the middle of nowhere," and in such a place, "suggestive of the end of recorded time," Harkness experiences "a splendid sense of remoteness" that "fir[es] my soul" (EZ 30): "[e]xile in a real place, a place of few bodies and many stones, is just an extension (a packaging) of the other exile, the state of being separated from whatever is left of the center of one's own history. I found comfort in West Texas. There was even pleasure in the daily punishment on the field. I felt that I was better for it, reduced in complexity, a warrior" (EZ 31). The minimal desert landscape, precision-tuned terms in the nuclear warfare textbooks, and the equally directional verbal orders given by the coach on the field all provide for Harkness a prophylactic of regulated simplicity that protects him from the dreadful chaos of the real. The ascetic convention of the desert as purifying space—a theo-geography of sanctified absence—is as abstract as the tactical jargons of sport and Cold War hostilities.

DeLillo has said that the characters in *End Zone* are "pieces of jargon. They engage in wars of jargon with each other."[16] Strategists like Staley and Herman Kahn, whose book *On Escalation* Staley draws on in his gaming, argues Mark Osteen, "actually prevent our thinking about nuclear holocaust by camouflaging it with pseudo-objective terminology. The habit of thinking in jargon encourages them to conceive of war as a perfect, rule-bound structure, occurring within white lines that demarcate the thinkable from the unthinkable." In this way, Osteen continues, "jargon itself is a weapon: the violence it does to meaning, and the simplifications it effects on morality and responsibility, harden the mind to accept, even welcome, apocalypse."[17]

In response to the paramilitary conception of football as a displaced mode of warfare, the novel offers biology teacher Alan Zapalac's more skeptical view that "[w]arfare is warfare. We don't need substitutions because we've got the real thing" (EZ 111). For Zapalac, as for DeLillo's "exemplary spectator," sport is merely an illusion "that order is possible" (EZ 112). Zapalac provides a resistant and ironic counterpoint to strategists like Creed and Staley, rejecting the closed systems that seek an abstract ideal order in favor of an open universe where millions of years ago "we were nourished by the heavens" as "tons of chemical materials" crashed to earth from outer space. While football combines atavistic warrior ritual and systems theory, Zapalac's compression of the ancient and futuristic is more in keeping with deep ecology; he imagines "the last living organisms, the spores and hydrozoans left behind after our protectors protect us into oblivion. We'll all end as astroplankton, clouds of dusty stuff drifting through space" (EZ 159). This tendency to script the event of nuclear war into a cosmic narrative of perpetual creation and destruction is also there in Harkness, who consoles himself by considering that the "universe was born in violence. Stars die violently. Elements are created out of cosmic violence" (EZ 121). For Zapalac, impending nuclear disaster is not a theologically sanctioned end-time that hygienically wipes the slate of a fallen humanity while a vengeful God retrieves the rapturous elect at the last minute. Instead, it is another historical contingency, as random and uncontrollable as the prehistoric comets that flung alien life-carrying carbons down on the planet millennia ago. For Zapalac what is interesting is the possible post-human life of unimagined futures.

Closer to home, Zapalac also rejects the Cold War demonization of the Soviets, arguing that it is America itself that poses the real threat: "[i]f anybody kills us on a grand scale it'll be the Pentagon. On a small scale, watch out for your local police" (EZ 159–60). Articulating a kind of countercultural fatalism grounded in a view of entropic decline, Zapalac believes that "[m]an's biotic potential diminishes as everything else increases" (EZ 160). Nuclearism, for Zapalac, is the point where science fiction "is just beginning to catch up with the Old Testament," and where the nineteenth century catastrophist argument backed a version of creationism, Zapalac's neocatastrophism hinges on the environmental collapse accelerated by science: "[s]ee artificial nitrates run off into the rivers and oceans. See carbon dioxide melt the polar ice caps. See the world's mineral reserves dwindle. See war, famine and plague. See barbaric hordes defile the temple of the virgins. See wild stallions mount the prairie dogs. I said science fiction but I guess I meant science. Anyway, there's some kind of mythical and/or historic circle-thing being completed here" (EZ 160). Zapalac's entropic vision of a scientifically produced end time is little more than a politically tuned-in version of Staley's reading of the "bombs as a kind of god." Out of nuclear proliferation comes a "theology of fear," Staley observes, and we "begin to capitulate to the overwhelming presence. It's so powerful. It dwarfs us so much. We say let the god have his way" (EZ 80). The nuclear threat has become so pervasive and incomprehensible that acquiescence in the face of an unimaginable and extra-human power has become the only possible response, both for critics like Zapalac and self-styled warriors like Staley.

Staley's father was one of the crew on the Nagasaki mission, and is thus well placed to understand how war is the "ultimate realization of modern technology" (EZ 83). Like the footballers, he is nostalgic for a time when war was "the great challenge and great evaluator" of manhood. Now, Staley complains, no one wants to fight and men prove themselves by making money or in displacement activities like skydiving or hunting. Even the contest of opposing ideologies can no longer be put forward as an honorable reason for war since "we can live with Communism; we've been doing it long enough" (EZ 84). This is precisely the stasis of deterrence strategy, where ideological conflict, for Staley, has been invented as a "grotesque" function of patriotism. All there is left is the disembodied "test of opposing technologies" (EZ 84). While once war "told men what they were capable of under stress," now it "informs the machines": "[i]t's the best test of a country's technological skills. Are all your gaseous diffusion plants going at top efficiency? Are your ICBM guidance and control mechanisms ready to work perfectly? You get the answers when war breaks out. Your technology doesn't know how good it is until it goes to war, until it's been tested in the ultimate way. I don't think we care too much about individual bravery anymore. It's better to be efficient than brave" (EZ 84). Ultimately, war has become abstracted—like Harkness the abstract noun—from any human meaning and simply "brings out the best in technology" (EZ 85).[18] Not only does no one invest meaning into the practice of warfare, but the compartmentalization of tasks, as at Los Alamos, means that no one feels guilt anymore since the "[r]esponsibility is distributed too thinly." It is only "old warriors" like Staley who "take the blame for what the so-called technocrats and multi-dimensional men are up to" (EZ 86).

Staley's conclusion here appears to suggest that "warriors" have become the fall guys of a military-industrial organization that is driven by the pursuit of maximum efficiency. Any drag on the system is put down to hot-blooded foot soldiers who are little more than disposable functionaries positioned at the sharp end of the power structure. Not only is nuclear war unfightable and only exists as a series of increasingly complex gaming hypotheticals, the individualization possible in combat is now completely voided by technology. All Staley can do is teach the history of a sort of warfare that no longer exists, and play elaborate nuclear war games with bright students like Harkness.

The big problem with war games, argues Staley, getting to the core of nuclearism's simulated condition of permanent war, is "the obvious awareness on the part of all participants that this wasn't the real thing" (EZ 219). The gaming environment can "never elicit the kind of emotions generated in times of actual stress," making it at best an inaccurate representation of "what might be expected from governments when armies were poised and the missiles were rising from their silos" (EZ 219–20). While Staley yearns for the adrenaline surge of enabling power provided by "real" war, for Harkness the appeal of football lies not in its promise of self-becoming but in the self-effacement of the codified plays. When Staley suggests he join the cadet wing, Harkness refuses, saying his interest is purely hypothetical.

Harkness is adept at renunciation because not doing most accurately confirms his situation within nuclearism's condition of proleptic dread. The elimination of purposeful action effected by the warfare state, whether through the withdrawal of land that ruins the ranch economy in McCarthy's Border Trilogy or through the displacement of human agency by technology, means that giving up remains the only decision left to be made. Before moving to Texas, Harkness had decided to give up football. While his Penn State coach explains to him that football is about sacrifice and preparation for the future, and that giving up now suggests a propensity to give up in the future, Harkness gives up (EZ 19). If nuclear war has already foreclosed on the future, the sacrifice has already been made and there can be nothing to prepare for. In the end, it is the threat of the draft that pushes Harkness back into football and to Texas, and herein, I think, lies part of the irony of End Zone's exploration of disembodied nuclear dread. The immediate threat to Harkness is not nuclear apocalypse but being sent to Vietnam, to a war still being fought by real soldiers and often described using the vocabulary of the Western.[19]

The Cold War's dematerialization of the warrior into the statistical calibrations of systems theorists did not prevent the mobilization of large armies, though the warrior ethos in its chivalric form now works as a legitimation effect for the manufacture and consumption of "substandard industrial robots." If football prepares for anything, it is for the performance of spectacular warrior moves that are, in fact, subordinate to an absent but controlling military bureaucratic order. Zapalac is right to say that there is no need for a substitution for war when the real thing exists, but for Harkness, football is literally a substitute for, and a necessary evasion of, real war. His obsession with nuclear annihilation is not merely, then, an appalled confrontation with the ineffable fact of nuclear dread, but a means of occluding the more proximate danger of death on an actual battlefield. The immensity of nuclear threat, in this way, could be said to serve as a pacifying screen that obscures the continuation of the more conventional kind of warfare nuclearism has allegedly made obsolete. It is worth remembering here that Billy Parham tries three times to enlist while Gary Harkness is intent on evading the draft. For Parham, during World War II there is still a vestigial promise of belonging to something honorable by joining the military; the war may be eviscerating Parham's home and way of life, but the legitimacy of the conflict remains intact. By the early 1970s the army is something to escape from, Harkness's retreat into football as a mode of empty signification marking a further distantiation of the citizen from the institutions of the state.

The loss of a viable code of honor in the United States that compels McCarthy's youths to move into the blank side of the map is echoed by the skepticism of Harkness, who wonders whether time is too compact to allow for a purging silence to be felt. What we must know, Harkness reasons, "must be learned from blanked-out pages. To begin to reword the overflowing world. To subtract and disjoin. To re-recite the alphabet. To make elemental lists. To call something by its name and need no other sound" (EZ 89). For Harkness, this desire to start over is not dissimilar to the end time thinking of evangelical Christianity, where a horror of the fallen contemporary world prompts a yearning for nuclear apocalypse as a form of righteous purgation. Gary Harkness's obsession with the strangely unambiguous yet persistently ineffable official discourse of nuclearism reveals the lure and the terror of the blank page: it may signify a new beginning but also implies evidence of a previous and ultimate erasure. While Harkness's more abstract eschatological meditations are leavened by the contingencies of draft evasion, in William Hauptman's *Storm Season* nuclear rapture is given a post-Vietnam valence in the confluence of conservative values and technological warfare that gave powerful shape to Ronald Reagan's presidency during the 1980s.

Not Stone but Fear

In *Blood Meridian*, McCarthy describes a storm so ferocious that it casts the land in such a light that it appears to be a place "of some other order . . . whose true geology was not stone but fear" (BM 47). *Storm Season* is a novel concerned with weather and politics, namely the storm manufactured by Reagan as the rainmaker of Cold War II. *Storm Season* registers, as Joseph Dewey has argued of other Reagan-era novels, "not the furious pride of the new patriotism, but unsettling fears, fears indeed keener than any felt in the American experience of post-Hiroshima since the delicate brinkmanship of the Cuban missile crisis."[20] While *End Zone* details the domestic performance of a warrior ethos considered obsolete under the dispensation of RAND corporation deterrence theory but belatedly reanimated in Vietnam, in *Storm Season* technocratic rationality has fused with the eschatology of the ascendant new right to produce a culture that seems less interested in deferring apocalypse than in calling it forth.

Burl Drennan, *Storm Season*'s protagonist, lives and works in the Texas panhandle town of Nortex, a place "on a border, a boundary, the edge of another world."[21] Situated in Burl's old schoolbook between the pink area of the "Great American Desert" and the rest of the United States, marked in green, the panhandle is the edge between conventional definitions of civilized and wild, the known and the unknown, the rational and the rapturous. In *Storm Season*, this is also the world where fundamentalist revivalism meets nuclear technology, and where extreme weather conditions rewrite local landmarks every few years. Nortex is on the cutting edge of the Reaganite 1980s, the apocalyptic "storm season" of the title, used to dealing with wildcat economies, catastrophic up and down swings of fortune, where revelation and revenue are tied into grand narratives of terrible power, and where aggressive individuals exploit communal fears and social instability.

Hauptman's Nortex is situated near Pantex, the final assembly point for all the nuclear weapons in the United States. The Pantex Army Ordnance Plant, a few miles from Amarillo, opened in 1942, and while it closed after the war, it was reactivated in 1950 by the Atomic Energy Commission for the assembly of nuclear warheads. Its functions are, as A. N. Mojtabai explains, the "fabrication and testing of conventional high explosives, nuclear weapons assembly, disassembly, modification and repair." During the mid-1980s, the plant was estimated to be producing around 1,500 new nuclear warheads a year, or roughly four a day.[22] Amarillo itself is a major railroad and highway junction and therefore an important trans-shipment point. As Mojtabai notes:

> Despite its apparent isolation, Amarillo is, in fact, the center of a vast web of connections with military-industrial operations throughout the nation. By truck, rail, sometimes by air, the components come in. From the Savannah River plant in Aiken, South Carolina, come plutonium and tritium for nuclear warheads; from the Rocky Flats plant in Golden, Colorado, come plutonium cores; from the Kansas City plant in Missouri, electronic arming, fusing, and firing switches; from the Mound Laboratory in Miamisburg, Ohio, detonators and times, from the Pinellas plant in Clearwater, Florida, neutron-generators; from the Y-12 plant in Oak Ridge, Tennessee, uranium and testing devices. . . . And from Pantex, the assembled weapons go forth. They go forth, ready for—whatever it is that they are ready for. . . . The white trains move slowly in and out of Pantex under cover of night; the stainless steel, unmarked trucks, bearing smaller but more frequent loads, moving in broad day, rumbling down the interstate where the traffic never stops.[23]

Storm Season, then, is positioned at a crucial hub of the West's open secret, a place where employees at the assembly plants and the entire transportation infrastructure are imbricated in the machinery of covert nuclear production.

A railroad worker with desires to escape, Burl is also a tornado chaser. His father, Willie, was a bully and a successful oilman until he told the local papers he had seen a UFO and took to drinking. Burl's workmate John, a blue-collar intellectual with strong socialist leanings as well as a survivalist streak, joined the railroad out of nostalgic dreams of freedom only to find himself transporting radioactive material and bits of nuclear weaponry back and forth from power plant to factory to installation. As a child, Burl is apparently predisposed to pick up on dread latent in the air: he is afraid of storms and has to lie down after watching The Wizard of Oz. This fear grows into a kind of lusty anticipation, and he is listless and bored except during the storm season. Alongside his fascination with tornadoes, Burl is also obsessed with "the whole classified world of defense technology he thought of as the Big Secret" (ss 27). Burl is, in short, attracted to impending catastrophe and thrives on dread of the unknown power latent in the everyday. Indeed, storms and military technology are both literally in the air; as Burl stares out into the night sky, he sees the blue lights of Pantex and, to the north, "flashes of lightning where the front was moving down" (ss 85).

After a big tornado destroys half of Nortex, Burl notes that everyone seemed happier and more content than they have ever been, even though the wrecked neighborhoods remind him of Hiroshima and Nagasaki. Ever since he was a child, we are told, "he had known there was going to be a nuclear war. . . . Now it had finally come" (ss 39). And with the arrival of disaster, there is relief and he can sit in the sun "with no past, no future" (ss 39). While the sense of community feeling experienced in the immediate aftermath of the storm soon wanes, the destruction of the tornado serves to energize the economy, which booms in the drive to honor the dead by rebuilding the town into a bigger and better version of itself. At the same time, even two years down the line, despite a surface prosperity, there is still a sense that "there was some sort of profound uneasiness, just under the surface" (ss 209). Meanwhile, local drilling companies and even the banks are gradually being absorbed into conglomerates.

Burl believes that since the invention of the atomic bomb the West has been tensely waiting for the apocalypse. Because of this, time has effectively stopped: there is no point in doing anything since any day the bomb could go off. This is what Burl understands as the "Big Secret": "[w]hen he was a boy, he had feared it. Now he longed for it. Because then the waiting would be over—and because knowing it could happen somehow made it harder instead of easier to change your life. Why even try, when it could happen anytime? It was easier to wait for the flash, to live for the moment" (ss 242).

Passivity like Burl's "makes sense," argues Jodi Dean, "if we lack perspective, if we lack even the possibility of perspective because all possible points from which to assess our situations have collapsed into one another."[24] This kind of resignation in the face of an infinitely more powerful force is strongly confirmed by the people A. G. Mojtabai interviewed in the early 1980s in Amarillo, many of whom worked at Pantex and were born-again Christians. For example, engineering technician Warren G. Brown, discussing the prospect of nuclear confrontation, is quite typical in thinking "that the things that are in God's timetable and these times are going to happen and ain't a whole lot we can do. We may—in our being for God—we might prolong it and hold it off a little while longer, but I think it's prophesized, and I think it's gonna come to pass."[25] As Dewey notes, "the awesome assurance of fundamentalism counseled its followers to accept as impermanent any secular system."[26] Comments like Brown's conflate, as Hauptman's novel does, nuclear anxiety and the so-called end-time thinking of fundamentalists who have abandoned the optimism of the New Testament as the failed project of the First Coming and headed back to the moral absolutes of the Old Testament. The reasoning is that humanity is so far gone that redemption is now too late; all there is to do is wait for the Rapture. This is a straightforward dispensationalist view that asserts that, as Mojtabai explains, "humans are powerless to build a just and peaceful future, powerless to avert the destruction to come. As a chronicle of defeat down the length of history and around the globe, its effects may be far more enfeebling than that of any 'Vietnam syndrome,' for it paralyzes not only our capacity for action, but our ability to think, even to conceive of ways to avert disaster."[27]

In *Storm Season*, the tornado may be a temporary respite from perpetually anticipating the end of the world, yet Reaganite apocalyptic fundamentalism is busy cleaning up the town in more prosaic ways: as small businesses go under, *Playboy* has been banned from convenience stores, the Cowboys for Christ hold revivals at the 4-H Club barn, and creationism is back in the curriculum (ss 43). The "war on drugs" and fear of Satanism help to maintain perpetual vigilance against unseen enemies.

John argues that the emphasis on the failure of the family, the demonizing of drug users and people with "loose morals" removes discussion of economic conditions and shifts the blame from politicians and businessmen to the working man. The radical atomization of society renders the individual as always the weakest link, and the self-surveillance of communities driven by a hysterical fear of nonconformity is successfully turning individual freedom into the enemy within.[28] The false dawn of economic renewal post-tornado becomes, two years later, a public fiction of survival and recovery so resolute that even a weatherman predicting more storms is sacked for being negative (ss 224).

Burl's need for the sublime proximity of the twister is a need for an authentic experience, a step into the nothingness of dread—to "become part of the energy that filled the air before a storm" (ss 59)—that can rupture the phony optimism of everyday life. Reading a storm spotter's guide, Burl discovers that storms are not formless but in fact have a shape and structure, "an intricate architecture of air" (ss 58), and at times even appear to be guided by an intelligence of their own (ss 129). As such, the storm provides an alternative model of order uncontaminated by the manipulations of small-town folk panics. Storm structure is dynamic and contingent, but as a form of primal energy it also places local circumstances into deep temporal context. Heading toward a tornado means "leaving the sunlit world behind" to enter a place where "[e]very living thing—birds, cattle, people—had disappeared, probably into shelter": "[t]he farmhouses looked haunted. Burl felt they were crossing the land of the dead, where things glowed with their own gray light. This, he thought, was the light that had shone on the Cretaceous extinction, when a comet had hit the earth, filling the atmosphere with ash, and the dinosaurs had died" (ss 129).

An observation like this is understood by the legendary tornado expert Dale Webster, a combination of meteorologist and minister, as "a moment of startling clarity" (ss 132). Burl is reading pre- and post-history into the dreadful anticipation of catastrophe that has driven every living thing into hiding. Webster offers some insight into the significance of storm chasing as a form of charting social as well as atmospheric turbulence. "Something is changing in our society or our atmosphere," he observes. "I'm not sure which" (ss 132). The atmosphere is a mirror, Webster explains: "[w]hen you study the atmosphere, you study everything" (ss 131). What is required is a new kind of meteorologist "with an understanding of change and things on a larger scale" (ss 133).

There are "no firm answers," Webster explains, only "indications" that need to be followed through a close interpretation of temporality: "[t]ime moved slowly, but at some point it speeded up." Like Zapalac, Webster is a catastrophist who insists on taking the long view; the ice age lasted for thousands of years, but now there is little trace of it. The question is, says Webster, "are the changes always gradual, or do they sometimes happen overnight? Is this the end of one climatic era, and will another come in our lifetime?" (ss 231). Webster thinks it will, but reading the signs correctly involves more than scientific rationality and involves developing "a feeling" for the situation. "Certain patterns appear, points of convergence." To watch tornadoes is to see "clear pictures scattered through nature" (ss 231). Stopping for gas, Burl and John come across a woman with a head "like vegetable matter, a purple cauliflower" of cancerous deformity. "There was a clear picture for you," thinks Burl, "of another kind" (ss 136).

Cancer is a point of convergence that reveals deep structural forces that are far from natural. Everyone in Nortex seems to be getting cancer, including Willie, who has the same kind as Ronald Reagan. While Willie's health fails, Burl, like Gary Harkness with his books on disaster, reads about the end of the universe in astronomy textbooks. "At the end of time," Burl reads, "the universe would be consumed by black holes, or scatter to nothingness, each star growing cold until it died the heat death" (ss 154). Burl recalls a story his father told him about an old cowboy who was taken by an Indian to a place out in the Medicine Mounds where there is a circle of stones. There the cowboy "saw the country the way it was before the white man came": giant buffalo and armadillos, mammoths, spouting volcanoes, and rivers of ice. "I found out later," says Willie, sipping on Ancient Age whiskey, "that's just the way this country was, back in the Ice Age" (ss 11). Medicine Mounds functions as both the site of revelation for Willie and his undoing. It is here that later Willie has what he calls, after the Indians, a "true dream," where time stops and Willie sees the story of his life. It is at Medicine Mounds that he strikes oil and here that he sees the flying saucer he believes is part of an alien intervention to save earth's atmosphere from the cancer-causing agents unleashed by the atomic bomb. The drinking starts because Willie cannot fathom the mysteries he has experienced, and as Willie is about to die, Burl realizes that all his father "ever wanted to do was get out of time" (ss 190).

Thinking cosmically about the end of the world does not provide a solution to more worldly points of convergence, as Willie's story reveals. Another character, Chaney, the ex-Pantex worker and survivalist biker who is slowly dying of plutonium contamination, also represents a kind of Reaganite knot of extremist contradictions. He is a nodal point in the network of values and experiences that include the threads of a nostalgic rugged individualism entwined with the effects of being a part of a proletarianized nuclear workforce. As a "Mountain Man" Chaney is positioned as a pioneering libertarian; as a cancer victim he is part of the collateral damage of the Cold War; and as a drug-user and blue-collar renegade he is part of the insidious creep against "family values." Chaney is certainly an expendable victim, but he is also untrustworthy. He tricks Burl into smoking crack, which provides another illusion that "nothing was real." The drug experience, though, leads Burl to think "of the caves burned out of the earth by underground nuclear explosions," fusing subjective experience with historical meltdown in an insight that fills his brain with "molten metal" and turns his thoughts "to light" (ss 239).

It is not timelessness itself that provides a means of escape from the structures of control, since the pursuit of oblivion—the end times of religion, drugs, and alcohol—cancels any critical function it might contain. Instead, it is thinking about time and scale that offers a perspective, as John explains to Burl how the structures of power—"the railroad. The liberals, the conservatives. The President of the United States"—gained control by destroying "our sense of time and trapp[ing] us in this damned continuous present" (ss 292). While John cannot work out how it started, Burl knows that it was the bomb that killed historical time as it had previously been understood. "I stopped thinking there was ever going to be a future at all" (ss 293), he reminds us. Fatalistically they conclude that eventually the bomb will go off. The "flying saucer people" cannot help since they are just here to watch the show. "Let it happen," says Burl, concluding with a line that recalls the doomed resignation of McMahon,

Morrow, McCarthy, and DeLillo: "I was born to see the end of the world" (SS 295). The novel ends with Burl studying meteorology and living in an Airstream trailer, the number 1 storm attractor; he has become a lightning rod.

In both *End Zone* and *Storm Season*, the negative storm of nuclear dread renders what Melville called the "glorious liberty of volition" redundant. In the desert, Gary Harkness seeks a place "suggestive of the end of recorded time," and Burl, viewing the calm before the twister, imagines that this "was the light that had shone on the Cretaceous extinction." Both are neutralized by the imagination of a disaster promised but withheld, effecting a retardation of agency and a collapse of historical time into a simultaneously pre- and post-historical vacuum. Zapalac's comment that nuclearism has caught up with the Old Testament is confirmed in *Storm Season*, but as John realizes, the destruction of time is itself a historical effect produced by the threat of the bomb and the inertia of containment. Exposed to the immensity of what Ulrich Beck calls "world society," the demands placed on the individual faced with nuclear threat can only be borne through "not listening, simplifying, and apathy."[29]

West Texas offers no sanctuary for Harkness or Burl; the remoteness of the place only reconfirms the inevitability of impending doom. The "points of convergence" Webster urges Burl to look for in weather patterns is a demand, as I see it, for a reengagement with history, to read which way the wind is blowing. Zapalac serves a similar function in *End Zone*, rejecting the symbolic rituals of containment culture in favor of a more historically grounded puncturing of the myth that rational order is possible or even desirable. Webster and Zapalac suggest that contingency can somehow be read in the broader patterns, that absent causes are a smokescreen that occludes understanding of real connections between policy and effect. The eschatological view of nuclear threat is but another mystification of politics as war by other means. The struggle "to get out of time," whether through some sort of religious experience, through imagining the end of the world, or through escape to the desert are, in the end, as productive of dread as they are relief from it. The proliferation of cancer in Nortex might be a more material sign of the invisible forces bringing an end to history for many people, and John's assessment that this is a "clear picture" that reveals "points of convergence"—the latter term is, of course, precisely the phrase used to describe Tayo's awakened under-standing of the constellation of intersecting global and local forces—is one way of grounding nuclear anxiety back in time. The absent cause of the cancer, when tracked historically rather than metaphysically, leads back to the bomb, and in the next two chapters it is precisely this conceal-ment of links between cause and effect that generates the toxic discourse produced in the aftermath of domestic nuclear testing in the West.

7. AFTER NATURE

Gothic Contamination

> For every kind of vampire, there is a kind of cross.
> And at least the physical things They have taken, from Earth and from us,
> can be dismantled, demolished—returned to where it all came from.
> Thomas Pynchon, Gravity's Rainbow

"It is in war, famine, and epidemic," claim Deleuze and Guattari, "that werewolves and vampires proliferate."[1] Less than a month after the Japanese attack on Pearl Harbor, dental surgeon and inventor Dr. Lytle S. Adams decided to write to FDR. In his letter he put forward a remarkable proposal: that the United States should look into the feasibility of dropping millions of bats, fitted with incendiary materials, onto Japanese cities. If dropped just before daybreak, the bats, according to Adams, would take refuge in hundreds of buildings that would, once the incendiary devices were ignited, create countless uncontrollable fires. "The effect of the destruction from such a mysterious source," Adams promised, "would be a shock to the morale of the Japanese people," and would render them homeless and their industries useless. A mere ten planes could carry, Adams calculated, two million "fire starters."[2] Thus began Project X-Ray, a series of secret experiments carried out in Bandera, Texas, Carlsbad, New Mexico, and El Centro, California, between 1942 and 1943. Though the experiments came to nothing, and the possibility of harnessing natural forces against the enemy took another turn at Los Alamos, this proposition of a plague of two million burning bats infiltrating Japanese cities reveals a gothic imagination at work in the deployment of Western nature as a weapon.

Adams conceives of the bat bomb not just as materially devastating but as strategically mysterious and shocking. Harvested from the subterranean places of the West, the creatures of the night would be recruited as America's own kamikaze unit. Despite the bizarre, even absurd nature of such a plan, the idea of something monstrous and shocking being awakened from the bowels of the earth is precisely what the atomic program instigated with the extraction of the uranium needed to produce the bomb. In this chapter, mineral extraction yields monsters from the underworld of Western space in the form of ancient bears and plagues of vampires that signify not just the nuclear era's toxic anxieties about the earth's gothic capacity to contain deadly secrets, but also the possibility that from within the mutations of the gothic might spring new modes of imagining "nature" that can animate resistance to despoliation.

As the development of nuclear weapons proceeded after World War II, the size of bombs and number of tests grew. While deterrence strategy may have fended off total war, the notion that no shots were fired in the Cold War is given the lie by the scale of America's record of nuclear detonation, which includes not just the devastation of two Japanese cities in 1945 but the pulverization of the Marshall Islands (66 explosions between 1946 and 1958) and other sites in the Pacific Ocean, and an over forty-year campaign of attrition at the Nevada Test Site (100 above-ground detonations between 1951 and the Limited Test Ban of 1963; 828 underground detonations until 1992). Worldwide, the United States has detonated 1,151 devices in total.[3]

Unsurprisingly, given the huge growth in weapons manufacture, not to mention the development of nuclear power, the extraction industries that shaped the economy of the Western United States since the nineteenth century enjoyed another, uranium-driven burst of speculative excavation of Western space. The vital material for the nuclear transformation of matter came from inside the earth, as if somehow it had been planted there for eventual discovery. It is finding the yellow-streaked uranium-bearing ore rock that produces Tayo's epiphany in *Ceremony* that the new world order has been produced by "beautiful rocks . . . laid down in a monstrous design" (Ce 246). The inversion of the natural order and the unleashing of an uncontainable power has been caused by forcing the inside into the outside.

Uranium, of course, has its own invisible properties, and like the bombs produced out of it, uranium mining generates airborne radioactive dust. Dread of nuclear war, as *Storm Season* reveals, has a material supplement in the corrupting cancers that have spread through the community that is economically as well as metaphysically tied to the bomb. The prospect of nuclear apocalypse may unite all human beings, as Tayo understands it, "in a circle of death," but there is a more banal threat to be faced by all who live and work in close proximity to the radioactive industries of the West. While nuclear war promises to end time, radiation lasts a long time, and the dilemma of how to imagine the persistence of contaminated matter surviving intact for thousands of years is barely more manageable than conceiving of the devastation of nuclear war itself. The invention of nuclear energy not only introduces the reality of there being no future, it also delivers an irreversible future of waste.

Burial is the most common solution for the long-term storage of radioactive materials, completing the sequence of discovery, extraction, employment, and interment involved in the production of nuclear energy.[4] This vertical process uncovers only to cover up, it reveals and then conceals. The earth is the repository of both the raw substance ("nature") and the spent substance ("nature" reshaped by human agency). While extraction is about finding, the point of burial is to hide, to make invisible the discarded waste from that which was made visible and valuable. The production of waste is not confined to the depleted materials of nuclear power, and human and environmental waste must be included in the category of matter reshaped by the process of extraction, employment, and interment of natural resources.

While the horizontal axis of Western space operates according to notions of open extension, exposure to sunlight, deep visibility, and directional movement across the surface of the earth, the vertical axis suggested by extraction and interment is one of hiddenness, darkness, secrecy, and sedimented geological time. If the visible, horizontal West provides the plane of expansion, the vertical bespeaks duration and persistence. The plain light of day yields an empirical knowledge of observation, a McCarthyesque "optical democracy" of discrete and separate objects, while the subterranean is more the realm of the gothic, where the unseen might be extracted into form or the undesirable concealed through burial. In fact, the gothic moment is precisely where the previously concealed appears from below or when the empirical descends into the darkness of the underworld. This intersection of the horizontal and the vertical might be said to produce the uncanny sense of something being simultaneously inside and outside, hidden yet almost visible, belonging to the world of known things but refusing the categories of empirical knowledge.

The nuclear industry in the West has produced precisely this kind of gothic epistemology. Not only is the industry, in its military and commercial forms, based on processes of extraction and burial, subsequently gaining business from the storage of the waste that it has itself produced from the extraction of matter from the earth and its conversion into energy, but the culture of the nuclear West is shot through with a discourse of exposure and concealment. Land and populations are unknowingly exposed to radiation; those who do know about the consequences of radiation often conceal that fact; vulnerable and undervalued populations—Native Americans, rural communities—are employed and/or contaminated by the industry; the relative isolation of the areas in which contamination occurs reinscribes the marginalization of those areas as extrinsic and expendable by-products of American economic and military power. The tropes of concealment and exposure also necessarily shape resistance to the despoliating influence of the military-industrial presence in the region, with activists and victims working to "bring to light" suffering and the indifference of corporations and authorities. In seeking to reveal evidence of contamination a counterdiscourse of secrecy and revelation is produced that also attempts an excavation of the unknown into the open.

One of the problems with concealment as a strategy for removing the unwanted is that, like Poe's telltale heart, it calls attention to itself. Total concealment is impossible since there must be one who conceals, and that person knows the site and object of concealment. If concealment cannot be achieved secretly, it is never really proper concealment, and merely a kind of calling attention to the fact that something is there but hidden from direct view: burying something requires a marker that announces the fact of burial. The marker, problematically, acts as an invitation to consider that which is now concealed and, since it is concealed, the precise nature of the concealed object can only be imagined. Again, the fact of concealment—intended to place out of sight that which is unwanted—actually calls forth the withheld object.[5] And once concealment is recognized as a strategy in one instance, who is to say that there are not other sites concealing things we did not even know were there to be buried. Concealment not only fails to conceal but it produces the specter of any number of cover-ups. If there is something hidden that is known to be hidden, we might argue, it is not unreasonable to assume that there are hidden things we know nothing about. From here, a gothic excess of paranoid meaning is only a step away.

The kind of sensibility produced by the permanent threat of invisible danger has given rise to what Lawrence Buell has called "toxic discourse." By this, Buell means the "rhetoric and ethics of imagined endangerment," an "expressed anxiety arising from perceived threat of environmental hazard due to chemical modification by human agency."[6] As is the case with nuclear weapons, the anxiety produced by fear of toxicity is never merely a purely imaginary danger but is produced at the intersection of "individual or social panic and from an evidential base in environmental phenomena."[7] While toxic discourse is "always immoderate," it is nevertheless "always being reinforced by unsettling events."[8]

Buell identifies four characteristics that define toxic discourse. First is the "shock of awakened perception," a rude confrontation with the fact of toxicity and the awareness that there can be no protection.[9] The disenchantment that follows awareness leads, in Buell's second topos, to what he calls "totalizing images of a world without refuge from toxic penetration"—like Tayo's realization in *Ceremony* that "human beings were one clan again, united by the fate the destroyers planned for all of them"—which in turn leads to a crusading "moral passion cast in a David versus Goliath scenario."[10] Faced with the enormity of threat, literary responses, in Buell's fourth category, become subject to "gothification" as everyday life increasingly becomes charged with unseen but intuitively sensed menace.[11]

It is this uncanny awareness of lurking danger that prompts Ulrich Beck to claim that perceived threats "are bringing about a kind of new 'shadow kingdom,' comparable to the realm of the gods and demons in antiquity, which is hidden behind the visible world and threatens human life on this Earth." In place of supernatural danger, radiation and thoughts of nuclear devastation, as evidenced in *End Zone* and *Storm Season*, come to haunt daily life. "Dangerous, hostile substances lie concealed behind the harmless facades," Beck observes, requiring a "double gaze" not unlike Nadel's conception of the nuclear gaze, whereby the visible world "must be investigated, relativized and evaluated with respect to a second reality, only existent in thought and concealed in the world":[12]

Like the gaze of the exorcist, the gaze of the pollution-plagued contemporary is directed at something invisible. The risk society marks
the dawning of a *speculative* age in everyday perception and thought.
. . . Not until the step to cultural risk consciousness is everyday
thought and imagination *removed from its moorings in the world of the
visible*. In the struggle over risks of modernization we are no longer
concerned with the specific value of that which appears to us in perception. What becomes the subject of controversy as to its degree of
reality is instead what everyday consciousness does *not* see, and *cannot perceive*: radioactivity, pollutants and threats in the future.[13]

The threat of the unseen, Beck claims, dismantles confidence in the
rational capacity to measure the world according to its visible limits. In
Ana Castillo's *So Far from God* (1993), a novel set in toxic New Mexico, people are faced with an "incomprehensible world" where livestock become
mysteriously sick and starlings fall from the sky like rain. They "didn't
understand what was slowly killing them, too, or didn't want to think
about it, or if they did, didn't know what to do about it anyway and went
on like that."[14] Like the blank spaces on the map produced by military
security's display of erased areas, apprehension of what cannot be seen
but is understood to be there must begin speculatively by addressing the
power of the invisible.

"Beneath our America lies buried another distinct continent,—an
archæan America," wrote Clarence King in 1877.[15] For this reason, as
Patricia Limerick warns, one needs to walk "with caution" in the West
because "land that appears solid may be honeycombed, and one would
not like to plunge unexpectedly into the legacy of Western history."[16] Limerick rightly combines the geographical and the historical here, as well
as signaling the hiddenness of the legacy that lay underfoot. The peril
of moving across that which appears solid but which is, in fact, full of
holes is that of a fall, a plunge into the subterranean space of the crypt.
The legacy of Western history is cryptic inasmuch as it lies hidden and is
encrypted in the sense that the hiddenness is encoded, written into the
land. The moment of the unexpected plunge, in these terms, is a fall into
the vertical, subterranean dimension of history, the subaltern or, as Pynchon would say, preterite history of the excluded and abandoned; it is a
fall into the unmarked grave of America's waste products.

The Enlightenment obsession with transparency, Anthony Vidler argues, is constructed out of a fear of the dark as the "domain of myth, superstition, tyranny, and above all the irrational." The well-lit transparency of the "rational grids and hermetic enclosures" characteristic of Enlightenment social and spatial organization was soon challenged by a growing fascination with concealed fantasy-worlds. What we see in the counter-Enlightenment sensibility, with its obsession with walls, darkness, hideouts, caverns, and grottoes, is the "invention of a spatial phenomenology of darkness."[17] If the Jeffersonian grid promises to make visible a regulated and containable spatial totality, its horizontal scopic dominion fails to register the honeycombed crypts beneath the surface plane of the map.

Sometimes, like the military's blank spots, failure to represent what is there is a willful demonstration of the power to withhold information. Similarly, the representational limitations of the gridded map can be put to use in the screening out of unwanted information, as Michael J. Shapiro argues when he suggests that treating dangerous occupations or industrial accidents as "environmental" rather than political issues reveals the "absence of a cartography of occupational danger." What Shapiro means is that, given the way maps represent "geopolitical or territorially-inflected sovereignty-oriented politics," populations or agencies not contained by such a map's coordinates—such as migrant workers or "illegal" immigrants, multinational corporations, and decentralized industries—are effectively unrecorded.[18] The promise of disciplinary transparency offered by the rational grid is, then, itself something of a bluff, its limitations providing a useful means of screening information anomalous to the project of containment. At the same time, however, Vidler's point about a counter-Enlightenment spatial phenomenology of darkness suggests the possibility of gaps in the disciplinary totality of transparent space that are not so easily recuperated as strategic omissions. As such, cryptic and anomalous spaces might be reconceived as sites of irrecuperable otherness that serve to activate the abject as an agent in the critical exposure of the grid's complicity in the politics of concealment.

The abandoned mine, the hidden cave, and the ancient burial site are all staples of Western fiction that call forth the prospect of this gothic history of concealment. Western novels of the nuclear era that draw upon the tropes of the cave, the disturbed graveyard, and the creatures of the night are working within a tradition that situates the subterranean as the dormant counter-space of America's horizontal, sunlit teleology of progress. In this chapter, three such novels—Jake Page's *Cavern* (2001), Martin Cruz Smith's *Night Wing* (1977), and A. A. Carr's *Eye Killers* (1996)—employ the gothic as a means of plunging into the legacy of mineral extraction in the West. They conjure out of the disturbed surface of the earth monsters awakened or produced by the invasive extraction and burial of matter, and locate in the exposed depths of Western space a notion of contamination that functions critically as a model of unpredictable mutation opposed to the rational control of a knowable "nature." "Those who travel in desert places," as McCarthy writes in *Blood Meridian*, "do indeed meet with creatures surpassing all description" (BM 282). Here, waste will not be buried as the recalcitrant toxic remainder of Western history but returns as the unsightly fact of a new, radioactive order of postnatural resistance.

Buried Alive

The Waste Isolation Pilot Plant (WIPP), tucked away in the southeastern corner of New Mexico near Carlsbad, is designed as the first deep geologic storage facility for transuranic waste. More than two thousand feet underground the Department of Energy (DOE) has carved out a labyrinth of chambers in the 250-million-year-old salt beds, intended to house 50 years of radioactive garbage so contaminated it must be contained for 240,000 years. The DOE, slightly less ambitiously, hopes to isolate the material from human contact for 10,000 years.[19] As Tom Vanderbilt observes, thus "will a weapons-building process that began with the mining of uranium end in a kind of mine in which the raw material is space itself, a real estate valued for its distance from civilization."[20] Some see WIPP not merely as the tomb of the Cold War but as the beginning of a new phase of nuclear development. Valerie Kuletz, for example, claims that since 70 percent of WIPP's capacity is reserved for the waste from weapons not even produced yet, the plant helps "prolong the production of nuclear weapons."[21]

The favorable properties of bedded salt for housing nuclear waste were first noted in 1957, but it was not until struggling potash miners in Carlsbad suggested that their former mines might be good for waste storage that the area became a prime site. Though the mines themselves turned out to be unsuitable, geologically (few underground disturbances and drilling holes) and politically (thin population, little alternative land use) the Delaware Basin was ideally suited for WIPP. While it is by no means clear that deserts are uniquely placed in terms of geology and climate as the best sites for nuclear and hazardous waste disposal, Charles Reith and Timothy Fisher's observations regarding the economic and political circumstances of the Carlsbad area during the 1970s and 1980s suggest good nonscientific reasons for the selection of the site. Recession in the extractive industries and high unemployment made the prospect of a big government employer attractive, overriding environmental and safety concerns.[22]

While the burghers of Carlsbad may have been willing, however reluctantly, to embrace the necessity of having a pioneering waste facility on their doorstep, Native Americans have not been so accommodating. The incursion of military-industrial nuclearism into the Southwest from the 1940s onward is described with characteristic directness by Ward Churchill as "radioactive colonization."[23] Indeed, Native Americans have been hosts to atomic imagineers from the start. Uranium mining and milling on Navajo, Hopi, Pueblo, and Ute land in the Navajoan Desert began in the 1940s. Los Alamos, as *Ceremony* reminds us, is located near Pueblo lands on the Pajarito Plateau of New Mexico. The first testing at Alamogordo, New Mexico, was near the Mescalero Apache reservation, while Western Shoshone and Southern Paiute lands at the intersection of the Great Basin and Mojave deserts were taken by the federal government in the early 1950s, in violation of the Treaty of Ruby Valley (1863), for use as the Nevada Test Site.[24] The only above-ground, temporary nuclear waste storage facilities considered have been on the Nevada Test Site and on the Mescalero Apache, Skull Valley Goshute, and Fort McDermitt Pauite-Shoshone reservations. WIPP is in the same general vicinity of the Mescalero Apache reservation.[25]

Sparse population and the promise of local economic gain have been cited to justify the use of the desert West as repository of nuclear waste, but the persistence of the "wasteland" fiction continues to ignore Native Americans and the particular relationship Indians have to place. The favored procedure of burying waste underground is in itself at odds with Indian attitudes toward the subterranean, with many origin stories featuring the emergence of the People from the earth. Native American places of origin are usually specifically located, known sites; for example, in the origin stories of the Laguna Pueblo peoples, the place of origin is a spring north of the village of Paguate. The land, then, is vividly sited as a birthplace, a maternal body to which one—individually and collectively—is corporeally related.

In the western European tradition, the internal space of the cave is also conceived as a source, whether of thought (Plato) or of art (the "presumed moment of primal visuality" of Paleolithic cave painting).[26] The cave is conversely, of course, a traditional site of burial, a return to the point of origin; the cave is the passage to the underworld, the location of possible "commerce between the living and the spectral shadow."[27] The cave, write Mark A. Cheetham and Elizabeth D. Harvey, placed "between inside and outside, makes it both a dangerous and privileged passageway between worlds or systems of representation."[28] Furthermore, caves are commonly spaces for the reception of prophetic utterances or revelations.[29] For Greek and Roman poets, caves were "transformative microcosms of the metamorphic essence of the world order."[30]

The difference between Indian and European understanding of subterranean space is revealingly noted in Willa Cather's *Death Comes for the Archbishop* (1927), where the Catholic bishop Latour and his Indian guide Jacinto retreat into a cave during a storm. The "peculiar formation in the rocks" suggest to Latour "two great stone lips, slightly parted and thrust outward." Into this obviously genital, and erotic, opening Jacinto enters quickly, its "footholds well known to him." Latour follows but is uneasy, "struck by reluctance, an extreme distaste for the place."[31] The cave is a sacred ceremonial place, Jacinto explains, and Latour experiences a "dizzy noise" in his head "like a heavy roll of distant drums."[32] While this is merely the sound of an underground river, to Latour it is "terrible" and the place is "remembered with horror."[33]

What is horrible and frightening to the Anglo mind is, for Cather, a place of refuge and reverence for the Indian, and these antagonistic positions toward the underworld animate fictions dealing with the politics of extraction and waste disposal in the West. In Jake Page's *Cavern*, an environmental thriller that deals directly with the impact of WIPP on the region, Jack Whittaker, a spelunking local hero, and his paleontologist ex-wife discover in unknown caverns inconveniently situated next to the plant the existence of prehistoric bears. Like *Death Comes for the Archbishop*, as well as, in a different register, Michael Crichton's *The Andromeda Strain* and *Jurassic Park*, which it superficially resembles, *Cavern* is concerned with time and power, with the violation of durational equilibrium by what Silko calls the "monstrous design" produced out of an excavated earth. Latour's horror at being exposed to the radical otherness of the cave is in part caused by exposure to the guts of a primal American space beyond the reach of European temporal models and historical ambitions. Jacinto's familiarity with the place functions to reveal the ethnocentrism of Latour's terror, and as such locates the horror in Latour's mind rather than in the cave itself. While the monstrous in *Cavern* is in the cave—bears and toxic waste—and not in the mind, the question of causation remains. Does secrecy produce monsters from within its dark recesses, or are the monsters already there?

For Joan Didion, the "sinister hysteria" felt in the nocturnal desert produces stories that "hint of the monstrous perversion to which any human idea can come." [34] She mentions reports of a diver sent to retrieve two drowned bodies from underground pools near Death Valley who comes to the surface babbling about water that gets hotter, flickering light, magma, and underground nuclear testing. Stories like this expose for Didion the extent to which the binary Cold War moral universe is predicated on the concealment of dark secrets. What happens in the mind—the rational categorization of "good" and "evil," us and them—is as monstrous as the real effects this folding of reason into morality produces. The diver brings back from the underworld a story that confirms the "ominous and terrible" condition of the nuclear West, where, for Didion "it is difficult to believe that 'the good' is a knowable quantity." [35]

Who knows, asks *Cavern*'s narrator, "what goes on, really, in so alien a place" as WIPP? [36] According to the engineers nothing goes on, just the salt slowly creeping around the containers. The paleontologist Cassie sees "[j]ust rocks. Just geology. Just endless, lifeless geophysics," yet others have a hunch that the earth "still held secrets" that human understanding might not recognize. [37] Jack's view is that the only way to understand the subterranean world is "to crawl around its natural nooks and crannies in the dark and the wet like a bacterium creeping through an intestine."[38] This organic metaphor figures the underworld as the habitat for a kind of counter-evolution, a parallel biosphere of self-regulating life forms. Just as no one used to believe life could exist at extremely high temperatures, places in the solid earth are now known, we are told, to host organisms that thrive on sulfur rather than sunlight: bacteria, spiders, midges, fish. Scientists and cavers stunned by the "plentiful life in a place where life should be impossible" have failed to ask whether the fish "represent the top of the food chain" or whether they are just a rung, that there could be something bigger "that likes the dark and prefers not to be seen or sensed."[39] If the biosphere is not a closed system and the impossible is now observable, then other impossibles also become possibilities. Once the known world unravels in this way, it is the short-termism of government officials, plant employees, and Carlsbad residents, all concerned primarily with career advancement and economic gain, that becomes the real threat.

The most dangerous monster in *Cavern*, of course, is not the prehistoric bear but the nuclear waste. What *Cavern* suggests is that the mistake made by the scientists is to believe that nonhuman nature, like the salt that encases the installation, is inert and predictable. Instead, the subterranean world is alive, independent, and unknown. Opening up the earth does not achieve the shadowless illumination of reason but instead releases a darkness that is not evil but definitely other: the place of the impossible. What excavation has inadvertently produced is, as David Mogen, Scott Sanders, and Joanne Karpinski have argued in relation to the Western gothic, "breaks in the logocentric history, of gaps in the authorized text of the past" where "the inscriptions of another history break through into meaning." This counterhistory "speaks, not from the history books, but from the landscape, which is no longer a locale, which opens itself as an unmediated text of the other filled with dark ruins and shadowy presences whose experience is queasy, uncertain, chaotic, and unknown."[40] The gothic landscape comprises forms that are "the immanent portents of the past and its other history that exist in a parallel reality," an affront to the official narrative of the state and a challenge to the "monstrous design" (Silko) crafted by its authors.[41] *Cavern*'s earth of "still held secrets" shares with *Ceremony*, and with two other novels set in New Mexico, Cruz Smith's *Night Wing* and Carr's *Eye Killers*, the view that the process of extraction that produces monsters—bears, bats, bombs, cancers—has unwittingly brought forth the countervailing power of the underworld.

In both *Night Wing* and *Eye Killers*, the gothic as repository for cultural anxieties finds a home in the Southwest.[42] In these novels the significance of the underworld as both sacred Native American site and abyss of capitalist devastation is explored through the related gothic tropes of the disease-carrying vampire bat. As with *Cavern*, these are tales of the collision of worlds, though here environmental despoliation is linked with the decimation of Native populations and the pollution of blood, both in terms of physical disease and also the compromising of Indian ethnic identity. As such, the conventional view of the vampire as rapacious imperialist is put to work in order to identify fossil fuel extraction and toxic waste management as a continuation of a racist American policy of extermination in the West.

As much as half of the uranium reserves in the United States is located on Indian-owned land in the West, mostly in Grants Belt of northern New Mexico, where the mining, processing, testing, and attempts at waste disposal and reclamation have taken place.[43] This area is also adjacent to some of the richest coal deposits in the country, located on Hopi and Navajo land in northeastern Arizona and the source of dispute since the nineteenth century. The conflict between Hopis and Navajos and between Indians and coal companies is the subject of *Night Wing*. While coal mining is a serious cause of aquifer depletion and water poisoning, as well as cultural vandalism (companies are allowed to mine on burial grounds), there are also over a thousand abandoned and unclaimed open-pit and underground uranium mines on Indian land. Taken together, coal and uranium mining have so devastated the Four Corners area that a 1972 report suggested that it be designated a "national sacrifice zone."[44]

Kuletz argues that the notional expendability of Indian land and Indians themselves underlies the failure to protect and provide for casualties of the nuclear industry. Since many scientists are under contract to mining companies, she suggests, it is hardly surprising that reports of birth defects, miscarriages, congenital or genetic abnormalities, and high incidence of cancers are often dismissed as anecdotal evidence rather than scientific proof.[45] She does go on to note, however, that increasingly, alternative studies are utilizing scientific methods against government and corporate interests and that there is developing a multicultural position that combines science and traditional knowledge into a hybrid discourse that can mediate between antagonistic binary positions.[46]

This complex interplay between "traditional" and "scientific" interests is a dominant feature of Native American fiction dealing with the politics of land use and echoes the broader literary work of constructing narrative models that effectively mediate between indigenous and Anglo cultural practices. In novels like *Ceremony*, *Night Wing*, and *Eye Killers*, social and environmental crisis is positioned as also a crisis of meaning that must involve a dialectical struggle toward some form of third position. As such, contaminated subject positions, often mixed-blood Indians or other abjected constituencies, are crucially mobilized to dismantle disabling and intransigent oppositions. While this sort of novelistic resolution may be a mode of narrative wish-fulfillment, it does speak to the kind of contingent decisions that must be made under circumstances of deep socioeconomic and cultural crisis. Furthermore, the gothic dimension of these texts is itself a deliberate incorporation of an aspect of Euro-American cultural discourse into Native American texts that interrogates buried anxieties and fears about the nature of the powers that structure everyday life in often incomprehensible ways. As such, these novels not only perform a kind of cultural analysis at the level of plot, they also embody the deep contradictions of that culture in their form.

The gothic, then, works in these texts to make visible the invisible networks of power that produce dread and also offers itself as an extra-rational mode of discourse that includes the unknown not as an enemy of reason but as a potentially liberating indeterminacy. As much as these novels are interested in utilizing indigenous myth and oral narrative forms, they also insist on historicizing the mystification of Indians in American culture as a function of their strategic marginalization by capitalist interests. What this does is preserve the Indian as other (as an alternative to Anglo domination) while exposing the process of othering as a politically expedient form of waste management. The contaminated subject position of the abjected and anomalous is therefore not only a favored model for effective social and political agency, but also the model for the text's condition as a mongrel literary form.

Return of the Bat Bomb

The plague-carrying bats in Night Wing have been summoned from Mexico by the outcast medicine man Abner, who lives like Silko's Betonie among the "junk of different civilizations" and understands the world according to the Aztec cosmology of worlds ending in catastrophe.[47] A redemptive apocalypse for Abner is preferable to coal mining on the reservation. Positioned between Abner and the mining companies is Youngman Duran, an orphaned Tewa Vietnam vet who has been given the job of deputy by tribal elders to keep him out of trouble and who is at home with neither Anglos or Indians. The dilemma faced by Duran is that to save the sacred caverns from mining and the community from the bats he must destroy the caves and the ancient pueblos they contain.

To do this Duran must, with the help of an obsessive bat expert and a reservation nurse who has rejected the military-industrial wealth of her family, combat the other unholy alliance of corporate mining interests and Navajo entrepreneurs. Abner's vengeance, it becomes clear, is directed not toward a straightforwardly invasive Anglo colonizer but at the already compromised integrity of tribal autonomy caused by deals stuck between Indians and business. The Hopis and Navajos had come to an agreement with the Peabody Coal Company in the mid-1960s, while the Navajo-Hopi Land Settlement Act of 1974 divided what had previously been a shared reservation between the two. Although there were few Hopis living on the Navajo side, there were many thousands of Navajos resident on what had now become Hopi land, which contained most of the coal. The government encouraged the Navajos on the Hopi side to relocate, but many lost their homes and became more prone to unemployment, alcoholism, and suicide than their tribal peers.

This intertribal conflict, generated by coal business intrusion, is the backdrop to Night Wing, which is set in the mid-1970s as the Arab oil embargo is beginning to bite and extraction companies are hungry for domestic alternatives to imported fuel. Thanks to NASA's launch of the

Landsat satellite in 1975, the novel tells us, previously undetectable oil reserves are discovered on land jointly owned by the Hopis and Navajos in
the Painted Desert. Previously invisible, the secret spaces of Pueblo territory are exposed by the new maps as another income stream, completing
the inventory of space begun with the nineteenth-century surveys.

It is here that Duran's anomalous hybrid position becomes vital, since
his army experience of reading aerial photographs of potential targets
makes him the only person qualified to understand the Landsat maps.
While a rejection of his complicity in the Vietnam War gets him court-
marshaled for deliberately misreading target photographs, back on the
reservation the same interpretive skill equips him to mount a realistic
challenge to the mining company. This is not to say that Duran has an
unalloyed allegiance to tribal culture. While contemptuous of white society, he also despises the ignorance, poverty, and superstition of reservation Indians. Because of his time away, part of him "would always be
white" (NW 37), yet the reservation is all he knows of home, and despite
his dismissal of Abner's datura-addled prophecies, he is fiercely loyal to
the old man. Duran's sense of angry powerlessness is clear when he dismisses Abner's delusional assumption that the Hopi are the "Chosen
People" by judging that they are, in fact, "marked for erasure" (NW 14).
Even toward the end of the novel, with the plague threatening to devas-
tate the entire Southwest, Duran is tempted to escape to California and
leave the Indians to their fate.

Self-loathing renders Duran passive and without hope, and his position at the crossroads of Anglo and Indian worlds provides just enough
insight to make him hate both: "[b]eing born a reservation Indian was
the same as committing a crime and being sentenced to life in isolation.
Quarantined with the perverse sickness that made life among the whites
the same as suffocation. The evidence-symptoms of this crime-disease:
self-pity, suspiciousness, stupidity, and pride. Was there an Indian of
the twentieth century, Youngman asked, who wasn't schizophrenic? And
who didn't use it as an excuse? Did anyone do it as well as him?" (NW 156).
Duran's sense of double deviancy, of being both criminalized and sick,
conflates social and biological pathologies in a self-damning articulation of the biopolitical exclusion of Indians as a condition of being. The
regulation and disciplining of Indian subjectivity here is so complete

that even Duran's ability to identify the contradictions of his circumstances does nothing to ameliorate the schizophrenia and merely renders him immobile.

By choosing to call Duran "Flea," Abner seems to reinforce this sense
of insignificance, and fleas feature in the novel as the passive carriers of
plague. But Flea is also, we are told, the name of Popay, the Tewa who led
the Pueblo revolt that drove the Spanish back into Mexico in 1680 (NW
25). In recalling the prior enslavement of Pueblo Indians as miners, the
novel reinforces Abner's view of history's cyclical movement. Fuelled by
datura, Duran experiences a vision of the long history of diasporic indigenous civilization in the Americas, signaling his awakened knowledge
of his place in that history. Yet his decision to kill the bats is not the outcome Abner demanded, and Duran in effect uses the powers of Indian
medicine against the cleansing apocalyptic momentum Abner has apparently generated, following through the Vietnam logic of destroying
in order to save. While Duran has thwarted oil company incursion—the
site is now valueless—he has not removed the threat of future exploitation, and like the original Popay, Duran has achieved only a temporary
victory over external domination.

To the extent that Duran has embraced the power of traditional Indian medicine he can be said to have overcome the self-pity and skepticism that have burdened him throughout the novel. But in rejecting Abner's apocalypticism he has accepted the limits of that power in favor of
an alliance with Anglo science and the conventions of romantic love. Beyond this, however, the only real allegiance Duran has is to place, a sense
of place beyond the exclusionary biopolitics of the reservation that has
deformed belonging into quarantine. Anne identifies Duran as a "desert
creature" (NW 112) and accepts that he can never leave, and the unstated
implication of the novel seems to be that a reinvigorated Duran must operate as a complex vector of forces directed toward a redefinition of what
it means to be indigenous. While this redefinition is not explicitly articulated by the narrative, Duran has clearly rejected the passivity he previously identified as the disabling schizophrenia of twentieth-century Indian life and has recast his "crime-disease" as a form of agency. As Flea,
Duran is the carrier of a new hybrid identity strain that is immune both
to the debilitating inertia of reservation life's containment of energy and
Anglo capitalism's tendency to read the lifeworld as resource.

What, then, are we to make of the bats? Whether they have been invoked by Abner or driven into Arizona by scientists, the vampires are curiously placed in the narrative as possible representatives of either a rapacious capitalism—all living things are potential food; their only drive is to consume—or the return of a repressed indigenous power. Emanating from Mexico and roosting in the ancient underground pueblo, the bats are an awakened underworld power capable of dismantling the Anglo social order. As such, the "invasion" of the vampires anticipates Silko's prophesy in *Almanac of the Dead* of the reclamation of the United States by the abjected multitude from the South. Like the much-feared "hordes" that haunt the imagination of nativist nationalism, the bats "seemed like a solid mass," flowing "unchecked" over all borders (NW 32), organized not by leaders but by a collective instinct "first carried out by the most aggressive individuals" (NW 66). The scientist Hayden Paine's obsessive desire to "know" and destroy the bats is likewise a version of Enlightenment science's will to dominate the "natural" akin to McCarthy's Judge Holden, who documents to destroy. At times, Paine accepts the reciprocal relationship between humanity and bat, explaining that plague is a consequence of civilization, with increased human population density producing epidemics that lead to adaptive social change that never eradicates the inevitable return of the disease. The bats, in a curious way, are the "natural" agents of cultural transformation, Paine's theory echoing Abner's view of successive worlds cyclically replacing the decadent old order. But Paine is not satisfied with this dialectical relationship, and craves a final annihilation of the vampires so humanity can take its place at the pinnacle of creation. The vampire, he believes, is the "freak" of nature that "gave nothing in return for its all-consuming thirst" and is therefore "evil" (NW 264). As his obsession leads him to conclude that "you are what you kill," Paine comes to see himself as part of the vampire, "one beast conceived in death" (NW 263).

Paine's identification of himself with the bats suggests that the drive to exterminate them is a form of self-annihilation, an uncanny recognition of the other as an inseparable property of himself. It may be, then, that the vampires in *Night Wing* simultaneously embody the destructive capacity of capitalism's power to consume and the fear of consumption's terrible other—the waste products never completely concealed in the dumping grounds (reservations, landfills, Third World countries) of the underworld.

Contagious Alliances

If *Night Wing* recalls *Ceremony*'s hybrid Euro-Indian sensibility, the similarity is likely accidental, the two books having been published the same year. In A. A. Carr's *Eye Killers* such similarities are much more deliberate and self-aware, the novel riffing on what by the 1990s had become staple characteristics of Native American fiction. A highly self-conscious and lurid hybrid of European vampire gothic and supernatural Navajo skinwalkers, *Eye Killers* is a rescue narrative in which an alienated urban Navajo/Keresan teenage girl is abducted by Falke, a nine-hundred-year-old Viennese vampire. After acquiring the requisite tribal wisdom necessary to do battle, Melissa's grandfather Michael and her teacher, the Irish woman Diana Logan, pursue Falke to his lair deep within an ancient cave in the desert outside of Albuquerque. While environmental damage is not foregrounded the way it is in *Cavern* and *Night Wing*, references to uranium mining and the vampire trope's overdetermined metaphorical baggage of defilement and extraction places *Eye Killers* squarely in the same contaminated genre space.

The elements of gothic thriller and *Ceremony*-like indigenous reintegration narrative in *Eye Killers* are further modified and synthesized by reference to various mass-cultural subgenres and their stock characters and situations, including the high school horror film, with its frustrated schoolteacher (also hijacked from the classic western), troubled pubescent girls, and the villain's jealous mistress. All the conventions of the Dracula story—old world evil, the taxonomy of sexual and sociological contamination, racism, exile, caves, grotesque servants, mysterious aristocracy, disused churches and theatres—are rewritten in *Eye Killers* as a fin de siècle slasher script. The classic counter-Enlightenment privileging of emotional over rational understanding is also deployed, with the suggestion that an overreliance on reason breeds a fascination with the things reason banishes, triggering a return of the repressed.

Alongside these familiar Euro-American tropes and conventions, Carr draws upon important strands of Indian culture and, as in Silko

195

and Momaday, *Eye Killers* approaches alienation among modern Indians through a syncretic ceremonial engagement with tradition that appropriates and modifies oral cultural forms into written narrative structure. The Euro-American and Native narrative conventions Carr deploys have much in common. Both share the sense of the mysteries of place, that the strange is embedded or concealed in the familiar. Both rely on repetition and transformation and are concerned with questions of intersubjectivity, with a sharing of thoughts that dissolves the discrete individual subject and the division between public and private. The gothic and the Indian concerns also revolve around questions of heritage, inheritance, and blood. The deep sense of palpable alienation registered by much recent Native American fiction also chimes with gothic themes of exile and powerlessness. In *Eye Killers* the vampires are exiled in the desert, having been marginalized in much the same way that Indians have been on reservations. Finally, both vampires and Indians are not only spatially positioned as exceptional threats to the integrity of the national body, they also share the burden of a history of representations that figure them as emanations from the past. While the vampire lives for hundreds of years, the figure of the Indian has also functioned in the American national imaginary as an artifact of pre-Columbian antiquity.[48]

It is in this sense of temporal duration that *Eye Killers* draws most heavily on the position articulated in *Ceremony*, for the restoration of peace, the reconstruction of family, and the eradication of evil in Carr's novel must, as for Silko, come through the power of storytelling as a means of survival through the perpetual presence of cultural memory. Storytelling is a crucial aspect of *Eye Killers*, both for the characters and their sense of their needs and duties and also in terms of the way the novel itself functions as a meditation on and celebration of narrative as a complex plastic form of cultural critique. As with *Ceremony*, the traditional narrative ritual must engage with changed circumstances and must itself be changed by those circumstances. This cannot be a "pure blood" Indian narrative, nor can it be a straightforward vampire novel; it must mutate convention into something other in order to absorb the problems of changed circumstances. As such, *Eye Killers* strategically and endlessly compromises distinctions between oral and written texts, between Indian and Anglo, between realistic and fantastic, the authentic and the absurd, between U.S. individualism and Indian communalism, ancient and contemporary, past and present.

While the vampires are clearly predatory invaders, feeding off the indigenous population and contemptuously referring to the Indians as "savages," Carr refuses to allow the vampires to simply stand in for Anglo culture. The Indians recognize the vampires as skinwalkers, acknowledging an Indian equivalent to the European monster and thereby establishing a continuity between cultures: Falke observes that "[t]he ancestors of your old savages . . . understood creatures such as me, though they gave us different names."[49]

While this may be seen as a political retreat from the critique of imperialism Carr has already set up into a metaphysics of evil, it is in keeping with the necessarily hybrid coalition he, along with Cruz Smith and Silko, promotes as the imperative form resistance must take in order to combat the disembodied power of the dominant order. Diana's initiation as a Navajo warrior is a recognition of the need to form new alliances when young Indians refuse to accept their traditional place within the tribe and a rejection of blood ties as the only legitimate pathway to communal inclusion.

As such, while the novel pivots on what has already or what is in danger of being lost—the innocence of young Indians, an organic Indian community, Diana's self-esteem and her marriage, an uncontaminated environment, Michael's memory—recovery is not configured as a clean return but as a preservation of the principle: broadly speaking, cultural memory and communal bonds. These may be reforged by the end of the narrative but not in any straightforward way. Identities are not bound by blood ties but renegotiated as a consequence of the struggle to make visible and throw off the influence of evil. As Eric Gary Anderson has written of the novel, "the routes and roots of human (and nonhuman) relationships" are seen "as pedagogical in nature." The vampires, Anderson suggests, "have to learn how to be vampires" just as "the Navajo have to learn how to be Navajo." Acts of cultural transmission "acknowledge permeable boundaries" that suggest that it is not merely narratives that are important but also the "relationships and transitions between stories."[50]

Falke's demise is, then, not so much due to his failure in battle but because, of all the characters, he is the one who stands alone and refuses to change; he becomes a living-dead cliché. As Diana spots straight away: "the man in black—perfect!" (EK 184). Diana and Michael triumph because their identities are precariously placed when faced with evil, keeping them open to contingency and advice from the most improbable sources. In order for Michael to remember the old ways he must move among the community, talk to all the people who can still remember the old stories, and proceed as the carrier of collective wisdom through a kind of contagious relay.

Diana and Michael, like Duran, Silko's Tayo, and Momaday's Abel, occupy the threshold or bordered position conventionally held by the sorcerer in that they live physically and emotionally on the outskirts of the community. Sorcerers, claim Deleuze and Guattari, are anomalous individuals who "haunt the fringes" between settlements.[51] They are capable of forming "assemblages" of alliance, collectivities that are not hierarchical and filiated like the biological family, but produced by contingent networks of association. Indeed, such assemblages, like wolf packs, "express minoritarian groups, or groups that are oppressed, prohibited, in revolt, or always on the fringe or recognized institutions, groups all the more secret for being extrinsic, in other words, anomic."[52]

Falke, who insists on the purity of the monoculture and resists contamination, is representative of oppressive regimes based on blood affiliation and hierarchy, while the forces of good in the novel embrace the pollution of blood and tradition. The figure of the vampire here is positioned both as negative parasite and as positive agent for the contamination of monological order. Falke is the clearly evil abductor, but the text itself is a vampiric cannibal of a more critical order, absorbing into itself the lifeblood of heterogeneous cultural conventions.

Donna Haraway has observed that "[f]ascination with mixing and unity is a symptom of preoccupation with purity and decomposition." The United States, she goes on, "like any expanding capitalist society that must continually destroy what it builds and feed off of every being it perceives as natural—if its strategies of accumulation of wealth are to continue to push the envelope of catastrophe—. . . is consumed with images of decadence, obsolescence, and corruption of kind." America's landscape discourse of gardens and wilderness is part of a "therapeutically crucial" narrative of "national innocence" that refuses to acknowledge the despoliation it generates and must bury the evidence.[53] In the face of this public fiction of purity the figure of the vampire, Haraway claims, is a powerful "vector of category transformation in a racialized, historical, national consciousness." He or she is "one who pollutes lineages," "promises and threatens racial and sexual mixing," and "feeds off the normalized human." The vampire, Haraway concludes, "insists on the nightmare of racial violence behind the fantasy of purity in the rituals of kinship."[54]

Certainly, in *Eye Killers* such "a fantasy of purity" is not reproduced in the rituals of kinship, which are reconfigured not along blood lines but through mutual respect and need. This is very much Haraway's position, which rejects kinship bonds in favor of "models of solidarity and human unity and difference rooted in friendship, work, partially shared purposes, intractable collective pain, inescapable mortality, and persistent hope."[55] The rejection of blood ties makes it possible to "theorize an 'unfamiliar' unconscious, a different primal scene, where everything does not stem from the dramas of identity and reproduction."[56] As such, Haraway is "on the side of the vampires, or at least some of them. But, then, since when does one get to choose which vampire will trouble one's dreams?"[57]

Haraway's final point here is apposite, signaling the doubleness of the trope of the vampire and the difficulty of knowing which allegiances it is safe to make. In the context of the toxic West, the decisions are no less complex. The monstrous presence of prehistoric bears or a plague of bats signals the eruption of hostile but natural forces caused by but also in opposition to the power of science. Indeed, Abner in *Night Wing* calls up this supernatural catastrophe in order to punish the unnatural defilement of the land. The novelists' refusal to align themselves with the purifying discourse of either Anglo or Indian racial integrity suggests a rejection of blood kinship and a reconception of community that is always already shot through with contagious and possibly lethal contamination of the other.

Alongside Haraway, Deleuze and Guattari have put forward a similar argument for the embrace of the gothic monster, a kind of counternature that approximates the deep subterranean or high temperature proliferation of life Page describes in *Cavern* that is indifferent to scientific orthodoxy. Positioning the bonds formed by the band or the pack against biological allegiance, Deleuze and Guattari claim that such collectivities "proliferate by contagion, epidemics, battlefields, and catastrophes" and do not reproduce themselves but begin "over again every time, gaining that much more ground."[58] If such "unnatural" unions are the "true nature," a kind of deep structure of transmutation, the vampire is a key trope since it "does not filiate, it infects." Contagion "involves terms that are entirely heterogeneous," like Michael and Diana in *Eye Killers*, producing combinations that "are neither genetic nor structural" but are instead "interkingdoms, unnatural participations."[59] Nature works "against itself," according to Deleuze and Guattari, not through the binary of hereditary reproduction but through a kind of polymorphous perversity where there are "as many differences as elements contributing to a process of contagion."[60]

The ad hoc gatherings of the pack stand in opposition to family or religious or state institutions, and are closer to peripheral social formations such as "hunting societies, war societies, secret societies, crime societies, etc."[61] This countercultural man of war, Deleuze and Guattari argue, is characterized by "multiplicity, celerity, ubiquity, metamorphosis and treason, the power of affect. Wolf-men, bear-men, wildcat-men, men of every animality, secret brotherhoods, animate the battlefields."[62] What distinguishes the "becoming-animal" is a kind of externalization not evident in conventional institutional collectivities; becoming-animal is a sum of its affects, a genuine semiotic agency stripped of the constraints of the symbolic order.

Within the pack as a kind of inside outsider is the sorcerer, the "exceptional individual" who is a "Loner" and a "Demon" standing at "the cutting edge of deterritorialization."[63] The seeming contradiction here between the collectivity of the pack and the individuated loner is, for Deleuze and Guattari, precisely the point: the anomalous is "a phenomenon of bordering" occupying a space between individual and species.[64] The anomalous protagonists of the fiction of gothic contamination are, in this sense, the excluded agents of collective reintegration. As the abjected remainder of filial attachments, they are not contained by regimes of biological or cultural purity and instead find allies according to shared purpose and collective pain rather than blood loyalty.

The open secret of environmental poisoning in the West may have centers of intensified race- or class-specific devastation, as the Native American experience in the Four Corners shows. At the same time, the nature of toxic contamination means that effects are impossible to contain. Alliances formed in the toxic West between the heterogeneous communities affected by fallout, strip mining, and other military-industrial damage confirm the model of collectivities that "proliferate by contagion, epidemics, battlefields, and catastrophes." Part of the price paid for the ascendancy of the military-industrial West has been, post-Trinity, the death of the "natural" as somehow a guarantor of things being in their rightful place. What the toxic discourse of gothic contamination introduces is the notion that in the collapse of an unreflective trust in the natural order lies an expanded and unpredictable conception of how "nature," even in its most monstrous forms, could function as a model for new modes of political engagement.

8. AFTER NATURE WRITING

Government ought to be all outside and no inside.
Woodrow Wilson

While the sometimes lurid excesses of contemporary Western gothic thrillers call attention to themselves as monstrous representations of equally monstrous facts, it is their very implausibility that signals the difficulty of grasping the unseen. These fictions attempt to construct an expanded field of what "nature" might mean after the military-industrial contamination of the Western environment. A similar challenge has presented itself to the generic limits of Western nature writing in recent years, as the effects of nuclear weapons testing and industrial exploitation have been increasingly felt. "Nowhere," writes Lawrence Buell, "is [the] blurring of standard genre distinctions more striking than in contemporary works of nature writing produced under pressure of toxic anxiety."[1] If the empirically observed is no longer an adequate basis upon which an understanding of the environment can be achieved, the verifiability of "nonfiction" as an account of what is there must be interrogated.

Three books published during the 1990s sought to rethink the relationship between nature writing as a form of spiritual autobiography and Western environmental politics. Terry Tempest Williams's *Refuge: An Unnatural History of Family and Place* (1991), Rebecca Solnit's *Savage Dreams: A Journey into the Landscape Wars of the American West* (1994), and Ellen Meloy's *The Last Cheater's Waltz: Beauty and Violence in the Desert Southwest* (1999) share the strategy of braiding personal narratives of emplacement with political awakening. All are enthralled by the physical, rather than simply retinal, experience of being in the West, and each text responds to the often uncanny realization of the concealed presence of military power in a landscape otherwise considered in some way to be redemptive or, at the very least, compelling in its intensities. The subtitles of these books make clear the nature of the collision of place and power that has occurred: Williams's history of family and place is "unnatural"; Solnit's journey is not into the West but into the "landscape wars" of the West; for Meloy, "beauty" and "violence" are on equal terms.

In some respects these are very different books with different agendas. *Refuge* combines Williams's work as a naturalist with the story of her mother's cancer and explores the extent to which private experience can be made public. There is clearly an analogy here with the need for secret or hidden knowledge about military testing to be brought to light, and Williams's private testimony is increasingly situated within the public discourse of "downwinder" politics.[2] *Savage Dreams* is more journalistic in its account of protests at the Nevada Test Site and the history of Indian "removal" at what is now Yosemite National Park. Solnit's book draws on first-person and firsthand accounts, historical records, novels, and other sources, and the text is heavily populated with activists, officials, and historical records. Meloy's work, by contrast, is characterized by solitude, driven by a more amorphous malaise to chart what she calls "the map of the known universe." The account is contextualized by the house-building project Meloy and her husband undertake in southeastern Utah, and the presiding emphasis is on the prospect of finding and making a home place, both literally and more expansively in terms of belonging. Each foray into the land, however, tends to produce anxiety and alienation rather than intimacy as the narrator encounters evidence of the military-industrial presence all around. What is discovered in each case is that what was considered secure—family, landscape, the democratic expectations of freedom of movement and protection from harm—is radically unstable and permeated by the fallout of postwar history.

What is clear in all of these books is the need to find a way of writing about the environment that includes the political struggles that take place within and about it. This is nature writing that, while maintaining a commitment to the representation of the nonhuman world, insists upon the interrelationship of "nature" and human activity in all its forms. At a mundane but necessary level, this includes accounts in all books of driving through the landscape, of moving between and through cities, towns, industrial sites, military bases, national parks, wildlife refuges, and uninhabited areas. There is no clear division between a notionally untouched "wilderness" and space shaped by human agency in these texts just as there is often an intentional blurring of distinctions between past and present. Indeed, while all the books contain passages that celebrate the powerful fact of the natural environment, its forms, scale, even its beauty, these are works that position "nature" as a complex term that cannot be extricated from the broader discourses of which it is part. Political, economic, and social concerns press hard on the "natural" here, as does the politics of representation. In each of these books, the open secret of the wasteland discourse becomes the fact of Western space that underwrites any apprehension of landscape, and the texts must work through the implications of a "nature" mediated, not just through the displacements of phenomenological and linguistic filters, but also through the occlusions of military-industrial screening. To write about the landscape is to become entangled in the representational politics of place, and Williams, Solnit, and Meloy all recognize and seek to respond to the always already constructed fact of the places they describe. The resulting texts necessarily corrupt the genre of "nature" writing, understood as a mode of addressing the relationship between the human and nonhuman, since they, however reluctantly, must include the effects of power on the land and, indeed, themselves, not just as a blight produced from elsewhere but as constitutive of Western space after World War II. In doing so, they expose, as Buell notes of *Refuge*, "how much even the previous generation of green activist writing about this region . . . has overlooked or suppressed."[3]

As with so many of the works discussed in this book, the environmental writing examined in this chapter develops an argument about state sovereignty even as its focus is ostensibly local. McCarthy's novels of violence, loss, and homelessness, for example, even at their most metaphysical and abstract, invite a consideration of the material causes of violence and abandonment rooted in the delimitation of space as territory. Similarly, novels concerned with Japanese American internment, even, and perhaps especially, when they seek to represent the effects of displacement on individual lives, are unavoidably involved in a meditation on the biopolitical construction of a subjectivity regulated by the political deployment of physical environment. The bats and bears in *Night Wing*, *Eye Killers*, and *Cavern* serve similarly to probe the limits of territorial sovereignty and provide symbolic material for a consideration of how "nature" might offer alternative models for recombinant social formations. In the same way, Williams, Meloy, and Solnit, while rooting their narratives in the particularities of family, home, and being in place, identify these local contexts as always already imbued with the atmosphere of sovereign power as it serves to give form to the meaning of those contexts.

Seth Shulman argues that the military's inability or unwillingness to deal with the environmental problems caused by its activities is a "perverse and unintended outcome" of the doctrine of sovereign immunity.[4] Since the very purpose of the military is to be able to fight wars, and because that ability demands security-driven secrecy, "the military has used the doctrine of sovereign immunity to bolster its claim to near autonomy in national security matters."[5] Shulman quotes a 1986 article by two Air Force lawyers who state that "due to the unique status of the military in our society" it should be expected that environmental laws, "like the public, stop at the installation gate."[6]

However, while it is it obvious that pollution does not respect gates or fences, President Carter did, in a 1978 executive order, attempt to waive sovereign immunity where environmental laws are concerned. Executive agencies, the order ruled, should apply the same standards that would apply to a private person and all applicable pollution control standards should be met. The government's failure to enforce environmental laws in line with Carter's order was, according to Shulman, due to Ronald Reagan's fondness for the so-called "unitary theory of the executive," a notion, incidentally, that has more recently found favor with the George W. Bush administration. In an executive order issued in 1987, Reagan limited the Environmental Protection Agency's (EPA) jurisdiction by claiming that the federal Justice Department must approve any actions undertaken by the EPA against federal facilities. Since, following the unitary theory, one part of the executive cannot sue another, enforcement of environmental laws was severely hampered.[7]

As we have already seen, the reciprocal relationship between executive and military authority has profoundly shaped the Western landscape and its meanings since Pearl Harbor. Here, deploying executive power in the name of national security enables the exemption of the military from environmental responsibility. The legal inscription of military land use as the blank space on the map is thus reinforced as that which is other to the environment that surrounds it, even as the effects of actions upon that space literally fall out beyond its parameters. While security contains the military within a demarcated zone of exclusion, with environmental law, like the public, stopped at the gate, the line between inside and outside is fatally compromised in the other direction. This bleeding of the exception into the "surroundings" is both an effect of security and a contamination of it. The openness of open space, as it is approached, experienced, and represented by Williams, Meloy, and Solnit, conceals the hidden effects of a porous exceptional space that is installed inside openness itself. The notional symbolic liberty embodied in open Western landscape—a "natural" expansiveness that confirms political freedom—must, then, be approached as a discourse underwritten by the legally sanctioned restriction of democratic law. The material effects of this apparent contradiction—restricted areas, irradiated terrain, poisoned populations, permanently harassed residents—becomes the material that comprises this nature writing.

Locate, Focus, Observe, and Identify

The relationship between home place and the political landscape is there from the beginning of *Refuge*, though the indications are at this point muted. As Nathaniel Lewis notes, when Williams refers in the prologue to "the country I come from and how it informs my life" she means primarily the Utah area around the Great Salt Lake but also, indirectly, the United States.[8] The sign-off date for the prologue is July 4, and this invocation of Thoreauvian independence folds the personal into the national as well as inserting her text into the tradition of politically animated naturalist writing.

While the themes that drive *Refuge* are laid out at the outset—landscape, conservation, sickness, family—the connections between them and the political assault on federal contamination of the environment and the population that follows are revealed slowly and incrementally. As the level of the lake rises with each chapter, elements emerge that start to gain weight and depth, and the different narrative threads begin to become braided together. The book is concerned with the visible and the invisible, the known and unknown, and takes great pains to show itself revealing what it knows. The prologue prepares the reader by opening with the statement that everything about Great Salt Lake "is exaggerated—the heat, the cold, the salt, and the brine"; it is "a landscape so surreal one can never know what it is for certain" (R 3). It is not explained whether this exaggeration refers to depictions of the conditions of the lake environment or whether the lake itself stands in excessive relation to what is held to be normal for lakes. Either way, it remains somehow unknowable.

One of the most common surrealist strategies is that of radical juxtaposition, the forcing together of unlikely and unrelated objects to produce a shock of misrecognition and a rupturing of familiar models of what constitutes ordinary life. It is the combination itself that produces the shock, and perhaps this is what Williams is thinking of in describing the landscape as surreal. The collision of heat, cold, salt, and brine produces an unexpected and unprecedented singularity of place that is at odds with what conventionally constitutes a landscape. The other thing about surrealist juxtapositions is that they function as a kind of unveiling of secret correspondences between things, showing a disturbing and grotesque relationship among ostensibly unrelated objects and phenomena. The surrealist fascination with dream states and the unconscious, "primitive" and extra-rational knowledge is manifested in the desire to make visible the hidden forces animating human action and social relations.

Refuge is a book about secret relationships and the attempt to bring to light the metaphorical, political, and historical interrelatedness of disparate forces, objects, and modes of knowledge and understanding. Williams, as a naturalist, is involved in a constant process of watching for signs. These signs may be easy to read—a particular bird may be common to the area and identified immediately; less common species may be found quickly in a reference book—or they may be oblique and variously occluded, such as a mirage's skewing of distance or when "what you know is hidden behind the weather" (R 141). Reading the environment involves interpretive complexity and an understanding that things may not be in plain sight. As such, the book is invested both in the processes of cataloguing and differentiating ("locate, focus, observe, and identify" [R 115]) that constitute scientific knowledge—species of birds, levels of the lake—and in a kind of divining, a probing into the folded spaces inside the knowable. *Refuge* constantly reminds the reader of the difficulties of unstable knowledge and the prospect of dissemblance. The Great Salt Lake is "exaggerated" but also, as "water in the desert that no one can drink," it is also the "liquid lie of the West" (R 5). The naturalist notation of bird names and precise details of lake level that give each chapter its title, then, imply a knowability that is constantly undercut by the sense of the unknowable nature of the events encountered.

The secretive and often deceptive nature of being in the desert is reiterated throughout *Refuge* and the sense of hiddenness is both an invitation and a blockage, a seduction and a rebuff. Sometimes secrecy is the refuge for a private identification with place: after a day bird-watching as a child, Williams falls asleep dreaming "of all that is hidden" (R 20); there are "female" dunes "hidden from interstate travelers" that entice her to "lie naked and disappear" (R 109). The paradox of the desert as secret refuge lies in the fact that "there is no place to hide, and so we are found" (R 148). At other times, the deception is a challenge to the affective power of looking. After watching a beautiful sunset, Williams must reconcile retinal pleasure with the knowledge of the pollution that has supplied it: "I can honor its beauty or resent the smog in this valley which makes it possible. Either way, I am deceiving myself " (R 52). The desire for aesthetic confirmation of nature's redemptive presence is compromised here, yet Williams acknowledges that denial of the optical pleasure of the sunset, despite the smog's corrupting influence, would also be a lie. Indeed, the necessary contradiction is in appreciating the scene while fully recognizing the toxicity that produces it. Even the knowledge of the hidden in this instance cannot overrule the retinal impact and its affective power.

Williams's willingness to note her own contradictory impulses and self-deception positions the narrator as akin, if not identical, to the landscape. The ambiguous status of the landscape as an object of knowledge, then, is not decided from the point of view of an otherwise stable subject position. Williams's insistence from the outset that her identity and that of her text are of a piece with the land that makes them possible suggests that the indeterminacy of the landscape is shared by the narrative position. The three interwoven narratives that drive *Refuge*—the flooding of the Great Salt Lake in 1983, the fate of the Bear River Migratory Bird Refuge, and the loss of Williams's mother and two grandmothers to cancer—are all signaled in the retrospective frame of the brief prologue. What is also plain at the outset is how the text itself is materially woven into these events. Williams describes sitting on the floor of her study with her journals spread out before her: "I open them and feathers fall from their pages, sand cracks their spines, and sprigs of sage pressed between passages of pain heighten my sense of smell—and I remember the country I come from and how it informs my life" (R 3).

This insistence on the inseparability of place, identity, and text as materially present, bits of the earth interleaved into the pages of writing, demands that the narrative be understood as an incarnation of a life, not merely a representation of it. On one hand, the text claims its authenticity on the grounds that it is part of the materials it describes, a kind of embodied utterance that conventionally works as a way of guaranteeing truth value. On the other, the very insistence *Refuge* makes that the subject, the place, and the text be conceived as of a piece must guide the reader to understand that every assertion of duplicity and inscrutability assigned to the land must also be an attribute of the narrator and the text. So if the Great Salt Lake is "exaggerated" with a "shifting shoreline" and a tendency to promise something by its appearance that it cannot deliver (drinkable water), then so too must it be inferred that the stability of the subject position of the narrator and the text itself tend toward duplicity, variability, and exaggeration.

These two assertions—that the text is authentic; that it is indeterminate—are not incompatible, but they do destabilize the reading process. The importance of the claim to authenticity must stand in order for the information *Refuge* conveys about the environment, sickness, and pollution to have any weight as criticism. The necessity of insisting on indeterminacy is also indispensable because it operates to undercut the confidence that anything can be fully and finally known, it rejects the notion of a fixed and stable narrative subject, and it acknowledges that the introduction of previously unforeseen or unknown information or events can reshape shorelines, family histories, and narrative accounts of them.

In fact, the slipperiness of the text belies its ostensibly straightforward structure, which also, I would argue, is a deliberate form of "liquid lie." The use of shoreline measurements as chapter headings and the tendency of chapters to be broken into short segments, sometimes of a single paragraph, produce the effect of the text being a diary or journal. This idea has already been implanted in the prologue with the image of the narrator sitting among her primary documents. While it is never admitted

overtly, the body of the text might be taken as the more or less unmediated contents of those journals, even though a glance at the acknowledg-
ments gives the lie to this notion: Williams's father, we are told, "read
each draft, edited and discussed the scaffolding of ideas built around
a tender . . . chronology" (R 291). The effect of the text's structure, as it
moves back and forth through time, interweaving aspects of natural and
family history, local and personal events, reinforces the impression of
the book as a collection of journal entries, seemingly related by a loose
thread of thought or by the accident of timing. There is, though, nothing accidental about this structure, and the journal effect produced by it
makes possible the kind of surrealist juxtapositioning of ostensibly dissimilar information in a way that sparks unanticipated connections for
the reader that are, in fact, deliberately paced.

Refuge is an "unnatural" history in the sense that all histories are re-
constructions of events shot through with retrospective narrative significance. The unfolding of a "natural" or unmediated series of events
as they happened through the unoccluded consciousness of "Terry Tempest Williams" is, in the very subtitle of Refuge, refused and challenged.
Instead, the text calls attention to its awkward relationship with "what
happened" even as it performs and insists upon the function of truth telling. The truth is, in Refuge, that knowledge must be gleaned through the
scrim of historical, environmental, political, and personal obstructions,
blockages, and screens. The seeding of the text with intimations of deception destabilizes the narrative's capacity to "locate, focus, observe, and
identify" even as it preserves these values as necessary in order to define
the shape of what cannot be directly seen. The accumulation of suggestions of various kinds of hiddenness, secrecy, and intended or accidental
occlusion (the obstructiveness of objects and climate, the self-conceal-
ment of birds and insects, the secret residuum of ancient tribes revealed
by the archaeological dig, the self-deception of the narrator) primes the
reader to understand this as an environment of unseen forces. The personal and political implications of cancer as it emerges as the focus of
the narrative are, then, extrapolated out of an environment that is always
already riven with invisible contingencies.

The family's response to Diane Dixon Tempest's cancer, like the
text's and the landscape's oscillation between moments of exposure

and concealment, is characterized by the double forces of confrontation and denial. Just as no one can say with certainty what caused the cancer, when or if it can be cured—what Williams calls the "curse and charisma of cancer" (R 36)—similarly, no one is sure how to speak of it and how much information to give. Discussion of the disease and its treatment is reticent and perforated with absences and omissions. Doctors ask "[h]ow much should I tell her?" (R 199), husbands and children worry about when to break news, even the patient admits that "I think I have denied having cancer for years" (R 200). Asked by her mother if treatment has succeeded in removing all the cancer, Williams admits it did not, provoking her father's rage because they had agreed to say nothing until the following day. "I could not lie," Williams responds (R 38). Later, she admits that she has "refused to believe that Mother will die" (R 75), yet "by denying her cancer, even her death, I deny her life" (R 76). Denial selfishly screens out "the potency of a truth we cannot yet bear to accept" (R 76). As a form of insidious occlusion of the unwanted truth, denial "flourishes in the familiar. It seduces us with our own desires and cleverly constructs walls around us to keep us safe" (R 76). The imperative not to lie is perpetually compromised and challenged by the desire, as with the smog-induced sunset, to screen off the devastating truth of what is really there.

What is really there, of course, is the repressed fact of environmental contamination caused by nuclear testing. This repression is not merely a form of collective and political amnesia, but also, as Williams eventually accepts, personal: only after her father explains her persistent dream of a flash of light in the night as a real memory of a witnessed explosion from 1957 does she realize "the deceit I had been living under" (R 283). "You were sitting on Diane's lap," her father explains. "Within a few minutes, a light ash was raining on the car" (R 283). Coming near the end of Refuge, this revelation—"I thought you knew that," her father says (R 283)—feeds back through the book to irradiate all that precedes it.

Refuge, I think, deliberately represses the fact of military contamination of the environment, which is, nevertheless, the absent presence that animates Williams's meditations on exposure and concealment throughout the book. The first mention of Utah's nuclear history does not come until more than forty pages into the narrative, following a meditation on the cultural meaning of cancer, and the possible significance of the introduction of what will become a crucial aspect of the book is suitably veiled. A business call about the availability for screening of a documentary about uranium tailings in the Four Corners area functions largely to break off the private musings of the narrator in the previous section. Williams is diverted by the call and reflects on the business of the museum as "a good place to be quietly subversive on behalf of the land." She closes the door and begins "to plot my strategy" (R 44). The strategy here is, however, already plotted, and this interlude, offered as relief from her grim thoughts on cancer, in fact advances those thoughts in a different register.

It is the history of nuclear activity in the West as repressed memory that will eventually emerge in the book's epilogue, the celebrated "The Clan of One-Breasted Women," originally published in the magazine *Northern Lights* a year before *Refuge*. As a coda to the preceding narrative that transforms *Refuge*'s meaning by making explicit what has been withheld or only partially considered, the epilogue paradoxically precedes the book in terms of chronological publication. "The Clan of One-Breasted Women" precedes *Refuge* and also completes it. Like Williams's childhood recurring dream of a flash that is actually the real flash of an above-ground nuclear explosion, the knowledge of contamination was there all along. Regardless of the order in which the texts were written, the epilogue "came to light" in advance of the narrative that leads up to it. The journal effect produced by the narrative form is here patently exposed as artifice: this is not a display of thoughts and events unfolding but rather a calibrated release of information that, by the epilogue, reveals itself to have strategically concealed the conclusions it knew in advance it would come to. As Lisa Diedrich explains: "*Refuge* is punctuated by glimpses of knowledge received only in flashes, and Williams must be a witness to these flashes even without fully knowing what they mean in the moment of their emergence. In attempting to capture in language our usual relationship to change, which is, in a sense, a relationship to new knowledge, Williams describes 'a sense of something tenuous.'"[9]

The text, then, is the incubator of secrets about itself, like a hidden cancer or the hidden history of exposure to nuclear testing. *Refuge* invites this comparison itself, comparing cancer to the creative process.

Quoting from the OED, Williams notes the definition of cancer as "anything that frets, corrodes, corrupts, or consumes slowly and secretly" (R 43). Cancer, as a "disease of shame," "encourages secrets and lies, to protect as well as to conceal" (R 43). The shame comes from the fact that the monstrous has emanated from within one's own body, as if called forth by the self, like an awful malignant double.

It is the military discourse that is used to describe the treatment of cancer—"the fight, the battle, enemy infiltration, and defense strategies" (R 43)—that prompts Williams to wonder how the illness can be rethought as somehow analogous to the creative. Of course, the probable cause of Williams's mother's cancer, while the notion of nuclear fallout has not yet been mentioned, is obliquely called forth in Williams's description of "rooms of secrecy" where "patient, doctor, and family find themselves engaged in war" (R 43). And the entire history of the post–World War II militarization of Western space is conjured up when she asks: "[c]an we be at war with ourselves and still find peace?" (R 43). Criticism of the language used in discussing cancer treatment is made to do so much more here, and these comments, like many other seemingly offhand remarks, recursively entwine the story of one diseased body with broader histories of place, nation, security, and secrecy.

To take cancer as a model for the creative process, then, is to retrieve from its shameful status a subversive valence feared by both its hosts and assailants. It is worth quoting Williams at length to demonstrate how the style here enacts the notion of cancer/creative process as deformed recombination:

> It begins slowly and is largely hidden. One cell divides into two; two cells divide into four; four cells divide into sixteen . . . normal cells are consumed by abnormal ones. Over time, they congeal, consolidate, make themselves known. Call it a mass, call it a tumor. It surfaces and demands our attention. We can surgically remove it. We can shrink it with radiation. We can poison it with drugs. Whatever we choose, though, we view the tumor as foreign, something outside ourselves. It is, however, our own creation. The creation we fear.
>
> The cancer process is not unlike the creative process. Ideas emerge slowly, quietly, invisible at first. They are most often abnormal

thoughts, thoughts that disrupt the quotidian, the accustomed. They divide and multiply, become invasive. With time, they congeal, consolidate, and make themselves conscious. An idea surfaces and demands total attention. I take it from my body and give it away. (R 43–44)

If, as *Refuge* insists, place, identity and writing are of a piece, then they must all be contaminated. Any attempt to articulate place must be toxic, infected with the capacity to dissimulate and mutate shared by fauna, cancer, and nuclear politics. The "unnatural," the "abnormal," and the disruptive must be embraced as the true face of the natural and the creative. The acceptance of cancer as part of the natural order, however, cannot extend to an acceptance of the aggressive and willful destruction of life and habitat by the military. What the book makes clear is that the real threat is less "cancer" as a disease, regardless of the pain and devastation it inflicts, but cancer-causing agents, military-industrial and chemical.

Williams's insistence that "I could not lie," as we have seen, is complicated by the fact that it is hard to tell the truth about something you cannot even see, let alone verify. The dilemma of the book emerges from the collision between the necessity for the truth of contamination to be spoken and the impossibility of proving links between bombs and cancer. Strategically, *Refuge* commits itself to the performance of this contradiction so that the inability to know anything for sure becomes its primary affective goal. Williams cannot prove that her mother or grandmothers and aunts "developed cancer from nuclear fallout in Utah. But I can't prove they didn't" (R 286). As Buell has persuasively argued, "[i]t is notoriously hard to demonstrate environmental causation of illness, given the limitation of preexisting research bases, not to mention the multiplicity of possible causal agents. The generation of conclusive data and accompanying regulatory codes is a lengthy and haphazard process," and in any case, science can only prove degrees of preexisting harm, not degrees of safety.[10] While there are clearly profound anxieties "about environmental poisoning for which there is often strong evidence," the kind of toxic discourse produced by Williams "is a discourse of allegation or insinuation rather than of proof."[11] Radiation, as Philip Fradkin observes, leaves no fingerprints.[12]

Just as the Tempest family's discussion of cancer is characterized by an oscillation between facing facts and denial, so too must Williams, in her condemnation of nuclear testing, propose a link between the tests and cancer in the downwind population only to withdraw from any categorical assertion that this is true: as Buell notes, "*Refuge* both levels charges and avoids claiming more than it can prove about the cause(s) of the family's illnesses." The tension generated by this frustration, for Buell, "produces a certain tortuousness" in the text.[13]

Just as the "blank spot on the map" translates as a "wasteland perfect for nerve gas, weteye bombs, and toxic waste" (R 241), the absence of a causal link between environmental contamination and cancer operates as an enabling gap opened up by the exceptional space of military occupation. The site is there but only negatively represented; the signs of the activity undertaken there are only seen indirectly through effects that cannot be verifiably traced back. Left high and dry by the logic of a unitary executive that can pass laws it can then exempt itself from, it is not surprising that the production of a narrative that seeks to unravel this knot becomes a meditation on provocative connections rather than provable causes. A similar "tortuousness" is evident in Ellen Meloy's *The Last Cheater's Waltz*, another work with cartographic ambitions thwarted by what Meloy calls "the silent chemistry of the desert."

A Map Broken into Pages

The prologue of *The Last Cheater's Waltz* opens with a boiled lizard. The narrator has inadvertently poured scalding water over it while making coffee, and the accidental killing prompts her to recognize that "matters of the mind had plunged to grave depths."[14] Whether the inattention is the cause of unease or a symptom is not clear, but despite living in a "much-loved, familiar place, . . . it and I floated apart from one another," and "I could no longer concentrate or hold life's focus or keep a coherent thought in my head" (LCW 4). The dead lizard is evidence of the dangers of inattention to place and comes, as the narrative proceeds, to represent in miniature the devastation caused to the environment when the mind is elsewhere. In order to deal with her "desensitized" (LCW 4) state, Meloy concludes that it is "time to get to know the neighborhood" (LCW 8). She takes a map of the region and marks her present location with an O, then draws a "manageable" two-hundred-mile circle around her home, placing the lizard at the center. In a notebook, she transcribes the contents of the circle into sections, "like an atlas" (LCW 8).

The book itself, then, stands at some remove from the process of what we might call the fieldwork that produces it, though the text suggests the necessary overlaying and transpositioning that takes place in the process of situating knowledge in place. The material fact of the dead lizard—"the small corpse" (LCW 8)—is laid on the O, ground zero, the "very dirt" of the home place. The map, which "offered a visual syntax of remembered journeys" and holds "a key to my somnambulance," ties representation to memory, and the sectioned notebook is intended to record the convergence of history (memory, geology, sites) and experience (the phenomenological event of being in place). The notebook is both a supplement to and an intensification of the map. The account of the process of getting to know the neighborhood that constitutes the text of *The Last Cheater's Waltz* is a further translation of the syntax of traversal. The lizard, the map, and the atlas are reflexively incorporated into the narrative's pursuit of reconnection with place as devices that signal the necessity of representation as a constitutive part of what it means to make the connection between being and emplacement. These devices are crucial but they are not, we are told, "blood": "the silent chemistry of the desert lay deep within me" (LCW 8). It is this lived interpenetration of land and self that animates the pursuit of a cause for the sense of "derailment" that is registered at the start of the book, but in many ways the answer, as in *Refuge*, is there all along.

The amorphous unease that is established in the prologue as the motor of the narrative is, in fact, produced by the "silent chemistry" that lay deep within the narrator. The sense of being removed from place—of ontological misalignment or of being beside oneself—is, as we soon learn, the very condition of that place as it has become the site of America's nuclear open secrets. The chemistry of the place contains unseen historical and biological contaminants. Identification with the land must entail a recognition of the disorder that has been produced by a fifty-year history of molecular rearrangement. The question posed only a few paragraphs into the book—"could I be repressing a fury so terrible, it had rendered me catatonic?" (LCW 4)—is a rhetorical one, for *The Last Cheater's Waltz* is nothing if not a confirmation of the weakly repressed history of uranium mining and nuclear testing. It is, then, given that the "silent chemistry" of the land lies "deep within," a book about the substantiation of a nuclear subjectivity and a nuclear body. The fact that this is known and felt but not understood—"the light [is] too often too bright to understand" (LCW 7)—is the necessary precondition of the narrative's latent drive to transcribe something about what it means to be of and in this particular place: "[a]s if by instinct I had long ago embraced the desert with the full knowledge that neither passion nor beauty comes without risk and that these conditions of being might well burn me right up" (LCW 5). The kind of risk referred to here is more than existential since "[i]n this abundant space and isolation, the energy lords extract their bounty of natural resources, and the curators of mass destruction once mined their egregious weapons and reckless acts" (LCW 6).

Given what the prologue sets us up to expect, it is no surprise that the journey detailed in the first chapter, ostensibly a quest for claret cup cacti—"Theirs is a wild and transient beauty of sweet, precise torture, an incarnation of the thin threshold between what the Zuni call the beautiful (tsoŷa) and the dangerous (attanni)" (LCW 12)—ends with the discovery of a curiously well-built road for which there is "no explanation" (LCW 17). As in the prologue, however, the reader is primed for this discovery not only by the ambivalent qualities attributed to the claret cup but also by a feeling of uneasy restlessness produced by the sight of "dark holes," of "mine shafts and waste piles" dotting the landscape (LCW 16).

The road ends "abruptly at an enormous field of disturbed soil, put back together and recontoured with earth-moving machinery." Next to it is an enclosure "surrounded by a chain-link fence about twelve feet high" (LCW 18). The fence contains a plastic-lined pit but little else. The entire site is "very strange" and produces in the narrator a sense of "unspecified dread" (LCW 18). Deciding that dread "can be part of the neighborhood," it too is entered into the "Map of the Known Universe" (LCW 19), though it is not specified whether what is sketched is dread itself or the fence and the pit that have produced the sensation. It is during the documentation that the connection between the site and the history of uranium mining in the area is made, suggesting that it is the active concentration involved in representing the observed environment that aids understanding. A short meditation on the name of the Tsé (rock) Valley and the immense age of the strata leads to the conclusion that "[i]n a strange convergence of human and geologic time, pieces of this valley had been deliberately unearthed, piled high, and exported to fuel an apocalypse" (LCW 20). The stress throughout this episode on strangeness lies in the uncanny effect produced by the inside literally being forced to the outside and its long-buried energy tapped for the purpose of unfathomable destruction. The "huge fence" that frames a seemingly innocuous pit signifies the threat posed by the energy to be found there, a kind of absurd gesture of containment that works largely as a symbolic barrier and offers no meaningful protection against the "querulous phantoms of mass death" (LCW 21).

Shaken by the discovery of evidence of contaminated ground, the narrator reminds herself of the lizard and its warning to "look closely and burn hotter"; understanding, if not peace of mind, must come by forging "the desert's sweetness and ferocity into my own, to find beauty" (LCW 21). This involves a search for the "missing pieces" of "the beds of fossil rivers removed from their deep burial in eternity" (LCW 21).

Meloy shares with Williams an "erotics of place" and longs for the kind of union with the landscape based on an intimacy with the environment that is thwarted at every attempt by the duplicity of the land as she finds it. The need for "soothing a persistent spiritual malaise by a renewed closeness to nature" is, as she visits the Trinity test site and White Sands Missile Range in order to track the destination of the uranium from the Tsé Valley rocks, "dimmed by further estrangement" (LCW 84). Lines on the map now join the home place with Trinity, Hiroshima, and Nagasaki. The map's concentric circles persist in expanding to connect in unwelcome but unavoidable ways the local and the global. Instead of helping "to instill more deeply the desert aesthetic that year after year reflexively seduces me," the map "itched. It did not stand still. Even though I had cast it over home terrain, it netted unsouled shapes and cruel angularities" (LCW 100). The more information that enters the map, the more it becomes a web of deception and hidden danger that produces anxiety and paranoia: "I was convinced that foreign armies occupied the Known Universe" (LCW 100). The familiar becomes "canted with new meaning," known territory now "husked and stripped bare, torn by flagrant episodes of the unfamiliar" (LCW 100). The Map of the Known Universe must contain the Southwest Defense Complex.

The old uranium mines a mere twenty miles from home lead Meloy to the "incongruous geography of wilderness and industrial warfare" at Trinity, and she feels her "most fervent loyalty" (LCW 100) to the land has been betrayed: "[m]y lover, my pure and faithful desert, was cheating" (LCW 101). Rattled by the experience of Trinity, the narrator repudiates "nomadic compulsions" and resolves to "find Home" (LCW 101) by staying put. With four survey pins she and her husband "fenced ourselves in" (LCW 102). In the "quintessentially western" act of establishing a boundary, steel posts and barbed wire "established 'control' over a parcel of ground" (LCW 102). Clocks and watches are hidden or thrown away and time is kept by reading the movement of the sun. Speaking for residents of the Four Corners, she explains that "[n]owhere—geographically speaking—is where a lot of us want to be. . . . The center of the world is elsewhere; the world has no other center but ours. No one is ever sure if we are hostages of isolation or the freest people in four states" (LCW 107).

The symbolic fencing in and erasure of the outside world performed here contains the awkward paradox at work within Meloy's text. On one hand the book is a self-consciously Western celebration of individual kinship with environment that irascibly rejects materialistic, urban American life. It draws on the plainspoken vernacular, the suspicion of authority, and the vaguely misanthropic isolationism that characterize much "nature" writing from Thoreau to Abbey. On the other hand, the empirical fidelity to experience demanded by that tradition compels Meloy to front the fact of a half-century of military-industrial enterprise in the region. She knows that her longing for an uncompromised "Western" freedom is close to becoming part of the simulated "Western" tourist experience produced in the national parks that stand as "wild" counterpoints to the barely contained wildness of the military sites. While returning home is a rejection of what Trinity represents and an embrace of the quotidian as the ground for understanding place, it is also in part a retreat into the myth of the atomized, self-reliant stake-claimer: "I wished to deny the Colorado Plateau's own history. I was ready for refuge. I was ready to stick the Map into the nearest sand dune and walk away" (LCW 100).

The local, as Meloy knows, is no refuge from the facts of history. When she asks if her home is "inside the lethal heart of Trinity?" (LCW 28), the answer is a foregone conclusion. ("Backyard," we are reminded later, is the name given to a hydrogen bomb so powerful it did not matter where it was detonated since it would destroy everyone on earth.) Any retreat to the home place is a return to the contradictions of the contemporary West. The enabling fiction of private self-becoming is soon dismantled as Meloy confronts local nostalgia for the uranium boom of the early 1950s as a thinly veiled desire for a reinstatement of frontier machismo. The boom, she suggests, "elevated the self-made man and his sense of control over women, children, and big-game animals. It built roads, schools, utilities, and a colossal myth" (LCW 116). The myth of pioneering uranium miners "free to be enriched or broken by their own labors in a free market" and unencumbered by federal authority denies the "unabashed government paternalism" that created and controlled the boom in uranium. As the sole buyer, the Atomic Energy Commission "ensured a market for ore by requiring big company mills to purchase a certain percentage from independent prospectors." The AEC also guaranteed prices and provided the infrastructure necessary to sustain the industry. It was, in fact, Meloy concludes, "the dreaded feds, propped by the frenetic arms race with the former Soviet Union [who] 'welfared' the uranium miners in every respect but their health" (LCW 116).

In applying "the instincts of Home," which she understands as looking for the "nearness of the unimagined" (LCW 119), Meloy comes to live inside the contradictions of place. The return home is not a retreat but a grounded engagement with the strategies of concealment that have come to permeate the culture. A trip to the town dump charts the shift in its function from a site that lays open the community—discarded household waste is voluntarily separated into actual garbage and stuff that others might find useful—into a "transfer station" with a "tidy row of Dumpsters" that can ferry the garbage to landfills elsewhere.[15] When "the debris of our lives falls into the chasm of a tidy steel box behind a chain link fence, we shall know a lot less about one another" (LCW 122), Meloy concludes. The new dump represents a local instance of the impulse Meloy identifies as characteristic of military-industrial practices: the imposition of an unnecessary and exclusionary level of secrecy over something that was once out in the open. The mundane things that bind communities together, like seeing each other's garbage, are predicated on the notion that there is nothing to hide. The clandestine removal of trash in tidy containers may be more sanitary, but it produces a division both between producers of garbage (neighbors) and between the producers and their garbage. Once garbage is assigned the status of the irredeemable, the implicit relationship between agent, act, and consequence is severed. While there is something utopian about the notion that in dumping garbage with an eye to its continued usefulness "we are not convinced that its life has truly ended" (LCW 120–21), the transfer station model of waste removal ensures the total abjection of garbage as en route to an invisible terminus.

Meloy reflects on the history of dumps used in the area dating back to nearby Anasazi middens that are also burial sites. While archaeologists have produced a wealth of information about the ancient inhabitants from the remains, Meloy recognizes the impossibility of translating the Basketmakers' experience, seeing the archaeological account as "a story told as if in an alien tongue or with a difficult speech problem" (LCW 128). Only the bones of the dead, as evidence of human presence, suggest a shared history of living in this place. Like modern garbage, however, the remains of the site have been dispersed. The bones have been reburied somewhere and the artifacts removed to museums. The site is covered with backfill, and a highway obliterates the midden. "Over it flow BMW sedans, Harleys, and truckloads of grapes, potato chips, floor wax, roof trusses, and the U.S. mail" (LCW 131–32). This is more than the inevitable overlay of historical sediment; like the buried uranium in the rocks, the bones and other Basketmaker remains have been extracted from their rightful resting place and reanimated to tell stories "in an alien tongue." Just as the improvised recycling of waste at the dump has been replaced with a rational compartmentalization of matter, the reordering of minerals and ancient remains literally displaces and mistranslates things into dangerous configurations.

The trust in home is finally betrayed when Meloy comes across a rock that appears to be the yellow cake from which uranium is milled. The latent dread produced by her forays into the nuclear West is now fully awakened, and Meloy resolves to run away from home, taking the rock with her. She heads for Los Alamos to bury the hot rock at ground zero, only to discover from a geologist friend that it is in fact a chunk of painted asphalt from an old road. Nevertheless, the damage to her faith in the land is confirmed by this scare, revealing the extent to which the paranoia and nosebleeds caused by visits to military sites have shaken Meloy's sense of belonging. She makes a final trip to a beloved mesa and, as an act of angry repudiation, in a parody of the Trinity test, intends to hurl the Map of the Known Universe over the edge while *The Nutcracker Suite* plays from the car stereo as a storm breaks.

Ravaged with disappointment, Meloy explains that her recent journeys have rendered the history of the region "foreign and unnervingly off-the-Map, even as I lived in its heart." The reader is invited to consider, from the vantage point of the mesa, what has become "my duplicitous lover." At the core of the desert's "timelessness" lies, "pressed into a nugget of inorganic matter, the single greatest threat to the continuity of life" (LCW 212). In one final entry to the map, she fills "empty space in the Known Universe with bits of Triassic point bars and channel sediments from my beloved homeland. From the air these pieces of Home took forty-three seconds to reach Hiroshima, a fraction less to reach Nagasaki" (LCW 213). Determined to dispatch the map in the direction of mine tailings below, she is overcome with vertigo and drops the map just as the lightning begins to flash. Faced with a dreadful sense of mortality and the prospect of losing "all those glorious ways to feel the world" (LCW 215), she scrambles for the map. The "Known Universe lay broken into pages," and as she "suture[s] the folios into a whole" she realizes that attending to the map has "turned my gaze away from the desert itself. I must raise my eyes" (LCW 216).

Instead of serving as a guide to place, the map has become part of the problem, an abstracting diversion from place itself. Despite Meloy's intention to draw an "antimap," the act of representation has perpetuated and reinforced the sense of separation that produced the need for it in the first place. *The Last Cheater's Waltz*, in the end, is not a book about mapping oneself into place but about the failure of mapping as a mode of orientation. If there is a cheater it is not the land so much as the representations of it that divert the eyes from what lies before them. The delirious, vertiginous moment that produces this insight is perhaps the first instance of embodied, sited being in the book, as the vortex of the waltz that has led Meloy around the Southwest's deadly spaces deposits her on the precipice of annihilation.

Tchaikovsky's *Nutcracker Suite* was inadvertently broadcast during the Trinity test as a storm caused the loudspeaker system to pick up a distant radio station. To waltz is to turn and be turned, and listening to Tchaikovsky on the mesa incites in Meloy a "heady state, a precarious union of delirium and control" (LCW 212). The music produces, as the cheating lover (the land) also produces, conflicting impulses of desire and repulsion, an enticement and a rejection. Transposed into the western vernacular by Sonny Throckmorton's song of the same name, *The Last Cheater's Waltz* is an embodiment of the "passionate and obsessive" (LCW 212) compulsion to be turned—waltzed—by place not despite but because of its contradictory nature as beautiful and violent. The malaise that drives the narrator's quest for attachment to place must in the end be the necessary nausea experienced by the waltzer, always cheated on but always returning to the dancer's embrace. This must be the condition upon which occupation can take place, a kind of perpetual ambivalence produced by the legacy of a violent past and a threatening present. Meloy's assessment of Trinity, despite her horror, sums up the text's position: "[t]his haunted real estate is neither beautiful nor terrifying. It is beautifully terrible. It conflates the ultimate with the intimate, poises a strange equanimity between the near-pristine lands and proving grounds for the extermination of life—a self-canceling proposition" (LCW 84). Awful as it is, the "conflict of the psyche" produced by Trinity might in the end be the most truthful articulation of "our century's troublesome relationship to the western deserts" (LCW 84).

To Fear Dust Everywhere

Refuge and *The Last Cheater's Waltz* are both, in different ways, forms of spiritual autobiography that lead the narrators toward a new dispensation in terms of their relationships with place. Both books chart the emergence, through a confrontation with the previously hidden connections between private and public realms, of a troubled recognition of toxicity as an inseparable part of contemporary Western experience. In *Refuge* this takes the form of an emergence into activism; in *The Last Cheater's Waltz* the more modest conclusion is to "try and live here as if there is no other place and it must last forever" (LCW 224). In both cases, though, the renewed tenacity of the narrator at the conclusion of the texts is a measure of the extent to which the "certain tortuousness" Buell rightly locates in toxic discourse yields to a hardened resolve. As Meloy says, everyone's home must be "the heartland of consequence" (LCW 224).

Rebecca Solnit's *Savage Dreams* takes a different approach to the issue of dwelling in the nuclear West, though her conclusions are much the same. *Savage Dreams* is less involved in the construction of a toxic subjectivity and the representation of its effects. This is not a conversion narrative, since Solnit is already a participant in the antinuclear left at the narrative's opening. Her position is from the outset that of a journalist participant-observer, and her text is peppered with passages, sometimes quite long passages, from research undertaken into the history and politics of the region. This is not to say that *Savage Dreams* does not speak of private investment in the West, for as Solnit acknowledges at the beginning, this is a book "about trying to come to terms with what it means to be living in the American West, learning as much from encounters with landscapes and people as from readings."[16] As such, the text works as a combination of memoir, journalism, and scholarly research, framed in part by the exploration narrative suggested by the subtitle: this is a "journey into" the West of the past and present.

The book is structured by the contrasting tropes of dust and water. The first half, "Dust, Or Erasing the Future" focuses on the Nevada Test Site while the second, "Water, Or Forgetting the Past" concentrates on Yosemite National Park. As these titles make clear, the act of erasure is seen to be the dominant practice in both places. As with Williams and Meloy, Solnit's concern is with the dangers of hiddenness in ostensibly open space.

Like the dust that pervades internment narratives and threatens to conceal all trace of the excluded Japanese population, for Solnit the desert dust is a pervasive hazard that conceals unknown dangers: "it became second nature to fear dust everywhere" at the test site, even though it "didn't look like anything special to the naked eye" (SD 4). It is the uncertainty that knowledge of nuclear activity produces that is perhaps the most worrying, fostering a suspicion of the quotidian that permeates Meloy's text and insinuates itself into Solnit's book from the beginning: "to see mortality in the dust by imagining in it the unstable isotopes of radioactive decay took an act of educated faith or perhaps of loss of faith in the government" (SD 4). The terms used here are revealing. The dust can only be imagined as dangerous, it is not immediately verifiable. Knowledge produces fear—an "educated faith" that what has been learned might raise awareness to the level of protection—but also distrust, an attendant "loss of faith" in political authority. Knowledge and power are entwined in a contradictory manner, as are belief and doubt. One form of belief—in government—must be lost in order for a belief in the facts of radiation to have meaning. It seems that one cannot believe in government and radiation at the same time. The politics of secrecy surrounding the nuclear program, legitimated by a discourse of security, has made even the most mundane aspects of one's surroundings—"ordinary dust"—suspect and a source of anxiety. As in Williams and Meloy, the self is estranged from that with which it is most familiar.

The protests at the test site during the 1980s and early 1990s invoke a Thoreauvian ethic of nonviolent civil disobedience that involves walking into the site as far as possible before being stopped and possibly arrested by security. Backed by the Nuremberg Principles of 1946, which "signal the end of obedience as an adequate form of citizenship" (SD 11), the protestors see nuclear testing as a violation of international law: a crime against peace, a crime against humanity, and a war crime. Solnit's explanation of this justification is powerful, but she is nevertheless ambivalent about the effectiveness of the protests, largely due to the failure of the actions to achieve much visibility. Even a big event in 1988, leading to over two thousand arrests (Terry Tempest Williams among them) and considered by Solnit to be "one of the biggest civil disobedience arrests in U.S. history," hardly makes local news (SD 27), though the Nevada protest did provoke a response in the Soviet Union, where antinuclear protestors in Kazakhstan initiated the Nevada-Semipalatinsk Anitnuclear Movement that by October 1989 had, through public protest, brought an end to testing in that country (SD 26).[17]

Solnit is dismayed by the indifference to protest in the United States, and she views the official practice of trivializing or ignoring dissent as effectively rendering it as invisible as the bomb tests and their radioactive effects. Buell's point about the frustration involved in trying to verify the harm done by military-industrial activity is expanded by Solnit to include the erasure of resistance as a visible response. Radiation, she suggests, "can make cells lose their memory, and loss of memory seems to be one of the cultural effects of the bombs too, for Americans forgot that bomb after bomb was being exploded here" (SD 6). She goes on to speculate that, more worrying than its forgetfulness, public indifference may not be down to memory loss at all but due to the fact that testing became so deeply learned it was no longer consciously considered: "[p]erhaps the bomb came to affect us as an invisible mutation in our dreams, a drama we could watch in our sleep instead of the Nevada skies" (SD 7). Like Williams's mysterious recurring dream of a flash of light from an absent cause, the bomb for Solnit pervades and regulates everyday life in ways only barely understood.

The importance of place becomes vital in the face of public indifference. Indeed, Solnit admits that the arms race and the Cold War "only became believable for me when they acquired a location, a landscape" (SD 15). While the protests may not function to contaminate the affirmative discourse of the mainstream media in any meaningful way, the symbolic act of trespass is essential for Solnit's Thoreauvian grounding of knowledge in place: "[w]alking claims land not by circumscribing it and fencing it off as property but by moving across it in a line that however long or short connects it to the larger journey of one's life, the surrounding roads and trails, that makes it part of the web of experience, confirmed by every foot that touches the earth" (SD 20). The "lines of convergence" that are imaginatively animated by the act of moving across the land make possible the work that the book itself undertakes:

> These lines of convergence are the lines of biography and history and ecology that come together as a site, as the history of nuclear physics, the Arms Race, anti-communism, civil disobedience, Native American land-rights struggles, the environmental movement, and the mysticism and fanaticism deserts seem to inspire in Judeo-Christians all come together to make the Nevada Test Site, not as a piece of physical geography, but of cultural geography, not merely in the concrete, but in the abstract. Such places bring together histories which may seem unrelated—and when they come

together it becomes possible to see new connections in our personal and public histories and stories, collisions even. A spider-web of stories spreads out from any place, but it takes time to follow the strands. (SD 24)

This is a good summation not only of *Savage Dreams* but also of *Refuge* and *The Last Cheater's Waltz*. In all cases, it is the fact of being in place that makes lines converge in ways they have otherwise been prevented from doing.

As Foucault reminds us, the point of counterhistory is to make visible the repressed condition of permanent war that structures relations of power the nation-state claims to have banished beyond its borders. The apparent fragmentation of order produced by permanent war is, in fact, the condition of possibility that constitutes the regulation and ordering of life under the permanent state of emergency. Understanding war not as the disruption of a prior order but as a form of ordering itself is what, according to Foucault, "makes society intelligible." The lines of convergence Solnit draws up in the quotation above—lines that link biography, history, ecology, foreign policy, and local struggle to provide a deep map of the West's "landscape wars"—represent precisely the kind of counterhistory Foucault describes when he says that a history that takes the fact of war as its starting point can relate "war, religion, politics, manners, and characters" and can "therefore act as a principle that allows us to understand history."[18]

Williams's journal and Meloy's "Map of the Known Universe" similarly, in having to embrace the fact of war as the precondition for an apprehension of place, are versions of the counterhistorical enterprise. Place itself, for Williams and Meloy, as it is for Solnit, stands in excessive relation to the condition of war's disorderly order and provides "a location, a landscape" where the fact of permanent war finally becomes "believable," not merely as empirical confirmation of an intuition or idea but through the material and affective pressures experienced by being in place. It is through this embodied realization of simultaneous "beauty" and "violence" that the force of beauty, however it is configured—as retinal pleasure, somatic attentiveness, a sense of belonging, or the dreadful seductions of the sublime—calls attention to the violence and makes it known as the otherwise repressed fact of despoliating sovereign power.

Part of the way that the test site and the protests are kept hidden is, for Solnit, due to the indeterminate status of the land the site occupies. While the Department of Energy operates the test site, local authorities take care of its legal aspects, meaning that the cost of processing large numbers of trespassers would be borne by the county. Since it is cheaper to simply move protesters on than charge them, most of the time the protests do not result in visible criminal prosecution. Furthermore, since the Western Shoshones claim never to have sold, leased, or given the land away, there is considerable dispute over the legitimacy of U.S. presence there in the first place. While the 1863 Treaty of Ruby Valley provides access to Western Shoshone land, it respects prior ownership. When offered money for the land that the Shoshones refused to accept, the U.S. government presumed acceptance on their behalf under the practice of "federal trusteeship." This action was upheld in the Supreme Court in 1985, but the Western Shoshones continue to contest the ruling. Solnit becomes embroiled in Carrie and Mary Dann's long-running battle with the government as they persist in rejecting the 1985 ruling.

The concealment of power, as Solnit comes to see it, is enabled at all levels by the kind of compartmentalization of roles that, as we have seen, regulated activity at Los Alamos. As a strategy of divide and rule, it is compartmentalization that disperses responsibility to the point where it becomes impossible to locate the source of any action, making it difficult to contest. Splitting responsibility for the test site enables the erasure of signs of dissent in the same way that the functionaries that originally administered the Indian treaties seem less to be carrying out a policy directive and more involved in the micromanagement of their own paperwork. Similarly, Solnit observes, "nobody makes bombs" in the weapons industry, they "work on the plutonium trigger assembly" (SD 166).

This compartmentalizing strategy also applies to the division and regulation of land into owned and managed parcels, enabling "geography itself " to become "undone," with landscapes "reduced to piles of rubble in which the original lay of the land is irrecoverable" (SD 190). What working with the Danns and participating in the test site demonstrations provide for Solnit is access to an alternative conception of land that is the material counterpart to the understanding of history as "lines of convergence" that dismantles the compartments of regularized knowledge and reattaches absent causes to their effects. This knowledge of place is premised on the "continuity of the surface of the earth" (SD 190). Instead of the "alienable, divisible objects" produced by the notion of land as possession, indigenous understanding of land is grounded in spatial and temporal continuities (SD 190). While Solnit admits that thinking about natural and human history at the same time "is like looking at one of those trick drawings" (SD 230) where two conflicting images are presented simultaneously but it is virtually impossible to see both at once, this double vision does, as it also does with Williams and Meloy, seem to be a requirement in attempts to produce an account of the duplicitous and abstracted history of the West's landscape wars.

What all three books discussed in this chapter reveal is the extent to which their authors have only been dimly aware of their own relationship to the nuclear West, despite years, even a lifetime spent there. Solnit's argument about public indifference to testing being evidence of a lesson learned so thoroughly that it becomes invisible is instructive, since each of the books discussed here is at pains to unlearn that lesson and, often painfully, by apprehending natural and human history at the same time, to embrace a fuller, if contaminated, attachment to place. The meaning of Williams's dream of a flash of light and Meloy's admission that she grew up oblivious to the Cold War despite the fact that it was happening nearby while "I listened to *Winnie the Pooh* in my flannel pajamas with little ducks on them" (LCW 156) are moments of belated recognition that the political has always been personal, that the regulation of life under the condition of permanent war has thoroughly imbricated itself into the structures of everyday life. For Solnit, time spent working near the Nevada Test Site as an activist and writer leads to a similar understanding of what has remained previously obscure. "I realized that I had been a Westerner all along," she writes, though "the fact had never imposed itself on my imagination" (SD 88). Claiming Westernness is accompanied by an attendant realization "that I'd been living in a war zone my whole life without noticing the wars, since they didn't match any of the categories in which I'd been instructed" (SD 88). Together, Western identity and the peculiarity of the West's ongoing war against itself position Solnit, Williams, and Meloy inside the kind of "tortuous" contradiction Buell notes as characteristic of toxic discourse. Each of these texts insists on both the beauty and the violence of the contemporary West as coterminous, but each, in working through the counterhistorical potentialities discovered by being in place, identify beauty as more than just a screen for covert despoliation but as the condition through which "nature" is put to work as critique.

Published after the end of the Cold War, *Refuge*, *The Last Cheater's Waltz*, and *Savage Dreams* all testify to the abiding legacy of that conflict as it was fought, not between states, but within the United States. As the continuing battles between Native Americans and the government over land rights, and downwinder struggles for recognition and restitution indicate, the Cold War has not ended but persists in the wasted lives and environments that bore the brunt of permanent preparedness for a "hot" conflict that, in the end, was played out at home. In Don DeLillo's *Underworld*, the "lines of convergence" of post–Pearl Harbor history again meet in the blasted landscapes of the West, where the wasted residuum of the Cold War is restructured as part of the new world order made possible by Sunbelt entrepreneurialism's capacity to convert waste into capital.

America, that surreal country, is full of found objects.
Our junk has become art.
Our junk has become history.
Susan Sontag, *On Photography*

There is a moment in DeLillo's *End Zone* when Gary Harkness, walking through the West Texas desert, comes across a terrifying "low mound" of "simple shit." Faced with this "terminal act," Harkness's thoughts spiral into a reverie of waste: dogs squatting, incontinent women in nursing homes, butchered animals' intestines, holy men, armies, scientists all obsessed with and immersed in shit. The turd is "strange and vile in this wilderness, perhaps the one thing that did not betray its definition." There was, he thinks, "the graven art of a curse in that sight," "self discontinued," "shit's infinite treachery, everywhere this whisper of inexistence" (EZ 88–89).

Peter Sloterdijk argues that the denial of human excrement "is the deepest training in order," providing a model for the shameful concealment of all refuse. Between the 1940s and the 1970s, as Mira Engler explains in her taxonomy of American attitudes toward waste management, despite the rise of consumerism causing a massive increase in waste, the sophistication of disposal methods meant that "waste itself passed under people's eyes virtually unnoticed."[1] By the 1970s, however, the oil crisis and economic recession, the rise of the environmental movement, and a growing skepticism toward the certainties of the postwar boom contributed to a shift in thinking about waste and an increased attention to the notion of waste as potential resource. Just as the repressed other Americas excluded during the maintenance of Cold War containment culture became increasingly visible after the 1960s, so too does the nonhuman waste produced by the modern military-industrial economy. An awakened environmental preoccupation with waste and recycling, then, coincides with the collapse of the Cold War consensus and the emergence of neoliberal strategies of borderless trade and new forms of biopolitical regulation. When waste becomes visible, as it does through the pressure exerted on the structures of containment, culture's abjected residuum returns as a challenge to the maintenance of social order. As Sloterdijk explains, the "grand act of ecology in the history of ideas" is its transformation "of refuse into a 'high' theme."[2]

DeLillo's Underworld (1997) is precisely engaged in thinking through the ramifications of waste as a "high" theme that speaks to the history of the postwar period and its legacy. While DeLillo is very much a New York writer, there is a longstanding preoccupation in his work with the desert Southwest as a trope and as a nodal site in the U.S. military-industrial matrix. From his first novel, Americana (1971), in which a disenchanted New York television executive lights out for the territory, to End Zone and Running Dog (1978), where the brutal demise of an intelligence operative takes place in at an abandoned silver mine previously used for government counterinsurgency training, the West has signified for DeLillo hidden military power. In Underworld, the elements of the desert West that have preoccupied DeLillo for over twenty years converge to produce a narrative that speaks powerfully of the region as integral to postwar American geopolitics.

The Archaeology of Garbage

Underworld is a reflection on what is left after the Cold War and what is to be done with its remains. As an archaeology of recent history, the novel is concerned with the status of objects, their function, durability, and meaning, after the evisceration of value produced by the end-time of the Cold War's political, military, and onto-epistemological stalemate. As such, Underworld is a curatorial project that produces out of debris a networked narrative made visible through inferred but not necessarily verified connections between fragments. In a way, Underworld is a literary version of so-called "garbology," a term used by the archaeologists who, since the establishment of the Garbage Project at the University of Arizona in 1973, have excavated the landfills of modern cities in order to understand social organization through an examination of its refuse.[3] The Arizona depicted in Underworld is a hotbed of garbage-related activity, and DeLillo probably had the Garbage Project in mind when imagining the reveries of "waste theorist" Jesse Detwiler. Certainly, the way some archaeologists describe their field is revealing of the ways in which DeLillo also approaches the relationship between the banality of refuse and the

234

larger social and historical forces of which is it a part: "the archaeological refers to ruin and responses to it, to the mundane and quotidian articulated with grand historical scenarios, to materializations of the experience of history, material aura, senses of place and history, choices of what to keep and what to let go (remember/forget), the material artifact as allegorical, collections and their systems, the city and its material cultural capitalizations (investments in pasts and futures), the intimate connection between all this and a utopian frame of mind (archaeology is not just about the past, but about desired futures too). And the stuff of it all is garbage."[4] If, as Michael Shanks and his associates claim, archaeology is the study of garbage, Underworld is a novel not merely about waste in all its forms but produced from waste: it is the novel as garbage—as Sontag writes, junk as art and as history.[5]

Underworld's excavation of the Cold War's general economy of matter operates inside and in opposition to that economy of expenditure and waste. In the face of the irradiated persistence of matter that cannot be disposed of, DeLillo offers acts of apparently pointless preservation, such as tracking down items of baseball memorabilia or reconfiguring bombers as art. Yet if Shanks is right, and archaeology is somehow by definition a utopian enterprise in that it implies that things are worth saving, and that, by extension, there is a future to save them for, then DeLillo's collectors and artists (and the novel itself as a form of bricolage made of found objects) are working dialectically inside and against the negativity of Cold War end-time and the capitalist logic of consumption and death.

The retrieval, rearrangement, reconfiguration, and reanimation of objects through artistic and curatorial manipulation are, along these lines, not the defeated scavengings of an exhausted culture doomed to piece together pale reproductions of past styles and shrines to former glories. Instead, the will to save and treasure, to reactivate the auratic power of the indexical object, positions preservation as an unlikely agent of radical resistance. What Underworld posits, I think, is a notion of the museum (imagined as any collection of retrieved objects) as the site of a defiant refusal of matter to expire and also as evidence of the ways in which the interpretation of objects is capable of active and unexpected mutation and transvaluation. As such, in a culture driven by the desire to use things up, DeLillo posits a counterculture—and a counterhistory—that

refuses to throw anything away. Oddly, this means that nuclear waste offers itself as the supreme embodiment of a stubbornly resistant matter,
primed to enter a museum of Cold War garbage that operates as evidence
of advanced military-industrial capitalism's radical contradictions. In a
way, by making something it cannot consume, Cold War America has invented its own critique. The dilemma for DeLillo is that his conception
of art as a mode of critical reappropriation of junk has also become part
of post–Cold War official culture's means of concealing its traces. Part
of the danger, as revealed in Klara Sax's desert art project, is that potentially critical cultural strategies remain imbricated in the power structures they ostensibly resist.

Sax's vast site-specific work, Long Tall Sally, comprises repainted de-
funct military aircraft in the middle of the Arizona desert. Sax is, like Nick
Shay, an expert in waste management, transmuting the excess and broken remains of military-industrial manufacturing into something else,
in this case, art. Sax has negotiated an interesting deal with the military,
who cooperate "up to a point," keeping the site isolated while the artists
paint the aircraft in order to "maintain the integrity of the project."[6] In a
significant sense here, the military provides for the art the same security
service it has provided for weapons testing and other Cold War activity in
the desert. The military guards the "integrity" of the project, maintaining its discreteness, mapping off a mile-deep circumference around the
work like the rope that prevents gallery-goers from getting too close to
a painting. And along with military aid, Sax's work is validated through
other forms of enterprise: "[w]e also have foundation grants, we have congressional approval, all sorts of permits," not to mention "[m]aterials do-
nated by manufacturers, tens of thousands of dollars' worth" (U 69).

Long Tall Sally is utterly reliant on official institutional networks of
support that financially and legally embed Sax's work within an emerging culture of historical recuperation that draws on what once would
have been seen as avant-garde strategies of political critique and subversion but which have become a legitimate branch of the culture industry.
Turning an unpleasant aspect of recent history into art is a useful way
of converting secrecy into openness, enabling the dark connotations of
military stockpiling to be bleached by the chromatic vibrancy of affirmative culture. By appealing to the conventional stance of the artist as

disinterested—"This is an art project, not a peace project"—Sax herself refuses to acknowledge the blindingly obvious content of the work, preferring instead to take shelter in formalist observations: "[t]his is a landscape painting in which we use the landscape itself. The desert is central to this piece. It's the surround. It's the framing device. It's the four-part horizon. This is why we insisted to the Air Force—a cleared area around the finished work" (U 70). For Sax it seems, in a kind of contradictory way, that the desert is central because it is the frame: both center and margin. What she suggests is that the work has to be where it is because it is set off by the open space that surrounds it, and that the openness of this space is guaranteed by the Air Force. It is open space because it is policed; open, then, but not accessible.

There is patently more to Sax's work, however, than the sculptural arrangement of forms in space, though her aesthetic explanation of the logic of the piece reveals how the conventions of landscape representation can serve to occlude even as they appear to show material histories. Sax is not unaware of the brute fact of the planes and the deep historical and cultural burden they embody, remarking that the Cold War produced a "number of postwar conditions without a war having been fought," and part of the motivation behind the project is to preserve and make visible what would otherwise be allowed to disappear.[7] She also notes that the desert "bears the visible signs" of war in its "craters and warning signs and no-go areas and burial markers, the sites where debris is buried" (U 70–71). Yet her concern with the uncanny (history that happened but events that did not) and the sublime (the "great machines" of awesome destruction) remains cordoned off so that, like any successful experience of the sublime, it can be viewed at a safe (physical and historical) distance.

Speaking at the end of the Cold War, Sax's interest in the planes and the desert is in danger of becoming a form of nostalgia for the clarity and thrill of what she calls "meaningful power." Reminiscing about the days when B-52s were on "permanent alert," Sax describes "feeling a sense of awe, a child's sleepy feeling of mystery and danger and beauty." This, she thinks, is real power, and the notion of "a force in the world that comes into people's sleep" recalls Williams's, Solnit's, and Meloy's comments on the insinuating dreamscape of buried nuclear fears, not to mention

Silko's and Momaday's psychologically damaged veterans and Otsuka's interned boy whose name is erased as he sleeps. As a "stable," "focused," and "tangible thing," such power "held us together," and having a worthy adversary meant that "[y]ou could measure things. You could measure hope and you could measure destruction" (U 75–76).

In the absence of the Cold War's "meaningful power," all that is left is what Oppenheimer called the bomb: merde. As Sax explains, the scientist knew that "something that eludes naming is automatically relegated . . . to the status of shit. You can't name it. It's too big or evil or outside your experience. It's also shit because it's garbage, it's waste material" (U 77). At this point, as Sax is beginning to enunciate the major theme of the novel—the power of American technological culture to turn itself into waste—she backs off and returns to the human response her painted aircraft offers. She discusses the actions of touch and applying pigment by hand, "putting our puny hands to great weapons systems" whose "millions of components" were "stamped out, repeated endlessly." The artwork, she claims, is "trying to unrepeat, to find an element of felt life, and maybe there's a sort of survival instinct here, a graffiti instinct—to trespass and declare ourselves, show us who we are. The way the nose artists did, the guys who painted pinups on the fuselage" (U 77).

The difference between Sax and the nose artists is that their art was not supported by the military, funded by foundations or given congressional support. There is very little in the way of real trespass or transgression here since the work has already been assimilated into the nostalgia of the culture industry. Sax's sentimental yearning for the human touch to somehow neutralize the brute industrial horror of the planes' actual purpose is a gesture from another age, drawing its legitimacy from the "primitive" craft of death-haunted airmen idling away the hours before a mission. This may be a severe assessment of Sax's position, since creative practice in Underworld is largely situated as a counterforce to the irrelevance of human life in the corporate worldview, whether this is Sabato Rodia's Watts Tower (like Sax's work, constructed from rubbish), graffiti, Lenny Bruce's improvisations, or a baseball game.[8] Sax's project is offered in part as a means of working through, of converting the nuclear sublime into a more benign rapture. This is certainly the reading of Nick Shay, who sees the planes, from a distance, meld into a "single mass, not a collection of objects," and this mass itself "invited us to see the land dimension, horizonwide, in which the work was set," the old weapons "so forcefully rethought" amid the "grim vigor of weather and desert" (U 84). For Shay, the painted planes "remark the end of an age and the beginning of something so different only a vision such as this might suffice to auger it" (U 126).

DeLillo is with Nick here, I believe, in seeing the work as a forceful rethinking of weaponry, but I also think there is enough ambivalence in Sax's position to suggest that the novel is straining between a desire to affirm the transformative power of art and a recognition of that power's absorption into a broader and more sinister cultural mode of therapeutic forgetting. Sax's assessment is ultimately too pat to accept completely, and the text's ambivalence is necessary, I would argue, to preserve the genuine grotesqueness of the airplanes' original function and to prevent an easy assimilation of the work into "heritage."

Sax's intuition concerning the uncanny fact of the non-event of the Cold War is important and bears comparison with Paul Virilio's articulation of the shift from the concept of total war experienced during World War II to the inertia of what he calls "pure war" caused by the bomb. The stasis of deterrence, according to Virilio, sublimated combat into a "techno-scientific explosion" of military-industrial creativity.[9] I think this is the paradoxical juncture occupied by *Underworld*, where the fact that things (weapons) are made to be destroyed but cannot be put to their proper use causes a collapse of the division between use and uselessness, art and waste, money and shit, preservation and destruction. The conventional relationship between the function and value of objects becomes voided and unforeseen possibilities—waste *as* art, destruction *as* culture— begin to present themselves.

The end of the Cold War has left tons of redundant materiel, as well as the contaminated effluent produced in the production of weapons never fired in anger, and the only industry left with potential for growth is the management of those things made but not used. The sense of things has become unhinged, as Sax recognizes when she notes that "[t]hings have no limits now. Money has no limits. I don't understand money anymore. Money is undone. Violence is undone, violence is easier now, it's uprooted, out of control, it has no measure anymore, it has no level of values" (U

76). What is registered here is Sax's anxiety when faced with what Joseph Masco calls the demise of the "purity of the Cold War narrative about the 'security' enabled by the nuclear complex."[10] In the post–Cold War period, Masco argues, revelations about environmental contamination, plutonium experiments on citizens, and the testing of fallout patterns across the United States through the atmospheric release of contaminating substances exposed the nature of the "kinds of national sacrifices that U.S. citizens were unwittingly subjected to in the name of 'national security' during the Cold War."[11] While the Cold War produced the screen of the nuclear sublime—or in Masco's terms, the "nuclear phantasmagoria"—that concealed real effects behind the spectacle of awesome and unthinkable power, the end of the Cold War prompted the leakage of information about the material facts of fifty years of contamination and devastation. It is at this point, as we have seen, that texts like *Refuge*, *The Last Cheater's Waltz*, and *Savage Dreams* begin to confront the terrors of the unseen and previously unknown. The limitlessness of the post–Cold War situation, as Sax sees it, means that what had been previously contained by the binary logic of nuclear stalemate is now "out of control." Like the dispersal of fallout into the atmosphere, other forms of power—money (capitalist enterprise) and violence (state or criminal)—are amorphous threats that can no longer be tracked or avoided.

Sax's modernist faith in the phenomenological redemption of waste through human recontextualization, specifically through her decision to paint the aircraft—a longing for the authenticity of gestural mark-making that now seems hopelessly romantic—figures her art as part of postwar culture's general waste-management strategy. But while there is a utopian dimension to this hope that squandered resources can be recuperated—as we have seen in Shanks's articulation of the archaeological project—there is also a bathetic quality to the postwar quest for value in the trash of discarded global ambitions. The gestural (literal and metaphorical) appropriation of redundant technology Sax attempts in *Long Tall Sally* in the end reveals a diminished sense of culture's critical power when dwarfed by the uncontrollable forces of the post–Cold War neoliberal world order.

A project like Sax's can be undertaken in the West because there is plenty of space there, yet the real avant-garde of the postwar years is the military itself, and *Long Tall Sally* is in danger of becoming merely another spot on the tourist map of the region, like the Meteor Crater and Ant Farm's *Cadillac Ranch* (which Sax's work echoes). If the project of radical modernism was to explode distinctions between "high" culture and everyday life, then as *Underworld* makes clear, it was the military-industrial complex that achieved it. The real transformations of consciousness post-1945 took place not in Manhattan art galleries but through the Manhattan Project's retooling of American life from its outpost in the middle of the desert.

A Remote Landscape of Nostalgia

In *Underworld* the culture of waste management is a desert culture, and the transplantation of characters like Nick Shay and Klara Sax from the Bronx to Arizona is a vital part of the novel's navigation of the impact of the Cold War on American life.[12] Nick Shay lives, he likes to tell people, a "quiet life in an unassuming suburb of Phoenix. Pause. Like someone in the Witness Protection Program" (U 66). Nick's flight from the Bronx is an escape from the past, from the mystery of his father's disappearance and from his own adolescent crime, the murder of George Manza. As Mark Osteen observes, "Nick is hiding from himself."[13] The consequences of past actions are now dealt with in the West, and Nick's job as waste manager signals his desire to take care of the evidence and keep hidden the toxic by-products of the culture. His choice of simile, though, suggests that Nick's position is a form of legitimate and justified secrecy: he is not on the run from the law but is in the Witness Protection Program for his own good. Nick's secrecy serves the machinery of the law just as Sax's sculpture helps recuperate weapons as heritage. As such, Nick is not only justifying his own private secrets as legitimately denied but also conceding that the business of managing waste is a necessary concealment of the facts of corporate and military-industrial activity.

Nick's presence in Phoenix is due to the West's massive post–World War II economic and demographic growth and the company he works for is part of the spin-off from the impact of Cold War technologies on the American economy. In this remapped political and economic space, the Bronx becomes emblematic of past times, a kind of new Old World: Nick has attempted to relocate his sense of himself in the new world order of the New West. Likewise, the transplantation of his mother is a further rejection of the old, immigrant environment of the East Coast: "[w]e took her out of the daily drama of violence and lament and tabloid atrocity . . . and we fixed her up in a cool room where she watched TV" (U 86).

While Nick's wife, Marian, wants to hear about the lurid old city of the East, the tales of old families and old criminality, Nick prefers "the way history did not run loose" in the West: "[t]hey segregated visible history. They caged it, funded it and bronzed it, they enshrined it carefully in museums and plazas and memorial parks. The rest was geography, all space and light and shadow and unspeakable hanging heat" (U 86). Without New York's sedimented history, Nick can enjoy the bleached pleasures of sheer geography, the broad, measured, and sanitized structuring of space. From his temperature-controlled "shimmering bronze tower" he can gaze out at the view and admire the "downtown hush," the "parks with jogging trails and its fairy ring of hills" (U 85–86). In his chilly corporate tower, Nick feels "assured and well defended" (U 119). The management of environment—space, temperature, hygiene—is accompanied and enabled by the slick management of rhetoric that has appropriated "the rhetoric of aggrieved minorities to prevent legislation that would hurt our business." In a form of recycling akin to Sax's deracinated mode of avant-garde critique, CEO Arthur Blessing is proud of the corporate "adaptation" of street-level protest: "[w]e learned how to complain, how to appropriate the language of victimization" (U 119). As Nick is aware, it is no longer necessary for corporate power to reveal itself as domination; instead it can "twist and swivel you" with "smiles and nods" (U 282). This clean corporate management of everyday life is, in fact, the finessed strategy of fifty years of America's Cold War containment culture—Sax's "meaningful power" that "comes into people's sleep"—and as such its smiling domination of the economically ascendant Southwest is evidence of the sleight of hand that reconstitutes nuclear stockpiling and environmental despoliation into capitalist triumphalism. The Southwest has become, in Underworld, the air-conditioned leisure complex for an amnesiac managerial culture that has learned to bronze its own shit.

The way America has managed to contain the excessive residue of Cold War militarism is, as we have seen in the case of Sax's artwork, through metamorphic transformations of waste into culture. The institutional critique of art begun with Duchamp's ready-mades and followed through since the 1960s with various nongallery artforms has enabled a reimagining of the relationship between spaces, objects, and modes of display and commemoration that has not so much achieved a utopian collapse of "high" art and everyday life but rather multiplied the opportunities through which material culture can be converted into culture-as-commodity, waste into value.

In his book *The Underground Heart* (2002), Ray Gonzalez returns to the Southwest after twenty years away to find a burgeoning heritage culture busily rearticulating the violence and atrocities of the past as part of a dominant narrative of America's triumphant post–Cold War achieved utopia. Gonzalez describes visits to, among others, the National Atomic Museum inside the Kirkland Air Force base in Albuquerque, the Albuquerque History Museum, the Alamo, and the Border Patrol Museum in El Paso, and he joins the Border Jumper tour of Columbus, New Mexico, to hear the tourist version of the U.S. operation against Pancho Villa. Conquest, he concludes, "is the main theme in Southwest museums."[14] While he muses that no one has yet thought of "creating a tour of devastated neighborhoods," which would undoubtedly "be of interest to the wave of tourists" that mill around other historical sites, the museums and themed sites Gonzalez visits have themselves been built out of previously devastated neighborhoods.[15] What is commonly achieved through the museum displays Gonzalez encounters is the erasure of violence by the staged unfolding of a teleological narrative of ascent from, in the case of the Atomic Museum, "Medieval Arms Control" (a glass case containing a bow and arrow) through to Fat Man and Little Boy. The conclusion of the Atomic Museum exhibit comprises bricks from the Berlin Wall, relics that testify to the success of American military spending in destroying the Soviet threat without dropping the bomb.

For Gonzalez each of these bricks "not only contains the history of the Cold War, but is made from the same grains of sand as White Sands National Monument, where Trinity was molded and exploded." The brick, like his desert homeland, is then "taken apart by the same hands that recreate and revise history to make sure we know how powerful we are and how we will dictate the future survival of mankind." In a final insight, Gonzalez also sees in the bricks an echo of America's "own Berlin Wall" along the international border with Mexico.[16] Like Meloy's rocks that connect for her the home place with Trinity and Hiroshima in a global network of destruction, Gonzalez reads the brick, against the grain of the museum's narrative, as a material signifier of how the local is imbricated in American world ordering. The brick, displaced from Cold War Europe to post–Cold War New Mexico, exceeds for Gonzalez its intended narrative function, allowing him to multiply connections otherwise denied by the logic of the exhibit. Squirreled away inside the exhibit, inside the museum, inside the Air Force base, in the desert, the potentially incendiary implications of the Berlin Wall brick ought to be properly contained. In activating the repressed connotations of the object, Gonzalez manages to both critique the reified triumphalism of the museum and deploy the relics within it to work against and beyond their official purpose.

The Southwest's post–Cold War waste management strategy, for Gonzalez as for DeLillo, centers on the cultural containment of the leaked material facts of domestic Cold War violence. In *The Underground Heart*, this process reaches back to include the rewriting of the Southwest's wars of conquest as the prehistory of U.S. global military and economic dominance. As the junk of history, indigenous and Mexican resistance, nuclear warheads, photos of captured illegal migrants, confiscated weapons, and bits of brick wall join Klara Sax's repainted bombers as part of the recycled spectacle of a culture able to extract value from its most wasted resources.

The ramifications of this notion of recuperating history, however violent and appalling, as cultural spectacle is further explored in a project by celebrated landscape photographer Richard Misrach. There are significant overlaps, I believe, between Sax's land art project and Misrach's images of military-industrial violence, particularly those collected in his book *Bravo 20: The Bombing of the American West* (1990). Following an essay by Myriam Weisang Misrach that tells a depressing tale of deception, destruction, and dispossession about the Bravo 20 bombing range near Fallon, Nevada, and Misrach's now famous sequence of images of the site, the final part of the book makes a curious turn. What Misrach proposes is the transformation of the sixty-four-square-mile range into "America's first environmental memorial: Bravo 20 National Park."[17]

It is worth considering Misrach's proposal here, since I think it registers the mix of irony and despair, optimism and gloom that is present in DeLillo's depiction of Sax's work and Gonzalez's account of Southwestern tourist sites. In consultation with landscape architects, Misrach unveils a series of maps, plans, architectural drawings, perspective renderings, and costings for a complete tourist venue, complete with campsite, picnic area, visitors' center, gift shop, and walking, driving, and climbing trails. The proposal is entirely plausible and echoes the kind of recycling of Cold War sites into tourist attractions, from underground bunkers to Minuteman Missile silos, that took place during the 1990s.[18] At the same time, the proposal is also an exercise in cognitive scrambling on a par with Robert Smithson's photo essay "A Tour of the Monuments of Passaic," where the artist-as-tour-guide leads the reader into the decrepitude of industrial New Jersey.[19] The point of Smithson's essay is partly caustic defamiliarization, exposing the invisible payment made by the land to the factory system, yet also deadly serious, and does indeed find such sites fascinating and picturesque. This is industrial archaeology as scripted by Duchamp.

Misrach's proposal operates in a similar way as both an environmental exposé and a surreal document, shot through with deadpan humor, and awed by the complex relationship between material destruction and aesthetic response. Misrach insists that the military ruins of Bravo 20 be understood within the same "sight-seeing circuit" that includes many of the natural wonders of the West. By doing so, the reader is reminded that military test sites sit geographically adjacent to national icons of romantic natural reverence.[20] The inclusion of Bravo 20 in this itinerary also introduces the issue of visibility and access, whereby the visual overload of the Grand Canyon or Las Vegas is matched by the absent presence of the nearby Nevada Test Site. The spectacle of "natural" or manufactured "sights" occludes the presence of other places.

Misrach's proposal brings into view that which remains obscured by the sublime view: the picturesque terrors of places like Bravo 20 as a form of "dark tourism."[21] If the "interpretive programs" of national parks train the visitor to view nature within particular aesthetic and political frames, so too will Bravo 20 National Park, which "will be devoted to the history of military abuse in peacetime," including "the military's illegal activities, its despoliation of the environment, its infractions of civilians' rights, and the incredible cost to the taxpayer."[22] The gift shop will contain maps of radioactive landfills and nuclear transportation routes, camouflage caps and T-shirts, models of the most advanced military hardware, postcards, calendars, and "fine art photography posters (but instead of glorious pictures of Yosemite in snow, how about images of bombing ranges?)"[23]

Bravo 20 National Park is a form of counterhistory that, as DeLillo writes, positions creative practice as "an agent of redemption, the thing that delivers us, paradoxically, from history's flat, thin, tight and relentless designs."[24] The doubleness of Misrach's proposal—a genuine proposition and a surreal blast of creative irony—retrieves destruction as critique in a similar way to DeLillo's novel and Gonzalez's reading of the Berlin Wall bricks. In each case, as DeLillo explains, "history and mock history ... form a kind of syncopated reality in which diverse human voices ultimately come into conflict with a single uninflected voice, the monotone of the state, the corporate entity, the product, the assembly line."[25]

One corporate entity that might be interested in following up Misrach's proposal for Bravo 20 is Nick Shay's employer, Whiz Co waste management. If picking through the garbage of history has become a dominant mode of cultural practice, the ex-radical Jesse Detwiler is "the visionary" whose "provocations had spooked the industry" (U 285). Converting his residual Vietnam-era paranoia to corporate gain, Detwiler's sense that "everything's connected" (U 289) enables him to think laterally enough to see a landfill as the "scenery of the future." His disquisition on the prospects for the business disturbingly echoes the utopian promise of Shanks's archaeology as an acceptance of the dialectical relationship between culture and garbage and Misrach's deadpan critique of toxic tourism: "[t]he more toxic the waste, the greater the effort and expense a tourist will be willing to tolerate in order to visit the site." Isolation of the most contaminated waste will make it "grander, more ominous and magical"; it will become "a remote landscape of nostalgia. Bus tours and postcards, I guarantee it" (U 286).

Here the political and economic programs of exploitation in the West converge with the aesthetic legacy of the visionary desert to produce a spectacle of apocalyptic grandeur that combines biblical and romantic desert rapture and late twentieth-century awe at Big Science. "Don't underestimate our capacity for complex longings," Detwiler warns. "Nostalgia for the banned materials of civilization, for the brute force of old industries and old conflicts" (U 286). Like Misrach, Detwiler identifies the twin core post–Cold War industries of the West as waste management and tourism, but in Detwiler's vision any prospect of critique is subsumed into the sublime: "[t]he way the Indians venerate this terrain now, we'll come to see it as sacred in the next century. Plutonium National Park. The last haunt of the white gods. Tourists wearing respirator masks and protective suits" (U 289). The triumphalism of Detwiler's capacity to imagine the Cold War as a marketing opportunity is symptomatic of capitalism's expanded field of operations after the collapse of the Soviet Union. Whiz Co is part of the advanced guard moving into new markets in ex-Soviet states where American imagineers can retool even enemy weapons and waste into part of the post-Fordist new world order.

What the end of the Cold War has made possible is the bringing together of the two sides of the nuclear stand-off. In 1990s Kazakhstan, where nuclear weapons are being developed as a form of waste disposal, Viktor Maltsev explains to Nick that weapons are the "mystical twin" of waste, just as Nick's brother Matt, the weapons expert, in an echo of Kip and Brice as the split nuclear Adams in Morrow's Los Alamos novels, is twinned with Nick the waste expert. Waste, Maltsev goes on, is the "devil twin" because it is the secret "underhistory" that is exposed "the way archaeologists dig out the history of earth cultures, every sort of bone heap and broken tool, literally from under the ground." But, unlike archaeologists, Maltsev says, people like himself do not dig it up but try—and fail—to bury it. In places like Kazakhstan, he explains, they are trying to fuse "two streams of history, weapons and waste" by blowing up contaminated nuclear waste with nuclear explosions (U 791).[26]

The American guests are given a tour of the old Kazakh test sites, where Nick senses "a spirit of old secrets gone bad" (U 792). The ex-Soviet site is the double of the desert sites scattered around New Mexico, Utah, and Nevada, a parallel world where test dwellings modeled on 1950s American domesticity—their accuracy a "point of pride with the KGB"—still contain the branded goods of a distant age, the "half-lost icons of the old life." Pricked by the old Oxydol and Rinso White packaging, Nick experiences waves of uncanny disorientation: "how strange it is, strange again, more strangeness" (U 793). The test dwelling has on Nick the kind of effect produced by a museum reconstruction of the recent past: familiar but entirely out of place, real things in an unbelievable setting, things preserved that are usually disposed of.

This relic of Cold War doubling, with the site as grave, memorial, dump, archaeological find, and exhibit, not only layers the significance of the once-hidden spaces of the Cold War. It also brings up the awkward question of how the awful residue of this unactivated conflict is to be addressed. Detwiler's theme park of waste acknowledges that there is always money in awe and dread; Misrach's proposal ironically knows this also, but inscribes a critique of landscape as tourist spectacle and leisure destination into his project of visibility as resistance. The Kazakhstan site is problematic for Nick because the test dwelling produces, even though it is evidence of old secrets gone wrong, a nostalgia for a time where good and evil could be clearly charted on the world map, where Rinso White did not apparently connect with U.S. weapons of mass destruction, where the secrets were still secret and the paranoia had a stable and legitimate object.[27] Now, such stability is gone, the corporations—and, in the ex–Soviet Union, the criminals: "fixing and hustling have come out of the shadows of black-market corruption to create a wholly open economy of plunder and corruption" (U 795)—have taken over what was once the preserve of the institutions of state, and the meaning of the past has itself become a commodity. In a sense, if the test site is to become a museum, the museum is also now a test site, a space where, as Misrach well knows, the interpretation of the past is contested, preserved, buried, or blown up.

The preservation of objects presents a constant counterpressure to the annihilation of matter (and therefore evidence of its ever having existed) in *Underworld*. Nick's sensitivity to objects is most pronounced in the structuring device of the baseball as relic of the real and even at the end of the novel, Nick walks "through the house and look[s] at the things we own and feel[s] the odd mortality that clings to every object" (U 804). The idiosyncratic and marginalized obsessions of collectors and hoarders are perhaps traces of resistance in this contaminated disposable culture, a kind of survivalist force of scattered individuals who persist in not throwing things away. As such, the contours of a life and of its contexts—a history—are embedded in the deep structure of private collections, archives, backstreet stores and loft spaces, a counterhistory of the late twentieth century, unofficial museums that preserve the unspoken, like the complex resonances of the Rinso White package.[28]

Certainly, it is often figures like Marvin Lundy, the baseball memorabilia collector, who, through the constant handling of "exhausted objects," offer the kind of insight that understands the structural necessity of the Cold War for the maintenance of power. Reflecting on the motives behind his acquisitiveness, Lundy understands that "it was some terror" that compelled him to "gather up things, amass possessions and effects against the dark shape of some unshoulderable loss" (U 191). When Brian Glassic visits Marvin in the early 1980s to talk about his collection, he gets instead an analysis of loss, even if it is concerning the Cold War: "when the tension and the rivalry come to an end that's when your worst nightmares begin. All the power and intimidation of the state will seep out of your personal bloodstream," and "other forces will come rushing in" (U 170).

Once the Cold War is over, perhaps the nightmares really do begin. The most disturbing consideration of the curatorial dilemma "after history" is the "Museum of Misshapens" the Americans visit in Kazakhstan, a long room of fetuses lined up in Heinz pickle jars (U 799). Here Nick and Glassic are finally confronted with the material ruins of the business they are in: the preserved monsters of postwar history, nameless victims of five hundred above-ground tests, not to mention the venting of radiation from underground detonations. From here they move on to a clinic that, we are told, is "not a museum this time," though it is an exhibit on Maltsev's toxic tour. Bald-headed children wait to be examined, a boy has skin grown over his eyes, a man has a growth under his chin with "a life of its own" (U 800). For years, Maltsev comments, "the word radiation was banned," and the villagers downwind of the tests, left behind to see what effect hydrogen bombs would have on them, didn't say it because they did not know such a word existed. Now, though, in these "wild, privatized times," all the banned words, secrets, and half-forgotten plots have been let out, Nick thinks to himself, "seeping invisibly into the land and air, into the marrowed folds of the bone" (U 802–3). "Once they imagine the bomb," Maltsev says, "it makes everything true" (U 801–2). What is collected "after history" is not evidence of triumphant technological rationality but the grotesque residuum of achieved catastrophe: the aftermath has superseded the event, for each invention yields also its own malfunction, the logic of its own capacity to destroy. As Virilio observes, the "riddle of technology . . . is also the riddle of the accident."

For Virilio, every technology "produces, provokes, programs" its own accident: the invention of the automobile, for example, was also the invention of the automobile crash.[29] It is in the production of war technology that this inversion of substance and accident is most vividly evident, since it reverses, as Patrick Crogan explains, the "commonsense notion that machinery is essentially productive." War machines, for Virilio, are "machines in reverse—they produce accidents."[30] The "beginning of wisdom," suggests Virilio, would mean "recognizing the symmetry between substance and accident, instead of constantly trying to hide it."[31] This is a theory of "hidden negativity," a counterhistory in opposition to the affirmative culture of progressive production.[32] One way to reveal the fact of the accident might be, suggests Virilio, the development of a new museography that "exposes the accident." Such a project of exposing "industry's other face" of "failure and breakdown" might establish a "public platform for what never gets exposed, but exposes us endlessly to major hazards."[33] This "accident museum" would "revers[e] the relationship to proof: proof through failure, exemplary refutation, and no longer through spectacular success."[34]

This is an argument for a kind of antisublime that refuses the triumphalism (and the awe) that accompanies the harnessing of forces and instead exposes the unlikely, the "unusual and yet inevitable."[35] A museum of this kind would not be a matter of exposing the objects of accidents "to the morbid curiosity of visitors in order to achieve some new romanticism of the technological ruin" but of "creating a new kind of scenography in which *only what explodes and decomposes is exposed*."[36] Indeed, such a museum would not be a museum in the conventional sense at all, "since the exhibition space would itself have lost its interest, its museographical appeal, in favor of an *exposure time*, of a time depth comparable to that of the widest horizons, the most immense landscapes."[37]

The dilemma of Sax's *Long Tall Sally* project, and Misrach's proposal, is that they do invite the morbid curiosity of those interested in Detwiler's "remote landscape of nostalgia" for the technological sublime. By the end of *Underworld*, a closed landfill emits gas that "produces a wavering across the land and sky that deepens the aura of sacred work. It is like a fable in the writhing air of some ghost civilization, a shimmer of desert ruin." At the vast recycling shed the kids love the machines, the parents watch the planes and trucks transport the garbage in and reprocessed goods out, "and we all feel better when we leave" (U 809–10). Misrach's National Park and Sax's painted aircraft are necessarily, and problematically, embedded within the discourse of leisure and optical recuperation, while the toxic waste in *Underworld* is reinscribed as global commodity. Perhaps these are not, after all, contenders for the accident museum.[38]

At the same time, neither *Long Tall Sally* nor Bravo 20 National Park, with their reminders of the bleak certainties of the Cold War, should be read as capitulations to the monumentalizing of the war machine's afterimage. In both cases, the exposure is not only of the hidden and lasting devastation of military-industrial power, but also of the more insidious process whereby devastation is retrieved and rebranded as evidence of righteous domination. The naturalization of Cold War secrecy and nuclear testing is what is really revealed here, the normalizing of extremism, both political and technological. As Virilio warns, "[a]ll 'limit situations' require vigilance against habituation."[39] *Underworld* is precisely such an attempt to probe the limit situation of the Cold War, and the novel's archaeological reconstruction of that irradiated history suggests that works of art, including the novel itself, are unavoidably and necessarily contaminated by the very logic of the history they simultaneously work to dismantle.

What is also clear from DeLillo's, Misrach's, and Gonzalez's attention to the material remains of histories of domination is the persistence of evidence, however much it is made to tell the story of the victorious. The capacity to read things against the grain and locate the "hidden negativity" within affirmative discourse puts to work the contradictions of the open secret in ways that ventilate the museum as a site that displays more than it intends. Beyond the management of past conflicts, however, as Gonzalez notes in his ironic suggestion that tours of devastated neighborhoods of El Paso might become a popular attraction, the clean-up operation that cultural recycling achieves also screens off the continuation of conflict elsewhere. When the Berlin bricks remind Gonzalez of the U.S.-

Mexican border, where tourist junkets to cities like Juárez and Tijuana confirm the asymmetrical relations between the achieved liberty of U.S. citizens and the thwarted movement of northbound migrants, he identifies another front in the post–Cold War perpetuation of violent histories the museums prefer to insist are over.

[J]ust know that everyone is everywhere now
so careful how you shoot.
Rubén Martínez, *The Other Side*

"When I was younger," writes Luis Alberto Urrea in *Across the Wire* (1993), "I went to war. The Mexican border was the battlefield."[1] Urrea is referring to his time spent dispensing poor relief among the barrios of Tijuana in the 1970s, where disease, crime, and random violence are everyday symptoms of structural poverty so deep it fuels a "seemingly endless circle of disasters."[2] Those who live among the hills of garbage can see the "big electric dream" of San Diego only twenty minutes away but remain invisible from the American side, interred by the "all-pervasive It" that refuses to show itself as a "specific enemy."[3]

Returning to Tijuana in the early 1990s, Urrea finds the dumps displaced by maquiladoras, yet the landfills upon which the factories stand remain full of toxic garbage that turns into a "noxious pudding" when it rains.[4] While the landscapes of trash are being reconstructed as feeder sites for the NAFTA-era global marketplace, this remains a place where people are so disconnected from the simplest forms of civic life—no address, no money for postage or paper—that a person "could move two miles away and vanish forever."[5]

Urrea's borderland recalls the open secret of DeLillo's toxic tourist sites—the dump as enterprise zone—where the waste from one order of domination is recycled as the resource for the next. In describing his missionary war on poverty as a "thrilling" battlefield, however, Urrea also, as José David Saldívar argues, "maps *la frontera* as a Vietnamlike spatial warzone" that dangerously invokes "the hallucinogenic excitement" and "military structures of eroticism" often associated with representations of that war.[6] Despite the authority with which Urrea lifts invisible suffering into view the text also contains what Saldívar calls Urrea's "imperial complicity" as a missionary and ethnographer.[7]

This sense of complicity is clear in McCarthy's *Border Trilogy*, where the sympathies John Grady Cole and Billy Parham hold toward Mexican culture are in the end overridden by their allegiance to the United States.

The asymmetrical political relations between the United States and Mexico that ultimately seal Magdelena's and John Grady's fate—and are negatively confirmed by the absence of Mexicans north of McCarthy's border—finally gives the lie to the continuities of geography and culture that are elsewhere reinforced by the ease with which the cowboys cross back and forth between the two countries.[8] John Grady's desire to work in Mexico—Alejandra playfully calls him a "mojado-reverso" (reverse wetback) (APH 124)—is predicated on a freedom to cross the border that is unavailable to either McCarthy's Mexicans or Urrea's garbage-picking Central American refugees.

The problem faced by texts like The Border Trilogy and Across the Wire is that any representation of North America's abjected other is already structured by the kind of totalizing rhetoric deployed by DeLillo's Detwiler, the waste theorist able to extract capital from the most implausible material. When even the concealed refuse of global capitalism can function as part of the covert spectacle that reinforces its legitimacy, the dilemma any project of critical unveiling faces is that it inadvertently reproduces the conditions it seeks to expose. This is clearly the case, it seems to me, in McCarthy's No Country for Old Men (2005) and Charles Bowden's A Shadow in the City (2005), two books that address the dissolution of the difference between crime and law enforcement caused by an escalating borderland drug trade. While in each case the extreme violence of the drug business is seen to have produced a crisis of national identity that can only be confronted by an intensification of policing, McCarthy and Bowden obscure as much as they reveal by relying on narrative conventions that replay political conflict as metaphysical struggle. In Leslie Marmon Silko's Almanac of the Dead (1991), by contrast, the security anxieties regarding the protection of national, racial, and gender integrity registered in McCarthy's and Bowden's books are viewed, from as it were the other side, as generative of new forms of dedifferentiated resistance to the U.S.-led neoliberal order. For Silko, the totalizing order of domination enforced by capitalism's permanent war contains within its own networks of power a countervailing potentiality it has as yet failed to neutralize. While McCarthy and Bowden tend to elevate the material to the transcendent, Silko works from the opposite direction and seeks to materialize the cosmic.

As Hardt and Negri argue, globalization, while productive of new modes of economic and political domination, "is also the creation of new circuits of cooperation and collaboration that stretch across nations and continents and allow an unlimited number of encounters."[9] These are terms that correspond to Almanac's subversive reading of contemporary border politics, which imagines an accelerated unraveling of binary thinking through what border artist Guillermo Gómez-Peña calls the "creative appropriation, expropriation, and subversion of dominant cultural forms" from within.[10] Constructed as a danger to American sovereignty that justifies a militarized response, including the deployment of technologies otherwise made redundant by the "enemy deficit" after the end of the Cold War, the broad coalition of smugglers, revolutionaries, shamans, eco-warriors, survivalists, hackers, homeless veterans, and other excluded populations of the Americas in Silko's novel functions as a kind of terrible wish-fulfillment of the permanent war economy's pursuit of new threats.

Anticipating the Zapatista uprising in Chiapas on the day NAFTA came into effect, January 1, 1994, Almanac of the Dead identifies the way the liberalization of trade signifies a market-driven neocolonialism that, at the same time, produces a counterforce that, as Hardt and Negri suggest, "emerges from within the new imperial sovereignty and points beyond it."[11] For Silko, one of the functions of resistance from the inside is to reimagine the militarized technologies of oppression through a synthesized indigenous Marxism that puts to work the constructed otherness of wasted populations and their repressed histories. In particular, as I will explore below, Almanac of the Dead variously conceives of the manufactured invisibility of the indigenous or otherwise excluded residuum of the American national imaginary as its primary strategic advantage. The technologies of surveillance intended to discipline and regulate perceived threats to security are, in Silko's novel, reanimated as guerrilla devices in the dismantling of biopolitical sovereignty. As such, ostensibly innocuous representational tools such as cameras, televisions, and maps become unglued from their function in the reproduction of normative values and instead serve to short-circuit the process that records in order to erase. If the border functions, as Mary Pat Brady claims, as an "abjection machine" that converts people into "undocumented" aliens and therefore "ontologically impossible," Silko feeds back this inscrutability as the enabler of revolt.[12]

Permanently Losing Control

"We are at war," claimed President George H. W. Bush in 1989. "Drugs are a terrifying, insidious enemy. They challenge almost every aspect of American public policy—the law, our national security, our public health. And the threats they pose touch deep into the nation's soul."[13] Even as the Berlin Wall fell the United States was engaged in a new kind of war. The terms Bush used in his speech to describe the enemy are familiar—it is an "insidious" threat to law, security, and health that demands total mobilization—but their object is no longer a state but something more abstract. Drugs are the enemy, a simple noun standing in for an indeterminate network of foreign and domestic forces that allegedly threaten the very soul of the nation.

While the criminal drug trade is a global phenomenon, in the United States, especially since the 1980s, the front line in the "war on drugs" has been the international border with Mexico. Reagan's heavy spending to counter the flow of cocaine from Colombia into the United States through Florida, while successfully increasing the amount of cocaine seized, did not reduce supply, with traffickers merely relocating routes through Mexico into the Southwestern United States.[14] As a result, spending on border policing followed the traffickers west, and Reagan officially designated drug smuggling a threat to national security in 1986.

If Reagan inadvertently made the border with Mexico a front line in the drug war, leading to the rise of Mexican drug cartels and an escalation of militarized drug enforcement agencies, he also turned immigration into a security issue by linking illegal immigration from Mexico with the perceived threat of communism in Central America. Without U.S. intervention, Reagan warned, America would become the destination for an unstoppable wave of refugees from "communist repression."[15] Links between drug smugglers and terrorists were also made during the 1980s, with Reagan again attempting to synthesize Central American insurgency, criminal activity, and threats to security: "terrorists and subversives are just two days' driving time from Harlingen, Texas," he warned in 1986.[16]

Richard Slotkin argues that the Reagan-Bush era's Central American counterinsurgency wars and the war on drugs invoke "the traditional myths of savage war to rationalize a policy in which various applications of force and violence have a central role." As a version of the frontier myth, crisis is confronted "by deploying the metaphor of 'war' and locating the root of our problem in the power of a 'savage,' captive-taking enemy."[17] For Urrea, apprehending "undocumented entrants" is also "an extension of the Indian Wars" since much of the "human hunting" happens on Indian land.[18] Once the war metaphor is established, explains Slotkin, it "spreads to new objects," producing "a narrative tension" that can only be properly resolved through "literal rather than merely figurative warfare," legitimizing "'cowboy' or (more properly) vigilante-style actions by public officials and covert operatives who defy public law and constitutional principles."[19]

U.S. policy toward Latin America during the 1980s was shaped, as Lars Schoultz has suggested, by certain long-held assumptions about the peculiar barbarism and disregard for the law characteristic of Latin Americans that reach back to early nineteenth-century Anglo views of Hispanic culture. Ambassador Jeanne Fitzpatrick, whose articles for *Commentary* magazine in 1979 and 1981 provided, according to Schoultz, the "intellectual foundation" for Reagan's policy, described endemic violence as "an integral part" of Latin America's authoritarian political regimes, where "[c]oups, demonstrations, political strikes, plots, and counterplots are, in fact, the norm." In particular, El Salvador's political culture emphasized, Kirkpatrick claimed, "strength and *machismo* and all that implies about the nature of the world."[20] We might recall at this point *Blood Meridian*'s Captain White, who complains that Mexicans "have not least notion in God's earth of honor or justice or the meaning of republican government" (BM 33).

A militarized border patrol, compromising as it does the legal protection of civilians from military action being used against them, coupled with attempts to withdraw public services from undocumented migrants like California's 1994 overturned Proposition 187, serve to construct, as José David Saldívar argues, a broad constituency of Latinos, Chicanos, Central Americans, and Asian Americans as "an illegal outside force, an alien nation 'polluting' U.S. culture."[21] American immigration policy and border control measures work to produce what Hardt and Negri call "fleeting and ungraspable" enemies that are the necessary "constitutive function of legitimacy."[22] The blurring of three distinct border issues—drug trafficking, undocumented immigration, and terrorism—into an overlapping problem of national security conflates economic migration, criminal activity, and political violence to produce an amorphous, externalized enemy who is permanently on the verge of invasion. As a consequence, the border is defined as a highly visible site in the maintenance of national sovereignty that justifies high levels of expenditure and the deployment of necessary force. Over the last twenty years, as Mike Davis argues, "immigration enforcement has merged with the War on Drugs and, now, the War on Terror to create what can only be described as a permanent state of low-intensity warfare along the U.S.-Mexican border."[23] Coinciding with increased levels of illegal crossings caused by Mexico's financial crisis and liberalized U.S.-Mexico trade agreements, the militarized border has produced the seemingly paradoxical situation of a border policy where movement is enhanced and encouraged (legal trade), while at the same time being restricted and rigorously policed (drug traffic, illegal immigration).

The border, then, embodies the contradictions of neoliberal restructuring and post–Cold War military realignment, with Defense Department resources redirected toward the regulation of legal trade and illegal smuggling. High-tech equipment—including infrared night vision scopes, low-light TV cameras, ground sensors, helicopters, all-terrain vehicles, magnetic footfall detectors and infrared body sensors used in Vietnam, an electronic fingerprinting system, giant X-ray machines, and, post-9/11, the 2002 introduction of the National Security Entry-Exit Registration System—as well as conventional barriers such as fences, checkpoints, and other fortifications, have been deployed to repel drug and immigrant traffic while protecting capital flows. The military-industrial investment in border policing is further indicated by the establishment, in 1995, of the Border Research Technology Center in San Diego, which specializes in developing technological aids for border management, and the doubling of the number of border patrol agents in the Southwest between 1993 and 1999 to over eight thousand.[24] In addition, the Joint Task

Force Six at Fort Bliss (established 1989) provides around seventy infantrymen for border policing, while the deployment of the National Guard has also remained a fixture since the late 1980s.

The huge cost of the militarization of the border suggests another contradiction: massive public spending on border control has been undertaken at a time when other state sectors are downsized and deregulated. As with Cold War military-industrial spending, this tends to harden allegiances between corporations invested in military and security technologies and the government agencies that fund security initiatives, producing what Peter Andreas calls a "policy feedback effect" whereby political, bureaucratic, and corporate structures become self-reinforcing. Justified as a national security issue, state funding of border policing enables the continuation of a form of military Keynesianism even as the rest of the market is exposed to the vagaries of deregulated free trade. This contradiction is especially apparent in A Shadow in the City, where Bowden's deep-cover drug agent Joey O'Shay comes to see law enforcement as a self-legitimizing business enterprise that is structurally dependent on the continuation of drug crime. The fact is that policies of containment along a two-thousand-mile stretch of terrain are unlikely to succeed consistently and permanently, and border policing, as Andreas has suggested, is largely an exercise in controlled failure, where failure itself escalates the level of police action and maintains the anxiety that control of the border is perpetually being lost. A war that is waged "to create and maintain social order can have no end," Hardt and Negri observe, and "has to be won again every day."[25]

This is certainly true of the "prevention through deterrence" strategy of the 1990s, which, beginning in El Paso in 1993 with Operation Blockade, later renamed Operation Hold the Line, eschewed the previous policy of apprehension in favor of literally blocking entry to prospective illegal migrants. While the policy did reduce illegal entries, and was subsequently adopted elsewhere, including San Diego (Operation Gatekeeper), the effect was to push migrants to more dangerous and remote areas, exposing them to the hazards of the desert and the often corrupt "coyotes" paid to get them into the United States. Some small border towns quickly became "major corridors of illegal crossing," leading to an influx of agents and new fencing projects; the mayor of Douglas, Arizona, complained that his town was becoming a "militarized zone."[26] Yet the main consequence of this increase in policing has been the rise in the death rate among those attempting to enter the United States, with a 78 percent increase in known deaths between 1998 and 2005.[27] The drug trade also continues to claim lives on the border, with more than two thousand Mexican deaths in gangland killings in 2006 alone.[28]

Andreas argues that there was never a time when the border was effectively controlled, and that the narrative of "loss of control" is an effect of the kind of policies instituted to contain the uncontainable. For both law enforcement advocates and critics alike, Andreas claims, the "loss of control" narrative reveals a basic misunderstanding about border policing and smuggling, which is that it "understates the degree to which the state has actually structured, conditioned, and even enabled (often unintentionally) clandestine border crossings, and overstates the degree to which the state has been able to control its borders in the past."[29] In fact, Andreas goes on, border policing is not just a strategy for preventing illegal crossings but, more fundamentally, it is "a symbolic representation of state authority" that signals a "commitment to marking and maintaining the borderline."[30] Even the failure to contain illegal crossings can, then, be symbolically effective in that displays of political resolve and public spending both reinforce the sense that there is indeed a threat and that it is being handled. At the same time, the deployment of highly visible border policing locates the threat to state sovereignty at the line of demarcation between inside and outside, externalizing the threat of drugs and immigrants and obscuring more complicated issues such as the huge domestic demand for drugs and cheap labor.

The border, like the internment camp and the blank space on the map, is another indeterminate zone of exception that marks the threshold between inside and outside, where state sovereignty shows itself in the regulation and discipline of space and bodies, and where bare life is manufactured through a response to perceived challenges to the integrity of the polis. In *Almanac of the Dead*, as we will see, this zone of exception becomes the place within which the anomalous products of hemispheric dispossession convert the condition of always already losing control into immanent critique.

History Is a Prophet Who Looks Back

Paul Virilio suggests that for God, "history is a landscape of events" in the sense that for him there is no sequence, only co-presence. This omnitemporal perspective is a "landscape of time in which . . . the past and the future loom up together in all their obvious simultaneity; a place where nothing follows on from anything else anymore and yet where nothing ever ends, the lack of duration of the perpetual present circumscribing the cycle of history and its repetitions."[31] We might pity God his awful view of the world were it not for the fact, Virilio claims, that this vision "has become the vision of each and every one of us."[32]

This spatialized view of history as a landscape of events provides an accurate and useful description of Silko's sprawling *Almanac of the Dead*. For Silko's ambition, with its focus on the militarized present of the U.S.-Mexico borderlands, is to track across the Americas the power lines of five hundred years of violent conquest and exploitation. In this book she pushes the ambivalence at the end of *Ceremony* to its awful limit. For Silko, the Americas is indeed a place "where nothing follows on" and "where nothing ever ends." The repetitions of history are, in *Almanac*, the endless waves of brutality, torture, and destruction wrought by outsiders upon a place and its inhabitants. However, while some might well fear the past, as Virilio writes, Silko locates in the past, alongside violence and destruction, the germ of future revolution. One of history's repetitions may well be the overthrow and demise of a great empire. The past that contaminates the present of the United States is, for Silko, the legacy of centuries of ethnic cleansing and environmental despoliation. At the same time, the persistence of indigenous populations, despite all efforts at containment and erasure, remains a latent threat, an active contaminant in the teleological history of Anglo-capitalist expansion. In Silko's novel the past is very much present; the ancient almanac is also a prophecy, predicting both the arrival of white conquerors and the end of European settlement in the Americas.

The U.S. government, wrote Eduardo Galeano in 1973, has "nightmares about millions of children advancing like locusts over the horizon from the third world."[33] This U.S. terror of invasion from "below" is precisely the subject of *Almanac*, a fear articulated by the white supremacist

Serlo, who believes that "the day would come when the world was over-run with swarms of brown and yellow human larvae called natives."[34] Silko has acknowledged the influence of Galeano's work on her novel, which is plain in terms of Galeano's notion of history as prophecy. For Galeano, the "ghosts of all the revolutions that have been strangled or be-trayed through Latin America's tortured history emerge" in new forms, as if "the present had been foreseen and begotten by the contradictions of the past. History is a prophet who looks back."[35] He notes the similari-ties between "the caravelled conquistadors and the jet-propelled techno-crats; Hernán Cortés and the Marines; the agents of the Spanish Crown and the International Monetary Fund missions; the dividends from the slave trade and the profits of General Motors."[36] But Galeano also sees the repetition in the present of "the defeated heroes and resurrected hopes: the fertile sacrifices." Referring to Alexander von Humboldt's study of the customs of the ancient inhabitants of the Bogotá plateau, Galeano writes that he found that the Indians called the victims of ritual ceremo-nies quihica, meaning "door." The death of each victim "opened the door to a new cycle of 185 moons."[37]

Almanac of the Dead develops the revolutionary prospect of the idea of the fertile sacrifice and the door to resistance that every victim opens. In these terms, death is the aperture through which might pass a dissemi-nated light of insurgent power. The view of history the novel presents is intended, like Galeano's elision of the slave trade and General Motors, to ignite recognition of past time as active in the present, both negatively and as potentiality. Like Virilio's God, Almanac of the Dead reads history not as sequence but as co-presence; the represented time of the novel is all there at once. The plot of Almanac does not so much unfold as develop in the manner of a photographic print: the form of the subject appears, at first lightly, gradually thickening until the entire surface is exposed. There is not much plot in Almanac, in the conventional sense of richly unfolding human relationships and complex motivations, but there are contours, channels, and passages through and across which characters and forces move.

The form of the novel, then, performs its own spatiotemporal recon-ceptualization: its digressions, numerous and scattered locations, mul-tiple protagonists, converging and diverging plot movements resist a

developmental process of understanding in favor of a kind of epistemological flux. Nothing is resolved by the end of the novel; the real action—the northward push into the United States of a revolutionary indigenous population—has not even started yet. What is evident by the
end of the novel, though, is a network of cross-referenced contingencies.
As Janet St. Clair has observed, the strands of plot in *Almanac* should be
understood not as lines but as "great looping convergences that encom-
pass more time, and more space, until time and space—those corner-
stones of modern Western thought—become the eviscerated signifiers
of a radically limited vision."[38]

Almanac is less interested in depth than in surface, and this is as true
of character as it is of history. The numerous characters become known
to us not so much through psychological insight as through where they
are geographically, their position within the prevailing social order, and
through their movements. As Zeta claims right at the very outset of the
novel, the "old ones" did not believe in the passage of time and thought
that it was not the years that aged people "but the miles and miles that
had been traveled in this world" (20). Silko's protagonists cannot be separated from time and place; they are nodal points through which local, national, and international interests are shaped and challenged. The novel
resists fetishizing "character" in order to elaborate on broader forces
and their part in the production of subjects. Indeed, the production of
the "individual" is precisely one of the colonialist categories *Almanac* is
at pains to disperse.[39]

In discussing *Almanac* as a surface, a map, and as a developing photograph it might be inferred that the technologies of representation utilized by the novel are coterminous with the disciplinary technologies of
conquest and as such reproduce the panoptic model of containment and
erasure of difference the book claims to resist. Indeed, the God's-eye-view
and pulverization of depth provided by the map as two-dimensional inventory, and the use of photography as a technology of surveillance and
captivity, are so deeply encoded in the colonization and policing of the
American West that it might be assumed that an appeal to such models
is to fatally miss the point.

Silko provides her readers with a map at the opening of her narrative,
however, and the novel is deeply invested in the production and reception

of photographic images. The novel positions itself in a complex relationship with the technologies of domination it seeks to undermine, and it retrieves from them possibilities for alternative interpretive practices. As Eva Cherniavsky has argued, while Silko certainly mobilizes "tribal affiliations and knowledges in an effort to define a transnational strategy of resistance to both the old and the new colonialisms," tribal knowledges in Almanac do not appeal to an ethnonationalistic "rhetoric of cultural purity" but are always situated "as contemporaneous with and internal to the forms, if not the ends, of capital."[40] This historicizing guerrilla strategy of reappropriation is, of course, at work at the literal level of the book itself, which writes itself into the American literary marketplace even as it acts as a critique of written language as a form of monocultural domination and imperial legitimation.

The squeamishness of some early critics of the novel, including the by now notorious review in the New Republic by Sven Birkets, reveals, perhaps, the extent to which Almanac antagonizes the culture's conventional expectations and presents itself as something unrecognizably other. Birkets complains that while the idea of the oppressed breaking their chains and retaking what is theirs "is not an unappealing idea (for some) . . . it is so contrary to what we know both of the structures of power and the psychology of the oppressed that the imagination simply balks." For Birkets, Silko's notion of revolt is "tethered to airy nothing" and "naive to the point of silliness." Appealing to prophecy simply "cannot make up the common-sense deficit."[41]

Partly, I think, the incredulity voiced by Birkets is due to Silko's explicit disavowal of common sense as it is generally understood: that is, everyday knowledge drawn so intimately from experience and so self-evident as to constitute a natural order of things. Even if only a fraction of the atrocities described in Almanac could be matched to actual events—and the murder, torture, sundry brutalities, fascist fantasies, snuff movies, depraved and vicious officials, porno cartels, drug rings, and the rest are unfortunately not outside the realms of most informed imaginations—then any purported natural order might legitimately be called into question. There is a common sense at work in Almanac, but it is a sense of the communal that is not always so reliant on rational empiricism and more willing to take a broader view of what might be garnered by the senses.

It is this counterlogic that enables Silko to claim maps and photographs, as well as novels, as part of the arsenal of a guerrilla epistemology that is, in a very important and literal sense, willfully naïve: native, born in and of a particular place. Far from being founded on an "airy nothing," Silko's conception of indigenous revolt emerges out of a very real understanding of how the policing of U.S. sovereign power through the related strategies of border control, counterinsurgency, and drug war operations are episodes in what the Yaqui drug smuggler Calabazas calls "the war that had never ended" (AD 178), namely, as Zeta says, "the war for the continents called the Americas" (AD 133). When she discovers, through a "message from the South" (AD 703), that the CIA are using drug money to fund counterinsurgency campaigns against indigenous rebels, Zeta kills her CIA-linked connection in the gunrunning business and is poised to join the rebellion. While smuggling, for Calabazas and Zeta, represents a refusal to abide by laws imposed by "illicit governments" that had to be "blasted away" (AD 133), discovering a government that breaks its own laws leaves Zeta complicit with the forces she has intended to destroy. The real war, as Silko suggests, is not fought by breaking laws that have already been broken but by being able to make the historical connections rendered invisible by the legitimation effects of the nation-state.[42]

The Crosshairs of Revolution

While photography has historically been used as a key recording device in the classification of the world, there is also, writes artist Robert Smithson, "something abominable about cameras because they possess the power to invent many worlds."[43] It is this power latent in technology to multiply rather than fix meaning that preoccupies Silko. "The Indian with a camera announces the twilight of Eurocentric America," she writes, not just because this inverts the colonial gaze whereby the "native" is positioned as an immobilized object, but because the function of technology itself becomes altered by a radically different epistemology.[44]

Discussing U.S. "blindness to the world," Apache elders during Geronimo's resistance remark, in Almanac, that Europeans often complain "in frightened tones that the hills and canyons looked the same to them" (AD 224–25). Yaqui and Apache strategists "quickly learned to make use of the Europeans' inability to perceive unique details in the landscape," in effect becoming cognitive guerrillas, destabilizing the grounds of European epistemological certainty (AD 225). Euro-American attempts at spatiotemporal structuring cannot contain the indigenous nomad's dispersed relation to place, as the drug-runner Calabazas explains: "[w]e don't believe in boundaries. Borders. Nothing like that. We are here thousands of years before the first whites. We are here before maps and quit claims. We know where we belong on this earth. We have always moved freely. North–South. East–West. We pay no attention to what isn't real. Imaginary lines. Imaginary minutes and hours. Written law. We recognize none of that" (AD 216). Maps and clocks function metonymically for Calabazas as signs of abstract thinking that seeks to divide and rule but also prevent Euro-Americans from seeing what is really taking place. Calabazas rejects the colonial process of verification through classification in favor of a primary empiricism: he already knows where he is because he is and has always been there; no method of authentication outside of himself can challenge this corporeal fact.

In arguing that "[w]e pay no attention to what isn't real," Calabazas is, ironically, more of a materialist than the colonizers: the Europeans saw "just a 'rock' whenever they found it, despite obvious differences in shape, density, color, or the position of the rock relative to all things around it" (AD 224). Lecha, by comparison, "had never seen any person, animal, place, or thing look the same twice" (AD 167), and Calabazas snarls that "I get mad when I hear the word identical. . . . There is no such thing. Nowhere. At no time" (AD 201). For Calabazas, the real can only be known in a particular time and place, and that knowledge cannot be held but must be known only in motion. As Cherniavsky claims, this "tribal epistemology levels an unsparing assault on the principles of equivalence, conversion, and exchange that underwrite identity and identificatory practices on the left and on the right."[45]

The nonidentity of Indian epistemological understanding is devastatingly revealed in the case of Menardo's body armor. The vest's instruction manual asserts the vest offers protection from all manner of terrorist and criminal attack but is ultimately useless since Menardo's belief in the identical nature of mass-produced goods is demonstrated to be empirically false. Explaining the virtues of the vest to Tacho, Menardo claims that it protected a man from a .38 Special. "This very same vest?" Tacho asks, disbelievingly. It is not, of course, exactly the same vest, it is "one just like it," but the difference is crucial because Menardo's "scientific" demonstration leads to his own death (AD 340).

The slipperiness of Indian countercultural onto-epistemology is developed more thoroughly in relation to the mechanical reproduction of images. Elsewhere, Silko has explained that she is interested in photographs "that obscure rather than reveal" and "don't tell you what you are supposed to notice."[46] As Eric Gary Anderson observes, "photographs for Silko do not necessarily or even primarily serve as documentary certifications or commemorations of some 'authentic' representational relationship in some specifiable time and place."[47] While she does not deny that photographs constitute evidence of some kind, Silko's conception of evidence is not consistent with Western notions of the documentary recording.

In Almanac, if Western thinking reduces all rocks to "rock," or all vests to this vest, the same applies to Indians: to whites, Calabazas recalls, "all Indians looked alike" (AD 225). When Geronimo is captured he is photographed in order to secure his identity, but he was probably not the real Geronimo since "there had been three different Apache warriors called Geronimo who ranged across the Sonoron desert south of Tucson" (AD 225). All the Geronimos had at various times been photographed, and while the accused often protested, denial was read as further sign of guilt. The mystery of the photographs, and the "heart" of the story as far as the Indians are concerned, is that while these various images were of different individuals, another, unidentifiable man's face appeared on the prints "where the faces of the other Geronimos should have been" (AD 228). The photographs are evidence for the Apache and Yaqui, but evidence of a metaphysical power somehow finding a passage into the world through the enemy's mechanisms of control rather than traces of Geronimo's likeness. Indeed, for White Ledge, an Apache medicine man, the photographs were merely "flat paper" that "had little smudges and marks like animal tracks across snow or light brown dust" upon them that were "supposed to 'represent' certain persons, places, or things" (AD 227). Even for the Americans they remain confusing and undecidable as evidence.

The undecidability of the image, however much it challenges the rationalizing project of the colonial power, can only in the end provide a temporary means of resistance for the Apaches, since the double function of documents—as self-evident truths and as open to interpretation—is ultimately the contradiction that serves to legitimate conquest by treaty, and then by ethnographic documentation—using photography—of the "vanishing" Indian culture that becomes the reified "evidence" of their "authenticity." Nevertheless, Silko's identification of the subversive potential of technologies intended to contain the monstrous refuses to accept that indeterminacy always favors the victor.

Television, like photography, is made in *Almanac* to produce unforeseen outcomes. Lecha's clairvoyant ability to locate the missing makes her perfect for TV talk shows. Her popularity is in part down to the "fascination the United States had had for the 'other'" (AD 142), but her TV revelations are tuned into mainstream tastes, sentimental performances of feigned emotion and expert timing. As the crew prepare for a broadcast, Lecha thinks of guerrillas "as quiet and smooth as snakes" breaking open "the dams and the electric motors of the machinery, machinery that belongs to the masters, stutter to a halt" (AD 162). Lecha had learned how technology, properly harnessed, could produce unexpected consequences years earlier in Alaska. During nights spent huddled around the communal television made possible by University of Alaska experiments with satellites, Lecha witnesses an old woman crash planes by running her fingers over the screen: "[w]hite people could fly circling objects in the sky that sent messages and images of nightmares and dreams, but the old woman knew how to turn the destruction back on its senders" (AD 156).

On the flight out of Alaska, Lecha sits next to an insurance adjustor working for petroleum exploration companies. He is investigating dozens of unexplained air crashes in the area and produces a map dotted with red crosses. While the adjustor claims that the disappearances can be explained, he inadvertently exposes the blindness of corporate interests. Alaska is nothing but a frozen waste, he thinks, empty of value except for the mineral wealth buried beneath the ice. While lives had been lost in the crashes, the insurance photographs he places on Lecha's lap focus on the "scattered, mangled electronic equipment," and conversation focuses on the cost of the losses (AD 159). Maps and photographs again, the latter "hastily" gathered up when a picture of a limb slips out, are presented here as evidence that explains little.

The recorded image is for Silko a channel or vehicle for forces that contain the same latent power as the vibrations generated by collective experience: "photographs are capable of registering subtle electromagnetic changes in both the subject and the photographer."[48] These changes are analogous to the transformations felt in a crowd, which, she claims, "emanate actual electricity" that alters perception and behavior and "binds and propels a mob as a single creature." Understood this way, "the greed and violence of the last century in the United States are palpable; . . . registered in the very atmosphere and effect, even in the light. 'Murder, murder,' sighs the wind over the rocks in a remote Arizona canyon where they betrayed Geronimo."[49] The movement Silko makes here from the photograph to the crowd relies on the recognition of picture "taking" as a form of communication and participation. As such, the imperial gaze of the photographer can be undermined by refiguring the photographer as both witness and agent of transformation rather than the taker of a still image. The same might apply to watching (or even being on) television, which, for Silko, can be a powerful collective experience, effecting a kind of energy transfer.

Menardo's all-night satellite TV sessions expose him to the electrical power of crowds transmitted through the tube: all over the world there are "what appeared to be larvae or insects swarming." These are in fact "mobs of angry brown people swarming like bees from horizon to horizon" (AD 481). Such scenes made Menardo nervous and angry: "television showed everything—it showed too much" (483). While the use of television technology in the novel maintains order, protects and enhances the interests of capitalism through the surveillance of criminals and terrorists, and by converting torture into commodity in the form of snuff movies, it is ultimately impossible to police the dissemination of TV images. The broadcasting of riots is "precisely what the terrorists had wanted" (AD 482). Menardo's conclusion is that television "spoiled secrecy" (AD 483): the light of a crowd's electricity, once broadcast, illuminates the revolutionary threat of collective anger.

Silko's reading of technology gives new valence to the possibility of repetition that is not merely a reproduction of the same. As Debora Horowitz suggests, the repetition of retelling is not a trope in the novel but "a meta-narrative device contouring the novel's structure through enactment."[50] While the technologies of representation have been deployed to replace the object with the document, in *Almanac*'s performative model, embodied repetition is intended to circulate felt knowledge rather than dead images.

Calabazas presents the power of narrative as a kind of swerve into knowledge through his "Indian style" of oratory. He "talks and talks before he turns at the last moment, to the point" he wants to make, the message being "in the route Calabazas took when he talked" (AD 215). This route does not "run in a line for the horizon but circled and spiraled" without apparent direction (AD 224). This is true also of the almanac itself, which incorporates the tales of the people entrusted to preserve and interpret it into itself, and of *Almanac of the Dead*: "with each retelling a slight but permanent shift took place" (AD 581). The story, in a sense, runs, is contingent to the process of its own creation. Like the corridos McCarthy celebrates, there is a significant connection in Silko between narrative and the body, the corporeal process of storytelling and the flow of the blood that roots the transmission of knowledge in the world as agent. The corrido, as we learn in *The Crossing*, is "the poor man's history. It does not owe its allegiance to the truths of history but to the truths of men" (C 386). The corrido represents the linguistic blood of the people infused with the dirt of history. The corridos run through the culture, transmitting a serial narrative, a relay of folk knowledge. The spiral narratives that Calabazas and others in *Almanac* tell (and that the novel itself tells) function in the same way, preserving but also altering (in the telling) the tale.

There is embedded in the notion of the tale, then, a dialectic of inside and outside, of the individual and the communal body, "official" and transgressive narrative histories. The maps, photographs, and other documents of conquest externalize or objectify domination as a process of normalization. As Gloria Anzaldúa argues, "in trying to become 'objective,' Western culture made 'objects' of things and people when it distanced itself from them, thereby losing 'touch' with them. This dichotomy is the root of all violence."[51] The enforcement of the borderline between experience and document, corporeal historical knowledge and normative discourse is, for Anzaldúa and Silko, a tactic that divides and conquers: it ruptures the body from history, sensation from sense, space from time. The struggle to resist this division is, for Anzaldúa an "inner" conflict performed in "outer terrains," with the psyche resembling a border-town.[52]

The swerve away from the narrative circle into the spiral is a practice that refuses the reproduction of the same that embeds the form of narrative into history: the swerve is always produced by context. It is, in effect, a form of violent resistance against the borders established by normative expectations. David L. Moore suggests that "the structural circulation of reader and text, past and future, reality and fiction, history and myth, as it eludes narrative closure in *Almanac of the Dead*, is rooted ultimately in a thematic circulation between life and death, a warrior's evasion of the final closure."[53] This evasion or swerve that takes place on the borderlines between structuring categories is, as Anzaldúa writes, a "place of contradictions" characterized by "[h]atred, anger and exploitation."[54]

Faced with anger and exploitation, Silko emphasizes the importance of patience and endurance in the struggle for liberation, what Moore calls a "radical patience" that must resist bloodshed in the face of violent domination.[55] The circulation of stories reinforces the importance of patience and understanding, stressing the perpetual struggle for nonrationalizing, counterimperialist interpretations of the power of blood, time, and space. Stories allow for blood to circulate, not to spill.

The struggle, then, intersects at the border between inner and outer, as Anzaldúa says, happening first in "the images in our heads" and "played out in the outer terrains." The relation between internalized ideological mechanisms of identification and self-definition and political, historical agency are part of the same struggle; one implies the other. In *Almanac*, as in Anzaldúa's work, the struggle is for the material body of the subject and for the body or form of the text. Silko has to acknowledge, indeed she celebrates, the always already hybrid condition of resistance. As Anzaldúa argues, the border dweller is "simultaneously insider/outsider," comprising "a geography of hybrid selves." As the embodiment of the peripheral, the hybrid subject is forced "to negotiate the cracks between realities."[56]

Silko's own recognition of the hybrid identity of the globalized subject seeks to wrest the machinery of oppression away from the "destroyers" in a creative act of appropriation. The understanding of the nonidentical nature of things and people she claims the Indian has preserved means that resistance to the commodification of the indigenous body (human and land) and the attendant erasure of difference into an amorphous and invisible underclass can be subversively reconfigured as a revolutionary return of the nonidentical. While Anglo culture is "fallen," Indian civilization, for Silko, retains a worldly acceptance of history's landscape of events. Affluent white people seek out Lecha in secret with a "deep sense that something had been lost" (AD 718). They fear physical change and illness, consciousness itself terrifies them, "and they had sought to control death by becoming killers themselves" (AD 718). This terror is hardly surprising to Lecha; after the destruction of the earth, "it was only logical" that the "earth's beings" would be next. Yoeme herself had doubted whether human life would survive, but then "humans would not be a great loss to the earth" (AD 719). Out of the dust grow plants that will be consumed to produce new life and "all the time, the energy had only been changing form, nothing had been lost or destroyed" (AD 719).

Starting to Lean Back the Other Way

Almanac of the Dead's taxonomy of the free trade underclass—a swarming population mobilized by aggressive economic forces into a kind of perpetual motion that traipses across the surface of the continent—is a version of Pynchon's preterite other America that coexists as the obverse of the official Sunbelt world of innocent consumption and legitimate freedoms but is only rarely seen in the peripheral vision of capitalism's majority stakeholders. For Ed Tom Bell, the middle-aged small-town West Texas sheriff in Cormac McCarthy's No Country for Old Men (2005), this world is as mysterious and alien as it is threatening. McCarthy largely eschews the lyricism of the Border Trilogy here in favor of a fast-paced chase narrative that leans heavily on genre clichés and gives little space for his characteristically ornate prose style. Nevertheless, there is something about No Country for Old Men—not least the premature demise of its chief protagonist, Llewellyn Moss—that suggests that McCarthy has little interest in the logical narrative arc the genre demands and is more concerned with how border politics has come to be read as a form of crime fiction. Throughout the novel, the first-person musings of Bell are offered as a counterpoint to the chase narrative, and in the final part of the book Bell's voice takes over once the action has ended. It is really Bell that McCarthy is interested in, I think, and through him McCarthy does pursue some of the themes that preoccupied him in his other Western works.

Bell's reflections on the state of the country position him as a man who is fearful of the changes he sees taking place and powerless, despite his elected position, to effect any influence over forces he cannot grasp. His observations betray the typical anxieties of small town conservatism, bewildered by the failure of traditional social structures of church, family, and the law to restrain and manage the seemingly atavistic, selfish drives of the society he is charged with protecting. Exposed because of his job to the rising levels of violent crime in the region, Bell longs for the certainties of his youth and the balance of rights and responsibilities he remembers enjoying as part of the paternalistic community built by his parents' generation. While he continues to follow a creed based on service and duty, he can only do so by paradoxically relinquishing his role as frontline law officer. Bell cannot and does not want to apprehend the brutal drug-warrior Chigurh, who operates at a level of lawlessness so beyond Bell's comprehension that he is little more than a satanic chimera to be avoided, and instead concentrates his efforts on trying to convince Moss, through his wife, Carla Jean, of the extent of the danger they are in.

In this self-confessed abdication of his duty as lawman—"somewhere out there is a true and living prophet of destruction and I dont want to confront him"—Bell's failure to grasp the political complexity of contemporary crime compels him to reframe it as an apocalyptic menace abroad in the country.[57] Asked if he believes in Satan, Bell concedes that he did as a boy and, after a waning of belief, he is "startin to lean back the other way. He explains a lot of things that otherwise don't have no explanation. Or not to me they dont" (NC 218). While it used to seem that drug runners were merely a modern version of the cattle rustlers of his grandfather's time, Bell is no longer "sure we've seen these people before. Their kind" (NC 79).

Readers of McCarthy have, of course, seen their kind before, and Chigurh's indifference to life, tendency to cod-philosophize on chance and fate, and capacity to survive the most bloody confrontation echo *Blood Meridian*'s Judge Holden. Bell's discomfort with the way his World War II–veteran peers, college-educated thanks to the GI Bill, came back home "with hard things to say about their people" (NC 195), measures the extent to which the historical path McCarthy charts in his Western works has led to some awkward compromises with the truth. If the free market in scalps helped to pay for the open range of the early twentieth century, Bell's outrage at revisionist criticism of "the early settlers" reveals how far the righteous stoicism embodied in John Grady Cole and Billy Parham has domesticated the legacy of violent conquest *Blood Meridian* so remorselessly reimagined. Bell is furious at the ingrate college boys who "didnt seem to know what I was talkin about" when he explains to them that "havin your wife and children killed and scalped and gutted like fish has a tendency to make some people irritable" (NC 195). The history of the West for Bell is a history of surviving violence from without, and it is this legacy, that of God-fearing small town communities under siege, that provides the attenuated vocabulary with which he attempts to establish contemporary drug crime as a modern version of the externalized savage menace that animates unreconstructed Western myth.

Set in the early 1980s, the book places Bell's conservatism as an articulation of the values and fears of the emergent political Right in the years following the election of Ronald Reagan. While Bell is certainly something of a caricature of the small town sheriff, his presence is remarkable in McCarthy's novels as a commentator who directly seeks to contextualize events within a definable historical frame. Bell is a mess of prejudices and ill-informed terrors, his confusion at the current state of things often boiling down to a despair at the young's contempt for authority and an abandonment of what he sees as "common sense" (NC 62). While he is unhappy about the criticism of his community as "a bunch of rednecks" by his college-educated peers, he is hopeful that the 1960s "sobered some of em up" (NC 195). For Bell, in line with the Reagan-Bush fantasy of "rollback," permissiveness has devastated the social fabric and can only be remedied by the invocation of the divine: "I know as certain as death that there aint nothing short of the second comin of Christ that can slow this train" (NC 159).

As with much of the information he gets regarding the world, Bell's views on the young are gleaned from the daily newspapers he reads "to try and figure out what might be headed this way" (NC 40). The appeal to "common sense" is also drawn in as a rebuttal to criticism of right-wing politics when Bell recounts a conversation he had with a woman who "kept talking about the right wing this and the right wing that" (NC 196). Bell claims he "aint even sure what she meant by it" because the "people I know are mostly just common people" (NC 196). Getting to the point, the woman complains that "I dont like the way this country is headed. I want my grand-daughter to be able to have an abortion" (NC 196). Bell's response encapsulates his disdain for the woman's identification of right-wing politics *as* politics and his own reactionary pessimism: "I'm goin to say that not only will she be able to have an abortion, she'll be able to have you put to sleep. Which pretty much ended the conversation" (NC 197).

This is a cheap shot, but it is the only kind Bell is capable of making in his diminished capacity as a lawman who can no longer catch criminals. What prevents him from remaining the ineffectual residuum of a lost Western white male hegemony, of course, is the success with which Reagan mobilized the values of people like Bell during the 1980s into a potent political force that claimed to reject ideology in favor of precisely the kind of "commonsense" values Bell is prone to articulate; that is, the restitution at the center of American life of the Cold War rhetoric of good and evil that leaned heavily on a lexicon of frontier myth and the cowboy code of honor. As Richard Slotkin explains, Reagan's reanimation of the frontier myth's linkages between "bonanza economics" and moral regeneration through "savage war" may be a "falsification of memory" but it gave historical legitimacy to the release of capital through the bonanza of deregulation and foreign policy cures for "Vietnam syndrome."[58]

In *No Country for Old Men*, McCarthy appears to have come full circle in his Western works. This last novel is set during the period of *Blood Meridian*'s composition and functions in some ways as a reflection on the recrudescence of the apocalyptic frontier rhetoric activated by Reagan's successful appeal to traditional values. While *Blood Meridian* explores the means by which Old Testament fire can be put to good imperialist use, *No Country for Old Men* exposes the reactionary impulse behind the rekindling of that flame in the 1980s. Bell's concession of defeat in the face of Chigurh's untouchable "evil" allows the criminal to remain at large as a largely symbolic threat that can be put to use in the construction and maintenance of an environment of fear. When the real villains are untouchable, surrogate targets in the form of perceived threats to social order are easily found, as Bell's tabloid-fuelled fear of moral deviancy indicates. Bell's nostalgia for the certainties of the postwar years is also shown to be flawed, and while his own sense of weakness, like John Grady's father, is produced by the war, World War II does not in and of itself destroy an uncontaminated pastoral Western socius, though it does contribute to the unraveling of the insulated mythos of small town self-legitimacy. What the drug war reveals is the perpetuation of violent conflict in the region that has as much respect for geopolitical boundaries and self-evident moral truths as Holden or Glanton. And just as expansionist violence remained unchecked and held at arm's length by a government prepared to concede its efficacy, so too are the drug cartels and their foot-soldiers free to roam across the borderlands due not just to their superior firepower and ferocity but because they serve a useful symbolic function in sustaining justification for counterinsurgent activities and low-intensity military operations. Bell knows that the only reason he is still alive is because the criminals "have no respect" for him (NC 216). Indeed, they do not merely lack respect for the law, they "dont even think about the law" (NC 216).

The Line between Them and Me

When Sheriff Bell concedes that he is not equipped to combat the new breed of criminal emerging from the drug business, he seeks an articulation of the threat in terms of satanic evil. Converted into a metaphysical power, Bell's reluctance to face men like Chigurh can be accommodated not as failure of leadership but as fear and trembling in the presence of evil. McCarthy and Silko both depict acts of seemingly motiveless casual violence by perpetrators who are oblivious to the law and apparently devoid of any identifiable traces of human feeling. The feral networks of drug dealers, gun runners, torturers, and assassins that compose Silko's invisible Americas can be hard to stomach, as Birkets's criticism shows, and McCarthy's willingness to countenance a kind of gnostic evil at work in the land pushes his work beyond the limits of conventional realism and toward the genre of gothic fable. Silko's interest in cosmic forces is bound up with an investment in indigenous modes of resistance to the long history of European domination of the Americas, and as such serves as an enabling function in the ongoing political struggle. Bell's move toward the biblical certainties of good and evil, however, is a retreat into myth as he recasts the sociopolitical terrors of organized crime as emanations of an evil force for which his only defense is rekindled faith. While both authors utilize the notion of something called "evil" to describe the immense destructive force at work, only Silko is able to conceive of a possible counterforce that drives a political response in this world. In McCarthy there is no one capable of challenging men like Holden and Chigurh, and the best course of action is stay out of their way.

If the "war on drugs" is constructed as a struggle against an amorphous evil, then the force of "good" requires a kind of warrior-king of a different order than the homely Sheriff Bell. In *A Shadow in the City: Confessions of an Undercover Drug Warrior* (2005), Charles Bowden offers a portrait of such a character in the form of Joey O'Shay. Like much of Bowden's work, this book is a willful confusion of genres, a combination of investigative journalism, hard-boiled noir, and pulp thriller. The nonfiction status of the book, however, is stressed from the outset. While names have been changed and the location rendered anonymous, "[i]t all happened," the reader is assured: "[t]he deals occurred. As did the killings, beatings, shootings, tortures, betrayals, suicide, and love."[59] As this certificate of authenticity suggests, however, the manner in which these events are to be represented is far removed from the strategic performance of objectivity relied upon in more conventional nonfiction accounts. Indeed, without this preemptive assurance, the text might be mistaken for a noir thriller by even the most assiduous reader—with a name like Joey O'Shay, the protagonist would be in good company in a James Ellroy novel. While there are a few moments when a secondary character appears to be addressing an external observer, perhaps an interviewer, such instances are rare and uncorroborated. Instead, the text positions itself as a free indirect discourse through which the contradictions of O'Shay's life as a deep-cover agent posing as a drug lord can be accessed. Short extracts of O'Shay's own journal are spliced into this account periodically in order to register some kind of distance between the narrative and the protagonist, but this is largely gestural and provides little in the way of "factual" support.

Evidently, what Bowden wants is for his readers to trust the veracity of events even as he constructs the text as a kind of novel. When the preface of the book claims that "[n]othing has been fabricated" the reader is clearly not supposed to include the hyperbolic performance of the narrative in the list of things that have not been made up. The reason that this matters is that the story Bowden tells is concerned with the same kind of palpable "evil" that preoccupies Silko and McCarthy and that is bound up with the hidden criminal world that is the uncanny peripheral presence in everyday American life. Birkets complains of Silko's "common-sense deficit" in imagining an indigenous uprising driven by prophecy, and the events of Bowden's tale are often as implausible as Silko's, if common sense is taken as the measure by which truth claims are judged.

Consider the example of a story from O'Shay's past concerning the magistrate faced with an apparently mute vagrant who struggles to communicate in wild gesticulations. Just as the man is about "[t]o be shipped to some state mental hospital," a wino steps forward claiming to be able to understand the gestures. The wino, we are told, used to be a professor of anthropology, and the vagrant is in fact an Indian from a Mexican tribe that evolved its own sign language, who had simply missed his contact at the bus station and was arrested (SC 101). For O'Shay, this event teaches him that "[y]ou can never be absolutely sure of anyone and you can never be absolutely sure that your read on what you're seeing is true" (SC 103). The same might be said of readers of Bowden's text, and while this works for O'Shay, who witnessed the event, the reader must surely remain challenged by the improbability of this astonishing coincidence, not to mention the wino's credentials.

What Bowden's book offers is a representation of the conditions of contemporary "evil" that seeks to make truth claims about those conditions even as it challenges, in its form and through the implausibility of many of its events, the reader to believe any of it. The back cover of A Shadow in the City offers a testimonial from Jim Harrison, who writes that Bowden's book "leaves you wishing it was a novel so it wouldn't be true." For Silko, McCarthy, and Bowden, "evil" as it is given form in their narratives is no less "true" because it is represented in implausible ways. Indeed, implausibility often functions as a way of destabilizing confidence in the truth claims of a dominant culture more comfortable with Sheriff Bell's nostalgia for a society underpinned by the respectful use of "Sir" and "Mam." Taken together, the depravity depicted in Silko, McCarthy, and Bowden, fabricated or otherwise, constructs an environment where the unthinkable happens daily. For some, like philosopher Richard Rorty, the pessimism of contemporary writers like Silko and Neal Stephenson (or McCarthy and Bowden) is a lamentable American version of anti-Enlightenment negativity similar to that found in Heidegger and Foucault. "When young intellectuals watch John Wayne war movies after reading Heidegger, Foucault, Stephenson, or Silko," he complains, "they often become convinced that they live in a violent, inhuman, corrupt country."[60]

One of Rorty's assumptions here is that "young intellectuals" are not convinced about the violence and corruption of their country before they read Heidegger and Silko, and given the "common-sense deficit" Silko's work allegedly suffers from, it is a wonder that they are so quickly taken in. The argument here is less about the plausibility of these narratives of negativity and more about their power to cast doubt over the transparency of the culture that has produced them. In the case of the "war on drugs," the notion of a seemingly untouchable international criminal class is the absent presence that makes possible the fabrication of "evil" as a timeless adversary that stands in opposition to and outside of mainstream American life. If "evil" is among us, it has invaded from elsewhere and has contaminated, to invert Rorty's terms, a peaceful, humane, and honest country. *No Country for Old Men*, through Bell's musings, tends to confirm this view that the drug barons are an unprecedented new breed of wickedness. But as we have seen, Bell's partial view of history obscures the fact of precursors like Holden, and Silko insists that unrestrained violent conquest is what continues to underpin social organization in the Americas.

What Bowden's text explores, through the conflicted and overwrought turbulence of O'Shay's immersion in the shadow world of the drug war, is the way "evil" is folded into the structures that are ostensibly in opposition to it. The crisis faced by O'Shay, who has spent over twenty years working his way to the top of the drug business, is that he finds it increasingly difficult to distinguish between drug trafficking and law enforcement. He has more respect for the work ethic of the dealers than for most of the "lazy" cops and agents who clock off and go home in the evening. He sees the drug business as only barely dissimilar to other forms of "legitimate" enterprise—"they seem twins to him" (SC 26)—and thinks decriminalization is the only serious way of dealing with the drug problem. In many ways, O'Shay's compromised position as a state-funded drug lord—he is rich, powerful, and violent—embodies the complicity of a system that turns crime-fighting into another form of business enterprise: "[e]veryone else around him is caught up in words he does not believe, words about waging war, keeping clean, enforcing a law, words about making cases, building a career, personal advancement, status, pay, words about money, money from agencies or money from the deals. Like any business, this one generates an interior logic, a series of operations with colorful names, a list of targets who have gained enough prominence to be worth destroying, various products of the moment that became the focus of crusades" (SC 180).

O'Shay's contempt for law enforcement is part of an all-encompassing obsession with the existential demands of the deal, which compels a honing of the will, mind, and body to the most extreme level of performance. It is not, in the end, the violence, the indifference to human life, the snuff movies, and the corruption that are hard to swallow in A Shadow in the City. Rather, it is the hypermachismo of O'Shay and his conception of himself (or at least the text's construction of that self-conception) as the finely tuned Übermensch that ultimately rings hollow. The punishing workouts, the violent apprenticeship, the quest for purpose, the fondness for wild and injured animals, the desire to paint, the references to Dostoevsky and Victor Frankl (whose Holocaust memoir Man's Search for Meaning comes to serve as a self-help bible for O'Shay), the endless insistence that worldly objects have no significance, the need to "touch the flesh and blood of the experience": O'Shay is a painful caricature of the worst kind of postwar American literary male hero. The disenchantment with "words he does not believe" is lifted from Hemingway, and O'Shay's contempt for the straight life and celebration of hard-body transcendence will be familiar to readers of Kerouac, Mailer, and their legion of pale imitators.

O'Shay's drive to realize himself as "a special predator" (SC 181) who moves beyond good and evil may be a function of the way he is able to move unconstrained (but legitimated) by the law in a world where dominance is achieved by the shrewdest lone wolf. The trouble for O'Shay is that he still worries about "evil" and his part in it. "Evil," he ponders, "seems the only way to explain ruining people for no reason other than appetite" (SC 164). If Holden or Chigurh had the inclination to consider their motives, this might be their conclusion, and O'Shay would no doubt concur with the judge's assessment that "[m]oral law is an invention of mankind for the disenfranchisement of the powerful in favor of the weak" (BM 250). Even McCarthy's less demonic characters are prone to doubt the usefulness of Christian values, as John Grady's father admits when he says that he is "a long way from bein convinced that it's all that good a thing" that the meek inherit the earth (APH 13).

To "touch the flesh and the blood of the experience," as O'Shay imagines it, is to enter into a ferocious struggle for ascendancy, and *No Country for Old Men* and *A Shadow in the City* insist on reiterating that only this kind of material knowledge of "evil" can lead to an authentic response to its reality. Formally, however, in order to articulate this plunge into the "truth" of the world in all its depravity, both writers lean so heavily on the conventions of the noir thriller that the texts at times collapse into parody. In McCarthy's case, Bell's mediating presence, his prejudices and failures, offer a useful means of framing the machismo of the novel's main plot as a largely intentional implosion of form into empty performance. In Bowden there is no such mechanism, and the prefatory insistence on the text's truthfulness rubs hard against the noir clichés of the narrative. What *A Shadow in the City* does is reproduce the metaphysics of evil and the rhetoric of the "war on drugs" even as it seeks to dispel them. Inadvertently, however, this does work, in a kind of double bluff akin to O'Shay's deep-cover persona. O'Shay's complaints that the world "has grown careless and fat" and the police "fail to appreciate excellence" (SC 81) are the grievances of a man so sucked into the asset-stripping capitalism of the high-rolling drug business that his tirades embody a disturbing synthesis of free-market economics and criminal braggadocio. If he can no longer "find that line between them and me" (SC 179) it may be that there is no line. The real line, as O'Shay intuits, is between ruthless predators and everyone else, and the law has nothing to do with it.

While the form of Bowden's book, like McCarthy's, seems to endorse a metaphysics of evil and ruthless masculinity as the only appropriate response, the plausibility of this endorsement—"Nothing has been fabricated"—is exposed by the self-evident fabrication of the form. The hard-boiled thriller, in the end, manufactures the threat and the solution and as such is complicit with the "evil" it seeks to convince is out there. Chigurh serves Bell's conservatism and confirms its validity just as O'Shay's Nietzschean fantasies serve the legitimate business that grows out of the drug war. The issue is not that Americans live in a "violent, inhuman, corrupt country" but rather that the forms fabricated to represent that country are able to dismantle the rhetoric of the hard-boiled free market. It is precisely the "common-sense deficit" of Silko's utopian reading of underclass resistance that distances Almanac of the Dead from the parodic pessimism of McCarthy and Bowden.

CONCLUSION
Endless War

The long, drawn-out dread is over.
George H. W. Bush, *State of the Union Address*, January 28, 1992

Our own generation is in a long war against
a determined enemy.
George W. Bush, *State of the Union Address*, January 31, 2006

There is, argues political theorist Michael Shapiro, a "cartographic component" to the "interpretive elaboration of danger" that attempts to identify on the map the location of threat. A correlation exists, Shapiro suggests, "between changing conceptions of the landscape of danger and engagement and alterations in approaches to the recognition and location of bodies."[1] What recent literature about the West since Pearl Harbor reveals is that the recruitment of the Western landscape as a key site and resource of the national security state has produced and intensified threat as a necessary component of its aim to maintain security. As we have seen, the identification of threats—Japanese Americans, Soviet nuclear attack, undocumented migrants, drug traffickers, and other potential subversives—has produced a landscape characterized as much by its disturbing absences as by its visibly demarcated borders and boundaries. These absences are sometimes, like the wasteland discourse that legitimizes their construction, part of the security apparatus itself, such as internment camps and secret weapons facilities. Other absences constitute what Agamben calls the "bare life" of political discourse under the state of permanent war: the included exclusions that are, at best, only ambiguously protected by law. Here we might include the interned, the downwinders, the undocumented, and the otherwise criminalized populations that are manufactured by the cartography of threat. The desert landscapes of the American West have been utilized, as I have argued throughout this book, to variously camouflage these absences, along with the other material waste products of postwar military-industrial enterprise.

On September 12, 2001, the *New York Times* described those responsible for the attacks on the World Trade Center and the Pentagon as the "kamikazes of the 21st century."[2] In the days following the attacks, the memory of Pearl Harbor was invoked repeatedly as a means of articulating the shock of an otherwise unprecedented violent assault on American soil. As Tom Engelhardt has observed, the reminder of Pearl Harbor also recalled "the victory weapon of 1945" that served as the ultimate retort to the Japanese aggressor and instituted fifty years of nuclear dread.[3] The site of the World Trade Center quickly became known as Ground Zero, a term previously synonymous with the Manhattan Project and the destruction of Hiroshima and Nagasaki but now mobilized to describe the place where the long-held fear of annihilation was consummated. Engelhardt writes that soon after Hiroshima, "Americans were already imagining versions of September 11th"; the events of 2001 were "strangely familiar."[4]

While the devastation of the World Trade Center has no obvious relation to World War II and the Cold War—indeed, the *Times* piece from September 12 pointedly notes that the "new kamikazes" bear "no flags or markings" and signal a new mode of warfare in which ordinary things like civilian aircraft can be turned into "guided missiles"—the mobilization of memories of those prior conflicts did provide a context within which an articulation of American resolve could be positioned within a history of successful U.S. responses to external aggression. The wars in Afghanistan and Iraq, the creation of the Department of Homeland Security and the passage of the Patriot Act, the extension of executive power, the incarceration of nebulously defined "enemy combatants" at Guantánamo Bay in Cuba, and intensified powers of domestic surveillance and border policing—after 9/11, observes Luis Alberto Urrea, "an open border suddenly seemed like an act of war"—all signal a return to Cold War models of military intervention and security-driven containment underwritten by a pervasive sense of amorphous threat.[5] Like the fear of Communist infiltration that so exercised Americans during the 1950s, the danger posed by terrorists is, as the *New York Times* was aware as early as September 12, 2001, that they seek to use an "open society" as a "weapon against itself."

It has been my contention throughout this study that "openness" has long been deployed as a weapon in the American West. The "open" spaces of the West are integral to the maintenance of security by concealing in plain sight the installations and facilities that manufacture, test, store,

and dispose of American military hardware; barrack military personnel; and provide an economic base for the region. The West, as we have
seen, also provides space for the detainment and disciplining of manufactured "threats" (Japanese Americans, nuclear and chemical waste).
For writers concerned with the legacies of the post–Pearl Harbor West,
the "open society" that has conventionally found its landscape analog in
the expansive desert regions of the United States is predicated upon the
included exclusion of wasted populations and habitat located precisely
within the space otherwise claimed to be empty. As I have already noted
more than once, it is one of the paradoxes of the discourse that would construct the desert West as "wasteland" that it denies the value of that upon
which it depends: a notionally radical "other" place and "other" people
extrinsic to, but simultaneously folded into, the polis. The manufacture
of waste as an externalized threat is, then, intrinsic to the consolidation
of power. As Zygmunt Bauman reminds us, waste is "the trade secret of
modern creation," the necessary by-product that stands in negatively va-
lenced structural relation to "what is."[6]

The invocation of Pearl Harbor and Ground Zero in the wake of 9/11
calls us back to the American West and its recent history as the fulcrum
of U.S. military power. George W. Bush's declaration of a global "war
on terror," not to mention his early, misguided but revealing preference
for Wild West analogies—Osama bin Laden is wanted "dead or alive"
and will be "smoked out"; Afghanistan is "wilder than the Wild West"—
similarly relies on a collective memory of the West as the overdetermined
site of American becoming, where legitimate force is invoked in the name
of justice and freedom. There is little here that has not already been effectively utilized by Ronald Reagan and George Bush Sr. in their attempts to
"roll back" to the future in Cold War II but, with 9/11 supplying the moral
legitimacy for FDR-style executive action, the "war on terror" has managed to combine the righteous mercenary imperial zeal so vividly delin-
eated in Blood Meridian and the inculcation of paranoid Cold War dread
mapped by DeLillo, Morrow, and many of the other writers discussed
here to a devastating effect not seen since the Vietnam era.

I opened this book with an epigraph from Benedict Anderson that
stated that from "profound changes in consciousness" come "characteristic amnesias."[7] If Pearl Harbor effected a profound change in the way

Americans perceived their place in the world, the amnesia has been, as the books examined above reiterate time and again, as politically and economically enabling as it has been environmentally and socially damaging. Out of the "oblivions" of amnesia, Anderson reminds us, "spring narratives," the "patterns and moirés" that Friedrich Kittler imagines seeping out through "obsolete media."[8] Narratives of the post–Pearl Harbor West, as we have seen, are dusted with the remains of poorly concealed adventures in nation-building and security-driven military-industrial enterprise. They insist on the persistence of the past in the present and on the long half-life of suffering, degradation, and fear.

Whether or not 9/11 has produced a "profound change of consciousness" of the magnitude of Pearl Harbor, the attendant amnesias have not failed to mobilize themselves, and the reawakened memories of that first attack have been accompanied by the strategic forgetting of the loss of civil liberties that attended America's entrance into World War II and the catastrophic loss of life that marked its end. This simultaneous remembering and forgetting recalls Ansel Adams's ruminations on Manzanar in 1944, where he imagines the "natural" erasure of the internment camp even as he notes that "America cannot deny its tremendous implications."[9] The very act of forgetting here carries inferences that suggest that amnesia does not void that which is forgotten but merely—as the word "implications" demonstrates—entangles and binds together the object of amnesia and the act itself. Like the waste that must remain an absent presence in order to define the positive against which it stands in negative relation, the forgotten necessarily gives shape to what is remembered and remains tangled up with it. It is not surprising, then, that 9/11 has called forth not just the selective, enabling memories of Pearl Harbor and World War II but also the countermemories of internment and apocalyptic dread.

In two recent novels, Perry Miyake's *21st Century Manzanar* (2002) and Cormac McCarthy's *The Road* (2006), the abiding legacies of World War II in the Western United States—the incarceration of citizens based on racial categorization and the permanent fear of annihilation brought about by the detonation of the atomic bomb—are recalled in narratives shot through with a post-9/11 awareness of the continuities and intensifications, as well as the ruptures, that characterize the "profound changes of consciousness" brought about by historical contingency. As such, these novels are not cited here to demonstrate a departure from earlier representations of the West as defense complex so much as they serve as contemporary iterations of the concerns already articulated at length above. Under the permanent state of emergency, as George W. Bush knows, there must continue to be "a long war against a determined enemy."

While inspired by the racially motivated murder of Vincent Chin by unemployed auto workers in Detroit in 1982—Chin was Chinese American but mistaken for Japanese by his murderers, who were resentful of the impact of Japanese manufacturing on the American economy—and written during the 1990s, Miyake's *21st Century Manzanar* is a prescient meditation on post-9/11 security anxieties. In fact, the novel's attempt to negotiate and keep up with the shifting realities of contemporary cultural politics means that the complex class and racial tensions that fueled the 1992 Los Angeles riots in the wake of the Rodney King beating can be folded into a post-9/11 environment where long-standing antagonisms are intensified and find articulation in an explicit policy of racialized exclusion. While the "war on terror" is largely a background concern in the near future of the novel's setting, the permanent war of the United States has extended to include an "Economic War" with Japan, and the United States is suffering high unemployment. As an emergency measure, Executive Order 9066 is reinstated in order to make sure jobs are filled by "real" Americans. Japanese products and cultural references are banned, and Japanese Americans are offered repatriation or internment in the revamped World War II camps.

21st Century Manzanar, then, identifies the production of enemies as a function of global economic realignment that leads to a defensive enforcement of national identity whereby the "homeland" is defined through the containment and expulsion of "foreign" surplus. Frustrated by the slow and endless hunt for terrorists, the "ReVac" of Japanese Americans gives domestic focus to the rage and anxiety produced by economic slump, itself exacerbated by the pursuit of an unwinnable war against invisible jihadists. Together, the amorphous permanent threat of "terror" and the "Economic War" with Japan have unraveled the already precarious social order of the novel's Venice Beach, and LA has become literally a war zone. Knowing he can longer remain at home, the novel's protagonist David

Takeda, a middle-aged record store worker still attached to the utopian promise of the 1960s counterculture, decides to deposit himself in Manzanar, where he has received orders to report and where his sister and her children have already relocated.

The journey to and subsequent struggle to escape from the camp give the novel the conventional tripartite structure of the captivity or incarceration narrative, which trades not only on the conventions of World War II internment texts but also on more generic thriller treatments of the themes of pursuit, capture, and escape. This is a replay of the recent past—the first part is called "Evacuation, The Sequel"—as imagined in a near future replete with the kind of apocalyptic features typical of films like Kathryn Bigelow's *Strange Days* (1995). In a nod to a countercultural predecessor it self-consciously invokes, Ken Kesey's *One Flew Over the Cuckoo's Nest* (1962), *21st Century Manzanar* also features a megalomaniac Nurse Ratched figure in the form of camp director Lillian Bunkum, whose own solution to the Japanese problem is compulsory sterilization.

While the satire in the novel is broad and the action somewhat frenzied, Miyake does have serious things to say about the mobilization of rumor as a means of hardening latent fear into policy. Longstanding animosity toward Japanese Americans in the West has historically found articulation in eugenicist arguments for sterilization, and rumors in the novel of a barely missed opportunity during World War II to implement such a project stand behind Miyake's imagined fulfillment of racist fantasy.[10] Together, insecurity and rumor provide an opening for the disciplining of scapegoated "enemies" whereby—like the absence of evidence of Japanese American subversion during World War II serving precisely as evidence—the target of suspicion is always already self-incriminating. Resistance to the camp regime in the novel merely confirms the dangerous nature of the incarcerated, and acts to accelerate and intensify strategies of repression.

Miyake makes the same point in relation to LA street gangs and draws an analogy between internment camps and the policing of the projects as an exercise in containment. David's nephew Graham, himself a gang member, is so thoroughly alienated by an upbringing characterized by exposure to violence and criminality that, once interned, he is easily converted by Bunkum into a terrorist threat and positioned as the leader of an uprising that is brutally snuffed out live on television.

The final escape from Manzanar is engineered by a gay Japanese American posing as a soldier, who escorts a convoy of buses out of the camp under the pretext that they are on their way to sterilization facilities. In fact, the buses disperse and head instead for Indian reservations that are still, as the Navajo Rodney Knifewing explains, "not only sovereign, but nontrespassable by any government forces under any circumstances."[11] Despite their isolation and technically independent status, Native Americans have not been immune to the ongoing U.S. wars; many have been killed by waves of a mysterious plague officially explained as being caused by rodent droppings. Here, in noting the years of "nuclear testing, toxic-waste dumping, polluted water," and, more recently the "threat of terrorist chemical or biological weapons," Miyake pulls the history of Western environmental racism into the complex of crises that are, like internment, constructed as "the victims' fault" (M 338).

The novel concludes with a ceremony on the Dineh reservation that functions to integrate the escapees into the excluded indigenous order. Stanley Greyhawk explains that the Dineh have "always been joined by other tribes," and in the ceremonial dancing David "thought he saw quick glimpses of old, familiar faces dancing next to the new faces" (M 373). Through this ritual of integration, past and present, dead and alive flare "into a big carousel of shining bursts of recognition" (M 373). Here, Miyake, in drawing upon the utopian capacity of ceremony so central to the works of Native American writers like Silko and Momaday, finds a means of constructing a collective alternative to the policies of waste management that the novel identifies as the modus operandi of the contemporary American warfare state. Greyhawk's assurance that "[y]ou may not be part of this country, but you are part of this land" (M 375) reiterates the claim made repeatedly by critics of U.S. military-industrial power discussed throughout *Dirty Wars*: that alongside the cartographic component of what Shapiro calls the "interpretive elaboration of danger" there remains an irreducible stubbornness among the dispossessed to persist in occupying the sites erased on and by the map.

In a consideration of Wovoka's legacy and the history of the Ghost Dance, Mike Davis echoes Silko's view in *Almanac of the Dead* that Anglo occupation of the United States might properly be seen as a temporary historical moment. What Davis locates in the apocalyptic desperation of the new religion and the diverse ways it was adapted to respond to the conditions of the many various tribes that were swept up in the fervor of the Ghost Dance is its utopian aspect. Discussing Wovoka with Paiute and Shoshone antinuclear activists in Nevada, Davis notes the "compelling" persistence of Wovoka's vision in the late twentieth century. Wovoka's descendents, Davis considers, live "with a keen awareness of the radical instability of this artificial [Anglo capitalist] world and its neon landscapes. It is a catastrophe to which they have painfully adjusted, which has transformed the outward trappings of their lives, but which they continue to resist inwardly." The "essence of the Ghost Dance," he concludes, "is, perhaps, precisely in the moral stamina to outlast this great mirage."[12]

Davis positions Wovoka the catastrophist in opposition to Frederick Jackson Turner's thesis of gradualist progressive expansionism. While Turner gave form to the evolutionary, "natural" process of the West's conquest and subjugation, the "heirs to Wovoka" are positioned by Davis as radically contingent counterhistorians who "reject the *telos* of the finished product, the conquered landscape, the linear historical narrative, the managed ecosystem."[13] In taking the long view they "see a chaos more ontological than the boom-and-bust cycle" and understand that the "permanent" structures and values of capitalism are provisional. Invoking Marx, Davis claims they are aware that "all that is solid melts into air," including the "most dearly held conceptions of the West as a region."[14] Davis explains that apocalyptic history—"literally the revelation of the Secret History of the world"—is "the alternate, despised history of the subaltern classes, the defeated peoples, the extinct cultures." As such, Wovoka offers "a neo-catastrophist epistemology" for reopening Western history "from the vantage point of an already visible future when sprawl, garbage, addiction, violence and simulation will have overwhelmed every vital life-space west of the Rockies." This is the Turner thesis "stripped down to its ultimate paranoia: the West become Los Angeles," but it is not the end, however, since, as in any truly apocalyptic narrative, the "end point is also paradoxically the point of renewal and restoration." For those who "retain the Ghost Dance tradition," it is "through this black hole that the West will disappear into the singularity of catastrophe, only to reemerge, on the other side, with streams full of salmon and plains black with bison."[15]

It is precisely the "moral stamina to outlast [the] great mirage" of the West as America, a mirage that has been projected by the permanent war economy as sublime spectacle, that Miyake celebrates at the end of *21st Century Manzanar*. This stamina is threaded through the texts explored in this book as the necessary refusal to construe waste as the terminus but as, instead, the very condition of resistance. Indeed, for Cormac McCarthy, moral stamina is all that remains in the post-catastrophic world of *The Road*, where even the spaces of exception identified by Miyake as sites of reprieve have been eradicated by an achieved, though unnamed, apocalypse.

The Road marks both a departure and an intensification of McCarthy's previous works. The geography of the novel is not Western, though the forlorn journey of a father and his son through an irretrievably devastated countryside retains the structure of the quest narrative that shapes McCarthy's earlier Western writing. Here, the journey is south toward the sea as the father and son seek to escape another winter they believe will kill them. Although the landscape is no longer the "ancient ossuary" (BM 175) of the Southwestern desert, there is a different kind of ash that blows off the ground and hangs in the air, obliterating all color and rendering the days "more gray each one than what had gone before."[16] The terrain of achieved destruction McCarthy so often saw in the geomorphology of Western space is, in *The Road*, made literal in a post-catastrophe America where nothing grows anywhere and where signs of whatever life there is left are to be avoided.

The Road is not directly concerned with the events of 9/11 or their aftermath, but the novel has entered American literary culture at a moment when the combined implications of an endless "war on terror" and the impact of climate change have contributed to a pervasive sense of apparently insurmountable crisis. The absence of relief from toil and suffering in *The Road* is suffocating and remorseless, the arduous journey to the sea bereft of any real inkling of hope. Indeed, the coast itself provides no succor, for the ocean is no longer blue but "vast and cold and shifting heavily like a slowly heaving vat of slag," and the horizon is "a gray squall line of ash" (R 181). Aside from the imperative to keep moving, all energy is dissipated in the depressing and increasingly fruitless search for food and shelter.

What human residue remains in this forsaken world comprises packs of thieves and cannibals. The bricolaged mercenaries and war parties of Blood Meridian have mutated here into a mask-wearing "army in tennis shoes" wielding "three-foot lengths of pipe with leather wrappings" threaded with chains "fitted at their ends with every manner of bludgeon" and spears "hammered out of trucksprings" (R 77). Further recalling the barbarism of Glanton's scalp hunters and Indian war parties, this nomadic band is followed by an appalling entourage of slaves, women (some pregnant), and "a supplementary consort of catamites" (R 78). These are, in the degraded private lexicon used by the father and son, "the bad guys" (R 78).

In my discussion of Blood Meridian in chapter 2, I argued that in that novel the moment of national consolidation marks a move into history that voids as prehistoric those wars that have functioned to define the parameters of the state. In The Road, the nation-state as such no longer exists, hurling the survivors back into a future of premodern chaos. To recall Hardt and Negri, "we seem to have been catapulted back in time into the nightmare of perpetual and indeterminate war."[17] For readers of Blood Meridian, not to mention McCarthy's Southern novels, the horrors of The Road might be understood as not merely a consequence of unprecedented catastrophe but as the repetition of a much longer history of barbarism in the United States that includes slavery and genocidal violence as intrinsic to the constitution of the nation-state. It is altogether appropriate, then, to detect echoes of Blood Meridian in The Road's depiction of precarious life after the end of nations. This is not to say that McCarthy is following through a long meditation on "human nature"—what happens, pace Hobbes, when human beings exist outside the law—but to insist that, just as extreme violence characterizes the birth of nations, so too must their demise produce equally savage convulsions. McCarthy's longstanding interest in "evil," then, must always be understood as conditioned by the depredations of political economy.

In his famous "Sinews of Peace" speech, delivered at Westminster College, Missouri, in 1946, Winston Churchill warned that "the Stone

Age may return on the gleaming wings of science, and what might now shower immeasurable material blessings upon mankind, may even bring about its total destruction." In this "breathing space" between the end of World War II and the Soviet Union's acquisition of the atomic bomb, though "time may be short," there is an opportunity, Churchill hoped, "to set our house in order."[18] A similar moment was identified by British prime minister Tony Blair in the days following the 9/11 attacks when, in a deliberate invocation of his predecessor, Blair saw a momentary opportunity: "[t]he kaleidoscope has been shaken. The pieces are all in flux. Soon they will settle again. Before they do so, let us reorder this world around us." Recalling Churchill's reference to the doubly utopian and catastrophic potential of science, Blair reminds his audience that "humankind has the science and technology to destroy itself or to provide prosperity to all."[19]

For Blair, Churchill's "Stone Age" has already returned on the "gleaming wings of science" in the form of hijacked passenger aircraft flown by Al-Qaeda operatives supported by "prehistoric" regimes like that of the Taliban. When Churchill thought of the return of the "Dark Ages," he had in mind the end-times of nuclear winter; for the supporters of the "war on terror," the Stone Age functions not only as a future scenario brought about by the criminal use of weapons of mass destruction but also to characterize the condition of the adversary. This imagining of a past that is also a future, of science as a means of reversing temporality, and of an enemy that seems to have been hurled out of deep time, in many ways characterizes something of the extent of contemporary anxieties not only concerning terrorism but also regarding the global threat posed by climate change. Blair's reading of the post-9/11 world order does not supersede Churchill's nuclear dread but adds to it, just as warnings of a coming environmental disaster do not diminish fears of suicide missions or so-called dirty bombs.

As commentators have been aware since the Trinity test, once unleashed, the danger of nuclear destruction can never be removed. The immensity of that threat has loomed over the postwar period, and the irreversible fact of the bomb has to some extent become a model for how other, largely unrelated dangers have come to be apprehended. Current anxieties over terrorism and the environment are often characterized by a sense of the permanence and ungraspability of the crisis. Part of the function of novels like Miyake's and McCarthy's—indeed, a function of all the works discussed in this book—is to imagine threat in terms of its material consequences rather than merely in terms of its unthinkable, abstract possibility. As such, fiction does not so much contribute to the ungraspable dread perpetrated by the circulation of threats of shock and awe, but instead seeks to seize those threats and, in doing so, make palpable the contradictions of crisis-as-normal that underpins the permanent state of emergency. To argue, for example—as DeLillo, Silko, Williams, Solnit, and Meloy, among others do—that the Cold War was, in fact, fought in the American West as a hot war, replays history from, as it were, the other side, not as a danger averted but as a catastrophe that did indeed take place. Understood this way, a novel like The Road advances in merely intensified form McCarthy's reading of American history as one of continuous despoliation and enforced homelessness.

Just as Blair's speech is rhetorically figured as a rerun of, and sequel to, Churchill's earlier speech, and Miyake's novel imagines a self-conscious sequel to World War II internment, so to is The Road a reiteration of McCarthy's previous work in the sense that the degraded Indians, Mexicans, and Americans wandering the Sonoran deserts in Blood Meridian prefigure the nomadic guerrilla bands of cannibals in the later novel. In Blood Meridian, the human presence in the desert is positioned as a kind of survivance, a residual trace scudding across the surface of an achieved geomorphological apocalypse. In The Road, the remaining population is literally left over from a real apocalypse, the sun- and wind-blasted terrain of the borderlands now expanded into a vision of a global ash heap. Taken together, Blood Meridian and The Road represent an uncanny doubling of before and after history, the mysterious traces of a dead civilization in The Road, like the discovery of an unopened can of Coca Cola, recalling the strewn potsherds and hieroglyphs that pockmark the landscape of the 1840s. The Border Trilogy and No Country for Old Men stand inside this pre- and post-historic continuum as the fulcrum of the post–World War II present, as the historical moment that embodies both the legacy of conquest—in the form of the inside outsider condition of the dispossessed Anglo rancher as the marker of compromised virtue—and, with the testing of the bomb at the end of The Crossing, the ground zero beyond which the catastrophe of *The Road* becomes inevitable. *Blood Meridian*, then, anticipates *The Road* as the end point of a movement that is triggered by the construction of the modern state through mercenary violence that is then subsequently absorbed into the national narrative as preceding its formation. Sheriff Bell's powerlessness in the face of the ascendant drug cartels in *No Country for Old Men* may be sublimated through an appeal to the religious and political apocalypticism of the New Right, but clearly, when the end-times actually come to pass, the eradication of fallen life does not expunge "evil" from the world but instead reduces the remaining population to the condition of homelessness already endured by John Grady Cole and Billy Parham.

The achieved apocalypse of *The Road* is not bereft of hope, however, and here the "moral stamina" Davis identifies in Native American persistence is located in the love between the father and son and in the son's seemingly uncontaminated love for others. The father's remaining duty on earth is to protect the son, whose own duty, the father tells him, is to "carry the fire" (R 234). Rescued after the father's death by people who assure the boy they are the "good guys," the novel ends with the ambivalent promise that somehow the hope for humanity embodied in the boy will survive. How this regeneration is to come about is, like the utopian promise of the imagined community of wasted souls in *21st Century Manzanar* or the hybrid army poised to reclaim the United States at the end of *Almanac of the Dead*, not revealed. The final lines of *The Road* instead recall Davis's vision of a West that appears from out of the other side of the "black hole . . . of catastrophe, . . . with streams full of salmon and plains black with bison." McCarthy's last words are a reminder that "in the world's destruction [it is] possible to see how it was made" (R 230–31); in the "ponderous counterspectacle of things ceasing to be" (R 231) is embedded the memory of "brook trout in the streams in the mountains" who carry on their backs "maps of the world in its becoming" (R 241).

The memory of trout that hum with the "mystery" of "all things . . . older than man" (R 241) recalls McCarthy's longstanding awareness of the earth's capacity to exist, in one state or another, before and after human occupation. Life on earth, including human life, is not over in *The Road*, but enough has happened for things "[n]ot to be made right again" (R 241). The function of what McCarthy calls the "counterspectacle of

295

things ceasing to be," and what I have imagined as a "counterhistory" of the West as it has been developed through a reading of the texts explored in this book, is not to make right what has been wronged during the "covert spectacle" or "open secret" of endless war since Pearl Harbor, but to make visible the "[m]aps and mazes" (R 241) of power that overlay the desert West like those McCarthy describes on the back of the trout. These are the tracks of history ingrained in the dirt of the desert upon which the Southwest Defense Complex has installed itself. In the literature of the post–Pearl Harbor West, what persists in the wasted lives and places of the permanent war economy, and what remains at the end of McCarthy's novel, is, as Davis writes, the "moral stamina to outlast this great mirage."

NOTES

Introduction

1. Richard Powers, *Prisoner's Dilemma* (1988; New York: Harper Perennial, 2002), 264–65.

2. Powers, *Prisoner's Dilemma*, 265.

3. Powers, *Prisoner's Dilemma*, 265.

4. Powers, *Prisoner's Dilemma*, 311.

5. Friedrich A. Kittler, *Gramophone, Film, Typewriter*, trans. Geoffrey Winthrop-Young and Michael Wutz (Stanford: Stanford University Press, 1999), xxxix–xl.

6. While the centrality of warfare in Western American history is clear, and the nature of America's relationship with the notion of war complex and contested, my purpose here is not to offer a broad analysis of the long historical view, though I will have occasion to consider these wider issues in the context of specific texts that themselves insist on linking recent events with deeper trends and attitudes. For an overview of U.S. military history, see Russell Weigley, *The American Way of War: A History of United States Military Strategy and Policy* (Bloomington: Indiana University Press, 1973). For a more detailed examination of America and warfare dealing with the period relevant to this study, see Michael S. Sherry's essential *In the Shadow of War: The United States since the 1930s* (New Haven: Yale University Press, 1995). On the military's participation in the construction of the West, see William H. Goetzmann's *Army Exploration in the American West, 1803–1863* (New Haven: Yale University Press, 1959), and *Exploration and Empire: The Explorer and the Scientist in the Winning of the American West* (Austin: Texas State Historical Association, 2000); and James P. Ronda, *Beyond Lewis and Clark: The Army Explores the West* (Seattle: University of Washington Press, 2003). For an overview of the Indian Wars, see Bill Yenne, *Indian Wars: The Campaign for the American West* (Yardley PA: Westholme, 2005). Richard Slotkin's trilogy remains the starting point for consideration of the representational politics of frontier violence and its part in the articulation of national identity. See Richard Slotkin, *Regeneration through Violence: The Mythology of the American Frontier, 1600–1860* (1974; Norman: University of Oklahoma Press, 2000); *The Fatal Environment: The Myth of the Frontier in the Age of Industrialization, 1800–1890* (1988; Norman: University of Oklahoma Press, 1998); *Gunfighter Nation: The Myth of the Frontier in Twentieth Century America* (1992; Norman: University of Oklahoma Press, 1998).

7. For a discussion of the "wasteland discourse," see Valerie L. Kuletz, *The Tainted Desert: Environmental and Social Ruin in the American West* (New York: Routledge, 1998), 13–14.

8. Frederick Dolan has argued that the 1947 National Security Act inaugurated a revolutionary transformation in the constitutional regime of the United States analogous to the nation's founding, the Reconstruction, and the New Deal. See

Frederick M. Dolan, *Allegories of America: Narratives, Metaphysics, Politics* (Ithaca: Cornell University Press, 1994), 60–61.

9. Joseph Masco, *The Nuclear Borderlands: The Manhattan Project in Post–Cold War New Mexico* (Princeton: Princeton University Press, 2006), 337.

10. Masco, *The Nuclear Borderlands*, 337.

11. W. J. T. Mitchell, *Picture Theory* (Chicago: University of Chicago Press, 1994), 366. Cold War policy, Dolan argues, "legislated or otherwise, was shaped by public fantasies and hysteria," and the enemy "was to an unusual degree an unverifiable creature of one's own imagination. The antagonists of the Cold War could never be certain that the enemy was not one of their own, reflected back to them in an uncanny register." See Dolan, *Allegories of America*, 61.

12. Guillermo Gómez-Peña, *Warrior for Gringostroika: Essays, Performance Texts, and Poetry* (Saint Paul MN: Graywolf, 1993), 55.

13. The notion of the West as America dates as least as far back as Turner's frontier thesis (1893) and surfaced again in the controversial 1991 Smithsonian exhibition "The West as America." See William Truettner, ed., *The West as America: Reinterpreting Images of the Frontier, 1820–1920* (Washington DC: Smithsonian, 1991). To the extent that Sunbelt neoliberalism's combination of market deregulation and welfare rollback has increasingly come to characterize the global economy, we might conclude that the postwar West provides a useful metonym for globalization.

14. For discussion of the notion of a "just" war, see Michael Waltzer's classic 1977 study *Just and Unjust Wars: A Moral Argument with Historical Illustrations*, 4th ed. (New York: Basic Books, 2006).

1. The Purloined Landscape

1. Michel Foucault, *Society Must Be Defended: Lectures at the Collège de France, 1975–76*, trans. David Macey, ed. Mauro Bertani and Alessandro Fontana (London: Penguin, 2004), 69–72.

2. Foucault, *Society Must Be Defended*, 73.

3. Foucault, *Society Must Be Defended*, 72.

4. Foucault, *Society Must Be Defended*, 76, 77, 78.

5. Foucault, *Society Must Be Defended*, 51.

6. On the New Western history, see Patricia Nelson Limerick's explanatory essay "What on Earth Is the New Western History?" in *Trails: Toward a New Western History*, ed. Patricia Nelson Limerick, Clyde A. Milner II, and Charles E. Rankin (Lawrence: University Press of Kansas, 1991), 81–88. The defining monographs remain Limerick's *The Legacy of Conquest: The Unbroken Past of the American West* (New York: Norton, 1988); Richard White's *"It's Your Misfortune and None of My Own": A New History of the American West* (Norman: University of Oklahoma Press, 1991); and Donald Worster's *Under Western Skies: Nature and History in the American West* (New York: Oxford University Press, 1992).

7. Michel Foucault, *Language, Counter-Memory, Practice: Selected Essays and Interviews*, ed. Donald F. Bouchard (Ithaca: Cornell University Press, 1977), 156, 189.

8. George Lipsitz, *Time Passages: Collective Memory and American Popular Culture* (Minneapolis: University of Minnesota Press, 1990), 214.

9. Foucault, *Language, Counter-Memory, Practice*, 139.

10. Lipsitz, *Time Passages*, 213.

11. Michel Foucault, "Collège de France Lecture," in *Culture, Power, History: A Reader in Contemporary Social Theory*, ed. Nicholas B. Dirks, Geoff Eley, and Sherry P. Ortner (Princeton: Princeton University Press, 1994), 206.

12. William Chaloupka, *Knowing Nukes: The Politics and Culture of the Atom* (Minneapolis: University of Minnesota Press, 1993), 114.

13. I have borrowed the notion of the "desert screen" as a site of visibility and also concealment from Paul Virilio's work of the same name. The screen, Virilio explains, "is the site of projection of the light of images—MIRAGES of the geographic desert like those of the CINEMA. It is also the site of projections of the force of energy—beginning with the desert in New Mexico, the first atomic explosion at the Trinity site, and leading up to the Persian Gulf War when the screens of Kuwaiti and Iraqi deserts were to be linked with the television screens of the entire world, thanks to CNN" (Paul Virilio, *Desert Screen: War at the Speed of Light*, trans. Michael Degener [London: Continuum, 2002], 135; emphasis in original).

14. The term "covert spectacle" is derived from Michael Rogin's essay "'Make My Day!': Spectacle as Amnesia in Imperial Politics," in *Cultures of United States Imperialism*, ed. Amy Kaplan and Donald E. Pease, 499–529 (Durham: Duke University Press, 1993). I discuss this notion in more detail below. The title of this chapter, with its allusion to Poe, is also indebted to Rogin's argument.

15. In Poe's tale, by way of explaining how he came to detect the presence of the letter, Dupin describes a "game of puzzles" played on a map. One player, explains the detective, invites another to find a word, "the name of town, river, state or empire," for example, "upon the motley and perplexed surface of the chart." While a "novice in the game" demands the opponent find the "the most minutely lettered names," the skilled player selects those words that "stretch, in large characters, from one end of the chart to the other." Such words "escape observation by dint of being excessively obvious; and here the physical oversight is precisely analogous with the moral inapprehension by which the intellect suffers to pass unnoticed those considerations which are obtrusively and too palpably self-evident." Thus, the best way to conceal the letter is by "not attempting to conceal it at all," its "hyperobtrusive situation" part of a "design to delude the beholder into an idea of [its] worthlessness." The suggestiveness of the invisible names stretched across mapped terrain, of course, not to mention the production of ideas of worthlessness, should be noted here in the context of U.S. enterprise in the West (Edgar Allan Poe, "The Purloined Letter," in *The Complete Stories* [London: Everyman, 1992], 697–99).

16. Patricia Nelson Limerick, *Desert Passages: Encounters with the American Deserts* (Albuquerque: University of New Mexico Press, 1985), 166.

17. Limerick, *Desert Passages*, 167.

18. Yi-Fu Tuan, *Topophilia: A Study of Environmental Perception, Attitudes, and Values* (Englewood Cliffs NJ: Prentice-Hall, 1974), 66–67. Tuan quotes Lieutenant J. H. Simpson's description of Navajo country from 1849 as typical: "But never did I have, nor do I believe anybody can have a full appreciation of the almost universal barrenness which pervades this country, until they come out as I did, to 'search the land' and beheld with their own eyes its general nakedness." Simpson sees the landscape as "sickening-colored" and impossible to look at "without loathing" until after an unfortunate but necessary period of acclimatization.

19. Limerick, *Desert Passages*, 168.

20. On the shifting status of U.S. "inland deserts," see Stephanie LeMenager, *Manifest and Other Destinies: Territorial Fictions of the Nineteenth-Century United States* (Lincoln: University of Nebraska Press, 2004), especially 23–69; and David W. Teague, *The Southwest in American Literature and Art: The Rise of a Desert Aesthetic* (Tucson: University of Arizona Press, 1997).

21. A site, suggests Edward S. Casey, is "the leveled-down, emptied out, planiform residuum of place and space eviscerated of their actual and virtual powers and forced to fit the requirements of institutions that demand certain very particular forms of building." The site's features of "homogeneity, planiformity, monolinearity, and seriality" conspire to work as "an antidote to place, its very antithesis—its *pharmakon*—the remedy that is its destruction" (Edward S. Casey, *The Fate of Place: A Philosophical History* [Berkeley: University of California Press, 1997], 183, 186).

22. Julia Kristeva, *Powers of Horror: An Essay on Abjection*, trans. Leon S. Roudiez (New York: Columbia University Press, 1982), 4.

23. Kristeva, *Powers of Horror*, 9. Abjection preserves "the immemorial violence with which a body becomes separated from another body in order to be" (10).

24. Roosevelt quoted in Sherry, *In The Shadow of War*, 65.

25. Sherry, *In The Shadow of War*, 66. Ulrich Beck points out that what he calls "risk consciousness" produces "interpretive diversions" in order to manage fear of unknown threats: "the very intangibility of the threat and people's helplessness as it grows promote *radical and fanatical reactions and political tendencies* that make social stereotypes and the groups afflicted by them into 'lightning rods' for the invisible threats which are inaccessible to direct action" (Ulrich Beck, *Risk Society: Towards a New Modernity*, trans. Mark A. Ritter [London: Sage, 1992], 75; emphasis in original).

26. The comparison between internment camps and Indian reservations is made by Roger Daniels in *Concentration Camps, USA: Japanese Americans and World War II* (New York: Holt, Rinehart and Winston, 1972), 105. Like reservations, the camps were located in isolated and otherwise "useless" areas. The position of

Native Americans as "foreign" politically and legally yet simultaneously "inside" the United States is discussed in Vine Deloria Jr. and David E. Wilkins, *Tribes, Treaties, and Constitutional Tribulations* (Austin: University of Texas Press, 1999), 28. In the nineteenth century, as Stephanie LeMenager argues, "Indian Territory was destined to remain a (shrinking) territory within the central United States that was neither a sovereign foreign nation nor a legitimate domestic polity" (LeMenager, *Manifest and Other Destinies*, 47). For a discussion of internal colonization, see Michael Hector's *Internal Colonialism: The Celtic Fringe in British National Development, 1536–1966* (Berkeley: University of California Press, 1975). The notion is developed in the context of Native Americans by Robert K. Thomas in "Colonialism: Classic and Internal," *New University Thought* 4, no. 4 (1966–67): 4–53; and by Ward Churchill, "Indigenous Peoples of the United States: A Struggle against Internal Colonialism," *The Black Scholar* 16 (1985): 29–35, and *A Little Matter of Genocide: Holocaust and Denial in the Americas 1492 to the Present* (San Francisco: City Lights, 1997).

27. See Gwenn M. Jensen, "System Failure: Health-Care Deficiencies in the World War II Japanese American Detention Centers," *Bulletin of the History of Medicine* 73, no. 4 (1999): 610: "Adverse environmental conditions contributed to health problems and could not have been further from what the internees were used to. Arid desert and high plains regions were selected for Manzanar, Poston, Topaz, Gila River, Amache, Minidoka, and Heart Mountain. Tule Lake was in the center of a dry lake bed. The remaining two, Rohwer and Jerome, were located on Arkansas swamp land that had severe drainage problems."

28. Carl Abbott, *The New Urban America: Growth and Politics in Sunbelt Cities* (Chapel Hill: University of North Carolina Press, 1981), 16.

29. Gerald D. Nash, *The Federal Landscape: An Economic History of the Twentieth Century West* (Tucson: University of Arizona Press, 1999), 52. The figures speak for themselves: sixty billion dollars of Federal money was spent on the West between 1940 and 1945 alone, half of which went on war materiel, five times the value of all manufacturing on the West in 1939. Nash, *Federal Landscape*, 42. For further discussion of the impact of World War II on the West, see also Nash's previous works: *The American West Transformed: The Impact of the Second World War* (Bloomington: Indiana University Press, 1985) and *World War II and the West: Reshaping the Economy* (Lincoln: University of Nebraska Press, 1990). For broader discussion of the twentieth century West, see Michael P. Malone and Richard W. Etulain, *The American West: A Twentieth Century History* (Lincoln: University of Nebraska Press, 1989) and Richard White, *"It's Your Misfortune and None of My Own."*

30. Nash, *Federal Landscape*, 52.

31. Nash, *Federal Landscape*, 46–47, 52.

32. Nash, *Federal Landscape*, 53. By 1960 Western cities held 16 percent of the national population. Some even believed that air conditioning contributed to the rising birth rate in the postwar years. See Nash, *Federal Landscape*, 59–60.

33. María E. Montoya, "Landscapes of the Cold War West," in *The Cold War American West, 1945–1989*, ed. Kevin J. Fernlund (Albuquerque: University of New Mexico Press, 1998), 17.

34. White, "*It's Your Misfortune and None of My Own*," 496.

35. Nash, *Federal Landscape*, 80. Referring to work by economist Roger Bolton, Nash claims that "military procurement and DOD payrolls provided at least 25 percent of the income from out-of-state sources in California, Washington, Hawaii, Alaska, Utah, and Colorado. Nevada, Arizona, New Mexico, Kansas, Oklahoma, and Texas received slightly less. Between 1950 and 1980, federal spending was relatively stable except for steep increases during the Korean and Vietnam Wars" (81). For Western politicians who were pro-defense and pro-growth, the Cold War was also, as Timothy M. Chambers writes, a "win-win situation" as "anti-communism was turned into defense dollars." In addition, "elected officials who represented America's western states were in a position to take on a considerable number of international issues because they had relatively fewer constituents to represent than politicians from eastern states" (Timothy M. Chambers, "Pro-Defense, Pro-Growth, and Anti-Communism," in *The Cold War American West, 1945–1989*, ed. Kevin J. Fernlund [Albuquerque: University of New Mexico Press, 1998], 101, 105).

36. Nash, *Federal Landscape*, 96.

37. See Nick Heffernan, *Capital, Class and Technology in Contemporary American Culture: Projecting Post-Fordism* (London: Pluto, 2000), 72–73. Abbott notes the above average proportion of workers in the West and South employed by the federal government, highlighting the economic dependence of the Sunbelt on federal investment even as Sunbelt politics favors free market individualism (Abbott, *The New Urban America*, 22). On the emergence of post-Fordism and the reorganization of the relation between capital and labor driven by Sunbelt politics, see Mike Davis, *Prisoners of the American Dream: Politics and Economy in the History of the U.S. Working Class* (London: Verso, 1986), esp. part 2, "The Age of Reagan."

38. Reed Way Dasenbrook, "Southwest of What?: Southwestern Literature as a Form of Frontier Literature," in *Desert, Garden, Margin, Range: Literature on the American Frontier*, ed. Eric Heyne (New York: Twayne, 1992), 123–32.

39. D. W. Meinig, *Southwest: Three Peoples in Geographical Change, 1500–1970* (New York: Oxford University Press, 1971), 3. Meinig's comment remains pertinent, and is quoted at the outset of two more recent, and exhaustive, attempts to locate the apparently unlocatable: James W. Byrkit's "Land, Sky, and People: The Southwest Defined," which comprises the entire autumn 1992 issue of the *Journal of the Southwest*, http://digital.library.arizona.edu/jsw/3403/index.html (accessed September 12, 2008); and Michael J. Riley's follow-up piece, "Constituting the Southwest, Contesting the Southwest, Re-Inventing the Southwest," *Journal of the Southwest* 36, no. 3 (1994), http://digital.library.arizona.edu/jsw/3603/riley .html (accessed September 12, 2008). For further discussion, see also Martin

Padget, "Travel, Exoticism, and the Writing of Region: Charles Fletcher Lummis and the 'Creation' of the Southwest," *Journal of the Southwest* 37, no. 3 (1995): 421–49; Barbara A. Babcock, "By Way of Introduction," *Journal of the Southwest* 32, no. 4 (1990): 383–99. For a broader discussion of how to define the "West," see Patricia Nelson Limerick, "The Realization of the American West," in *The New Regionalism: Essays and Commentaries*, ed. Charles Reagan Wilson, 71–98 (Jackson: University Press of Mississippi, 1998).

40. See, in particular, Byrkit's disapproving remark that disagreement in precisely locating the area in part derives from "an attraction to a mirage, a 'romance' about the region, a romance custom-tailored to their own appetites and proclivities and background and training, together with the fantasies about the region that these influences engender." Byrkit's response to this "laziness" is an extensive and rigorous delineation of the region according to its geometric, bioregional, geologic, climatic, anthropological, ethnographic, historical, political, and cultural characteristics. See Byrkit, "Land, Sky, and People."

41. Riley, "Constituting the Southwest."

42. For a discussion of the structural inequalities of power produced by a touristically attractive lack of development in some regions, see John Frow, "Tourism and the Semiotics of Nostalgia," *October* 57 (1991): 123–51.

43. Sylvia Rodriguez, "Art, Tourism, and Race Relations in Taos: Toward a Sociology of the Art Colony," *Journal of Anthropological Research* 45, no. 1 (1989): 79.

44. Rodriguez, "Art, Tourism, and Race Relations in Taos," 79.

45. This is a point made by Riley, who, in discussing Rodriguez's argument, reminds us of "the post–World War II mass-culture Southwest and its hospitable climate, lack of isolation, profuse development, high-tech industrial base, major universities, and large-scale government nuclear research and defense projects that represent the dominant institutions and characteristics of an economic order which constructs people as cultural Others so as to consume them (or their symbolic representations) in the form of othered objects" (Riley, "Constituting the Southwest").

46. Zygmunt Bauman, *Modernity and Ambivalence* (Cambridge: Polity, 1991), 100.

47. Bauman, *Modernity and Ambivalence*, 100.

48. Arjun Appadurai, *Modernity at Large: Cultural Dimensions of Globalization* (Minneapolis: University of Minnesota Press, 1996), 190.

49. Appadurai, *Modernity at Large*, 190.

50. Dasenbrook, "Southwest of What?" 124.

51. William E. Riebsame, et al., eds., *Atlas of the New West: Portrait of a Changing Region* (New York: Norton, 1997), 58.

52. Southwest Defense Alliance, http://swda.us/complex.html (accessed July 30, 2007). The alliance, formed in 1997, is "a private, nonprofit, nonpartisan group of citizens, elected officials, counties, cities, businesses, retired defense

and military experts, and supporters of a strong national defense" from Arizona, California, Nevada, New Mexico, Texas, and Utah. The idea for a Southwest Defense Complex came from a proposal by General Colin Powell to focus joint service testing and training in the Southwest. Powell argued in 1993 that "in the southwestern U.S. all four services have training, test and evaluation ranges that provide a land, airspace, sea area, and offshore supersonic operating domain that could accommodate a major portion of our joint test and evaluation needs." Quoted at GlobalSecurity.org, http://www.globalsecurity.org/military/facility/southwest.htm (accessed July 30, 2007).

53. "Southwest Range Complex," GlobalSecurity.org, http://www.globalsecurity.org/military/facility/southwest.htm (accessed July 30, 2007).

54. At a recent meeting hosted at the University of Arizona, a "timely and valuable" presentation was delivered "by the leader of a 9-university collaboration looking into ways to enhance border security," the alliance Web site reports. The announcement continues that "this is the first time a 'host' university . . . has included the SWDA in its advocacy efforts. With these greetings, acknowledgements and presentations, the Defense Alliance has taken a big step, and has taken a seat at the table of key advocates" (Southwest Defense Alliance, http://swda.us/complex.html [accessed July 30, 2007]). In fact, as Luis Alberto Urrea argues, the borderland is militarized in advance of any new policing measures since much of the territory migrants enter on crossing the border is military land (Luis Alberto Urrea, The Devil's Highway [New York: Back Bay, 2004], 78–79).

55. Appadurai, Modernity at Large, 189.

56. James Madison, Political Observations, April 20, 1795, in Selected Writings of James Madison, ed. Ralph Ketcham (Indianapolis: Hackett, 2006), 236. In the case of the United States and its relation to war, Michael Hardt and Antonio Negri argue that the notion of exceptional powers is bound up in and complicated by the notion of American exceptionalism. The ethical dimension of American exceptionalism—that it is a state founded on its difference from the corruptions of European sovereignty and embodies the civic virtues of democratic social organization—gives special purchase to the notion of the state of exception. It enables the claim that because America is virtuous, it can exempt itself from the constraints of international law since its motives and actions will be good. America's ethical exceptionalism—no one, not even the ruler, is above the law—however, is in direct contradiction with the wartime state of exception whereby the ruler stands above the law in order to take control. In a manner that recalls Madison's prescient fear for freedom "in the midst of continual warfare," Hardt and Negri argue that the "exceptional role of the United States in the global state of exception serves only to eclipse and erode the republican tradition that runs through the nation's history" (Michael Hardt and Antonio Negri, Multitude: War and Democracy in the Age of Empire [London: Penguin, 2006], 9).

57. Chalmers Johnson, "Republic or Empire: A National Intelligence Estimate

on the United States," *Harper's Magazine* (January 2007), 66. While the target of Johnson's assessment of enlarged presidential power is George W. Bush, he notes that "Few, if any, presidents have refused the increased executive authority that is the natural byproduct of military Keynesianism" (67).

58. While the War Powers Resolution (1973) sought to obtain congressional approval for military action undertaken without formal declaration within sixty days, the constitutionality of the resolution remains undecided. During the Korean and Vietnam wars, no formal declaration of war was issued.

59. Following Michel Foucault, Judith Butler has recently observed that "state power is not fully exhausted by its legal exercises: it maintains, among other things, a relation to law, and it differentiates itself from law by virtue of the relation it takes." Drawing also on Georgio Agamben, Butler notes that "contemporary forms of sovereignty exist in *a structurally inverse relation* to the rule of law, emerging precisely at that moment when the rule of law is suspended and withdrawn." In the state of exception, Butler explains, space for the "extra-legal field of policy" is opened up and given authority by a sovereignty that calls the exception into being: "As law is suspended, sovereignty is exercised; moreover, sovereignty comes to exist to the extent that a domain—understood as 'the exception'—immune from law is established." See Judith Butler, *Precarious Life: The Power of Mourning and Violence* (London: Verso, 2004), 60–61.

60. Georgio Agamben, *State of Exception*, trans. Kevin Attell (Chicago: University of Chicago Press, 2005), 21.

61. See Timothy J. Dunn, *The Militarization of the U.S.-Mexico Border, 1978–1992: Low-Intensity Conflict Doctrine Comes Home* (Austin: CMAS Books, 1996), 57–58: A proposed Immigration Emergency Act of 1982—drafted in response to the 1980 Mariel boatlift crisis that brought 125,000 Cuban refugees to the United States—sought to give the president the authority to declare an "immigrant emergency" under certain conditions that would have allowed for the indefinite detainment of "illegal aliens" and protected executive decisions from a dissenting judiciary. While this bill did not pass, its provisions reemerged as part of the Immigration Reform and Control Act (IRCA) of 1986, which made $35 million available for an "Immigration Emergency Fund" for border patrolling and enforcement: "It gave the president the authority to determine whether or not an emergency exists and stipulated that the president must certify that fact to the Senate and House judiciary committees. This provision was made operational in 1990."

62. David Loomis, *Combat Zoning: Military Land-Use Planning in Nevada* (Reno: University of Nevada Press, 1993), 10, 30. The figure of thirty million acres was given by California representative Clair Engle in 1957. See Richard Misrach and Myriam Weisang Misrach, *Bravo 20: The Bombing of the American West* (Baltimore: Johns Hopkins University Press, 1990), 4. Roosevelt and Truman, by executive orders in 1942, 1943, and 1952, had delegated the broad authority of the executive branch to issue land withdrawals to the secretary of the interior. As Loomis

suggests, the process of applying to the Department of the Interior was largely a formality, and defense officials claimed that the military had never had a request turned down (33–34).

63. Take, for example, the Air Force control of entry to the Groom Range area in 1978. Located next to Area 51, the Air Force established a buffer to protect security, including checkpoints in 1984, in advance of congressional approval that was only sought belatedly due to public demand. While the withdrawal was granted, and the Air Force retrospectively complied with the Engle Act and the National Environmental Policy Act, which, along with the Federal Land Policy and Management Act of 1976, were intended to regulate and manage the use of federal lands, such preemptive withdrawal demonstrates how legal safeguards against unilateral military action are easily waived if the condition of "emergency" is invoked. See Loomis, *Combat Zoning*, 46–47. From World War II until the Carter administration the Atomic Energy Act exempted the military from environmental legislation. See Alexander Wilson, *The Culture of Nature: North American Landscape from Disney to the Exxon Valdez* (Oxford: Blackwell, 1992), 281.

64. Loomis, *Combat Zoning*, 96–98.

65. Agamben's discussion of the concentration camp is instructive here and will be discussed more fully in chapter 3. For now, it is sufficient to note that as the space of exception, "the camp is . . . the structure in which the state of exception—the possibility of deciding on which founds sovereign power—is realized *normally*" (Georgio Agamben, *Homo Sacer: Sovereign Power and Bare Life*, trans. Daniel Heller-Roazen [Stanford: Stanford University Press, 1998], 170).

66. Bauman, *Modernity and Ambivalence*, 56.

67. Agamben, *Homo Sacer*, 15.

68. Bauman, *Modernity and Ambivalence*, 65. As Henry A. Giroux has argued in a different context, "Under the logic of modernization, neoliberalism, and militarization, the category 'waste' includes no longer simply material goods but also human beings, particularly those rendered redundant in the new global economy, that is, those who are no longer capable of making a living, who are unable to consume goods, and who depend on others for the most basic needs." This "biopolitics of disposability" is "conditioned by a permanent state of class and racial exception" that renders entire populations largely invisible. When they are seen, they are "defined as redundant, pathological, and dangerous" (Henry A. Giroux, "Reading Hurricane Katrina: Race, Class, and the Biopolitics of Disposability," *College Literature* 33, no. 3 [2006]: 187, 175, 182).

69. Hardt and Negri, *Multitude*, 30.

70. Paul Virilio and Sylvere Lotringer, *Pure War*, rev. ed., trans. Mark Polizzotti (New York: Semiotext(e), 1997), 30–31: "[T]he Second World War never ended. Legally, furthermore, it's not finished. It hasn't been put out. There's no state of peace. It isn't over because it continued in Total peace, that is in war pursued by other means."

71. Seymour Melman, *The Permanent War Economy: American Capitalism in Decline* (New York: Touchstone, 1974). Melman's thesis is that the emphasis on defense spending since World War II has led to the neglect of capital investment in other vital areas, draining the initiative from American industry and causing the stagnation of the economy. He could not, of course, have foreseen that Reagan's answer to 1970s "stagflation" would be further massive investment in defense during the 1980s, but Melman would probably argue that this also must come at the expense of other areas of investment, not least in social welfare programs. Indeed, until his death in 2004 Melman continued to argue that the Permanent War Economy, in its neoliberal form, is devastating other sectors of the economy, with enormous social repercussions. See, for example, Seymour Melman, "In the Grip of a Permanent War Economy," *CounterPunch*, March 15, 2003, http://www.coun terpunch.org/melmano3152003.html (accessed September 12, 2008). The term Permanent War Economy is often attributed to Charles Wilson, CEO of General Electric and Einsenhower's secretary of defense between 1953 and 1957.

72. Daniel Bell, *The Coming of Post-Industrial Society: A Venture in Social Forecasting* (London: Heinemann, 1974), 253. For more on Bell, see Brian Jarvis, *Postmodern Cartographies: The Geographical Imagination in Contemporary American Culture* (London: Pluto, 1998), 14–23.

73. Chalmers Johnson, *The Sorrows of Empire: Militarism, Secrecy and the End of the Republic* (London: Verso, 2004), 56.

74. Thomas Pynchon, *Gravity's Rainbow* (London: Picador, 1973), 645, 105.

75. Foucault, *Society Must Be Defended*, 50, 51.

76. See Hardt and Negri, *Multitude*, 8–9. For an earlier assessment, see Randolph Bourne, "The State" (1918), in *War and the Intellectuals: Collected Essays, 1915–1919*, ed. Carl Resek, 65–104 (Indianapolis: Hackett, 1999).

77. Madison, *Political Observations*, 236.

78. War, Foucault explains, "is a general economy of weapons, an economy of armed people and disarmed people within a given State, and with all the institutional and economic series that derive from that." It is "a war that begins before the battle and continues after it is over." War as such is "an internal institution, and not the raw event of the battle" (Foucault, *Society Must Be Defended*, 159–60).

79. Foucault, *Society Must Be Defended*, 163.

80. Madison, *Political Observations*, 236.

81. Hardt and Negri, *Multitude*, 13. Foucault first discussed the notion of biopower in his courses at the Collège de France, and the term first appeared in the first volume of *The History of Sexuality*.

82. Foucault, *Society Must Be Defended*, 246–47. For Foucault, sovereign power's "most obvious and most spectacular manifestation" before the emergence of the nation-state was the power to take life or let live. With the emergence of democratic government, the power to take life is at odds with the function of the state, which is to foster life. Since, as Agamben notes, "death is power's limit,"

the administration of life must find ways of working that fall short of actually taking life. See Agamben, *Homo Sacer*, 138.

83. Michel Foucault, "Governmentality" (1978), in *Power*, vol. 3 of *Essential Works of Foucault, 1954–1984*, ed. James D. Faubion (London: Penguin, 2001), 219. Governmentality comprises "the institutions, procedures, analyses, and reflections, the calculations and tactics that allow the exercise of this very specific albeit complex form of power, which has as its target population, as its principal form of knowledge political economy, and as its essential technical means apparatuses of security." On Foucault's theory of governmentality, see Graham Burchell, Colin Gordon, and Peter Miller, eds., *The Foucault Effect: Studies in Governmentality* (Hemel Hempstead: Harvest Wheatsheaf, 1993); and Thomas Lemke, "'The Birth of Biopolitics': Michel Foucault's Lecture at the College de France on Neo-liberal Governmentality," *Economy and Society* 30, no. 2 (2001): 190–207.

84. Chaloupka, *Knowing Nukes*, 18.

85. For an extensive and revealing account of the power of Hiroshima as the shaping event of postwar cultural politics, see Donald E. Pease, "Hiroshima, the Vietnam Veterans War Memorial, and the Gulf War: Post-National Spectacles," in Kaplan and Pease, *Cultures of United States Imperialism*, 557–80.

86. Michel Foucault, *The History of Sexuality*, vol. 1, *An Introduction*, trans. Robert Hurley (New York: Vintage, 1980), 137.

87. Foucault, *Society Must Be Defended*, 255.

88. Foucault, *Society Must Be Defended*, 255–56.

89. Rogin, "'Make My Day!'" 516.

90. Rogin, "'Make My Day!'" 516–17.

91. Rogin, "'Make My Day!'" 517–18.

92. Rogin, "'Make My Day!'" 518.

93. Hardt and Negri, *Multitude*, 38. The treaty was in force for thirty years, from 1972 until 2002, when the United States withdrew.

94. Hardt and Negri, *Multitude*, 38.

95. Hardt and Negri, *Multitude*, 39.

96. See Hardt and Negri, *Multitude*, 39: "It is no coincidence that the ABM Treaty was signed midway between the delinking of the U.S. dollar from the gold standard in 1971 and the first oil crisis in 1973."

97. Hardt and Negri, *Multitude*, 39.

98. Paul N. Edwards, *The Closed World: Computers and the Politics of Disclosure in Cold War America* (Cambridge MA: MIT Press, 1996), 276–77.

99. Edwards, *The Closed World*, 278–79.

100. Rogin, "'Make My Day!'" 518.

101. Edwards, *The Closed World*, 275.

102. Edwards, *The Closed World*, 275. Edwards borrows the term Cold War II from Fred Halliday, *The Making of the Second Cold War* (London: Verso, 1986), modifying Halliday's periodization: Cold War I, 1947 (containment) to 1969 (Nixon

administration); Cold War II: 1979 (Carter's right turn) to 1989 (fall of the Berlin Wall).

103. See Edwards, *The Closed World*, 280–81. Projects included strategic nuclear forces, the B-1 bomber program, the MX missile, Trident submarine, communications, logistics, and intelligence. Defense spending rose by over 50 percent from $197 billion in FY 1980 to FY 1985's $296 billion. During the middle years of Reagan's administration, defense spending commonly exceeded $300 billion a year. The Reagan New Right ideology of tax cuts, supply-side economics, and massive military buildup, all couched in fundamentalist Christian apocalyptic Cold War rhetoric, backed counterrevolutionary campaigns in Afghanistan and throughout Central America during the 1980s.

104. Rogin, "'Make My Day!'" 512.

105. Rogin, "'Make My Day!'" 519, 504.

106. Henri Lefebvre, *The Production of Space*, trans. Donald Nicholson-Smith (Oxford: Blackwell, 1991), 164.

107. Lefebvre, *The Production of Space*, 143.

108. Hardt and Negri, *Multitude*, 334.

109. Hardt and Negri, *Multitude*, 364 n.37. For a discussion of the differences between Foucault and Agamben, see Mika Ojakangas, "Impossible Dialogue on Bio-power: Agamben and Foucault," *Foucault Studies* 2 (May 2005): 5–28. For an application of the notion of biopower that addresses Foucault, Agamben, and Hardt and Negri, see Giroux, "Reading Hurricane Katrina."

110. The word "facsimile" is derived from the Latin *fac*, imperfect form of *facere*, to make, do, and *simile*, similar.

111. Miller accepts that for many southerners, African Americans, and new leftists, there were good reasons to harbor skepticism toward government, but he argues that such disquiet failed to reach the broad majority of citizens. "Even when Eisenhower was caught in a lie about the air surveillance of the Soviet Union during the U-2 incident, the nation had no way of contextualizing the information, and the incident did not affect Eisenhower's reputation" (Stephen Paul Miller, *The Seventies Now: Culture as Surveillance* [Durham: Duke University Press], 4).

112. Miller, *The Seventies Now*, 4.

113. Peter Bürger, *Theory of the Avant-Garde*, trans. Michael Shaw (1974; Minneapolis: University of Minnesota Press, 1984), 50.

114. Philip Nel, "'A Small Incisive Shock': Modern Forms, Postmodern Politics, and the Role of the Avant-garde in *Underworld*," *Modern Fiction Studies* 45, no. 3 (1999): 731.

115. Nel, "'A Small Incisive Shock,'" 731. See also David Wise and Thomas B. Ross, *The Invisible Government* (1964; New York: Bantam, 1965).

116. Don DeLillo quoted in Nel, "'A Small Incisive Shock,'" 731.

117. See Pynchon, *Gravity's Rainbow*, 645: "[T]he truth is that the War is keeping

things alive. *Things.* . . . The Germans-and-Japs story was only one, rather surrealistic version of the real War. The real War is always there."

118. I am borrowing the phrase from Patrick O'Donnell's *Latent Destinies: Cultural Paranoia and Contemporary U.S. Narrative* (Durham: Duke University Press, 2000).

119. Lefebvre, *The Production of Space*, 28.

120. Lefebvre, *The Production of Space*, 29–30.

121. The payments were $50,000 for individuals downwind of the Nevada Test Site; $75,000 for workers participating in above-ground nuclear tests; and $100,000 for uranium miners. An amendment in 2000 extended coverage to include uranium mill workers and ore transporters, included more compensable diseases, and added additional geographical areas to the downwinder category. For full information on the act, including a list of compensable diseases, eligibility requirements, and summary of claims received, see the Justice Department's webpage, http://www.usdoj.gov/civil/torts/const/reca/about.htm (accessed September 12, 2008).

122. William M. Hix, *Taking Stock of the Army's Base Realignment and Closure Selection Process* (Santa Monica CA: Rand, 2001), 1. See also Dianna Gordon, "Base Closings: Panic or Potential?" *State Legislatures* 21 (September 1995): 1.

123. Ann Scott Tyson, "Military Is Consolidating into Large Installations," *Washington Post*, May 14, 2005, A10.

124. Tom Englehardt, "Bases, Bases Everywhere," TomDispatch.com, June 1, 2005, http://www.tomdispatch.com/index.mhtml?pid=3025 (accessed September 12, 2008).

125. Even the financial savings promised by military base closure is elusive, as Rachel Woodward observes: "the U.S. Department of Defense, between 1990–2001, spent US$23 billion on closures under the BRAC actions; only in 1996 did some savings (US$100 million) overtake costs, and cumulative savings only eventually overtook closure costs in 1998" (Rachel Woodward, *Military Geographies* [Oxford: Blackwell, 2004], 69).

126. Lorna Dee Cervantes, "Freeway 280," in *Emplumada* (Pittsburgh: University of Pittsburgh Press, 1981), 159.

2. The Prehistory of the Permanent War Economy

1. Jay Ellis has dismissed the notion that McCarthy's scalp hunters are "the gleaming white bad guys of revisionist history," pointing out that they "are hardly all white (whatever that is)" and that "they kill anyone they please, for a variety of reasons that are only provisionally connected to anything so ephemeral or quotidian as a local political agenda." See Jay Ellis, *No Place for Home: Spatial Constraint and Character Flight in the Novels of Cormac McCarthy* (New York: Routledge, 2006), 176, 175. My argument in this chapter is that it is precisely the feral and non-instrumental nature of the violence performed by the scalp hunters that

underwrites it as an action constitutive of state formation. The very construal of violence as mythic or primal serves to externalize and dehistoricize acts of violent conquest as outside political legitimacy even as the state is called into being by such violence. In short, the members of Glanton's gang do not need to be white nor do they have to know what they are doing. The fact that they appear to be operating outside of any historical imperative is a condition of their historical efficacy. The pursuit of unreflective libidinal violence does not have to have a reason in order to have an effect. The agents of Manifest Destiny are not required to be conscious of their actions as politically effective—any more than military service personnel are required to have a view as to the political legitimacy of their duties—so long as the results do indeed achieve that destiny. In fact, Ellis later comes to much the same conclusion when he writes that the Glanton gang is "beyond the pale of civil authority even as they enact that authority," reminding us that "ignorance on the part of the gang as to their violent function does not alter the function itself " (191). The utilization, official or otherwise, of expendable human resources in the furtherance of political aims is hardly invented by nineteenth century U.S. expansionism, but it would be mistaken to assume that legitimate force is the only means at the state's disposal.

2. Hardt and Negri, *Multitude*, 7.

3. Hardt and Negri, *Multitude*, 37.

4. In a revealing discussion, Ellis has perspicuously noted how *Blood Meridian* "describes a shift in time" from "antinomian space" to "historical place" (*No Place for Home*, 170).

5. Cormac McCarthy, *Blood Meridian, or, The Evening Redness in the West* (London: Picador, 1985), 50. Further references are cited in the text with the abbreviation BM.

6. For an extensive discussion on the historical sources of the novel, see John Sepich, *Notes on Blood Meridian* (Louisville KY: Bellarmine College Press, 1993).

7. Dana Phillips, "History and the Ugly Facts of *Blood Meridian*," in *Cormac McCarthy: New Directions*, ed. James D. Lilley (Albuquerque: University of New Mexico Press, 2002), 38.

8. Thomas Pughe, "Revision and Vision: Cormac McCarthy's *Blood Meridian*," *Revue française d'études américaines* 62 (November 1994): 381.

9. Phillips, "History and the Ugly Facts," 38.

10. Richard Godden and Colin Richmond, "'Blood Meridian', or the Evening Redness in the East: 'Itinerant Degenerates Bleeding Westwards,'" *Comparative American Studies* 2, no. 4 (2004): 448.

11. Phillips, "History and the Ugly Facts," 23.

12. Vereen Bell, *The Achievement of Cormac McCarthy* (Baton Rouge: Louisiana State University Press 1988), 132. Phillips argues that McCarthy's similes "seem designed to increase the intensity and accuracy of focus on the objects being

described rather than to suggest that they have double natures or bear hidden meanings" (Phillips, "History and the Ugly Facts," 36).

13. Susan Kollin, "Genre and Geographies of Violence: Cormac McCarthy and the Contemporary Western," *Contemporary Literature* 42, no. 3 (2001): 562.

14. I am not saying that Kollin is necessarily redeeming *Blood Meridian* in this way, but in setting oppositions between the Western's conventional tropes and McCarthy's refusal of them, the way is cleared for such an unproblematic revisionist reading of the novel.

15. Kollin, "Genre and Geographies of Violence." 561. For a discussion of the Western's "self-subverting" tendency, see Forrest G. Robinson, *Having It Both Ways: Self-Subversion in Western Popular Classics* (Albuquerque: University of New Mexico Press, 1993).

16. Peter Josyph, "Blood Music: Reading *Blood Meridian*," in *Sacred Violence: A Reader's Companion to Cormac McCarthy*, ed. Wade Hall and Rick Wallach (El Paso: Texas Western Press, 1995), 186; Steven Shaviro, "'The Very Life of Darkness': A Reading of *Blood Meridian*," in *Perspectives on Cormac McCarthy*, ed. Edwin T. Arnold and Dianne Luce, 2nd ed. (Jackson: University of Mississippi Press, 1999), 152.

17. Shaviro, "'The Very Life of Darkness,'" 147.

18. Shaviro, "'The Very Life of Darkness,'" 147.

19. David Holloway, *The Late Modernism of Cormac McCarthy* (Westport CT: Greenwood, 2002), 16.

20. Holloway, *Late Modernism*, 44.

21. Frederic Jameson, *The Seeds of Time* (New York: Columbia University Press, 1994), 1, 52, quoted in Holloway, *Late Modernism*, 54.

22. For studies that position *Blood Meridian* as a novel with things to say about Vietnam, see Vince Brewton, "The Changing Landscape of Violence in Cormac McCarthy's Early Novels and the Border Trilogy," *Southern Literary Journal* 37, no. 1 (2004): 121–43; Godden and Richmond, "Blood Meridian."

23. Godden and Richmond, "Blood Meridian," 449.

24. Holloway, *Late Modernism*, 47.

25. Godden and Richmond, "Blood Meridian," 451.

26. Godden and Richmond, "Blood Meridian," 452.

27. John C. Van Dyke, *The Desert: Further Studies in Natural Appearances* (London: Sampson Low, Marston, 1901), 200.

28. Van Dyke, *The Desert*, 26–27.

29. Van Dyke, *The Desert*, 27.

30. The first use of the word "prehistory" in English, according to Alice Beck Kehoe, was in Daniel Wilson's *The Archaeology and Prehistoric Annals of Scotland* (1851). See Alice Beck Kehoe, *The Land of Prehistory: A Critical History of American Archaeology* (New York: Routledge, 1998) xiii.

31. Kehoe, *The Land of Prehistory*, xiii.

32. Kehoe, *The Land of Prehistory*, xi.

NOTES TO PAGES 60-63

33. Kehoe, *The Land of Prehistory*, 40.

34. On degeneration theory, see Gregory Moore, *Nietzsche, Biology and Metaphor* (Cambridge: Cambridge University Press, 2002), 117: "Theories of descent not only suggested that human and ape shared a common ancestor; they implied a hierarchy leading from the simian primogenitor, through primitive peoples to civilized Europeans. At the same time, the concept of *dégénérescence* served to characterize other races as degenerate deviations from the ideal white type. These purportedly inferior races could be identified by atavistic skull and brain sizes which revealed their more immediate relation to the ape than those races at a more 'advanced' stage of cultural development. Racial biology, in other words, became a science of boundaries between groups; when these boundaries were transgressed, degeneration threatened. New anxieties about the proper place of different classes, nationalities and ethnicities, as well as the sexes, in society allowed racial biology to become a model for the analysis of the distances that were supposedly 'natural' between the various peoples." Among the many examples of this kind of racial thinking in *Blood Meridian*, the judge's argument that "you can't be all Mexican. It's like being all mongrel" is typical (159).

35. Godden and Richmond, "Blood Meridian," 451.

36. Godden and Richmond, "Blood Meridian," 451.

37. Ellis makes a similar point when he notes how the kid's discovery of dead babies hanging from a tree is repeated in *All the Pretty Horses* when John Grady finds birds impaled by the wind on the thorns of a cholla cactus: "From babies to birds: the violence is still there, but stepped down several levels" (*No Place for Home*, 180).

38. *Blood Meridian*'s heliocentrism invokes the age-old belief in the heliotropic myth that imagines history as a succession of civilizations moving, like the sun, from East to West. In many versions of the myth, America is often conceived as the last empire. For a thorough cultural history of the heliotropic myth, see Jan Willem Schulte Nordholt, *The Myth of the West: America As the Last Empire*, trans. Herbert H. Rowen (Grand Rapids MI: Eerdmans, 1995). I am grateful to William Handley for drawing my attention to this book.

39. Georges Bataille, "Rotten Sun," in *Visions of Excess: Selected Writings, 1927– 1939*, ed. Allan Stoekl, trans. Allan Stoekl, Carl R. Lovitt, and Donald M. Leslie Jr. (Minneapolis: University of Minnesota Press, 1985), 57–58. See also T. E. Hulme, "Cinders," in *Selected Writings*, ed. Patrick McGuinness (Manchester: Carcanet, 1998), 24: "The eyes, the beauty of the world, have been organised out of the faeces. Man returns to dust. So does the face of the world to primeval cinders."

40. See Shaviro, "'The Very Life of Darkness,'" 147: "Zenith and horizon continually exchange places, without mediation or delay; what is most dim, distant and uncertain abruptly appears as an inescapable fatality." See also Neil Campbell, "Liberty Beyond Its Proper Bounds: Cormac McCarthy's History of the West in *Blood Meridian*," in *Myth, Legend, Dust: Critical Responses to Cormac McCarthy*, ed.

Rick Wallach (Manchester: Manchester University Press, 2000), 221: "*Blood Meridian* is the point at which one reaches the climax of life and simultaneously recognizes the proximity, even the inevitability of its end."

41. Ellis discusses the title of the novel at length. See *No Place for Home*, 188–91.

42. See Ellis, *No Place for Home*, 188–89: "The book's secondary title is 'The Evening Redness in the West.' Numerous references to 'blood' indicate that redness, and we may remember that our perception of a single color is in itself a trick of the perceiver's selective perception of the full spectrum of light. The second title, then, points again backwards. Rather than providing us with a reliable reference point (a meridian, the sun), against which we might measure the actions of the book, we are instead thrown back on a realization that all we can do is to perceive, and in perceiving, we see something that is not objectively true."

43. See Ellis, *No Place for Home*, 191: The Glanton gang "cross the meridian of blood between lawless killing and the legal, civilized, near-holocaust carried out not only by the United States, but also by the local Mexican government, by creating a trade in dead human beings."

44. James D. Lilley refers to McCarthy's rendering of the "horizontal, physical, factualness of things." See "Representing Cormac McCarthy's 'Desert Absolute': Edward Weston, Ansel Adams, and the Dynamics of Vision," *Proceedings of the Second International Conference on the Emerging Literature of the Southwest*, September 13–15, 1996, El Paso, Texas (El Paso: University of Texas at El Paso, 1996), 163. For extended discussion of optical democracy, see for example, Phillips, "History and the Ugly Facts," 30, 37: "The suggested independence of light and dark reinforces the lack of precedence, of referential order, in the natural world." The book's "odd power derives from its treating everything and everybody with absolute equanimity." See also Holloway, *Late Modernism*, 135: "the style of 'optical democracy' connotes a writing that renders all preference among objects 'whimsical' (moral preference, epistemological preference, aesthetic or political preference), until anything beyond the uniform facticity of the moment is crowded out from view."

45. Georges Bataille, *The Accursed Share*, trans. Robert Hurley (1967; New York: Zone, 1991), 1:58; emphasis in original.

46. Bataille, *Accursed Share*, 1:52–53.

47. See Ellis, *No Place for Home*, 188–91.

48. The most commonly held interpretation is that the actions described in the epilogue are those of a posthole digger, signifying the fencing off of the West. Harold Bloom prefers a Promethean reading and refuses the Western allegorical view of the end of the novel. Ellis's argument for a combination of the historical and mythic interpretations seems, as my own claims here for a folding of the prehistoric into historical time would suggest, the most appropriate way of approaching the epilogue. See Peter Josyph, "Tragic Ecstasy: A Conversation with

Harold Bloom about Cormac McCarthy's *Blood Meridian*," *Southwestern American Literature* 26, no. 1 (2000): 14–15; Ellis, *No Place for Home*, 192–98.

49. Holloway, *Late Modernism*, 171. See also Harold Bloom, *How to Read and Why* (New York: Scribner, 2001). Bloom concurs that the novel does not allow Holden "the last word" (262–63). Similarly, for Godden and Richmond the epilogue reveals the judge's belief that he will never die as "delusional" (458).

50. Phillips, "History and the Ugly Facts," 40.

51. Ellis, *No Place for Home*, 171. Ellis does valuable historical work locating the practice described in the epilogue within the context of the surveying and fencing of the West. See especially 194–97.

52. William H. Goetzmann, *Exploration and Empire: The Explorer and the Scientist in the Winning of the American West* (Austin: Texas State Historical Association, 2000), 303.

53. Goetzmann, *Exploration and Empire*, 305.

54. Hulme, "Cinders," 22.

3. Dust Breeding

1. Quoted in Tetsuden Kashima, *Judgment without Trial: Japanese American Imprisonment during World War II* (Seattle: University of Washington Press, 2003), 134.

2. Discussing the wartime documentary *Japanese Relocation* (1942), Sumiko Higashi observes that in the voice-over, Milton S. Eisenhower, director of the WRA, "invokes the Western tradition of pioneering. Indeed, the music on the soundtrack at the beginning of the film signifies both mysterious Orientalism and frontier experience. But the internees are forced to move to uninhabitable areas inland, in a reversal of the westward movement, so that most of the panning and tracking in the film, as well as the movement of buses and trains, is toward the right. And despite the narrator's claim that the Japanese 'were in a new land that was raw, untamed, and full of opportunity,' men sit idly as new arrivals enter the concentration camp" (Sumiko Higashi, "Melodrama, Realism, and Race: World War II Newsreels and Propaganda Film," *Cinema Journal* 37, no. 3 [1998]: 50).

3. John Y. Tateishi, "Memories from Behind Barbed Wire," in *Last Witnesses: Reflections on the Wartime Internment of Japanese Americans*, ed. Erica Harth (New York: Palgrave, 2001), 130.

4. Miné Okubo, *Citizen 13660* (1946; Seattle: University of Washington Press, 1983), 123.

5. Edward T. Miyakawa, *Tule Lake* (Victoria BC: House By the Sea Publishing, in cooperation with Trafford Publishing, 1979), 88.

6. Miyakawa, *Tule Lake*, 91.

7. Miyakawa, *Tule Lake*, 93–94.

8. Jeanne Wakatsuki Houston and James D. Houston, *Farewell to Manzanar* (1973; New York: Bantam, 1995), 25–26.

9. Peter T. Suzuki, "Desertification in Hiroshi Nakamura's Treadmill," Asian Profile 21, no. 6 (1993): 472.

10. Patricia Nelson Limerick, "Disorientation and Reorientation: The American Landscape Discovered from the West," Journal of American History 79, no. 3 (December 1992): 1040.

11. Limerick, "Disorientation and Reorientation," 1040. Gwenn M. Jensen notes that "the green wood used for construction warped and shrank, leaving knotholes and cracks—depriving people of personal privacy, and allowing dust and sand to fly in unfettered during the rousing dust storms that were common to most sites." Amache, Poston, and especially Gila River all suffered from regular dust storms, causing high levels of respiratory illness. See Gwenn M. Jensen, "Systems Failure: Health-Care Deficiencies in the World War II Japanese American Detention Centers," Bulletin of the History of Medicine 73, no. 4 (1999): 604–5, 611–13.

12. Ansel Adams, Born Free and Equal: Photographs of the Loyal Japanese-Americans at the Manzanar Relocation Center Inyo County, California (New York: U.S. Camera, 1944), 9.

13. One of the most famous photographs made at the camps is Dorothea Lange's 1942 image of a dust storm at Manzanar, the frame vertically bisected by a pole flying the American flag as two small figures in the middle distance flee from the weather. For a discussion of this image, see Melody Graulich, "'Cameras and Photographs Were Not Permitted in the Camps': Photographic Documentation and Distortion in Japanese American Internment Narratives," in True West: Authenticity and the American West, ed. William R. Handley and Nathaniel Lewis (Lincoln: University of Nebraska Press, 2004), 226–27. The image is also discussed by Nancy J. Peterson in Against Amnesia: Contemporary Women Writers and the Crises of Historical Memory (Philadelphia: University of Pennsylvania Press, 2001), 138, and provides the cover image for the book.

14. Mary Douglas, Purity and Danger: An Analysis of Concepts of Pollution and Taboo (London: Routledge, 2002), 44.

15. Douglas, Purity and Danger, 45, 47.

16. Kristeva, Powers of Horror, 4.

17. For a revealing discussion of the relationship between the terms "domestic" and "foreign" as they pertain to the construction of national identity, see Amy Kaplan, The Anarchy of Empire in the Making of U.S. Culture (Cambridge MA: Harvard University Press, 2002). On dirt and the politics of domestic labor, see Phyllis Palmer, Domesticity and Dirt: Housewives and Domestic Servants in the United States, 1920–1945 (Philadelphia: Temple University Press, 1989).

18. Jake Kennedy, "Dust and the Avant-Garde," in "New Papers in American Cultural Studies," ed. Joanne Morreale and P. David Marshall, thematic issue, CLCWeb: Comparative Literature and Culture 7, no. 2 (2005), http://docs.lib.purdue.edu/clcweb/vol7/iss2/4 (accessed September 10, 2008).

19. After the photograph was taken, Duchamp wiped The Large Glass almost

entirely clean, leaving a section of the cones covered with dust that he permanently fixed to the glass.

20. Agamben, *Homo Sacer*, 19.

21. Agamben, *Homo Sacer*, 17.

22. Agamben, *Homo Sacer*, 17–18.

23. Agamben, *Homo Sacer*, 170.

24. Agamben, *Homo Sacer*, 174.

25. Agamben, *Homo Sacer*, 175.

26. Caroline Chung Simpson, *An Absent Presence: Japanese Americans in Postwar American Culture, 1945–1960* (Durham: Duke University Press, 2001), 9.

27. Simpson, *An Absent Presence* 21. Donna K. Nagata lists practical and organizational difficulties, lack of representation, a sense of having been betrayed by the government, stoicism, and public ignorance among the reasons for nisei silence about internment. "Although the Nisei were aware of the unjust nature of the internment," Nagata argues, "breaking the silence could be dangerous. The danger was felt at a personal level (not wanting to revive painful memories) as well as at a societal level (not wanting to stir up anti-Japanese sentiments)." See Donna K. Nagata *Legacy of Injustice: Exploring the Cross-Generational Impact of the Japanese American Internment* (New York: Plenum, 1993), 188.

28. Simpson, *An Absent Presence*, 2.

29. Simpson, *An Absent Presence*, 2–3.

30. Simpson, *An Absent Presence*, 2–3.

31. Simpson, *An Absent Presence*, 5.

32. Adams, *Born Free and Equal*, 25, 29.

33. Adams, *Born Free and Equal*, 29.

34. Adams, *Born Free and Equal*, 22.

35. On *No-No Boy*, see Lisa Lowe, *Immigrant Acts: On Asian American Cultural Politics* (Durham: Duke University Press, 1996), 51: "Virtually ignored when it was published in 1957 and rejected by the reading public for its uncompromisingly unconventional style, *No-No Boy* was reissued in 1976 by the University of Washington Press after an excerpt of it was featured in the anthology *Aiiieeeee!* *No-No Boy* may be characterized as a realist narrative to the extent that its action proceeds chronologically. But it is antidevelopmental in the sense that its condensed, almost static portrait takes place within the small period of several weeks, and it repeatedly undermines uniperspectivalism by alternating inconsistently between a third person omniscient narration and despairing, angry, or confused interior monologues."

36. Sau-ling Wong, *Reading Asian American Literature: From Necessity to Extravagance* (Princeton: Princeton University Press, 1993), 128.

37. Sumiko Higashi, for example, argues that Guterson's "highbrow representations mask a great deal of stereotyping, not to mention fantasizing, about Asian American women." See "Melodrama, Realism, and Race," 61 n.58.

38. On the prohibition of photography and Okubo's singular response, see Graulich, "'Cameras and Photographs Were Not Permitted in the Camps.'"

39. Krista Comer, Landscapes of the New West: Gender and Geography in Contemporary Women's Writing (Chapel Hill: University of North Carolina Press, 1999), 209.

40. Rahna Reiko Rizzuto, Why She Left Us (New York: HarperCollins, 1999), 20. Further references are cited in the text with the abbreviation WSL.

41. Marianne Hirsch, "Surviving Images: Holocaust Photographs and the Work of Postmemory," Yale Journal of Criticism 14, no. 1 (2001): 8–9. On the importance of silence in Asian and Asian American culture, see King-Kok Cheung, Articulate Silences: Hisaye Yamamoto, Maxine Hong Kingston, Joy Kogawa (Ithaca: Cornell University Press, 1993).

42. Hirsch, "Surviving Images," 10.

43. Hirsch, "Surviving Images," 12.

44. David Leiwei Li, Imagining the Nation: Asian American Literature and Cultural Consent (Stanford: Stanford University Press, 1998), 3.

45. Li, Imagining the Nation, 4.

46. The notion of shikata ga nai is a common feature of narratives of internment. Wakatsuki Houston devotes a chapter to the term, which is, as it is in Why She Left Us, associated with issei stoicism: "You would hear the older heads, the Issei, telling others very quietly, 'shikata ga nai' (It cannot be helped). 'Shikata ga nai' (It must be done)." See Farewell to Manzanar, 16.

47. Michiko Kakutani describes the final pages as "bluntly didactic" and "ill-conceived." See Michiko Kakutani, "War's Outcasts Dream of Small Pleasures," The New York Times, September 10, 2002.

48. Julie Otsuka, When the Emperor Was Divine (New York: Knopf, 2002), 3. Further references are cited in the text with the abbreviation WED.

49. Hisaye Yamamoto, "Death Rides the Rails to Poston," in Seventeen Syllables and Other Stories, rev. ed. (New Brunswick: Rutgers University Press, 2001), 131–41.

50. I am indebted to William Handley for pointing out some of the connections in this passage.

4. Learning From Los Alamos

1. Peter Bacon Hales, Atomic Spaces: Living on the Manhattan Project (Urbana: University of Illinois Press, 1997), 13.

2. The internment camp and the secret Los Alamos project could be described, following Erving Goffman, as "total institutions," where individual contact with the rest of society is severed and everyday life is regulated and controlled. On Goffman, see Hugh Gusterson, Nuclear Rites: A Weapons Laboratory at the End of the Cold War (Berkeley: University of California Press, 1996), 81.

3. See Gusterson, Nuclear Rites, 81. "Total institutions," Gusterson explains, "have a powerful ability to 'deself' people: to alter their position in a field of social relationships and thus to peel away their old identities and create new ones."

4. Gusterson, *Nuclear Rites*, 68. On the continuing importance of Los Alamos in shaping America as a nuclear state, see Masco, *The Nuclear Borderlands*.

5. For a survey of Los Alamos novels that includes brief discussion of a number of these novels, see David L. Caffey, *Land of Enchantment, Land of Conflict: New Mexico in English Language Fiction* (College Station: Texas A&M University Press, 1999), 146–62.

6. Frank Waters, *The Woman at Otowi Crossing*, rev. ed. (1966; Athens: Ohio University Press/Swallow Press, 1987), 240.

7. David E. Nye, *American Technological Sublime* (Cambridge: Massachusetts Institute of Technology Press, 1994), 230.

8. Waters, *Woman at Otowi Crossing*, 159. Waters is borrowing here from his earlier comparison of old and new in *Masked Gods*: "The oldest forms of life discovered in this hemisphere, and the newest agent of mass death. The oldest cities in America and the newest. The Sun Temple of Mesa Verde and the nuclear fission laboratories of the Pajarito Plateau. The Indian drum and the atom smasher" (Frank Waters, *Masked Gods: Navaho and Pueblo Ceremonialism* [Athens: Ohio University Press/Swallow Press, 1950], 425). Here, just a few years after the Trinity explosion, it seems too early to tell what the new atomic order will bring, and Waters is ambivalent: the bomb "may be a Monster Slayer or a Monster Bomb, a new faith or a new fear. Only the guiding philosophy determines whether it be constructive or destructive" (422).

9. Other novels involving a culture clash between archaeology and science include Robert Olen Butler's *Countrymen of Bones* (1983) and Ron Querry's *Bad Medicine* (1998).

10. Hales, *Atomic Spaces*, 14.

11. As Restricted Data, all ideas produced by weapons scientists "are automatically and immediately classified and continue to be classified until they are explicitly unclassified." See Gusterson, *Nuclear Rites*, 69.

12. While the work Tim is doing is far from the top secret science his father did at Los Alamos, his attempt to hide in the toilet is an indication of the extent to which Tim has internalized the high-security regime of the weapons lab. See Gusterson, *Nuclear Rites*, 70: "The laboratory is an enormous grid of tabooed spaces and tabooed topics. These taboos become part of the everyday practical consciousness of all laboratory employees as the practice of secrecy is encoded in their daily routines in ways that soon come to be taken for granted. Every time employees move from one part of the laboratory to another, discuss their work with other employees, go to the bathroom, or take a coffee break, observance of the taboos is part of their routine. It is, on a daily basis, engraved and reengraved into their practical consciousness."

13. Hales, *Atomic Spaces*, 73.

14. See Peter Bacon Hales, "Topographies of Power: The Forced Spaces of the Manhattan Project," in *Mapping American Culture*, ed. Wayne Franklin and Michael Steiner (Iowa City: University of Iowa Press, 1992), 272–73: "Compartmentalization

was the military's system for assuring security in the workplace. Its model was straightforward, simple, elegant. Two workers stand at a laboratory table. They may not speak to each other, only to their immediate superiors. These superiors may only speak to their superiors who may . . . and so on up the line, until finally the two superiors turn out to be the same person." This system was not only good for security but suited the military's hierarchical structure, rewarding those locked into the system rather than those who knew the whole plan. The system "fragmented social and informational networks, isolating individuals in their cells, where they did as they were told." Naturally, this benefited the managerial elite at Du Pont and the military elite most and the scientists the least. Compartmentalization, Hales goes on, was not only the workplace model, but "defined every social relation" in the project.

15. Gusterson, *Nuclear Rites*, 70.

16. Hales, *Atomic Spaces*, 221.

17. Thomas McMahon, *Principles of American Nuclear Chemistry* (1970; Chicago: University of Chicago Press, 2003), 47. Further references are given in the text with the abbreviation PNC.

18. Hales, *Atomic Spaces*, 214.

19. The three-legged dog seems to anticipate the crippled dog Billy Parham scares off at the end of McCarthy's *The Crossing*. After witnessing the Trinity explosion, Parham calls for the dog, but it does not return.

20. Hales, *Atomic Spaces*, 29.

21. Hales, *Atomic Spaces*, 30.

22. Hales, *Atomic Spaces*, 32.

23. Bradford Morrow, *Trinity Fields* (London: Flamingo, 1995), 26. Further references are abbreviated in the text as TF.

24. Alan Nadel, *Containment Culture: American Narratives, Postmodernism, and the Atomic Age* (Durham: Duke University Press, 1995), 14.

25. Hales, "Topographies of Power," 251–52.

26. Gusterson explains that "we must partly understand laboratory practices of secrecy as a means of creating a disciplinary distance between weapons scientists and their families. Often working in concert with traditional American notions of appropriate roles in marriage, they open a space between the laboratory and the domestic sphere that, to some extent at least, insulates weapons scientists from questions and challenges about their work and maintain a seal between the values of the public and domestic spheres" (*Nuclear Rites*, 98–99).

27. This kind of "internalized surveillance," Gusterson observes, creates an "expansionary inertia," since people become unsure about what is and is not being monitored and are not sure what is permissible. As such, surveillance becomes a "generalized mechanism for disciplining amorphous political deviance." See Gusterson, *Nuclear Rites*, 85.

28. Hales, *Atomic Spaces*, 259.

29. Gusterson, *Nuclear Rites*, 80.

30. Masco explains that the Santuario and the Los Alamos labs have, since

1943, been engaged in a "symbolic regional dialogue." An interfaith Pilgrimage for Peace has taken place annually since 1983, involving the taking of soil from the Santuario, which is then ceremonially distributed in the center of Los Alamos at Ashley Pond. The pilgrimage, Masco suggests, is an effort "to contain the foreignness of Los Alamos." See Masco, The Nuclear Borderlands, 170–75.

31. Bradford Morrow, Ariel's Crossing (New York: Viking, 2002), 53. Further references are abbreviated in the text as AC.

32. Jacques Derrida, "No Apocalypse, Not Now (full speed ahead, seven missiles, seven missives)," Diacritics 14, no. 2 (1984): 23.

33. Derrida, "No Apocalypse," 24.

34. Delfino's defiance recalls the long battle with the government fought by David McDonald for the return of the ranch leased by the military during World War II and never returned. This scenario is also played out in novels by Edward Abbey and Alexander Parsons, which are discussed in the next chapter. On David McDonald, see, Ferenc Morton Szasz, The Day the Sun Rose Twice: The Story of the Trinity Site Nuclear Explosion July 16, 1945 (Albuquerque: University of New Mexico Press, 1984), 30–31.

35. Martin Heidegger, "The Question Concerning Technology," in The Question Concerning Technology and Other Essays, trans. William Lovitt (New York: Harper and Row, 1977), 13.

36. Heidegger, "The Question Concerning Technology," 14.

37. Heidegger, "The Question Concerning Technology," 17.

38. Heidegger, "The Question Concerning Technology," 27.

39. Rob Wilson, The American Sublime: The Genealogy of a Poetic Genre (Madison: University of Wisconsin Press, 1991), 260.

40. Martin Heidgger, "The Turning," in The Question Concerning Technology and Other Essays, 36–37. Pynchon makes the same strikingly Heideggerian argument in Gravity's Rainbow, 412: "Kekulé dreams the Great Serpent holding its own tail in its mouth, the dreaming Serpent which surrounds the World. But the meanness, the cynicism with which this dream is to be used. The Serpent that announces, 'The World is a closed thing, cyclical, resonant, eternally-returning,' is to be delivered into a system whose only aim is to violate the Cycle. Taking and not giving back, demanding that 'productivity' and 'earnings' keep on increasing with time, the System removing from the rest of the World these vast quantities of energy to keep its own tiny desperate fraction showing a profit: and not only most of humanity—most of the World, animal, vegetable and mineral, is laid waste in the process."

5. Gridlocked and Homeless

1. Thomas Pynchon, Vineland (London: Minerva, 1991), 250.

2. Terry Tempest Williams, Refuge: An Unnatural History of Family and Place (New York: Vintage, 1991), 241.

3. Don DeLillo, *Underworld* (London: Picador, 1998), 404.

4. Zygmunt Bauman, *Wasted Lives: Modernity and Its Outcasts* (Cambridge: Polity, 2004), 39.

5. Bauman, *Wasted Lives*, 18.

6. Bauman, *Wasted Lives*, 21.

7. Bauman, *Wasted Lives*, 22.

8. Edward Abbey, *Fire on the Mountain* (1962; New York: Avon, 1992), 79. Further references are abbreviated in the text as FM.

9. Bauman, *Wasted Lives*, 50.

10. Agamben, *State of Exception*, 35.

11. Agamben, *State of Exception*, 35.

12. Bauman, *Wasted Lives*, 31.

13. Alexander Parsons, *In the Shadows of the Sun* (New York: Nan A. Talese/Doubleday, 2005), 58. Further references are indicated in the text by the abbreviation ISS.

14. Ross also identifies with Apaches in his resistance to eviction, arguing that they "wouldn't have nothing if they hadn't fought." Baylis points out, however, that the Apaches were shot in the end (ISS 78).

15. See John Wegner, "'Wars and Rumors of War' in Cormac McCarthy's Border Trilogy," in *A Cormac McCarthy Companion: The Border Trilogy*, ed. Edwin T. Arnold and Dianne C. Luce, 73–91 (Jackson: University of Mississippi Press, 2001); Jacqueline Scoones, "The World On Fire: Ethics and Evolution in Cormac McCarthy's Border Trilogy," in Arnold and Luce, *A Cormac McCarthy Companion*, 131–60. All references to the books of *The Border Trilogy* will be given in the text using the following abbreviations: *All The Pretty Horses* (APH), *The Crossing* (C), and *Cities of the Plain* (CP).

16. Robert L. Holmes, *On War and Morality* (Princeton: Princeton University Press, 1989), 3, quoted in Wegner, "Wars and Rumors of War," 81.

17. Bauman, *Wasted Lives*, 50.

18. Beck, *Risk Society*, 137.

19. Beck, *Risk Society*, 137.

20. Bauman, *Wasted Lives*, 39–40.

21. Gail Moore Morrison, "*All the Pretty Horses*: John Grady Cole's Expulsion from Paradise," in *Perspectives on Cormac McCarthy*, ed. Edwin T. Arnold and Dianne C. Luce, rev. ed. (Jackson: University Press of Mississippi, 1999), 177–78. For further discussion of chivalry in *The Border Trilogy*, see Ellis, *No Place for Home*, chap. 6; and Jay Ellis and Natalka Palczynski, "Horses, Houses, and the Gravy to Win: Chivalric and Domestic Roles in *The Border Trilogy*," in *Sacred Violence*, vol. 2, *Cormac McCarthy's Western Novels*, ed. Wade Hall and Rick Wallach (El Paso: Texas Western Press, 2002), 105–25.

22. Michel Foucault, *Discipline and Punish: The Birth of the Prison*, trans. Alan Sheridan (Harmondsworth: Penguin, 1977), 135.

23. Richard Slotkin's *Gunfighter Nation* is a good place to start for an analysis of the Western film's engagement with Cold War politics.

24. Foucault, *Discipline and Punish*, 135.

25. Harold Lasswell quoted in Sherry, *In The Shadow of War*, 75.

26. Foucault, *Discipline and Punish*, 138.

27. Slotkin, *Gunfighter Nation*, 644.

28. Vince Brewton has argued that the various "rescues" performed by Cole and Parham are similar "to the popular rescue fantasies of the 1980s where American POWs from Vietnam are snatched from work camps by selfless and patriotic (but antiestablishment) commandos." In particular, Billy's expedition to retrieve Boyd from Mexico, according to Brewton, recalls the desire to repatriate the remains of soldiers killed in action and save surviving MIAs as a means of kicking the "Vietnam Syndrome": "Bringing the POWs home became a part of a new national narrative, culturally significant if election results are an indicator, whereby rescuing brave Americans from the netherworld of POW camps marked a symbolic movement analogous to rescuing national identity from the miasma of defeat in Southeast Asia and self-division at home. The narrative of the guerito and the narrative of American MIAs are similar in their role in the continuous reproduction of national identity, and both incorporate 'real' events into a self-serving myth necessary for their respective communities." See Vince Brewton, "The Changing Landscape of Violence in Cormac McCarthy's Early Novels and the Border Trilogy," *Southern Literary Journal* 37, no. 1 (2004): 137, 138.

29. Daniel Cooper Alarcón places *The Border Trilogy* within what he calls the tradition of writing about Mexico as an "infernal paradise," a Manichean, ahistorical space that provides "a symbolic backdrop against which a spiritual quest is played out." Daniel Cooper Alarcón, "All the Pretty Mexicos: Cormac McCarthy's Mexican Representations," in Lilley, *Cormac McCarthy*, 143.

30. Bauman, *Modernity and Ambivalence*, 54. "Being a friend, and being an enemy," claims Bauman, "are the two modalities in which the *Other* may be recognized as another *subject*, construed as a 'subject like the self,' admitted into the self's life world, be counted, become and stay relevant."

31. Bauman, *Modernity and Ambivalence*, 56.

32. José E. Limón, *American Encounters: Greater Mexico, the United States, and the Erotics of Culture* (Boston: Beacon, 1998), 195.

33. N. Scott Momaday, *House Made of Dawn* (1966; New York: Signet, 1969), 25. Further references are indicated in the text by the abbreviation HMD.

34. Leslie Marmon Silko, *Ceremony* (New York: Viking, 1977), 6–7. Further references are indicated in the text by the abbreviation Ce.

35. Rudolfo Anaya, *Bless Me, Ultima* (1972; New York: Warner Books, 1994), 19–20. Further references are indicated in the text by the abbreviation BMU.

36. For more on the importance of the bomb in the novel, see Alex Hunt, "Right

and False Suns: Cormac McCarthy's *The Crossing* and the Advent of the Atomic Age," *Southwestern American Literature* 23, no. 2 (1998): 31–37.

37. Hirchfelder's text reads: "we came to a small store at the crossing of two dirt roads. [We] rang the door bell and an old man came out. He looked quizzically at us. Then he laughed and said, 'You boys must have been up to something this morning. The sun came up in the west and went on down again.'" Joseph O. Hirschfelder, "The Scientific and Technological Miracle at Los Alamos," in *Reminiscences of Los Alamos 1943–1945*, ed. Lawrence Badash, Joseph O. Hirshfelder, and Herbert P. Broida (Boston: D. Reidel Publishing Company, 1980), 77.

38. Ryan Bishop and John Phillips, "Sighted Weapons and Modernist Opacity: Aesthetics, Poetics, Prosthetics," *boundary 2* 29, no. 2 (2002): 167.

6. Loomings

1. See Paul Boyer, *By the Bomb's Early Light: American Thought and Culture at the Dawn of the Atomic Age* (New York: Pantheon, 1985), 334: "For a fleeting moment after Hiroshima, American culture had been profoundly affected by atomic fear, by a dizzying plethora of atomic panaceas and proposals, and by endless speculation on the social and ethical implications of the new reality. By the end of the 1940s, the cultural discourse had largely stopped. Americans now seemed not only ready to accept the bomb, but to support any measures necessary to maintain atomic supremacy"; and Allan M. Winkler, *Life Under a Cloud: American Anxiety about the Atom* (New York: Oxford University Press, 1993), 4: "As hydrogen weapons replaced atomic bombs in the 1950s and kilotons gave way to megatons in the decades that followed, . . . fear grew even more pronounced, and speculation about the dismal or nonexistent future became more common. Scientists in the 1970s and 1980s predicted deadly epidemics of radiation-related illnesses, devastating climatic adjustments, and the death of life as we know it."

2. Herman Melville, *Moby-Dick; or, the Whale* (Harmondswoth: Penguin, 1985), 387.

3. Paul K. Saint-Amour, "Bombing and the Symptom: Traumatic Earliness and the Nuclear Uncanny," *Diacritics* 30, no. 4 (2000): 61.

4. Saint-Amour, "Bombing and the Symptom," 61.

5. Saint-Amour, "Bombing and the Symptom," 61.

6. H. G. Bissinger, *Friday Night Lights: A Town, a Team, and a Dream* (1990; London: Yellow Jersey Press, 2005), 32.

7. Bissinger, *Friday Night Lights*, 33.

8. Bissinger, *Friday Night Lights*, 33.

9. Nadel, *Containment Culture*, 14.

10. Nadel, *Containment Culture*, 24.

11. Martin Heidegger, "The Thing," in *Poetry, Language, Thought*, trans. Albert Hofstadter (New York: Harper and Row, 1971), 170. William Chaloupka argues

that nuclearism "organizes public life and thought so thoroughly that, in another era of political theory, we would analyze it as an ideology." See Chaloupka, *Knowing Nukes*, 1.

12. Derrida, "No Apocalypse," 29.

13. See Nadel, *Containment Culture*, 39.

14. Don DeLillo, *End Zone* (1972; New York: Penguin, 1986), 30. Further references are to this edition and cited in the text as EZ.

15. On the reciprocal relationship between discourses of sport and warfare, see Michael J. Shapiro, "Representing World Politics: The Sport/War Intertext," in *International/Intertextual Relations: Postmodern Readings of World Politics*, ed. James Der Derian and Michael J. Shapiro (Lexington MA: Lexington Books, 1989), 69–96.

16. Don DeLillo with Thomas LeClair, "An Interview with Don DeLillo," *Contemporary Literature* 23 (1982): 21.

17. Mark Osteen, *American Magic and Dread: Don DeLillo's Dialogue with Culture* (Philadelphia: University of Pennsylvania Press, 2000), 40–41.

18. On the end of the warrior, see Peter Sloterdijk, *Critique of Cynical Reason*, trans. Michael Eldred (Minneapolis: University of Minnesota Press, 1987), 129: "All modern military ethics . . . have abolished the image of the aggressive hero because it would interfere with the defensive justification for war." For further discussion, see Chaloupka, *Knowing Nukes*, 23–42.

19. On the deployment of Western tropes in Vietnam, see Slotkin, *Regeneration through Violence*, 562–65, and *Gunfighter Nation*, part 4. One of the best known accounts of Vietnam that uses Western history critically to approach the war is Michael Herr's *Dispatches* (1977).

20. Joseph Dewey, *In a Dark Time: The Apocalyptic Temper in the American Novel of the Nuclear Age* (West Lafayette: Purdue University Press, 1990), 180.

21. William Hauptman, *Storm Season* (1992; Austin: University of Texas Press, 2000), 128. Further references are cited in the text with the abbreviation SS.

22. A. N. Mojtabai, *Blessèd Assurance: At Home with the Bomb in Amarillo, Texas* (Boston: Houghton Mifflin, 1986), 47.

23. Mojtabai, *Blessèd Assurance*, 48.

24. Jodi Dean, *Aliens in America: Conspiracy Cultures from Outerspace to Cyberspace* (Ithaca: Cornell University Press, 1998), 173.

25. Mojtabai, *Blessèd Assurance*, 80. Mojtabai's interviews with Amarilloans reveal only a slow dawning of realization that their town was host to the only final assembly plant for nuclear weapons in the entire United States, despite relatively high public exposure since the 1970s. While most residents appeared to know that something bomb related went on at the Pantex plant, many did little to find out exactly what it was, and even once it was obvious, the facts seemed to be rarely discussed. The general sense given from the interviews is of a known presence just out of view that, because it is always there, is mostly ignored even though its potential danger is known. Largely because of Pantex, of course, Amarillo was a

prime Soviet target throughout the Cold War, a fact that one interviewee claims was a source of pride in high school: "We thought that was pretty neat." Most of the others interviewed stoically accepted the situation. A 1982 survey commissioned by the Los Alamos National Laboratory disclosed "an unusually high refusal rate" with regard to the significance of Pantex and, as Mojtabai notes, while the vast majority of the population thought Amarillo a good place to raise children, significant numbers also believed there was a good chance of there being an accident of some kind at Pantex or along the transportation routes. The Los Alamos survey noted: "One somewhat surprising result was that *not one* respondent pointed to a moral position as the cause for stress resulting from Pantex." See Mojtabai, *Blessèd Assurance*, 56–62.

26. Dewey, *In a Dark Time*, 181.

27. Mojtabai, *Blessèd Assurance*, 149. We are, Mojtabai concedes, "increasingly powerless to control our collective fate. Over nature, we have gained some control, over human nature—none at all. Dispensationalism codifies a sense of the drift of history, and a mood, with which most of us are familiar" (150).

28. See Mojtabai, *Blessèd Assurance*, 220–21. The pastor of a Lutheran church in Amarillo believes that there is an insularity in the panhandle that is a vestige of frontier living: "the reason for which people came [here originally] was to move on one more place where they couldn't see the smoke of their neighbor's chimney. That kind of isolation is very close to alienation . . . the psychological sense of being not accountable and not depending on anybody else. And that carries into their churches. . . . I think the church is simply captive to it. It's just been captured by the local heritage and simply reinforces it, and, oftentimes, at its very worst point." This convergence of local temperament and religiosity leads to a narrow, "highly privatistic, individualized . . . hyperindividuality . . . [that is] so overwhelmingly important that they do not hear the calls for brother-keeping and justice and peace-keeping."

29. Beck, *Risk Society*, 137.

7. After Nature

1. Gilles Deleuze and Félix Guattari, *A Thousand Plateaus: Capitalism and Schizophrenia*, trans. Brian Massumi (London: Athlone, 1988), 243.

2. Jack Couffer, *Bat Bomb: World War II's Other Secret Weapon* (Austin: University of Texas Press, 1992), 7.

3. Matthew Coolidge, *Nuclear Proving Grounds of the World* (Culver City CA: Center for Land Use Interpretation, 1998), not paginated. For a detailed account of every series of above-ground tests, including maps of fallout trajectories, see Richard L. Miller, *Under the Cloud: The Decades of Nuclear Testing*, 2nd ed. (The Woodlands TX: Two-Sixty Press, 1991).

4. On the history of uranium mining, weapons production, and their impact on the region, see Raye C. Ringholz, *Uranium Frenzy: Saga of the Nuclear West*, rev. ed. (Logan: Utah State University Press, 2002).

5. For a pertinent discussion of secrecy and display in the context of marking the site of the Waste Isolation Pilot Plant (WIPP) in New Mexico, see Peter C. van Dyke, "American Monument: The Waste Isolation Pilot Plant," in *Atomic Culture: How We Learned to Stop Worrying and Love the Bomb*, ed. Scott C. Zeman and Michael A. Amundson, 149–72 (Boulder: University Press of Colorado, 2004).

6. Lawrence Buell, *Writing for an Endangered World: Literature, Culture, and Environment in the U.S. and Beyond* (Cambridge MA: Belknap Press of Harvard University Press, 2001), 27, 31.

7. Buell, *Writing for an Endangered World*, 31.

8. Buell, *Writing for an Endangered World*, 34.

9. Buell, *Writing for an Endangered World*, 35.

10. Buell, *Writing for an Endangered World*, 35–40.

11. Buell, *Writing for an Endangered World*, 42.

12. Beck, *Risk Society*, 72.

13. Beck, *Risk Society*, 73; emphasis in original.

14. Ana Castillo, *So Far from God* (New York: Norton, 1993), 172.

15. Clarence King, "Catastrophism and Evolution," *American Naturalist* 11, no. 8 (1877): 454.

16. Limerick, *The Legacy of Conquest*, 18.

17. Anthony Vidler, *The Architectural Uncanny: Essays in the Modern Unhomely* (Cambridge MA: MIT Press, 1992), 168–69.

18. Michael J. Shapiro, "The Discursive Spaces of Global Politics," *Journal of Environmental Policy and Planning* 7, no. 3 (2005): 228.

19. For official information on WIPP, including fact sheets on subjects such as the project's history, the rationale behind the installation, and transportation issues, refer to the WIPP Web site: http://www.wipp.energy.gov/ (accessed February 7, 2009). For a discussion of the WIPP project from a geological and design point of view, see Charles C. Reith and N. Timothy Fisher, "Transuranic Waste Disposal: The WIPP Project," in *Deserts as Dumps?: The Disposal of Hazardous Materials in Arid Ecosystems*, ed. Charles C. Reith and Bruce M. Thomson, 303–18 (Albuquerque: University of New Mexico Press, 1992). A more critical view is expressed in Kuletz, *The Tainted Desert*, 97–101. Useful comments on the position of WIPP among subterranean nuclear installations are made in Tom Vanderbilt, *Survival City: Adventures Among the Ruins of Atomic America* (Princeton NJ: Princeton Architectural Press, 2002), 185–91.

20. Vanderbilt, *Survival City*, 186.

21. Kuletz, *The Tainted Desert*, 99.

22. Reith and Fisher, "Transuranic Waste Disposal," 308.

23. Ward Churchill, *Struggle for the Land: Indigenous Resistance to Genocide, Ecocide and Expropriation in Contemporary North America* (Monroe ME: Common Courage Press, 1993), 261–328. See also Kuletz, *The Tainted Desert*, 112.

24. Kuletz, *The Tainted Desert*, 12. For detailed discussion of the impact of the

nuclear West on Native Americans, see Peter H. Eichstaedt, *If You Poison Us: Uranium and Native Americans* (Santa Fe NM: Red Crane Books, 1996). The long battle fought by the Western Shoshone over the Nevada Test Site is explored at length in Rebecca Solnit's *Savage Dreams*, discussed in the next chapter.

25. Kuletz, *The Tainted Desert*, 12. In addition to WIPP, various other nuclear waste sites are on or near numerous tribal lands. Radioactive waste from Los Alamos National Laboratory is stored at "Area G," which borders the San Ildefonso Pueblo and is near Santa Clara Pueblo's lands. Storage of low-level waste is planned for Fort Mojave Indians and the Chemehuevis of the Colorado River Indian tribes, while the proposed major permanent site for high-level waste is Yucca Mountain, affecting the Western Shoshones, Southern Pauites, and Owens Valley Pauites.

26. Mark A. Cheetham and Elizabeth D. Harvey, "Obscure Imaginings: Visual Culture and the Anatomy of Caves," *Journal of Visual Culture* 1, no. 1 (2002): 105.

27. Cheetham and Harvey, "Obscure Imaginings," 106.

28. Cheetham and Harvey, "Obscure Imaginings," 106.

29. Cheetham and Harvey, "Obscure Imaginings," 106.

30. Cheetham and Harvey, "Obscure Imaginings," 112.

31. Willa Cather, *Death Comes for the Archbishop* (1927; London: Virago, 1981), 125–27.

32. Cather, *Death Comes*, 129.

33. Cather, *Death Comes*, 130, 133.

34. Joan Didion, "On Morality" (1965), in *Slouching toward Bethlehem* (Harmondsworth: Penguin, 1974), 134.

35. Didion, "On Morality," 133.

36. Jake Page, *Cavern* (Albuquerque: University of New Mexico Press, 2001), 70.

37. Page, *Cavern*, 82.

38. Page, *Cavern*, 7.

39. Page, *Cavern*, 72.

40. David Mogen, Scott P. Sanders, and Joanne B. Karpinski, eds., introduction to *Frontier Gothic: Terror and Wonder at the Frontier in American Literature* (London: Associated University Presses, 1993), 16–17.

41. Mogen et al., *Frontier Gothic*, 16–17.

42. See Mogen et al., *Frontier Gothic*, 16: "When the ethos of a culture's past is integrated with the ethos of the present culture, the identity of the culture at that moment is at its zenith, and its literature may produce its definitive epic. . . . Understood in this cultural sense, gothicism results when the epic moment passes, and a peculiar rift in history develops and widens into a dark chasm that separates what is now from what has been. The history that suffers this rift is the inscripted past, the literal re-presentation to ourselves of a [hi]story that integrates people, events, and places, and makes of the world and its landscape

a locale, a *locus civilis* whose experience is comfortable, coherent, and known. This inscripted history is privileged; it functions as a logocentric past, the point of seemingly solid, objective, and true reference that exists as the sure foundations of the present civilization."

43. Helen Jaskoski, "Thinking Woman's Children and the Bomb," in *The Nightmare Considered: Critical Essays on Nuclear War Literature*, ed. Nancy Anisfield (Bowling Green: Bowling Green State University Popular Press, 1991), 159.

44. Kuletz, *The Tainted Desert*, 27.

45. Kuletz, *The Tainted Desert*, 28–29.

46. Kuletz, *The Tainted Desert*, 32–33.

47. Martin Cruz Smith, *Night Wing* (New York: Norton, 1977), 2. Further references are given in the text with the abbreviation NW.

48. For further discussion of the parallels between vampires and Indians, see Rebecca Tillett, "'Your Story Reminds Me of Something': Spectacle and Speculation in Aaron Carr's *Eye Killers*," *Ariel* 33, no. 1 (2002): 149–74.

49. A. A. Carr, *Eye Killers* (Norman: University of Oklahoma Press, 1996), 317. Further references are given in the text with the abbreviation EK.

50. Eric Gary Anderson, *American Indian Literature and the Southwest: Contexts and Dispositions* (Austin: University of Texas Press, 1999), 194.

51. Deleuze and Guattari, *A Thousand Plateaus*, 246.

52. Deleuze and Guattari, *A Thousand Plateaus*, 247.

53. Donna J. Haraway, "Universal Donors in a Vampire Culture: It's All in the Family: Biological Kinship Categories in the Twentieth-Century United States," in *Uncommon Ground: Toward Reinventing Nature*, ed. William Cronon (New York: Norton, 1995), 322.

54. Haraway, "Universal Donors," 322–23.

55. Haraway, "Universal Donors," 366.

56. Haraway, "Universal Donors," 366.

57. Haraway, "Universal Donors," 366.

58. Deleuze and Guattari, *A Thousand Plateaus*, 241.

59. Deleuze and Guattari, *A Thousand Plateaus*, 242.

60. Deleuze and Guattari, *A Thousand Plateaus*, 242.

61. Deleuze and Guattari, *A Thousand Plateaus*, 242.

62. Deleuze and Guattari, *A Thousand Plateaus*, 243.

63. Deleuze and Guattari, *A Thousand Plateaus*, 243–44.

64. Deleuze and Guattari, *A Thousand Plateaus*, 245.

8. After Nature Writing

1. Buell, *Writing for an Endangered World*, 46.

2. For another Utah-based text that, like Williams's, situates awakening environmental and political consciousness as a response to the incremental erosion of domestic security as the concealed facts of contamination come to light,

see Chip Ward, *Canaries on the Rim: Living Downwind in the West* (London: Verso, 1999). For a powerful documentary overview of "downwinder" experience in the West, see Carole Gallagher's essential *American Ground Zero: The Secret Nuclear War* (Cambridge MA: MIT Press, 1993). For an overview of the political and representational issues of nuclear politics that includes a discussion of Gallagher's work, see Mike Davis, "Dead West: Ecocide in Marlboro Country," *New Left Review* 200 (July–August 1993): 49–73.

3. Buell, *Writing for an Endangered World*, 46.

4. Seth Shulman, *The Threat at Home: Confronting the Toxic Legacy of the U.S. Military* (Boston: Beacon, 1992), 45.

5. Shulman, *The Threat at Home*, 46.

6. Shulman, *The Threat at Home*, 46.

7. Shulman, *The Threat at Home*, 46. See also Sharon K. Weiner, "Environmental Concerns at U.S. Overseas Installations," DACS Working Paper, July 1992, http://18.48.0.31/ssp/Working_Papers/Working%20Papers/WP-92-2.pdf (accessed September 12, 2008).

8. Williams, *Refuge*, 3. Further references are cited in the text as R. See Nathaniel Lewis, *Unsettling the Literary West: Authenticity and Authorship* (Lincoln: University of Nebraska Press, 2003), 162–63.

9. Lisa Diedrich, "'A New Thought in Familiar Country': Williams's Witnessing Ethics," in *Surveying the Literary Landscapes of Terry Tempest Williams: New Critical Essays*, ed. Katherine R. Chandler and Melissa A. Goldthwaite (Salt Lake City: University of Utah Press, 2003), 219.

10. Buell, *Writing for an Endangered World*, 48. The same dilemma faces Ana Castillo's Fe in *So Far from God*, who cannot sue the company that has poisoned her because it is discovered that she had skin cancer before starting work there.

11. Buell, *Writing for an Endangered World*, 48. On the frustration not being able to verify the cause of alleged contamination-related conditions and how this enables military "denial, cover-ups, and resistance to accountability," see Ward, *Canaries on the Rim*, 75–77.

12. Philip L Fradkin, *Fallout: An American Nuclear Tragedy*, 2nd ed. (Boulder CO: Johnson Books, 2004), 9. For an account of the tests that contaminated southeast Utah in the 1950s, see John G. Fuller, *The Day We Bombed Utah: America's Most Lethal Secret* (New York: New American Library, 1984).

13. Buell, *Writing for an Endangered World*, 47.

14. Ellen Meloy, *The Last Cheater's Waltz: Beauty and Violence in the Desert Southwest* (Tucson: University of Arizona Press, 1999), 3. Further references are cited in the text as LCW.

15. Meloy's celebration of the dump recalls Wallace Stegner's recollection of the town dump of his youth, which he describes as "our poetry and our history." See Wallace Stegner, "The Town Dump," *Atlantic Monthly*, October 1959, 80.

16. Rebecca Solnit, *Savage Dreams: A Journey into the Landscape Wars of the American*

West (1994; Berkeley: University of California Press, 1999), x. Further references are cited in the text as SD.

17. The twinning of Nevada and Kazakhstan is a feature of Don Delillo's *Underworld*, which is discussed in the next chapter. For a firsthand account of the Western Shoshone campaign and the Nevada-Semipalatinsk Movement, see Corbin Harney, *The Way It Is: One Water . . . One Air . . . One Mother Earth* (Nevada City CA: Blue Dolphin, 1995).

18. Foucault, *Society Must Be Defended*, 163.

9. The West as Cold War Museum

1. Mira Engler, "Repulsive Matter: Landscapes of Waste in the American Middle-Class Residential Domain," *Landscape Journal* 16, no. 1 (1997): 73.

2. Peter Sloterdijk, *Critique of Cynical Reason*, trans. Michael Eldred (Minneapolis: University of Minnesota Press, 1987), 151.

3. For an overview of the Garbage Project, see William Rathje and Cullen Murphy, *Rubbish! The Archaeology of Garbage: What Our Garbage Tells Us about Ourselves* (New York: HarperCollins, 1992).

4. Michael Shanks, David Platt, and William L. Rathje, "The Perfume of Garbage: Modernity and the Archaeological," MODERNISM/*Modernity* 11, no. 1 (2004): 64.

5. The subject of waste in *Underworld* has understandably been a preoccupation for critics of the novel. For extended discussion of the topic, see especially Ruth Helyer, "'Refuse Heaped Many Stories High': DeLillo, Dirt, and Disorder," *Modern Fiction Studies* 45, no. 4 (1999): 987–1006; Jesse Kavadlo, "Recycling Authority: Don DeLillo's Waste Management," *Critique* 42, no. 4 (2001): 384–401; Todd McGowan, "The Obsolescence of Mystery and the Accumulation of Waste in Don DeLillo's *Underworld*," *Critique* 46, no. 2 (2005): 123–45; and Paul Gleason, "Don DeLillo, T. S. Eliot, and the Redemption of America's Atomic Waste Land," in *UnderWords: Perspectives on Don DeLillo's Underworld*, ed. Joseph Dewey, Steven G. Kellman, and Irving Malin (Newark: University of Delaware Press; London: Associated University Presses, 2002), 130–43.

6. Don DeLillo, *Underworld* (London: Picador, 1998), 69. Further references are given in the text with the abbreviation U. The space provided for Sax's work reproduces the modernist gallery's austere neutrality, the "piece" defined and given significance by the blankness of its context.

7. While conservation has, according to Michael Shanks, David Platt, and William L. Rathje, been a driving concern of archaeologists since the late nineteenth century, the wider acceptance of preservation as something of a cultural duty is clearly more recent: "The Soviet occupation chose to obliterate traces of Hitler's bunker in Berlin in 1945; this kind of destruction of history would be unthinkable now" (Shanks et al., "The Perfume of Garbage," 63).

8. For DeLillo, according to Jesse Kavadlo, "at bottom, recycling is pragmatic, designed to counter hopefully a physical reality of diminishing resources." Perhaps,

331

like Sax, "the author-as-waste-manager can create something beautiful and meaningful out of the dangerous debris" instead of allowing it "to fester into the waste land that the modernists feared" (Kavadlo, "Recycling Authority," 386).

9. Paul Virilio quoted in John Armitage, "From Modernism to Hypermodernism and Beyond: An Interview with Paul Virilio," in *Paul Virilio: From Modernism to Hypermodernism and Beyond*, ed. John Armitage (London: Sage, 2000), 36. For further discussion of Virilio and *Underworld*, see Nicholas Spencer, "Beyond the Mutations of Media and Military Technologies in Don Delillo's *Underworld*," *Arizona Quarterly* 58, no. 2 (2002): 89–112.

10. Masco, *The Nuclear Borderlands*, 17.

11. Masco, *The Nuclear Borderlands*, 17.

12. For discussion of *Underworld* as a narrative of westward migration, see Marni Gauthier, "'Better Living through Westward Migration': Don DeLillo's Inversion of the American West as 'Virgin Land' in *Underworld*," in *Moving Stories: Migration and the American West, 1850–2000*, ed. Scott E. Casper, 131–52 (Reno: Nevada Humanities Committee, 2001).

13. Osteen, *American Magic and Dread*, 223.

14. Ray Gonzalez, *The Underground Heart: A Return to a Hidden Landscape* (Tucson: University of Arizona Press, 2001), 96.

15. Gonzalez, *The Underground Heart*, 27.

16. Gonzalez, *The Underground Heart*, 167.

17. Richard Misrach and Myriam Weisang Misrach, *Bravo 20: The Bombing of the American West* (Baltimore: Johns Hopkins University Press, 1990), 95. For a wider discussion of Misrach's photography, see John Beck, "Blown Away: Wars Visible and Invisible in Richard Misrach's *Desert Cantos*," *European Journal of American Culture* 19, no. 3 (2000): 156–66.

18. There is certainly a market for nuclear tourism, and Misrach's proposal increasingly looks less like satire and more like a viable business opportunity. The deadpan "Bureau of Atomic Tourism" Web site http://www.atomictourist.com/ (accessed September 12, 2008) offers a list of likely destinations and provides a rundown of what the visitor can expect to see and how to get there. A more extensive and detailed itinerary is provided by James M. Maroncelli and Timothy L. Karpin in their CD-Rom book, *The Traveler's Guide to Nuclear Weapons: A Journey through America's Cold War Battlefields* (Bremerton WA: Historical Odyssey, 2002). Vanderbilt's *Survival City* adds valuable architectural and social analysis. Every tourist of toxic America ought, one would hope, to benefit from some degree of ironic self-awareness, and a suitable mixture of fascination and bewilderment is registered by Douglas Coupland in his view of the nuclear trail: Los Alamos is a "must-see destination," and the town has its own memorabilia shop that sells "non-radioactive cast-offs from the Laboratory." See Douglas Coupland, "Acid Canyon," *New Republic*, February 7, 1994, http://www.geocities.com/SoHo/Gallery/5560/nr1.html (accessed September 12, 2008). The Department of Energy is

presumably not being ironic when, on the Nevada Test Site Web page detailing its own guided tours, visitors are advised not to "remove soil, rock, plant samples or metal objects" (http://www.nv.doe.gov/nts/tours.htm [accessed September 12, 2008]). For more detailed discussion of nuclear tourism, see Jenna Berger, "Nuclear Tourism and the Manhattan Project," *Columbia Journal of American Studies* (2006), http://www.columbia.edu/cu/cjas/print/nuclear_tourism.pdf (accessed September 12, 2008); Arthur P. Molella, "Exhibiting Atomic Culture: The View from Oak Ridge," *History and Technology* 19, no. 3 (2003): 211–26; and Nathan Hodge and Sharon Weinberger, *A Nuclear Family Vacation: Travels in the World of Atomic Weaponry* (London: Bloomsbury, 2008).

19. See Robert Smithson, "A Tour of the Monuments of Passaic," in *Robert Smithson: Collected Writings*, ed. Jack Flam (Berkeley: University of California Press, 1996), 68–74.

20. Discussing an abandoned magnesium mine as "horrifyingly beautiful," William L. Fox observes that the "nineteenth-century century convention of viewing a tortured landscape as romantic ruins is so pervasive in the West that it doesn't matter if the landform is the Grand Canyon or a mine, so long as it's big." *The Void, the Grid, and the Sign: Traversing the Great Basin* (Salt Lake City: University of Utah Press, 2000), 147. Both the Grand Canyon and the magnesium mine are, as Heidegger argues, "enframed" by technology; both are objects "on call for inspection by a tour group ordered there by the vacation industry." See Heidegger, "The Question Concerning Technology," 16.

21. See John Lennon and Malcolm Foley, *Dark Tourism: The Attraction of Death and Disaster* (London: Continuum, 2000). David Nye is also instructive on the recuperation of Three Mile Island as a tourist attraction: the cooling towers have become world famous, "as identifiable as the Eiffel Tower or the Stature of Liberty." The site is surrounded by grass, including picnic tables. Visitors are told that nuclear power is under control and all systems work. The visit culminates in a trip around the plant in a minibus, complete with choreographed spontaneity whereby the guide stops the bus and allows guests into the cooling tower, at which point the visit, in Sharon O'Brien's words, "becomes invested with religious meaning as awed tourists enter." See Nye, *American Technological Sublime*, 237.

22. Misrach, *Bravo 20*, 95.

23. Misrach, *Bravo 20*, 96. A trip to any military base's visitor center and gift shop will confirm that Misrach's list of "Bombs Away" mugs, tote bags, and bumper stickers is far from being a perverse fantasy.

24. Don DeLillo, "The Power of History," *New York Times*, September 7, 1997, http://www.nytimes.com/library/books/090797article3.html (accessed September 12, 2008).

25. DeLillo, "The Power of History."

26. The Soviet nuclear test reported alongside Bobby Thomson's homer on the front page of the *New York Times* in 1951 that prompted DeLillo to pair the

two events in *Underworld* occurred in Kazakhstan. DeLillo discusses this in "The Power of History."

27. For a revealing discussion of stable and unstable paranoia in *Underworld*, see Peter Knight, "Everything Is Connected: *Underworld's* Secret History of Paranoia," *Modern Fiction Studies* 45, no. 3 (1999): 811–36.

28. As Walter Benjamin wrote, the collector "takes up the struggle against dispersion." See *The Arcades Project*, trans. Howard Eiland and Kevin McLaughlin (Cambridge MA: Harvard University Press, 1999), 211.

29. Paul Virilio and Sylvere Lotringer, *Pure War*, trans. Mark Polizzotti, rev. ed. (New York: Semiotext(e), 1997), 32.

30. Patrick Crogan, "The Tendency, the Accident and the Untimely: Paul Virilio's Engagement with the Future," in Armitage, *Paul Virilio*, 171.

31. Paul Virilio, *A Landscape of Events*, trans. Julie Rose (Cambridge MA: MIT Press, 2000), 54.

32. Crogan, "The Tendency, the Accident and the Untimely," 171.

33. Virilio, *A Landscape of Events*, 55.

34. Virilio, *A Landscape of Events*, 56.

35. Virilio, *A Landscape of Events*, 56.

36. Virilio, *A Landscape of Events*, 59; emphasis in original.

37. Virilio, *A Landscape of Events*, 59; emphasis in original.

38. Virilio's ultimate example is of a TV broadcast of a Parisian high-rise destroyed live on air, a de-realized instant of collapse happening.

39. Virilio, *A Landscape of Events*, 56.

10. The Fringe of Empire

1. Luis Alberto Urrea, *Across the Wire: Life and Hard Times on the Mexican Border* (New York: Anchor, 1993), 9.

2. Urrea, *Across the Wire*, 11.

3. Urrea, *Across the Wire*, 31, 10.

4. Urrea, *Across the Wire*, 167.

5. Urrea, *Across the Wire*, 168.

6. José David Saldívar, *Border Matters: Remapping American Cultural Studies* (Berkeley: University of California Press, 1997), 140.

7. Saldívar, *Border Matters*, 138.

8. The Mexicans McCarthy's protagonists do encounter north of the border are not necessarily interested in a transnational borderlands. Asked what he knows about Mexico by John Grady's sidekick Rawlins, a young Mexican American in *All the Pretty Horses* spits and replies that "I never been to Mexico in my life" (APH 34).

9. Hardt and Negri, *Multitude*, xiii.

10. Gómez-Peña, *Warrior for Gringostroika*, 43.

11. Hardt and Negri, *Multitude*, xvii.

12. Mary Pat Brady, *Extinct Lands, Temporal Geographies: Chicana Literature and the Urgency of Space* (Durham: Duke University Press, 2002), 50.

13. George Bush, naming William Bennett as the new Drug Czar in 1989, quoted in David Thoreen, "The President's Emergency War Powers and the Erosion of Civil Liberties in Pynchon's *Vineland*," *Oklahoma City University Law Review* 24, no. 3 (1999): 794.

14. See Peter Andreas, *Border Games: Policing the U.S.-Mexico Border* (Ithaca: Cornell University Press, 2000), 43–44.

15. Dunn, *The Militarization of the U.S.-Mexico Border*, 2.

16. Ronald Reagan quoted in Dunn, *The Militarization of the U.S.-Mexico Border* 3. Connecting drugs with terrorism has more recently also become a favored rhetorical strategy of George W. Bush. Two advertisements broadcast by Fox during the 2002 Super Bowl explicitly made the connection between the "War on Drugs" and the "War on Terror" for the first time. See Frank Ahrens, "New Pitch in Anti-Drugs Ads: Anti-Terrorism," *Washington Post*, February 4, 2002.

17. Slotkin, *Gunfighter Nation*, 650.

18. Urrea, *The Devil's Highway*, 38.

19. Slotkin, *Gunfighter Nation*, 651. A number of military operations have been undertaken as part of the War on Drugs, including the 1989 invasion of Panama on the pretext that the head of the Panama government, General Manuel Noriega, was involved in drug trafficking. As part of Plan Colombia, the United States has funded coca eradication through private contractors such as Dyn-Corp and helped train the Colombian armed forces to eradicate coca and fight left-wing guerrillas such as the FARC (Revolutionary Armed Forces of Colombia) and right-wing paramilitaries such as the AUC (United Self-Defense Forces of Colombia), both of which have been accused of participating in the illegal drug trade in their areas of influence.

20. Jeanne Kirkpatrick quoted in Lars Schoultz, *Beneath the United States: A History of U.S. Policy toward Latin America* (Cambridge MA: Harvard University Press, 1998), 378.

21. Saldívar, *Border Matters*, x.

22. Hardt and Negri, *Multitude*, 30.

23. Mike Davis, "The Great Wall of Capital," in *Against the Wall: Israel's Barrier to Peace*, ed. Michael Sorkin (New York: New Press, 2005), 93.

24. Andreas, *Border Games*, 90.

25. Hardt and Negri, *Multitude*, 14. As Rubén Martínez writes, "To truly 'hold the line,' as American politicians say, the United States would have to spend hundreds of billions of dollars . . . to either build the Great Wall of America or amass all along the line . . . thousands of troops and all manner of physical obstacles, weaponry, and technology. . . . After all the rhetoric, the line is still more of an idea than a reality" (Rubén Martínez, *Crossing Over: A Mexican Family on the Migrant Trail* [New York: Picador, 2001], 7–8).

26. Andreas, *Border Games*, 94.

27. Brady McCombs, "Barriers Have Failed Before," *Arizona Daily Star*, September 25, 2006, http://www.azstarnet.com/sn/border/147884 (accessed September 12, 2008). For an extensive assessment of the dangers faced by migrants pushed to the most dangerous border crossing areas, see Urrea, *The Devil's Highway*, and John Annerino, *Dead in Their Tracks: Crossing America's Desert Borderlands* (New York: Four Walls Eight Windows, 1999).

28. Hector Tobar and Cecilia Sanchez, "Mexico's Drug War Death Toll Tops 2000," *Los Angeles Times*, November 14, 2006.

29. Andreas, *Border Games*, 7.

30. Andreas, *Border Games*, 8.

31. Virilio, *A Landscape of Events*, x.

32. Virilio, *A Landscape of Events*, xiii.

33. Eduardo Galeano, *Open Veins of Latin America: Five Centuries of the Pillage of a Continent* (1973; New York: Monthly Review Press, 1997), 6. Silko acknowledges Galeano in Thomas Irmer and Matthais Schmidt, "An Interview with Leslie Marmon Silko," (1995), in *Conversations with Leslie Marmon Silko*, ed. Ellen Arnold (Jackson: University Press of Mississippi, 2000), 155. The convergence of Galeano's and Silko's interests is discussed in Virginia E. Bell, "Counter-Chronicling and Alternative Mapping in *Memoria del fuego* and *Almanac of the Dead*." *MELUS* 25, nos. 3/4 (2000): 5–30.

34. Leslie Marmon Silko, *Almanac of the Dead* (New York: Penguin, 1992), 545. Further references are given in the text with the abbreviation AD.

35. Galeano, *Open Veins of Latin America*, 8.

36. Galeano, *Open Veins of Latin America*, 8.

37. Galeano, *Open Veins of Latin America*, 8.

38. Janet St. Clair, "Uneasy Ethnocentrism: Recent Works of Allen, Silko, and Hogan," *Studies in American Indian Literatures* 6, no. 1 (1994): 87.

39. As William Bevis writes of the Laguna people, "Individuality is not even the scene of success or failure; it is nothing" (William W. Bevis, *Ten Tough Stripes: Montana Writers and the West* [Seattle: University of Washington Press, 1990], 102).

40. Eva Cherniavsky, "Tribalism, Globalism, and Eskimo Television in Leslie Marmon Silko's *Almanac of the Dead*," *Angelaki* 6, no. 1 (2001): 111.

41. Sven Birkets, "Apocalypse Now," review of *Almanac of the Dead*, by Leslie Marmon Silko, *New Republic*, November 4, 1991, 41. For an effective unpacking of the implications of Birkets's review, see Caren Irr, "The Timeliness of *Almanac of the Dead*, or a Postmodern Rewriting of Radical Fiction," in *Leslie Marmon Silko: A Collection of Critical Essays*, ed. Louise K. Barnett and James L. Thorson, 223–44 (Albuquerque: University of New Mexico Press, 1999). A similar charge of implausibility is directed at John Rechy's novel about Chicano/a experience in southern California, *The Miraculous Day of Amalia Gómez*, published the same year as *Almanac*, by a review in the *New York Times*. See Saldívar, *Border Matters*, 111–12.

42. For an insightful discussion of *Almanac of the Dead*'s reading of the drug war, see Curtis Marez, *Drug Wars: The Political Economy of Narcotics* (Minneapolis: University of Minnesota Press, 2004), 247–83.

43. Robert Smithson, "Art Through the Camera's Eye," in *Robert Smithson: The Complete Writings*, 371.

44. Leslie Marmon Silko, "The Indian with a Camera," in *Yellow Woman and the Beauty of the Spirit: Essays on Native American Life Today* (New York: Touchstone, 1996), 178.

45. Cherniavsky, "Tribalism, Globalism, and Eskimo Television," 113.

46. Leslie Marmon Silko, "As a Child I Loved To Draw and Cut Paper," in *Yellow Woman and the Beauty of the Spirit*, 169.

47. Anderson, *American Indian Literature and the Southwest*, 64.

48. Leslie Marmon Silko, "On Photography," in *Yellow Woman and the Beauty of the Spirit*, 180.

49. Silko, "On Photography," 182.

50. Debora Horowitz, "Freud, Marx and Chiapas in Leslie Marmon Silko's *Almanac of the Dead*," *Studies in American Indian Literatures* 10, no. 3 (1998): 50.

51. Gloria Anzaldúa, *Borderlands/La Frontera: The New Mestiza* (San Francisco: Spinsters/Aunt Lute, 1987), 37.

52. Anzaldúa, *Borderlands/La Frontera*, 87.

53. David L. Moore, "Silko's Blood Sacrifice: The Circulating Witness in *Almanac of the Dead*," in Barnett and Thorson, *Leslie Marmon Silko*, 171.

54. Anzaldúa, *Borderlands/La Frontera* preface, not paginated.

55. Moore, "Silko's Blood Sacrifice," 153.

56. Gloria Anzaldúa quoted in AnaLouise Keating, ed., *Gloria Anzaldúa: Interviews/Entrevistas* (London: Routledge, 2000), 254–55.

57. Cormac McCarthy, *No Country for Old Men* (London: Picador, 2005), 4. Further references are cited in the text with the abbreviation NC.

58. Slotkin, *Gunfighter Nation*, 645, 655.

59. Charles Bowden, *A Shadow in the City: Confessions of an Undercover Drug Warrior* (Orlando: Harcourt, 2005), preface (unpag.). Further references are cited in the text with the abbreviation SC.

60. Richard Rorty, *Achieving Our Country: Leftist Thought in Twentieth-Century America* (Cambridge MA: Harvard University Press, 1998), 7.

Conclusion

1. Michael J. Shapiro, *Methods and Nations: Cultural Governance and the Indigenous Subject* (New York: Routledge, 2004), 177.

2. Michael R. Gordon, "When an Open Society Is Wielded as a Weapon against Itself," *New York Times*, September 12, 2001, A24. Gordon goes on to remind readers that "During the Second World War, the Japanese pioneered the use of kamikaze planes. The kamikazes sank 34 ships and damaged hundreds or others. During the battle off Okinawa, they killed almost 5,000 men."

3. Tom Engelhardt, *The End of Victory Culture: Cold War America and the Disillusioning of a Generation*, rev. ed. (Amherst: University of Massachusetts Press, 2007), 306.

4. Engelhardt, *The End of Victory Culture*, 306, 308.

5. Luis Alberto Urrea, *The Devil's Highway* (New York: Back Bay, 2005), 204.

6. Bauman, *Wasted Lives*, 21.

7. Benedict Anderson, *Imagined Communities: Reflections on the Origin and Spread of Nationalism* (London: Verso, 1991), 204.

8. Kittler, *Gramophone, Film, Typewriter*, xl.

9. Adams, *Born Free and Equal*, 29.

10. For a discussion of the history of anti-Japanese proposals for preserving American racial purity, see James A. Tyner, "The Geopolitics of Eugenics and the Incarceration of Japanese Americans," *Antipode* 30, no. 3 (1998): 251–69.

11. Perry Miyake, *21st Century Manzanar* (Los Angeles: Really Great Books, 2002), 347. Subsequent references are given in the text with the abbreviation M.

12. Mike Davis, *Dead Cities and Other Tales* (New York: The New Press, 2002), 30.

13. Davis, *Dead Cities*, 31.

14. Davis, *Dead Cities*, 31.

15. Davis, *Dead Cities*, 31.

16. Cormac McCarthy, *The Road* (New York: Knopf, 2006), 3. Subsequent references are given in the text with the abbreviation R.

17. Hardt and Negri, *Multitude*, 7.

18. Winston Churchill, speech delivered at Westminster College, Fulton MO, March 5, 1946.

19. Tony Blair, speech delivered at the Labour Party conference, Brighton, October 2, 2001.

economy (continued)
302n37; Sunbelt as model for
global, 12, 298n13; threats to,
along Mexican border, 12; trans-
formation of, in 1970s, 41; in
Underworld, 235, 241, 248; and
uranium boom, 26, 221; in wake of
disaster, 170, 172; and wasted human lives, 136; during World War
II, 25–26. *See also* permanent war
economy
Edwards Air Force Base, 30
Ehrlich, Gretel: *Heart Mountain*, 83
Eisenhower, Dwight, 36, 309n111
Eisenhower, Milton S., 315n2
El Centro CA, 177
Ellis, Jay, 69, 71, 310n1, 311n4,
313n37, 314n48, 315n49
El Paso TX, 25, 243, 251, 259
El Salvador, 257
El Santuario de Chimayó, 115, 117,
119, 320n30
emptiness: in *Blood Meridian*, 51, 56,
60–61, 73; in *End Zone*, 167–68; federally constructed, in Southwest,
30, 31; on maps, 126–27, 140–41;
perception of, 22, 23, 285, 300n18;
as representation of exclusion,
127; in *Storm Season*, 172–74;
through clearing and dispossession, 125–26; in *When the Emperor
Was Divine*, 95
End Zone (DeLillo), 9–10, 40, 157–59,
163, 175–76, 181, 233, 234
"enemy combatants," 284
"enemy deficit," 11
enemy production, 41
Engelhardt, Tom, 46–47, 284
Engle, Clair, 305n62
Engle Act (1958), 34–35, 306n63
English language, 86

Enlightenment, 65–66, 71, 183, 194,
195
environmental contamination:
caused by military-industrial complex, 10–11, 47; effects of warnings
of, 293; in *End Zone*, 164; and illness, 190, 215–16, 330n10; in *Last
Cheater's Waltz*, 217; and national
security, 240; in Native American
fiction, 190; open secrets of, 201;
post–9/11, 12; in *Savage Dreams*,
225–31
environmental legislation, 206, 216,
306n63
environmental memorial, 244–46
environmental politics, 203–7, 329n2
Environmental Protection Agency
(EPA), 206
erasure: in *Almanac of the Dead*, 255,
263, 272; in *Blood Meridian*, 60,
61; in internment narratives, 73,
75, 93, 95–96, 98, 225, 286; in *In
the Shadows of the Sun*, 131; at Los
Alamos, 108, 122–23; on maps,
128; in national security technologies, 4; in *Night Wing*, 192; in *Savage
Dreams*, 225, 229; in Southwest museums, 243; of wartime violence,
15; in West, 4. *See also* concealment
ethnic identity, 189
evil: in *Eye Killers*, 197, 198; in *No
Country for Old Men*, 273, 275–79,
281, 282, 295; in *The Road*, 292; in
Shadow in the City, 277–82
exception, state of: in *Border Trilogy*,
132, 133; dimensions of, 33–34,
304n56, 305n59; and internment,
77, 79, 94, 102; at Los Alamos,
102, 108; on Mexican border, 260;
during wartime, 87; wasted populations in, 35, 306n68; and withdrawn land, 35, 126–32

In the Postwestern Horizons series

Dirty Wars
Landscape, Power, and Waste in Western American Literature
John Beck

The Rhizomatic West
Representing the American West in a Transnational, Global, Media Age
Neil Campbell

True West
Authenticity and the American West
Edited by William R. Handley and Nathaniel Lewis

Postwestern Cultures
Literature, Theory, Space
Susan Kollin

Manifest and Other Destinies
Territorial Fictions of the
Nineteenth-Century United States
Stephanie LeMenager

Unsettling the Literary West
Authenticity and Authorship
Nathaniel Lewis

María Amparo Ruiz de Burton
Critical and Pedagogical Perspectives
Edited by Amelia María de la Luz Montes
and Anne Elizabeth Goldman

To order or obtain more information on these or other
University of Nebraska Press titles, visit www.nebraskapress.unl.edu.